WILLIAM MORRIS

HIS LIFE, WORK AND FRIENDS

THIS IS THE PICTURE OF THE OLD HOUSE BY THE THAMES TO WHICH THE PEOPLE OF THIS STORY WENT. HEREAFTER FOLLOWS THE BOOK ITSELF WHICH IS CALLED NEWS FROM NOWHERE. OR AN EPOCH OF REST & IS WRITTEN BY WILLIAM MORRIS.

Kelmscott Manor. The frontispiece from 'News from Nowhere'
printed by the Kelmscott Press in 1892

PHILIP
HENDERSON

WILLIAM
MORRIS

HIS LIFE
WORK AND FRIENDS

ANDRE DEUTSCH

To John and Julian

First published 1967 by
Thames and Hudson

This edition published 1986 by
André Deutsch Limited
105 Great Russell Street London WC1B 3LJ

Copyright © 1977 by Philip Henderson

ISBN 233 97855 0

Printed in Great Britain by
Ebenezer Baylis and Son Ltd, Worcester

Contents

List of Illustrations

PREFACE

Part One: Romance
1834–1876

CHAPTER ONE
1834–1852
WALTHAMSTOW TO MARLBOROUGH
Page 3

CHAPTER TWO
1853–1856
OXFORD · RUSKIN, ROSSETTI AND PRE-RAPHAELITISM
Page 11

CHAPTER THREE
1856–1859
RED LION SQUARE · THE OXFORD UNION · 'ISEULT' AND 'GUENEVERE'
Page 39

CHAPTER FOUR
1859–1865
RED HOUSE · MORRIS, MARSHALL, FAULKNER & CO. FINE ART WORKMEN
Page 58

CHAPTER FIVE
1865–1871
QUEEN SQUARE · 'OF UTTER LOVE DEFEATED UTTERLY'
Page 79

CHAPTER SIX
1871–1875
KELMSCOTT AND ICELAND
Page 117

CHAPTER SEVEN
WALLPAPERS · TEXTILES · EMBROIDERY ·
'SIGURD THE VOLSUNG'
Page 152

Part Two: Commitment
1876–1890

CHAPTER EIGHT
1876–1879
THE ANTI-TURK CAMPAIGN · KELMSCOTT
HOUSE · VISITS TO ITALY · EXPERIMENTS
IN WEAVING
Page 173

CHAPTER NINE
ARCHITECTURE AND THE ARTS OF LIFE
Page 194

CHAPTER TEN
1879–1883
HAMMERSMITH · KELMSCOTT ·
MERTON ABBEY
Page 214

CHAPTER ELEVEN
1883–1884
THE SOCIAL DEMOCRATIC FEDERATION
Page 244

CHAPTER TWELVE
1885–1887
THE SOCIALIST LEAGUE
Page 273

CHAPTER THIRTEEN
1887–1890
'A DREAM OF JOHN BALL · 'THE ODYSSEY' ·
BLOODY SUNDAY AND THE END OF
THE SOCIALIST LEAGUE
Page 301

Part Three: Utopia
1890–1896

CHAPTER FOURTEEN
1890–1893
'NEWS FROM NOWHERE'
THE KELMSCOTT PRESS
Page 327

CHAPTER FIFTEEN
1894–1896
LAST YEARS
Page 346

CONCLUSION
Page 367

NOTES AND SOURCES
Page 370

ACKNOWLEDGEMENTS
Page 380

INDEX
Page 381

Illustrations

between pages 100 and 101

William Morris aged 23 (1). Drawing by Rossetti (2)

Early influences: Merton College, Oxford (3), G. E. Street (4), Great Coxwell (5), John Ruskin (6). The Oxford Union ceiling (7), the Oxford Museum (8)

Dante Gabriel Rossetti: self portrait (9), Morris's 'Iseult on the ship' (10), 'Arthur's Tomb' (11), 'The Blue Closet' (12)

Jane Burden: 'The Blue Dress' (13), a photograph posed by Rossetti (14), at Kelmscott Manor (15), a drawing by Morris (16), 'Janey Morris and the Wombat' (17)

Red House, Bexleyheath: the staircase (18), 'Si je puis' (19), Philip Webb (20), exterior (21), the drawing-room (22)

Morris, Marshall, Faulkner & Co.: Morris (23), Burne-Jones (24) and C. J. Faulkner (25). 26 Queen Square (26), 'Daisy' (27), the 'St George' cabinet (28), 'Wreath' (29), stained glass panel for Harden Grange (30). 499 Oxford Street (31). Some important commissions: All Saints, Dedworth (32), the Armoury, St James's Palace (33), All Saints, Jesus Lane, Cambridge (34), 'The Sermon on the Mount' (35), St Michael and All Angels, Brighton (36), 1 Palace Green (37), 'Woodpecker' tapestry (38), 'Pilgrim in the Garden' (39), the Green Dining Room (40), Buscot Park (41) and the 'Clouds' carpet (42)

between pages 324 and 325

Morris in the 1880s painted by W. B. Richmond (43), stone plaque by George Jack (44)

Kelmscott Manor, Oxfordshire: the staircase (45), exterior (46), the Tapestry Room (47), the attic (48) and the four-poster bed (49)

Woven and printed textiles: Merton Abbey (50), Morris at the loom (51), 'Tulip' (52), 'Crown Imperial' (53), 'Rose and Lily' (54), 'African Marigold' (55)

Kelmscott House, Hammersmith: the drawing-room (56, 58), the river front (57) and the dining-room (59)

Burne-Jones and The Grange: 'Topsy and Ned settled on the settle' (60), and in the garden of The Grange (61). The studio (62) and the drawing-room (63)

The Democratic Federation: 'Chants for Socialists' (64), 'Labour's May Day' (65), Bernard Shaw (66), Walter Crane (67), 'The Attitude of the Police' (68), membership card (69)

Books and printing: the library at Kelmscott House (70), 'Love is Enough' binding (71), 'The Story of the Glittering Plain' (72), printing the Kelmscott Chaucer (73)

Family and friends: Mrs Morris senior (74), the Morris and Burne-Jones families (75), Jenny Morris (76), Rossetti in later life (77), Mrs Burne-Jones (78), Mrs Coronio (79), members of the Kelmscott Press in 1895 (80)

Morris's funeral cart (81). Kelmscott churchyard (82)

Preface

MUCH of what can be said and written of William Morris, it may be thought, has been written and said already. We have the original study of his work and public life by Aymer Vallance, the spacious Victorian biography of J. W. Mackail, the prefaces and memoranda of May Morris and, more recently, the well-nigh exhaustive account of his political activities in Edward Thompson's *William Morris: Romantic to Revolutionary*. No subsequent biographer can hope to compete with Mackail's classic achievement, which must remain to a large extent his primary source. Nevertheless, we know Mackail to have been in possession of material of a more intimate and revealing nature, which he could not hope to use during the lifetime of other members of the Morris family, and all that he did write was subject to the approval of Sir Edward and Lady Burne-Jones, at whose request he undertook his biography in the first place. He was compelled, as he complained with some bitterness, to be 'tactful' and so finally leaves us with an image of Morris, even in the face of his own evidence, as a man who moved through life 'in a dream, isolated, self-centred, almost empty of love or hatred'.

Such a view is demonstrably untrue. It is one purpose of this book to show Morris as the highly nervous, emotional and complex character that he actually was: a man very much in contact with the world of his time, however he may have felt himself to be out of tune with it: a business man who made a success of an unlikely undertaking, an association of 'art workmen', which became under his guidance the flourishing Morris & Co., with works at Merton Abbey and a showroom in Oxford Street – above all, a man whose passionate concern with the whole problem of art and society makes him, as Raymond Williams has said, 'a pivotal figure' of our time.

For art, Morris was never tired of saying, depends on the quality of the society which produces it. The very fact that his designs have once more come back into favour in a predominantly urban and scientific society is sufficient to show that his thought and work has a direct appeal to our utilitarian age. We find ourselves driven back to Morris and his emphasis on the spontaneous and creative spirit for refreshment and renewal. He was not a dreamer lost in sentimental visions of the Middle Ages, but a man determined to preserve all that is most valuable in our heritage. This alone makes his example of inestimable value in a time of ruthless 'development' and the often thoughtless destruction of that heritage. It is, in fact, hardly an exaggeration to say that almost every attempt to make life more worth living in a standardized environment hostile to the creative spirit derives from Morris and the things he fought for. Indeed, Henri Nocq in his *Tendances Nouvelles* records Toulouse-Lautrec as saying: 'Je crois qu'il n'y a qu'à regarder William Morris, pour avoir une réponse à toutes vos questions.'

Many books have been written about Morris and many more will be written, for those who came into contact with him during his lifetime declared that he was the greatest man they had ever known. This book is primarily a biography, rather than a study of each aspect of Morris's work, since that, as Edward Thompson has justly remarked, 'must be the result of the collaboration of many specialist opinions', though a very adequate survey has recently been written by Dr Paul Thompson under the title of *The Work of William Morris*. To a great extent Morris's work *was* his life. But it still remains to see the man himself, and the men and women who surrounded him, in a modern perspective.   P.H.

PART ONE

ROMANCE

1834–1876

CHAPTER ONE

1834–1852

Walthamstow to Marlborough

I was born at Walthamstow, in Essex, a suburban village on the edge of Epping Forest, and once a pleasant place enough, but now terribly cocknified and choked up by the jerry builder.

THE MORRISES originally came from the Welsh Marches, the upper valley of the river Severn and its tributaries. William Morris's paternal grandfather, 'a man excellent in every relation of life, and very religious',[1] when he settled in business in Worcester at the end of the eighteenth century, was the first of his family, it is said, to drop the Welsh Ap from his name. About 1820 he moved to London and entered his son, another William Morris, as a clerk in a firm of discount brokers, Harris, Sanderson & Harris of Lombard Street. The Harrises were Quakers and related to the Morrises by marriage. When he was a little over thirty, this son became a partner of the firm and in 1826 married Emma Shelton, a Worcester-shire neighbour of prosperous merchant and land-owning stock, several of whom had distinguished themselves in the Church and at the Bar. It was a family with strongly developed musical tastes. Several of the Sheltons had been singing canons of Worcester Cathedral and Westminster Abbey; another became a music teacher in Worcester and a part of the musical tradition of that city which, in the middle of the century, was to produce the great figure of Edward Elgar. Emma Shelton's father, it is said, threw up every-thing for music.

Mr and Mrs Morris, according to the business custom of the time, set up house over the office in Lombard Street and here their two eldest daughters, Emma and Henrietta, were born in 1830 and 1832 respectively. Next year, in 1833, they moved to Clay Hill, Waltham-stow, then a pleasant village to the east of London, within a mile or so of Epping Forest. Here William Morris, poet, designer and pioneer socialist, was born on 24 March 1834.

Six years later, the family moved to Woodford Hall, a Palladian

3

mansion standing within its own park of fifty acres with twice that amount of farmland. Only a fence separated the park from Epping Forest. Woodford Hall was very much the squire's house, with a garden gate opening into the churchyard, the church itself a small red brick building with a few fine Georgian houses next to it. 'From the Hall', Mackail writes, 'the course of the Thames might be traced winding through the marshes, with white and ruddy-brown sails moving among cornfields and pastures.'² It was a peaceful and almost Flemish scene. In *News from Nowhere*, Morris writes of 'the wide green sea of the Essex marshland, with the great domed line of the sky, and the sun shining down in one flood of peaceful light over the long distance'. It was the type of landscape to which he always felt most drawn and not unlike that of his later home at Kelmscott in Oxfordshire.

The move to Woodford Hall had been made possible by the rise in the price of copper shares, William Morris senior being the fortunate possessor of 272 shares in a Devonshire copper mine, the famous Devon Great Consols. These shares, originally valued at £1 each, were at one time changing hands at £800 and Mr Morris's holding rose to the value of £200,000. Those who actually mined the copper did not, of course, share in this wealth, though their children also worked alongside them in the mine. In the year in which William Morris was born, six Dorset-shire farm labourers were sentenced to seven years' transportation in the unspeakable convict ships of Botany Bay, for forming a union in an attempt to raise their weekly wage from seven to ten shillings.

Meanwhile Mr Morris drove up daily to the City by coach, along one of Telford and McAdam's excellent new roads. He had already, as befitted his new status, obtained a grant of arms from the College of Heralds – 'Azure, a horse's head erased argent between three horse-shoes or'.

Like other business families of the time, the Morrises were staunch Evangelicals. 'I was brought up', Morris wrote later, 'in what I should call rich establishmentarian puritanism; a religion which even as a boy I never took to.'³ The Nonconformist conscience mani-fested itself chiefly among Morris's sisters; his brothers conformed to a more conventional pattern. At the age of nineteen, Emma, his eldest sister, married the Rev. Joseph Oldham and devoted her life and money to working with her husband among the coal miners of

Derbyshire. Henrietta never married, but became a Roman Catholic later in life during a visit to Rome with her mother. Isabella, his third sister, after forty years of marriage to a naval officer, Archibald Gilmore, trained as a hospital nurse at Guy's, for which she was ostracized by her family. She devoted the remaining twenty years of her widowhood to working in the slums of South London, becoming Deaconess and head of the Rochester and Southwark Mission with headquarters on the north side of Clapham Common. Physically, Isabella closely resembled her brother William and shared with him the same sort of missionary fervour that impelled him to become a socialist in middle life. She is commemorated by a plaque in Southwark Cathedral. The youngest sister, Alice, married Reginald Gill, a banker, of Bickham, Devon, who was subsequently killed in the hunting field. After his death, Alice went to live at Tunbridge Wells.

Little is known of Morris's four brothers. Hugh lived as a gentleman farmer near Southampton and bred Jersey and Guernsey cattle. Thomas went to a German university and is said to have shown literary talent, but joined the Gordon Highlanders. He left three sons and five daughters, with descendants living in Australia and Canada. Among his daughters was Effie, who in 1958 presented her notes concerning the family to the Morris museum at Walthamstow.[4] There is a mention of Colonel Arthur Morris of the 60th Royal Rifles in a letter of 3 March 1881 in which Morris writes of going to Much Hadham, where his mother was then living at Lordship Place next to the church, 'to see the last of Arthur before he goes to India. Lucky he, that he didn't have to run down hill at Majuba, though I see that his old battalion seem to have run the fastest and so lost fewest men' – a sardonic reference to the British defeat by the Boers. Later Arthur went to China and was present at the sack of Peking. Edgar, who also married and had two sons and two daughters, lived in Herefordshire, but lost all his money and later joined Morris at Merton Abbey, working as a dyer. There are references to him in several of Morris's letters and in Wilfrid Scawen Blunt's diary.

The Sheltons were a sturdy and long-lived stock, whereas the Morrises were of a more delicate constitution. Early in life, Morris took after his father's side of the family and had, at first, to be kept alive on a diet of calves-foot jelly and beef tea. An elder brother, the first-born of the family, had already died in infancy. Even in later life, Morris's burly physique and aggressively masculine manner was by no means an infallible index to his constitution.

Beneath the thick-set exterior was a nervous, excitable disposition, a feminine tenderness and sensitivity which drew him emotionally rather towards his own sex than to women. This manifested itself in intimate friendships formed at Oxford with Edward Burne-Jones, Cormell Price, Charles Faulkner and Philip Webb, and maintained for the rest of his life. Though he went to women for sympathy and was very close indeed to Georgie Burne-Jones, Morris appeared to Wilfrid Scawen Blunt, who met him in later middle-age, to be 'absolutely independent of sex considerations'.[5] The more sensuous side of his nature, it would seem, found satisfaction in the textures of wood and rough stone mellowed by time and weather – there was something almost personal in Morris's love for ancient buildings – in the feel of woven and embroidered stuffs, delight in flowers and foliage and the intertwined lines of natural growth. When he married, one of his Oxford friends remarked: 'he has lately taken a strong fancy for the human'.[6] There is, indeed, passionate feeling in *The Defence of Guenevere* – soon to be cut off short and dammed at the source – but even so, Morris's idea of romance was, as he admitted, to have a feeling for history. The second half of his life was largely devoted, once more, to the service of an idea, a concept of social and historical development in which the mainspring was a feeling for history and what he called 'the arts of life'.

At an early age, Morris began visiting the old Essex churches, with their memorial brasses of knights and clerics, and when, at the age of eight, his father took him to Canterbury Cathedral, it was, he said later, as if the gates of Heaven had been opened to him. By the age of seven, he had, he tells us, read all Scott's novels and even had a miniature suit of armour in which to ride through Epping Forest – anticipating the armour he had a local blacksmith make for him when decorating the walls of the Oxford Union Debating Hall.

But probably nothing in his childhood made such a lasting impression on Morris as Epping Forest itself. 'Well I remember as a boy', he says in his first lecture 'The Lesser Arts', 'my first acquaint-ance with a room hung with faded greenery at Queen Elizabeth's Lodge by Chingford Hatch in Epping Forest . . . and the impression of romance that made upon me! a feeling that always comes back on me when I read, as I often do, Sir Walter Scott's "Antiquary", and come to the description of the Green Room at Monkbarns amongst which the novelist has with such exquisite cunning of art embedded the fresh and glittering verses of the summer poet Chaucer.' In fact, it is hardly an exaggeration to say that this room set the pattern for many of the rooms he was later to decorate. Everything in Morris's childhood contributed to what he was later to become. In his case, even more than in most lives, it can be said that the child was father to the man: the pattern, once established, never changed.

At the age of nine, Morris was sent to a preparatory school at Walthamstow. It was two miles from Woodford and he rode over to it on his pony. In the autumn of 1847, when he was thirteen, his father died and next year he went to Marlborough, one of the new public schools founded for the sons of the middle classes. Started in 1843 with two hundred boys, within the first three years their number had doubled and there were more than a hundred entrants in 1848.

Fortunately for Morris, life at Marlborough was far freer and less regimented than it became at other public schools. Above all, there were no compulsory games. Instead of standing on a cricket field all the afternoon or kicking a leather ball about in the mud in winter, he was free to explore Savernake Forest and the strange, bare Wiltshire countryside, the stone circles of Avebury, Silbury Hill and the pre-Celtic long barrows on the ridges above Pewsey Vale.

The school library was also well stocked with books on archaeology and medieval architecture, and before he left school, Morris had picked up most of what there was to be known about English Gothic. 'His power of assimilation', Mackail tells us, 'was prodigious.'[7] Doubtless, Pugin's *Contrasts* was among the books he studied, and its effect reinforced the High Church character of the school, where the newly-discovered Elizabethan church music was sung. Otherwise, Morris said later that he 'learned next to nothing' at Marlborough, 'for indeed next to nothing was taught',[8] all the boys under the fifth form being crowded into one big class-room. But there was at least no prefect system, no organized ragging of new boys, and none of the bullying and beating that, for the sensitive boy, could make life at an English public school not unlike a concentration camp. Moreover, Morris was not the sort of boy who could be bullied. A schoolfellow describes him at this time as already 'a thick-set, strong-looking boy, with a high colour and black curly hair [actually his hair was brown], good-natured and kind, but with a fearful temper'.[9] But even then his outbursts of temper were as brief as they were violent.

The restlessness of his hands was his most noticeable character-istic, for which he sought relief in endless netting. 'With one end of the net fastened to a desk in the big school-room he would work at it for hours together, his fingers moving almost automatically.'[10] For Morris was never happy unless he was using his hands, which accounts for the large number of crafts he practised during his life, to say nothing of the amount of poetry he wrote, which sometimes seems to have been almost another form of manual exercise. In the last year of his life, he told Wilfrid Scawen Blunt that at Marl-borough 'he was neither high nor low in his form, but always last in arithmetic; hated Cicero and Latin generally, but anything in the way of history had attracted him'.[11]

More ordinary boys at Marlborough considered Morris 'Welsh and mad', as they encountered him 'mooning and talking to him-self. . . . On his walks he invented and poured forth endless stories, vaguely described as "about knights and fairies", in which one adventure arose out of another, and the tale flowered on from day to day over a whole term.'[12] With such stories he would entertain his dormitory at night. Once more, Morris may be said to have begun his life as he ended it, with tales and romances. Yet his eye missed nothing in his surroundings. It was an eye which, while it appeared unobservant, took in everything at a glance. A letter written to his elder sister at the age of fifteen, with its careful des-cription of a water meadow, is evidence of the precision with which he already registered outside impressions.

During the autumn of 1848 the family moved from Woodford Hall to Water House, Walthamstow, another Georgian mansion on a slightly smaller scale, within half a mile of their old house on Clay Hill. Fortunately, this house is still standing and has been taken over by Walthamstow Borough Council as a Morris museum and memorial gallery. Its rather lumpish exterior of yellowish brick is not particularly attractive, but within there is a spacious hall, paved with marble flags, and a broad staircase of Spanish chestnut. On the first landing is the large window with the window-seat in which Morris used to spend whole days reading both before and after he went up to Oxford. Before the garden was turned into a recreation-ground, with asphalted paths, seats and a pavilion for refreshments and concert parties, a broad lawn led down to a moat some forty feet in breadth and an island planted with a grove of aspens and thickly wooded with hollies, hawthorn and chestnuts. In this moat the boys fished and bathed, boating in summer and skating in winter.

Meanwhile, Dr Wilkinson's rule at Marlborough had become so deplorable that, in November 1851, it culminated in a rebellion of the whole school. Accordingly it was arranged that Morris should leave at Christmas and prepare for Oxford with a private tutor. He was not high up in the school and, Mackail tells us, was 'more of an expert in silkworms' eggs and old churches than in exact scholarship'.[13] The tutor chosen was the Rev. F.B.Guy, an assistant master of the Forest School, Walthamstow, of which he became headmaster a few years later, and then Canon of St Alban's. At that time he took a few pupils in his own house in Hoe Street. Guy was a High Churchman, with a wide knowledge of painting and architecture. Morris remained with him a year and under his sympathetic tuition developed into a very fair classical scholar. From 1850 to 1852 Guy had been the first headmaster of Bradfield College, where Burne-Jones's earliest window (done in 1856 for Messrs Powell on Rossetti's recommendation) may be seen in the timbered dining-hall, built by Gilbert Scott under the direction of that remarkable man the Rev. Steevens, founder of the college and Lord of the Manor of Bradfield.

By this time Morris had become such a formidable opponent at singlestick that his friend W.H.Bliss, a fellow pupil at Guy's house, records that, in order to guard himself against his impetuous attacks, it was necessary to place a table between them when they played. Bliss recalls Morris's great bodily strength, his intense love of nature, his outdoor tastes. Together the two friends would drag the moat at Water House for perch, with a net of Morris's own manufacture, and go for almost daily rides in Epping Forest. When the other pupils went up to London for a day's amusement, Morris would go off into the forest by himself. On the day of the Duke of Wellington's funeral, instead of taking part in the national mourning, he rode across country to Waltham Abbey, and when his family visited the Great Exhibition of 1851 in Hyde Park, he is said to have sat down and refused to go inside. He had already formed the curious habit of tilting his chair backwards, twisting his legs round it, and then straightening them out till the frame split with a resounding crack. His manners were brusque and impetuous, and he spoke in a husky shout.

At the beginning of June 1852, Morris sat for the matriculation exam in the hall of Exeter College, Oxford. The pale, thin youth sitting next to him was Edward Jones (the prefix 'Burne' was not added until later), the son of a poor Birmingham picture-framer and gilder, who was to become Morris's most intimate, life-long friend. At that time the college was full and their entry had to be deferred until the Lent term of 1853.

CHAPTER TWO

1853–1856

Oxford: Ruskin, Rossetti and Pre-Raphaelitism

WHEN MORRIS came into residence in January 1853, Oxford was still in its outward aspect a medieval city, 'a vision of grey-roofed houses and a long winding street and the sound of many bells', as he later described it in *A Dream of John Ball*. 'On all sides, except where it touched the railway', wrote Burne-Jones,

> the city ended abruptly, as if a wall had been about it, and you came suddenly upon the meadows. There was little brick in the city, it was either grey with stone or yellow with the wash of the pebble-dash in the poorer streets. It was an endless delight to us to wander about the streets, where were still many old houses with wood carving and a little sculpture here and there. The Chapel of Merton College had been lately renovated by Butterfield, and Pollen, a former Fellow of Merton, had painted the roof of it. Many an afternoon we spent in that chapel. Indeed I think the buildings of Merton and the Cloisters of New College were our chief shrines in Oxford.[1]

New College cloisters are still enchanted ground, and it is there and at Merton that one can feel the spirit of the Middle Ages perhaps more than elsewhere at Oxford. R. W. Dixon, who had been up a term already, says that he remembered being taken by Morris 'to look at the Tower of Merton'.[2]

To all appearances the Oxford of 1853 still breathed from its towers what Matthew Arnold called 'the last enchantments of the Middle Age', though, since the shock of Newman's reception into the Church of Rome, little remained, except aesthetically, of the ardours of the Anglo-Catholic revival known as the Oxford Movement. It was only nine years before, in the teeth of fierce opposition from the university, that the railway had been extended from Didcot. In the year that Morris went up to Exeter, Gilbert

Scott built his monster chapel there. It was said to be modelled on the Sainte Chapelle, but whereas that is all soaring grace and light, Scott's chapel is gloomy and ponderous. Indeed, Exeter itself is rather depressing altogether with its dull Gothic Revival buildings in the Turl and Scott's dreary block on Broad Street. The last extension on the corner of Broad Street and the Turl, in shiny black brick, looks like a bank – indeed, the ground floor *is* a bank, symbol of the growing commercial vulgarization of the city as a whole. As Ruskin was to write with extraordinary prevision: 'You shall draw out your plates of glass and beat out your bars of iron till you have encompassed us all . . . with endless perspective of black skeleton and blinding square.'[3]

The undergraduates at Exeter were divided, Mackail tells us, between 'the reading men, immersed in the details of classical scholarship or scholastic theology', and the rest, who 'rowed, hunted, ate and drank largely, and often sank at Oxford into a coarseness of manners and morals distasteful and distressing in the highest degree to a boy whose instinctive delicacy and purity of mind were untouched by any of the flaws of youth'.

Thus, while the royal commissioners of 1850 conceded that 'the grosser exhibitions of vice, such as drunkenness and riot, have, in Oxford, as in the higher classes generally, become rare', the most obvious evils among undergraduates were 'sensual vice, gambling in its various forms and extravagant expenditure. . . . External decency, on the whole, is well preserved in the town of Oxford, but in the villages round Oxford, and in places still more remote from the Proctors' jurisdiction, the opportunities to vice are abundant. The metropolis itself is not beyond the reach of ill-disposed or weak young men who . . . may often have the whole day at their command.' The commissioners also complained of the growing taste among undergraduates for 'totally unsuitable' furniture and decorations, leading to ruinous expense, and 'the excessive habit of smoking', their bills for tobacco amounting in many cases to as much as £40 a year.

Though undergraduates were forbidden to keep horses without the sanction of the head of their college, there was nothing to prevent them from hiring them and, on the grounds that riding may often take the place of worse pursuits, the commissioners noted that it was often overlooked by the authorities. Indeed the blameless Burne-Jones himself was a keen rider, as was Morris. But what they rode forth to see in the surrounding villages were not complaisant maidens (if that is what the commissioners meant by 'opportunities to vice'), so much as Gothic churches and memorial brasses, of which they took rubbings to decorate their rooms.

Nevertheless, for Morris and his new friend Jones, the tall, frail and witty young man from King Edmund's School, Birmingham, their first term's experience was disillusioning. 'The place was languid and indifferent', says Burne-Jones. 'Scarcely anything was left to show that it had passed through such an excited time as ended with the secession of Newman. So we compared our thoughts together upon these things and went angry walks together in the afternoons and sat together in the evenings reading.'[4]

Burne-Jones also recorded his first impressions of Morris:

From the first I knew how different he was from all the men I had ever met. He talked with vehemence and sometimes with violence. I never knew him languid or tired. He was slight in figure in those days; his hair was dark brown and very thick, his nose straight, his eyes hazel-coloured, his mouth exceedingly delicate and beautiful. Before many weeks were past in our first term there were but three or four men in the whole college whom we visited or spoke to. But at Pembroke there was a little Birmingham colony, and with them we consorted when we wanted more company than our own.[5]

These were: Charles Faulkner, a mathematician, a gentle, sensitive man, destined to become one of Morris's closest friends and associated with him in his firm; R. W. Dixon, an old school-friend of Jones, and later Canon of Carlisle, but remembered now as a minor poet and the friend of Gerard Manley Hopkins; and William Fulford, an overwhelming conversationalist, superficially the most brilliant of the whole group, and their senior by about two years.

'But our common-room was invariably Faulkner's,' says Burne-Jones, 'where about nine of the evening Morris and I would often stroll down together, and settle once for all how all people should think.'[6] They were soon to be joined by Cormell Price ('Crom' for short), who had been Burne-Jones's closest school-friend at Birmingham. 'Crom', a young man of captivating charm, soon became another of Morris's intimate friends and the recipient of some of his most enthusiastic early letters. In later life he became head-master of the United Services School, Westward Ho, about which

Rudyard Kipling wrote in *Stalkey & Co.* As Montague Weekley suggests, had it not been for Burne-Jones, who drew him into this group of friends, it is doubtful whether Morris, 'with his instinct for solitude and self-absorption', would have enjoyed Oxford at all,[7] for he is not known to have made any friends outside this immediate circle, which was soon to become an exclusive set known to its members as the Brotherhood.

In the Michaelmas term of 1853 Morris and Burne-Jones moved into rooms in college. 'Morris's rooms were in the little quadrangle affectionately known among Exeter men as Hell Quad, with windows overlooking the small but beautiful Fellows' Garden, the immense chestnut tree that overspreads Brasenose Lane, and the grey masses of the Bodleian Library.'[8] Here, in the evenings, Morris would read to Burne-Jones (he could not bear to be read to himself) largely from works of theology, ecclesiastical history, and ecclesiastical archaeology, as befitted young men destined for the Church. This habit of reading to Burne-Jones continued throughout their lives. Now he read *Tracts for the Times*, medieval chronicles, Neale's *History of the Eastern Church*, Milman's *Latin Christianity*, and, secretly and rather shamefacedly, Kenelm Digby's *Mores Catholici*. Indeed, it was not very long before both Morris and Jones, already Anglo-Catholic in sympathy, were themselves on the verge of going over to Rome.

But their reading was not entirely ecclesiastical. One of Burne-Jones's earliest recollections was of hearing Morris read 'The Lady of Shalott' in a curious, half-chanting voice, with immense stress laid on the rhymes. At this time too, with the publication of the second volume of *The Stones of Venice* in 1853, Ruskin became for them both hero and prophet. In fact, Morris's whole attitude to the arts may be traced to the famous chapter 'Of the Nature of Gothic', which he later described, when reprinting it at the Kelmscott Press, as 'one of the very few necessary and inevitable utterances of the century'.

All Morris's subsequent lectures on art and socialism are, in their general argument, a repetition and expansion of Ruskin's central thesis – that there was an essential virtue in the roughness of the work of the medieval sculptors and carvers, this being the sign of 'the life and liberty of every workman who struck the stone', whereas the fine craftsmanship of the eighteenth century was in comparison dead and the product of the slavish copying of pattern books, while its architecture was 'rigid, cold, inhuman . . . full of insult to the poor in every line'. As for the mechanical finish demanded of modern mass-produced goods, this could only be achieved by reducing the workman to a tool.[9]

But, with his narrow Evangelical Protestantism, Ruskin was also engaged in the thankless task of attempting to free medieval art from all taint of 'Romish error'. The splendour of medieval craftsmanship derived, he argued, solely from the craftsman's pleasure in his work – that is, from the status of the workman himself. Ruskin's art criticism thus became increasingly involved with sociology and economics and it was at this point that Morris was later to take it up and develop it into one of his principal arguments for socialism. Again, Morris's whole attitude to the restoration of ancient buildings derives from Ruskin's *Seven Lamps of Architecture*. 'I never intended to have republished this book', says Ruskin in a preface to a later edition, 'which has become the most useless I ever wrote: the buildings it describes with so much delight being now either knocked down or scraped and patched up into smugness and smoothness more tragic than uttermost ruin.' Here we find the spark which later produced Morris's Society for the Protection of Ancient Buildings, which came to be known familiarly as 'Anti-Scrape'. Again, annotating the splendid description of an English cathedral in Chapter IV of *The Stones of Venice*, for the words 'the great mouldering wall of rugged sculpture', Ruskin advises us to read 'the beautiful new parapet of Mr Scott, with a gross of kings sent down from Kensington'.

For Morris and Burne-Jones at Oxford, Ruskin's *Modern Painters* was a sacred text. Next to Ruskin in their estimation stood the Carlyle of *Past and Present*, with its angry confrontation of the twelfth and the nineteenth centuries. Malory was as yet unknown to them, but a new world opened to Morris in the pages of Thorpe's *Northern Mythology*, a world which, as he grew older, was to dominate his whole imagination, whereas Burne-Jones practically moved and had his being in the world of Malory. Morris was already studying medieval design from illuminated manuscripts in the Bodleian, a splendid Apocalypse of the thirteenth century becoming his ideal book. His letters of this time are decorated with drawings of floriated capitals, windows, arches and gables.

In those days reproductions of great paintings were practically unknown, and Morris and Burne-Jones became very excited by a woodcut copy of Dürer's engraving of *The Knight and Death*, which they discovered in a translation of Fouqué's *Sintram*, a book which supplied Morris with the germ of some of his own early romances. Fouqué was discovered via Charlotte Yonge, whose *The Heir of Redclyffe* mirrored many of the religious ideals and social enthusiasms of the years between the decline of Tractarianism and the outbreak of the Crimean War. For Morris the pious, refined and chivalrous hero, Sir Guy Morville, became something of a model.

It was from Ruskin's Edinburgh Lectures that Morris first heard of the Pre-Raphaelites. 'I was reading in my room', writes Burne-Jones of the year 1854, 'when Morris ran in one morning bringing the newly published book with him: so everything was put aside until he read it all through to me. And there we first saw about the Pre-Raphaelites, and there I first saw the name of Rossetti. So many a day after that we talked of little else but paintings which we had never seen. . . .' Soon after that Millais's *The Return of the Dove to the Ark* was on view at a shop in the High Street, 'and then,' says Burne-Jones, 'we knew.' In the Edinburgh Lectures, Ruskin had stated:

> Pre-Raphaelitism has but one principle, that of absolute, un-compromising truth in all that it does, obtained by working everything, down to the most minute detail, from nature only. (Or, where imagination is necessarily trusted to, by always endeavour-ing to conceive a fact as it was really likely to have happened, rather than as it most prettily *might* have happened.) Every Pre-Raphaelite landscape is painted to the last touch, in the open air from the thing itself. Every Pre-Raphaelite figure, however studied in expression, is a true portrait of some living person. Every minute accessory is painted in the same manner. And one of the chief reasons for the violent opposition with which the school has been attacked by other artists, is the enormous labour which such a system demands from those who adopt it, in contradistinction to the present slovenly and imperfect style.

It is curious that such an admirer of Turner as Ruskin should not have seen how utterly unnatural the brightly and artificially illumin-ated paintings of the Pre-Raphaelites, with their carefully copied detail, actually are. But here, of course, he is adopting moral and scientific rather than aesthetic standards, for obviously photographic literalness does not make a good painting, however great the pains expended on achieving it may have been. Holman Hunt's *The Awakened Conscience* may be a remarkable painting; put it beside a Rembrandt and it will appear as crude as a poster. But, as Burne-Jones wrote later of that time: 'Of painting we knew nothing.' It was enough to read Ruskin on the Pre-Raphaelites: 'With all their faults, their pictures are, since Turner's death, the best—incomparably the best – on the walls of the Royal Academy: and such works as Mr Hunt's "Claudio and Isabella" have never been rivalled, in some respects never approached, at any period of art.' To read this must have been very exciting to young men in 1854, when the Pre-Raphaelites were still a revolutionary body and true to their original principles.

At first, according to Dixon, Morris was regarded by other Pembroke men simply as 'a very pleasant boy . . . who was fond of talking . . . and fond of going down the river with Faulkner, who was a good boating man. He was very fond of sailing a boat. He was also very fond of singlestick and a good fencer.' But, as time went on, they began to notice other things about him too:

> his fire and impetuosity, great bodily strength, and high temper . . . were sometimes astonishing. As, e.g., his habit of beating his own head, dealing himself vigorous blows, to take it out of himself. . . . But his mental qualities, his intellect, also began to be perceived and acknowledged. I remember Faulkner remarking to me, 'How Morris seems to know things, doesn't he?' And then it struck me that it was so. I observed how decisive he was: how accurate, without any effort or formality: what extraordinary power of observation lay at the base of many of his casual or incidental remarks, and how many things he knew that were quite out of our way.

To his tutor, however, Morris appeared as 'a rather rough and un-polished youth, who exhibited no special literary tastes or ability. . . .' Dixon tells us that at a time when most young men at Oxford thought that poetry had reached a final perfection with Tennyson, Morris perceived his limitations. 'The attitude of Morris I should describe as defiant admiration. . . . He said once, "Tennyson's Sir Galahad is rather a mild youth." Morris would often read Ruskin aloud. He had a mighty singing voice, and chanted rather than read those weltering oceans of eloquence as they have never been given before or since, it is most certain.' His reading of Shakespeare was, apparently, equally impressive. 'I remember Morris's Macbeth and his Touchstone particularly; but most of all his Claudio, in the scene with Isabel. He suddenly raised his voice to a loud and horrified cry at the word "Isobel", and declaimed the awful follow-ing speech, "Aye, but to die, and go we know not where" in the same pitch. I never heard anything more overpowering.'[10]

Otherwise Morris worked off his superabundant energy at Mac-laren's gymnasium in Oriel Lane, in fencing, boxing and singlestick. Maclaren once said that Morris's bills for broken foils and sticks equalled those of all the rest of his pupils put together.

During the Long Vacation of 1854 Morris visited Belgium and Northern France, where he saw for the first time the work of Memling and Van Eyck, who, Mackail tells us, remained for him ever after 'absolute and unapproached masters of painting'. In Paris he went to the Musée de Cluny; he also saw the cathedrals of Amiens, Beauvais, Chartres and Rouen. Later he wrote of this experience in 'The Aims of Art':

> Less than forty years ago, I first saw the city of Rouen, then still in its outward aspect a piece of the Middle Ages: no words can tell you how its mingled beauty, history, and romance took hold of me: I can only say that, looking back on my past life, I find it was the greatest pleasure I have ever had: and now it is a pleasure which no one can ever have again: it is lost to the world for ever.

Morris brought back with him, too, an abiding love of the French poplar meadows and the little villages and the waters about the Somme. The very smell of beeswax, wood-smoke, and onions, which greeted the traveller landing in France, was, he said, enough to set his blood tingling in anticipation.

At the beginning of the October term, Morris and Burne-Jones moved into new rooms next-door to each other. They were in the part of Exeter known as the Old Buildings, overlooking the Broad across a little open space with trees and long since pulled down, to be replaced by the dreary Gothic Revival front we now know. They were described by Burne-Jones as: 'Tumbly old buildings, gable-roofed and pebble-dashed, little dark passages led from the staircase to the sitting-rooms, a couple of steps to go down, a pace or two, and then three steps to go up—your face was banged by the door, and then, inside the rooms, a couple of steps up to a seat in the window, and a couple of steps down into the bedroom – the which was bliss.'[11]

It was in October 1854 that Cormell Price came up to Brasenose. 'Morris loved him from the first,' writes Burne-Jones, 'and was always fond of him and tender about him, as we all were.' During this winter term, too, we hear for the first time of Morris's poems. Canon Dixon's account has often been repeated of how one night, when he and Cormell Price went to Exeter, Burne-Jones greeted them with the exclamation: '"He's a big poet!" "Who is?" asked we. "Why Topsy."' [the name his friends gave Morris on account of his abundant curly hair], and how Morris then and there read to them

> the first poem he had ever written in his life. It was called 'The Willow and the Red Cliff'. As he read it, I felt that it was something the like of which had never been heard before . . . perfectly original, whatever its value, and sounding truly striking and beautiful, extremely decisive and powerful in execution. . . . He reached his perfection at once. . . . I expressed my admiration in some way, as we all did, and I remember his remark, 'Well, if this is poetry, it is very easy to write.' From that time onwards, for a term or two, he came to my rooms almost every day with a new poem.[12]

When making a final selection for *The Defence of Guenevere*, Morris destroyed many of his early poems; among those destroyed was 'The Willow and the Red Cliff'. He was wise to do this. Unfortunately, however, he had sent copies of many of them to his sister Emma, who kept them, and 'The Willow and the Red Cliff' was printed by May Morris in Volume XXI of the *Collected Works*. Its survival makes the enthusiasm of Morris's Oxford friends a little suspect. It begins:

> *About the river goes the wind*
> *And moans through the sad grey willow*
> *And calls up sadly to my mind*
> *The heave and swell of the billow.*
>
> *For the sea heaves up beneath the moon,*
> *And the river runs down to it.*
> *It will meet the sea by the red cliff,*
> *Salt water running through it.*

> *That cliff it rises steep from the sea*
> *On its top a thorn tree stands,*
> *With its branches blown away from the sea*
> *As if praying with outstretched hands*
>
> *To be saved from the wind, from the merciless wind*
> *That moaneth through it always,*
> *And very seldom gives it rest*
> *When the dark is falling pallwise.*
>
> *One day when the wind moaned through that tree,*
> *As it moans now through the willow,*
> *On the cliff sat a woman clasping her knee*
> *O'er the rise and fall of the billow.*

When Morris said: 'If this is poetry, it is very easy to write', one can see what he meant. Soon the woman begins to sing about her misery, telling the sun that her lover had plighted his troth to her under 'the happy willow tree'. She then turns to the sea and lets her hair down – 'And the west wind blew it but wearily'. She begins singing again and asks the willow tree if it still has the ring she hung on one of its branches when her lover left her. She then throws a picture of herself and her lover into the sea and soon after follows it over the side of the cliff. The poem ends with the image of the golden ring hanging on the branch of the willow.

'The Willow and the Red Cliff' recalls nothing so much as George du Maurier's parody of Pre-Raphaelite verse 'A Legend of Camelot', with its refrain 'O miserie!' in Gothic type. Of the other early pieces, 'The Kisses', copied out in a letter to Cormell Price next year, is rather better and might even be said to suggest Fra Angelico in feeling. The best of them, 'The Midnight Tilt', he did include, with slight alterations, in *The Defence of Guenevere* as 'Riding Together'.

In the letter to Cormell Price, already referred to, written from Walthamstow in Easter Week 1855, in which he had enclosed 'The Kisses', Morris said: 'I have been in a horrible state of mind about my writing, for I seem to get more and more imbecile as I go on.' Morris was always pretty realistic in his attitude towards his own writing and never thought much of his poetry. In any case, 'The Willow and the Red Cliff' was certainly not 'the first poem he had ever written in his life'. As May Morris has shown,[13] he wrote an ambitious poem on 'The Dedication of the Temple' during his first term at Oxford, this being set as the 'Prize Poem on a Sacred Subject' in the competition open to Bachelors of Arts. Morris was, of course, not eligible, so he must have written it for his own amusement. It was among the poems found by Effie Morris in Aunt Emma's drawer in 1921.[14] It is untitled, but its subject is clear enough.

In March 1855 Morris came of age and inherited £900 a year in his own right. To a young man of his simple tastes, this represented wealth. More important, it meant that he was now free to do as he liked.

The Crimean War was in progress and its awakening effect on opinion at home can be judged from Tennyson's *Maud* and Kingsley's *Two Years Ago*. And then came the news, through *The Times* dispatches, of the appalling sufferings of the wounded and the unspeakable conditions in the field hospitals. 'The terrible cholera epidemic of the autumn of 1854 seemed the climax of a period of physical and moral stagnation', Mackail tells us, 'from which the world was awakening to something like a new birth.' Something of this feeling, and also the exhilaration of discovering his own creative powers, is reflected in the first of the stories Morris began to write this year.

Till late that night I ministered to the sick in that hospital; but when I went away, I walked down to the sea, and paced there to and fro over the hard sand: and the moon showed bloody with the hot mist, which the sea would not take on its bosom, though the dull east wind blew it onward continually. I walked there pondering till a noise from over the sea made me turn and look that way; what was that coming over the sea? Laus Deo! The WEST WIND: Hurrah! I feel the joy I felt then over again now, in all its intensity. How came it over the sea? first far out to sea, so that it was only just visible under the red-gleaming moonlight, far out to sea, while the mists above grew troubled, and wavered, a long level bar of white; it grew nearer quickly, it rushed on toward me fearfully fast, it gathered form, strange, misty, intricate form – the ravelled foam of the green sea; then oh! hurrah! I was wrapped in it – the cold salt spray – drenched with it, blinded by it, and when I could see again, I saw the great green waves rising, nodding and breaking, all coming on together; and over them from wave to wave leaped the joyous WEST WIND; and the mist and the plague clouds were sweeping back eastward in wild swirls; and right away were they swept at last, till they brooded over the face of the dismal stagnant meres, many miles away from our fair city.

At one time Morris had seriously thought of devoting the whole of his fortune to the foundation of a monastery. Newman's community at Littlemore, near Oxford, was already a place of pilgrimage and similar communities had sprung up in other parts of the country. George Edmund Street, the Gothic Revival architect, in whose office Morris was to work next year, had at one time also considered founding an institution, on the model of that founded in Rome by the German Nazarene painters Cornelius and Overbeck (who so strangely anticipated the early Pre-Raphaelites), that would combine college, monastery and workshop for students of the theory and practice of religious art. Street had been living in Oxford since 1852; he had restored several of its churches and was even then building SS Philip and James for the families of married dons in North Oxford, described by Mackail as 'one of the purest examples of a return to the architecture of the 13th century'. Meanwhile, in London, Butterfield was building the harshly ostentatious All Saints, Margaret Street, the exemplar of mid-Victorian High Church sentiment.

The first reference to the idea of a brotherhood occurs in a letter of 1 May 1853, from Burne-Jones to a schoolfellow at Birmingham, who was preparing for Oxford. At that time, May Day morning was still celebrated in Oxford not only by the singing of hymns from Magdalen Tower (a subject of one of Holman Hunt's paintings) but by the blowing of whistles and hunting horns. The day concluded with rowdy celebrations in the streets, more reminiscent of the fifth of November. 'Ten o'clock, evening', writes Burne-Jones. 'I have just been pouring basins of water on the crowds below from Dixon's garret – such fun, by Jove. I have set my heart on founding a Brotherhood. Learn 'Sir Galahad' by heart; he is to be the patron of our Order. I have enlisted one in the project here, heart and soul.' This is probably Morris. A few months later he writes: 'We must enlist you in this crusade and holy warfare against the age.' In October, a year later, he writes to the same correspondent: 'The monastery stands a fairer chance than ever of being founded: I know that it will be some day.'

But by the end of the year monastic ideals began to fade away in face of the more pressing social situation. Price and Faulkner came to Oxford with accounts of the squalor and misery of the great industrial centres festering in the heart of England. Things were at their worst, writes Cormell Price, in the 1840s and 1850s.

There was no protection for the mill-hand or miner – no amuse-ments but prize-fighting, dog-fighting, cock-fighting and drink-ing. When a little boy I saw many prize-fights, bestial scenes: at one a combatant was killed. The country was going to hell apace. At Birmingham School a considerable section of the upper boys were quite awake to the crying evils of the period. . . . We were nearly all day boys, and we could not make short cuts to school without passing through slums of shocking squalor and misery, and often coming across incredible scenes of debauchery and brutality. I remember one Saturday night walking five miles from Birmingham into the Black Country, and in the last three miles I counted more than thirty lying dead drunk on the ground, nearly half of them women.[15]

It is this that lay behind the splendours of the Crystal Palace, with its triumphs of Victorian manufacture, which were to institute such a glorious era of prosperity and peace. So we find Price writing to a friend in May 1855: 'Our Monastery will come to nought I'm afraid. . . . Morris has become questionable on doctrinal points, and Ted [Burne-Jones] is too Catholic to be ordained. He and Morris diverge more and more in views though not in friendship.' Burne-Jones had, in fact, reached an impasse and took up one of the com-missions open to university men during the Crimean War. 'I wanted to go and get killed', he said. But he was rejected as medically unfit.

Lady Burne-Jones recalls her first meeting with Morris, who was to become her hero, at the Royal Academy this year. She saw him standing before Millais's *The Rescue*, examining it closely: 'as he turned to go away, Heeley said, "That's Morris", and introduced us to each other; but he looked as if he scarcely saw me. He was very handsome, of an unusual type – the statues of medieval kings often remind me of him – and at that time he wore no moustache, so that the drawing of his mouth, which was his most expressive feature, could be clearly seen. His eyes always seemed to me to take in rather than to give out. His hair waved and curled triumphantly.'[16]

While in London, Morris and Burne-Jones went to 'a very pretty old fashioned house on Tottenham Green' to call on a Mr Windus, to see Madox Brown's *The Last of England*, the idea of emigration to the colonies being very much in the air just then and invested with a sort of religious sanction. At the end of the summer term that year at the house of Thomas Combe, the head of the Clarendon Press, they also saw two pictures by Holman Hunt. But their greatest admiration was reserved for Rossetti's water-colour of Dante drawing the head of Beatrice. 'We had already fallen in with a copy of *The Germ* containing Rossetti's poem "The Blessed Damozel"', notes Burne-Jones, 'and at once he seemed to us the chief figure in the Pre-Raphaelite Brotherhood.'

As soon as term was over, Morris and Burne-Jones went to Cambridge to see the latter's friend Wilfred Heeley of Trinity, who next year became one of the editors of *The Oxford and Cambridge Magazine*. During the train journey up to Cambridge from London, the two friends talked of 'old French chronicles' and on their first evening in Cambridge they 'went before any other place to see the little round church; and there Heeley showed us the first edition of Tennyson's poems with the "Hesperides" in it and the earlier "Mariana of the South", to our great delight and content. Three or four very happy days we passed.'

In a letter to Cormell Price written from Walthamstow after the Cambridge visit, Morris discusses the contents of the first number of *The Oxford and Cambridge Magazine*, which he was to finance:

I have finished the tale I began last term and failed signally therein. I am afraid that it won't do for the 'Brotherhood' [the original title of the magazine]: I am going to send it to Dixon and Ted to look at, and see if it is altogether hopeless, will you look at it too? . . . If you remember, you were to review 'North and South' [by Mrs Gaskell]: are you thinking of it?

As to Cambridge, it is rather a hole of a place, and can't compare for a moment with Oxford; it is such a very different kind of place too, that one is inclined to laugh, at least I do when I think of it. I suppose by this time Ted has told you about it, and how we went to see Ely, which disappointed me somewhat, it is so horribly spoilt with very well meant restorations, as they facetiously term them . . . outside happily it has been hardly touched, which makes the exterior much more beautiful and interesting than the interior.

He goes on to discuss the Royal Academy exhibition.

Millais's picture is indeed grand, how gorgeously the dawning is painted! I had been sitting up late the night before, and saw the dawn break, through the window in our hall, just as it might have been there, minus the smoke. There was a very sweet little picture by Collins in the Octagon room called 'The Good Harvest of '54' did you notice it? I think Maclise's picture [of the wrestling scene in *As You Like It*] about as bad as possible, fancy the brute spoiling one of the best scenes in your favourite comedy, don't you hate him therefore? . . .

He signs himself 'Yours most lovingly Topsy'.

Two previous letters from Walthamstow to Cormell Price of April this year mention several brass-rubbing expeditions to Essex and Surrey churches.

The other day I went 'a-brassing' near the Thames on the Essex side: I got two remarkable brasses and three or four others that were not remarkable: one was a Flemish brass of a knight, date 1370, very small; another a brass (very small, with the legend gone) of a priest in his shroud: I think there are only two other shrouded brasses in England.

I am going a-brassing again some time soon: to Rochester and thereabouts, also to Stoke D'Abernon in Surrey. . . .

This magnificent brass of a mailed knight, Sir John d'Aubernoun of 1277, being, in fact, the earliest in England and still in a remarkable state of preservation.

On 19 July 1855 Morris went to France with Burne-Jones and Fulford, crossing by Folkestone and Boulogne and going straight to Abbeville, where they arrived late in the evening. Next day he was up before the others and called them to come out and see the town before breakfast. They climbed the tower of St Wolfram's to get a clear view of 'the high-pitched roofs and irregular streets of the town and the low hills and the bright fields of the country round'. In the afternoon they left for Amiens and spent an hour in

the cathedral before dinner, returning to it afterwards. 'Morris sur-
veyed it with calm joy', wrote Fulford in one of his letters home,
'and Jones was speechless with admiration. It did not awe me until
it got dark, for we stayed till after nine, but it was so solemn, so
human and divine in its beauty, that love cast out fear.' In an account
he wrote for *The Oxford and Cambridge Magazine* Morris said:

> I think I felt inclined to shout when I first entered Amiens
> Cathedral. It is so free and vast and noble that I did not feel the
> least awestruck or humbled by its size and grandeur: I have not
> often felt thus when looking on architecture, but have felt at all
> events at first, intense exultation at the beauty of it. That, and a
> certain kind of satisfaction in looking at the geometrical tracery
> of the windows, and the sweep of the huge arches, were I think
> my first feelings in Amiens Cathedral.

The tour was originally meant to be a walking tour – 'for cheapness
sake,' says Burne-Jones, 'not that we walked far, but started with
fine ideas of economy, necessary to me and conceded by him
[Morris] who never said whether he had, or had not, money'. But
at Amiens Morris fell lame, 'filling the streets with imprecations on
all bootmakers'. He bought a pair of carpet slippers and in these
walked from Clermont to Beauvais, a distance of about eighteen
miles. But he grew so footsore that they were forced to continue
their journey either by diligence or train.

The thought of the restorations going on at Notre-Dame made
Morris urge his companions not to stop at Paris, but to go straight
on to Chartres. Burne-Jones, however, wanted to go to the Louvre
and Fulford wanted to see Paris itself, and after all, there was the
Musée de Cluny to pacify Morris. But, as he had warned them,
they found the sculptures of Notre-Dame 'half taken down and lying
in careless wreck under the porches'. At the Sainte Chapelle they
saw restoration in all its glory. They were, however, delighted to
find no less than seven Pre-Raphaelites at the Beaux-Arts: three by
Hunt, including *The Light of the World*; three by Millais, and one by
Collins. But only Millais's *The Order of Release* seemed to be attract-
ing any attention, perhaps because of the Ruskin scandal. At Burne-
Jones's special desire, they went to the opera to hear *Le Prophète*,
but Morris 'seemed a good deal bored'.

In fact, he was so fidgety in Paris that after three days they left.
They spent two days at Chartres, nearly all the time in the cathedral,

and then went north to Rouen. On 10 August Morris wrote ecstatically to Cormell Price from Avranches:

> O! the glories of the Churches we have seen! for we have seen the last of them now, we finished up with Mont S. Michel yesterday and we are waiting here (which is a very beautiful place, however) till Saturday evening or Sunday morning when we shall go back to Granville and take steamer for Jersey and Southampton. Crom, we have seen nine Cathedrals, and let me see how many non-Cathedral Churches; I must count them on my fingers; there, I think I have missed some but I have made out 24 splendid Churches some of them surpassing first-rate English Cathedrals.

From Avranches they went by rail to Maintenon and then by a little one-horse conveyance

> through the beautiful country to Dreux, for a distance of about 17 miles. . . . I almost think I like that part of the country better than any other part of the lovely country we have seen in France; so gloriously the trees are grouped, all manner of trees, but more especially the graceful poplars and aspens, of all kinds; and the hedgeless fields of grain, and beautiful herbs that they grow for forage whose names I don't know, the most beautiful fields I ever saw yet, looking as if they belonged to no man, as if they were planted not to be cut down in the end, and to be stored in barns and eaten by the cattle but that rather they were planted for their beauty only, that they might grow always among the trees, mingled with the flowers, purple thistles, and blue cornflowers, and red poppies, growing together with the corn round the roots of the fruit trees, in their shadows, and sweeping up to the brows of the long low hills till they reached the sky, changing sometimes into long fields of vines, or delicate lush green forage; and they all looked as [if] they would grow there for ever, as if they had always grown there, without change of seasons, knowing no other time than the early August.

And of their ride from Louviers to Rouen he wrote:

> O! the trees! it was all like the country in a beautiful poem, in a beautiful Romance such as might make a background to Chaucer's Palamon and Arcite; how we could see the valley

winding away along the side of the Eure a long way, under the hills: but we had to leave it and go to Rouen by a nasty, brim-stone, noisy, shrieking railway train that cares not twopence for hill or valley, poplar tree or lime tree, corn poppy, or blue corn-flower, or purple thistle and purple vetch, white convolvulus, white clematis, or golden S. John's wort: that cares not twopence either for tower, or spire, or apse, or dome, for it will be as noisy and obtrusive under the spires of Chartres or the towers of Rouen, as it is [under] Versailles or the Dome of the Invalides; verily railways are ABOMINATIONS; and I think I have never fairly realised this fact till this our tour. . . .

Ah me! if only you had been here, how I have longed for you! so very, very much.

It was at the conclusion of this holiday that, walking together on the quays at Le Havre late into the August night, Morris and Burne-Jones decided definitely not to take Holy Orders, but to devote themselves for the rest of their lives to art; that their undergraduate lives should be wound up as soon as possible, Jones to be a painter, Morris an architect. 'It was a resolve only needing final conclusion', says Burne-Jones, 'we were bent on that road for the whole past year, and after that night's talk we never hesitated more. That was the most memorable night of my life.'[17] Mackail has told us, in an eloquent passage, what this meant to Morris. 'For him, then and always, the word architecture bore an immense, and one might almost say a transcendental, meaning. Connected at a thousand points with all the other specific arts which ministered to it out of a thousand sources, it was itself the tangible expression of all the order, the comeliness, the sweetness, nay, even the mystery and the law, which sustain man's world and make human life what it is.'[18]

Soon after returning to England, Morris went to Birmingham to stay with Burne-Jones. Fulford and Price were there too, and Wilfred Heeley, who had just passed into the Indian Civil Service. Three weeks were spent in Birmingham 'in furious reading and talking' and discussions of the magazine. 'Ted, Top and Fulford came over to tea and supper', reads an entry in Price's diary for 7 September. 'Had much talk with Top about architecture and organization of labour. Discussed the tone of reviews in general, and "Blackwood" in particular. It is unanimously agreed that there is to be no showing off, no quips, no sneers, no lampooning in our Magazine.' The reference is to a review in *Blackwood's* of Tennyson's *Maud*, which had aroused much indignation among 'the set', *Maud* being a poem they all greatly admired. On 9 September Price noted: 'Saw Ted and Topsy. Talked chiefly about the review. Politics to be almost eschewed: to be mainly Tales, Poetry, friendly Critiques, and social articles.'

According to the *Memorials*, the idea of *The Oxford and Cambridge Magazine* as a medium for the expression of their principles and enthusiasms, and also as a place for the publication of original work, had originally come from Dixon. Price's diary also mentions a meeting at Heeley's house, where Carlyle's *Past and Present* and *The French Revolution* were the chief subjects of discussion.

When Morris and Burne-Jones were alone together, they communed with each other in their own world of imagination. 'Of course imagination doesn't end my work', said Burne-Jones, 'I go on always in that strange land that is more true than real.' And now he discovered a book which seemed to belong entirely to that strange land – the *Morte d'Arthur*. He had come upon Southey's edition in Cornish's bookshop one day, but had been unable to buy it. Morris bought it, however, as soon as he set eyes on it and had it bound in white vellum, and so great did their love and veneration for this book become that he and Burne-Jones were almost too shy to speak of it, even among their intimate friends.

It was not till a year later, when they heard Rossetti say that the two greatest books in the world were the Bible and the *Morte d'Arthur* that their tongues were unloosed. 'I sometimes think', writes Lady Burne-Jones, 'that the book never can have been loved as it was by those two men. With Edward it became literally a part of himself. Its strength and beauty, its mystical religion and noble chivalry of action, the world of lost history and romance in the names of people and places – it was his own birthright upon which he entered.'[19] In the case of Morris it inspired a large part of his first and most passionately felt book, *The Defence of Guenevere*, which has a flaming imaginative intensity he was never again to recapture.

From Birmingham, Morris went to Worcester, now practically demolished by developers, like so many of our old towns. Having taken the decision to become an architect, he wrote to George Edmund Street, with a view to entering his office. He also began to read hard for his Finals, writing to Price on 29 September from Walthamstow:

> I went to Malvern the day after I parted from you, it certainly is a very splendid place, but very much spoiled by being made into a kind of tea gardens for idle people. The Abbey bells rang all day for the fall of Sebastopol, and when I went by railway to Clay Cross the next day, they hoisted flags up everywhere, particularly on the chimneys at Burton – at Chesterfield they had a flag upon the top of their particularly ugly twisted spire – at Clay Cross, by some strange delusion, they had hoisted all over the place the *Russian* tricolour (viz., horizontal stripes of blue, red and white) thinking, honest folks, that it was the French flag; they had no peal of bells at Clay Cross, only one bell of a singularly mild and chapelly nature, said bell was tolled by the patriotic inhabitants ALL day long, the effect of which I leave you to imagine. My life is going to become a burden to me, for I am going (beginning from Tuesday next), to read for six hours a day at Livy, Ethics &c. – please pity me.

Evidently Morris had given the impression that he intended to leave the university without taking his degree, for Price records in his diary under 28 September: 'Wrote to Morris two sheets abusing him roundly for thinking of leaving Oxford.' A week later, Morris replied:

> make your mind easy about my coming back next term, I am certainly coming back, though I should not have done so if it had not been for my Mother: I don't think even if I get through Greats that I shall take my B.A., because they won't allow you not to sign the 39 Articles unless you declare that you are 'extra Ecclesiam Anglicanam' which I'm not, and don't intend to be, and I won't sign the 39 Articles. Of course I should like to stay up at Oxford for a much longer time, but (I told you didn't I?) I am going, if I can, to be an architect, and I am too old already and there is no time to lose, I MUST make haste, it would not do for me, dear Crom, even for the sake of being with you, to be a lazy, aimless, useless, dreaming body all my life long, I have wasted enough time already, God knows; not that I regret having gone to Oxford, how could I? for I should be a very, poor helpless kind of thing without Ted and you. Didn't I tell you that I meant to ask Street of Oxford if he would take me?

But Mrs Morris did not take kindly to the idea at all, for it had always been understood that William was intended for the Church. Besides, an architect was, after all, a kind of artist. It is true that an architect did work in an office and was thus safeguarded from the worst dangers to which painters, in their more bohemian way of life, were exposed. So when he returned to Oxford in the autumn, Morris wrote to reassure his mother about his intentions. In the course of a long letter, he said:

> First I suppose you think that you have as it were thrown away money on my kind of apprenticeship for the Ministry; let your mind be easy on this score; for, in the first place, an University education fits a man about as much for being a ship-captain as a Pastor of souls: besides your money has by no means been thrown away, if the love of friends faithful and true, friends first seen and loved here, if this love is something priceless, and not to be bought again anywhere and by any means: if moreover by living here and seeing evil and sin in its foulest and coarsest forms, as one does day by day, I have learned to hate any form of sin, and to wish to fight against it, is not this well too? Think, I pray you, Mother, that all this is for the best: moreover, if any fresh burden were to be laid upon you, it would be different, but as I am able to provide myself for my new course of life, the new money to be paid matters nothing. If I were not to follow this occupation I in truth know not what I should follow with any chance of success, or hope of happiness in my work; in this I am pretty confident I shall succeed, and make I hope a decent architect sooner or later: and you know too that in any work that one delights in, even the merest drudgery connected with it is delightful too. I shall be master too of a useful trade; one by which I should hope to earn money, not altogether precariously, if other things fail. . . . Will you tell Henrietta that I can quite sympathise with her disappointment, that I think I understand it, but I hope it will change to something else before long, if she sees me making myself useful; for that I will by no means give up things I have thought of for the bettering of the world in so far as lies in me.

He concludes by apologizing to his mother for 'speaking somewhat roughly to you when we had conversation last on this matter, speaking indeed far off from my heart because of my awkwardness, and I thought I would try to mend this a little now: have I done so at all?' Mackail says that Morris wrote to his mother 'with an un-surpassable delicacy of tenderness'. As a matter of fact, economic arguments are well to the fore and doubtless impressed Mrs Morris more than anything else with the seriousness of his intentions.

Morris passed his Final Schools in the autumn of 1855 and arranged to begin work in Street's Beaumont Street office at the beginning of the next year. Then he saw Dalziel's woodcut from Rossetti's drawing *The Maids of Elfenmere* in Allingham's *Day and Night Songs*, and at once set to work drawing on wood and cutting the designs himself. Rossetti, however, was disgusted with Dalziel's woodcut; yet it still dominates the book with its strange romantic appeal and should be compared to the mawkishly pretty illustrations by Arthur Hughes, though these faithfully reflect the spirit of Allingham's verses.

Meanwhile *The Oxford and Cambridge Magazine* was in active preparation. 'Ground out a prospectus with Top', records Cormell Price in his diary under 22 November. 'In the evening to Pembroke and go on with the prospectus, Fulford joining in and doing lion's share.' The prospectus appeared in nearly all the other monthlies. 'We have thoroughly set ourselves to work now and banded our-selves into an exclusive Brotherhood of seven', Burne-Jones wrote to his cousin Maria Choyce.

> Mr Morris is proprietor. The expense will fall very heavily upon him, I fear, for it cannot be published under £500 per annum, exclusive of any drawings which we shall sometimes give: he hopes not to lose more than £300, but even that is a great deal. . . . Not one magazine in a hundred pays, but we are full of hope. Two of the ablest young writers of Cambridge have joined us, and for three of our Oxford contributors I should look long up and down the world before I could name their peers.

The Oxford and Cambridge Magazine, conducted by Members of the two Universities was published by Bell & Daldy at a shilling monthly. The first number appeared on 1 January 1856, seventy-two closely printed pages set in double columns. It contained the first instalment of a long essay by Heeley on Sir Philip Sidney, Fulford on Tenny-son, 'The Cousins, a Tale' by Burne-Jones, 'The Story of the Unknown Church' by Morris, the best of his early prose romances, 'The Rivals, a Tale' by Dixon, Macdonald on *Hiawatha*, Burne-Jones on Thackeray's *The Newcomes*, Heeley on Kingsley's sermons, and 'Winter Weather', a poem by Morris. On 9 January Miss Price recorded in her diary: 'Morris does not like being Editor of the O. and C. Magazine, so gives Fulford £100 a year to be Editor.' Fulford took a lodging at 20 Montpelier Square, Brompton Road, with Heeley and this became the regular meeting-place of the contributors. 'On Tuesday I dined at Brompton', Burne-Jones writes to Cormell Price, 'Topsy and Macdonald were there, five of us together, like old times.'

It was Fulford who saw that the magazine appeared regularly on the first day of every month for a year. It appeared without illustrations, as these were found to be too expensive after all, though two photographs of medallion portraits by Woolner of Carlyle and Tennyson were printed and sold separately. Eight hundred copies of the first number were printed, a great many of these being for presentation, and the circulation of the succeeding numbers slowly fell off. By the end of the year there was a large stock of unsold copies on the publisher's shelves. But Ruskin praised it warmly and half-promised to contribute, though he said in a note to Burne-Jones that 'people don't want honest criticism' and that he had 'never known an honest journal get on yet'. Tennyson wrote to Fulford: 'I find in such articles as I have read, a truthfulness and earnestness very refreshing to me. . . . As to your essay on myself, you may easily see that I have some difficulty in speaking: to praise it, seeming too much like self-praise.'

Later numbers contained three poems by Rossetti: 'The Burden of Nineveh', a revised version of 'The Blessed Damozel' and 'The Staff and Scrip'. In the course of his essay on *The Newcomes*, Burne-Jones had written that Rossetti's illustration to Allingham's *Day and Night Songs* was 'the most beautiful drawing for an illustration I have ever seen, the weird faces of the maids of Elfenmere, the musical timed movements of their arms together as they sing, the face of the man, above all, are such as only a great artist could conceive'. No wonder Rossetti was pleased when he read it, even though he had never heard of 'young Jones' before.

Apart from the essays on Ruskin, Tennyson and Thackeray, there were thoughtful articles on Mrs Gaskell's Lancashire, the position of women, Charlotte Brontë and, for that time, an unusual choice of Shakespearean subjects – the poems, *Timon of Athens* and *Troilus and Cressida*. One of the articles (probably by Fulford) speaks of the necessity for 'young men of the present age' to meditate upon 'social wrongs, their causes, and the best way in which they, each in their several spheres, may help to heal them', an obligation which extends 'even to those who love the life of the recluse, and would strive to conjure up images of the Middle Ages as they pore in some quaint Gothic work over the stirring chronicle of the olden days'.[20]

Morris's contributions were, besides those of the January number already mentioned: 'The Churches of Northern France. No. 1. Shadows of Amiens' (February); 'A Dream' (prose romance) and a review of Browning's *Men and Women* (March); a tale of modern life, 'Frank's Sealed Letter' (April); the poem 'Riding Together' (May); the chivalric prose romance 'Gertha's Lovers' and the poem 'Hands' – that is, the Prince's song in 'Rapunzel' (July); the stories 'Death the Avenger and Death the Friend', 'Svend and his Brethren' and the continuation of 'Gertha's Lovers' (August); 'Lindenborg Pool' and 'The Chapel in Lyonesse' (September); part of 'The Hollow Land' and 'Pray But One Prayer for Me', later called 'Summer Dawn' (October), and 'Golden Wings' (December).

Most of these tales are immature, with an adolescent feverishness, though they all have striking passages, particularly in the observation of nature, as in the beautiful description of the garden in 'The Story of the Unknown Church' and the evil, stricken landscape of 'Lindenborg Pool', where the priest is tricked into giving Extreme Unction to a pig. But it was the essay on Amiens which gave Morris the most trouble; the poems came naturally as breathing and so, apparently, did the dream-like tales. In January he had written to Burne-Jones from Walthamstow about the Amiens essay: 'It is very poor and inadequate, I cannot help it: it cost me more trouble than anything I have yet written. I ground at it the other night from nine o'clock till half-past four a.m., when the lamp went out, and I had to creep upstairs to bed through the great dark house like a thief.'

The essay is a most detailed and laborious description of the cathedral. Originally Morris had intended to write a series of articles on the cathedrals of Northern France, but work in Street's office now took up too much of his time. So he wrote a story about a mason working on the west front of Amiens instead – 'The Story of the Unknown Church'. The description of the garden in this story is very Pre-Raphaelite in its detail and its feeling for primary colours. It is an early example of the meticulous accuracy of vision that went into the later designs for wallpapers and textiles; the trellises anticipate those he was to erect later in his own garden at Red House:

> . . . in the garden were trellises covered over with roses and con-volvulus, and the great-leaved fiery nasturtium; and specially all along by the poplar trees were there trellises, but on these nothing grew but deep crimson roses; and hollyhocks too were all in blossom at that time, great spires of pink, and orange and red, and white, with their soft, downy leaves. I said that nothing grew on the trellises by the poplars but crimson roses, but I was not quite right, for in many places the wild flowers had crept into the garden from without; lush green briony, with white-green blossoms, that grows so fast, one could almost think that we see it grow, and deadly nightshade, La bella donna, O! so beautiful; red berry, and purple, yellow-spiked flower, and deadly cruel-looking, dark green leaf. . . .

In the review of Browning's *Men and Women* we can hear the ardent, earnest young Morris talking to his friends at Oxford:

> but now Childe Roland passes straight from our eyes to the place where the true and brave live for ever; and as far as we go, his life flows out triumphantly with that blast he blew. And was it not well to leave us with that snatch of old song ringing through our ears like the very horn-blast that echoed all about the windings of that dismal valley of death? . . . In my own heart I think I love this poem the best of all in these volumes.

Indeed, it was the hopeless, knightly quest of Childe Roland, the unavailing courage that appealed to him, as it always would.

On 21 January 1856, Morris signed his articles and began work in Street's office, taking rooms in St Giles, in a house opposite St John's. Street's senior clerk, or chief assistant, was Philip Webb, who describes Morris when they first met as 'a slim boy like a wonderful bird just out of his shell'. Morris only stayed with Street nine months and for most of that time was occupied in copying a drawing of the doorway of St Augustine's Church, Canterbury. He found great difficulty, we are told, in delineating the many archmouldings, and 'at last the compass points nearly bored a hole through the drawing-board.'

The general atmosphere of the office was gay and light-hearted. Because one of Street's pupils stuttered and could sing better than he could speak, it became customary to chant to him in Gregorian plainsong through rolls of foolscap. On Ascension Day they were given the day off provided they went to church, Street remarking: 'Some of you, I know, have voices.'

The atmosphere was very different from the gloomy oppressiveness prevailing in Butterfield's office in the Adelphi. All the repellent characteristics of Butterfield can be seen in Keble Chapel, whereas the charm of Street is evident in St James-the-Less, Thorndike Street, Westminster, which he was designing in 1858 as an answer to Butterfield's All Saints, Margaret Street, for which he nevertheless had a great admiration, referring to it as 'not only the most beautiful, but the most vigorous, thoughtful and original of them all' – that is, of the new churches then being built on Tractarian principles. But the remarkable wrought-iron railings of St James-the-Less anticipate designs associated with Art Nouveau. Street believed that an architect should not be just a builder, but a blacksmith, a painter, a fabric worker and a designer of stained glass. In this he was the original inspiration of Morris and Webb and of the whole Arts and Crafts movement.

In his spare time, besides writing poems and stories, Morris was modelling in clay, carving in wood and stone and working at illumination and embroidery. Thus the pattern to be followed all his life of running a number of different crafts simultaneously, and jumping from one to the other as the humour took him, was estab-lished quite early. Both Street and Webb were embroidery enthusiasts. Webb was a personal friend of Agnes Blencowe, who, with Street's sister, founded the Ladies' Ecclesiastical Embroidery Society.[21] In 1855 Morris had an embroidery frame made, Jane Morris told Mackail, and some worsteds dyed for him by an old French couple. The experimental piece of embroidery done at this time used to hang in Red House, Bexley Heath. The design was a repeating pattern of a flowering tree with birds and a scroll bearing the motto 'If I can'.

Burne-Jones had gone down to London at Easter this year to begin painting under Rossetti's guidance, and Morris went down almost every week-end to spend Sunday with him and then caught the early train back to Oxford in order to be at Street's office by ten o'clock. Saturday evenings were spent with Rossetti roaming about

the streets or going to a play, which Rossetti usually found too
boring to sit out, and then they would go back to his studio at
Chatham Place and sit talking or reading with him until three or
four o'clock in the morning. Sunday Morris would spend reading
Morte d'Arthur with Burne-Jones, and Rossetti would join them
during the afternoon.

At the Academy that summer Morris was much struck by Arthur
Hughes's *April Love* and on 17 May he wrote to Burne-Jones: 'Will
you do me a favour, viz. go and nobble that picture called "April
Love", as soon as possible lest anybody else should buy it.' He would
also have seen five paintings by Millais, Hunt's *Scapegoat* and Wallis's
Death of Chatterton. Rossetti had already introduced him to Holman
Hunt and to Madox Brown; he was falling more and more under
the influence of Rossetti's view that the only thing worth doing in
life was painting. In July he wrote somewhat breathlessly from
Oxford to a friend, probably Cormell Price:

> I have seen Rossetti twice since I saw the last of you; spent almost
> a whole day with him the last time, last Monday, that was. Hunt
> came in while we were there, a tallish, slim man with a beautiful
> red beard, somewhat of a turn-up nose, and deep set dark eyes:
> a beautiful man. . . . Rossetti says I ought to paint, he says I
> shall be able; now as he is a very great man, and speaks with
> authority and not as the scribes, I *must* try. I don't hope much, I
> must say, yet will try my best – he gave me practical advice on
> the subject. . . . So I am going to try, not giving up the architec-
> ture, but trying if it is possible to get six hours a day for drawing
> besides office work. One won't get much enjoyment out of life
> at this rate, I know well, but that don't matter: I have no right
> to ask for it at all events – love and work, these two things only.
> . . . I can't enter into politico-social subjects with any interest, for
> on the whole I see that things are in a muddle, and I have no
> power or vocation to set them right in ever so little a degree. My
> work is the embodiment of dreams in one form or another. . . .
> Yet I shall have enough to do, if I actually master this art of
> painting. . . . Ned and I are going to live together. I go to London
> early in August.

Under 24 August 1856, Madox Brown recorded in his diary:
'Yesterday Rossetti brought his ardent admirer Morris of Oxford,
who bought my little "Hayfield" for £40.' At this time Rossetti

did a study of Morris's head for the King David in the Llandaff Cathedral triptych.

After a visit to the Low Countries with Street that autumn, Morris returned more fired with enthusiasm for painting than ever, and adopted Van Eyck's motto, 'Als ich kanne', in a French form of 'Si je puis'. When Street moved his office to Montague Place, Bloomsbury, Morris and Webb went with him. Morris then took rooms at Upper Gordon Street, Bloomsbury, with Burne-Jones, near to Street's office and also to the various drawing schools known as Gandish's in the neighbourhood of Fitzroy Square, where Madox Brown lived. 'Topsy and I live together in the quaintest room in all London', wrote Burne-Jones in August, 'hung with brasses of old knights and drawings of Albert Dürer. . . . Topsy will be a painter, he works hard and is prepared to wait twenty years, loves art more and more every day . . . he is now illuminating "Gwendolen" for Georgie. . . . The Mag. is going to smash – let it go !'

CHAPTER THREE

1856–1859

Red Lion Square: The Oxford Union: Iseult and Guenevere

IN NOVEMBER 1856 Rossetti suggested that Topsy and Ned should take over the rooms at 17 Red Lion Square he had shared with Deverell. If Red Lion Square was dark and dirty, it was at least more interesting than Upper Gordon Street. As Morris and Burne-Jones were only too ready to fall in with anything the master suggested, they took over the first floor. This consisted of three rooms, the window of the large room overlooking the square having been extended to the ceiling to admit 'a painting light'. The tenants of the house were some French feather-dressers named Fauconnier, who carried on their business below.

It is from the time of this move to Red Lion Square that Morris's work as a decorator and manufacturer really begins. Unable to buy even a tolerable chair or a table with which to furnish his rooms, we are told, he at once set about designing his own and having them made by a local carpenter. 'Morris is rather doing the magnificent there,' Rossetti wrote to William Allingham on 18 December 1856, 'and is having some intensely mediaeval furniture made – tables and chairs like incubi and succubi. He and I have painted the back of a chair with figures and inscriptions in gules and vert and azure, and we are all three going to cover a cabinet with pictures.'

The great settle had been designed by Morris on such a scale that the carpenter could not get it up the stairs and the two friends came home one evening to find all the passages and the staircase choked with vast blocks of timber. 'I think', remarked Burne-Jones, 'the measurements had perhaps been given a little wrongly and that it was bigger altogether than he [Morris] had ever meant, but set up it was finally, and our studio was one third less in size. Rossetti came. This was always a terrifying moment to the very last. He laughed, but approved.'[1] Moreover, he straightway made designs for paintings to be done on its central panels: 'Love between the

Sun and Moon', 'The Meeting of Dante and Beatrice in Florence', and their meeting in Paradise. On the backs of the two vast chairs ('such as Barbarossa might have sat in') he painted subjects from Morris's poems – Gwendolen in the witch tower and the prince below kissing her golden hair, from 'Rapunzel', and the arming of a knight from 'Sir Galahad, a Christmas Mystery'.

Rossetti did well to approve of the settle. Now at Red House, Bexley Heath – though deprived of Rossetti's painted panels – it is indeed a splendid piece of furniture and compares well with any-thing produced later for the firm by Webb or Madox Brown. There was also a large round table 'as firm, and as heavy, as a rock', as Rossetti described it. Nor were the chairs lightly to be moved. One of them, mentioned in a note from Burne-Jones to Madox Brown, had a large box overhead in which Rossetti suggested they might keep owls – 'Dear Bruno, Come tonight and see the chair, there's a dear old fellow – such a chair! ! ! ! ! ! Gabriel and Top hook it tomorrow, so do come. Hughes will come, and a stunner or two to make melody. Come soon, there's a nice old chap – victuals and squalor at all hours, but come at 6.'

They were looked after by good-hearted Red Lion Mary, who later became Mrs Nicholson. Her originality, says Lady Burne-Jones, 'all but equalled that of the young men, and she understood them and their ways thoroughly. Their rough and ready hospitality was seconded by her with unfailing good temper; she cheerfully spread mattresses on the floor for friends who stayed there and when mattresses came to an end it was said that she built up beds with boots and portmanteaux.' Morris's quick temper annoyed her, but she said: 'though he was so short-tempered, I seemed so necessary to him at all times, and felt myself his Man Friday'.

It is to this Red Lion Square period, which lasted until 1859, that many of the earlier Morris legends belong. His boisterousness, eccentricity and endearing moments of helplessness, as when he stood rubbing his back against the door like a sheep when bored, became the subject of endless stories among his friends. There is the story of Morris opening the door one morning after breakfast and roaring to Mary: 'Those six eggs were bad. I have eaten them, but don't let it occur again.' He even taught Mary, as he seems to have taught nearly every woman he came into contact with, to embroider his designs for hangings. As well as everything else, she sewed draperies for their models and would have posed for them herself

40

had she not been too short and too plain for a 'Ladye in a Bower'. Burne-Jones reports the following conversation with Mary. 'I shouldn't think Mr Morris knew much about women, sir.' 'Why not, Mary?' 'I don't know, sir, but I should think he was such a bear with them.'[2]

For the two years or so during which he worked hard at painting, Mackail tells us, Morris was moody and irritable. 'He brooded much by himself, and lost for the time a good deal of his old sweetness and affectionateness of manner.' Morris did not really feel that he was a painter, yet he had abandoned architecture after only nine months, finding it impossible to combine the two vocations. Another objection against architecture was that 'he could not get at it at first hand'. Characteristically, he announced in an offhand way to his mother that he was leaving Street's office, while on a visit to her with Burne-Jones. Mrs Morris seems to have thought Burne-Jones responsible for this.

By this time, too, Morris had ceased to shave and was beginning to present the shaggy appearance familiar from later photographs. Mrs Morris must have felt that her worst fears were now confirmed and that her son had after all become a good-for-nothing Bohemian and 'an idle objectless man'. But, in fact, as well as working hard at drawing and painting from the figure – an occupation he detested – Morris was already developing his natural facility for pattern designing, in which he at first followed the example of illuminated manuscripts in the Bodleian Library and the British Museum. 'In all illumination and work of that kind', Rossetti wrote of him in 1856, 'he is quite unrivalled by anything modern that I know.'[3] He was also working at wood-carving. 'I can still see in my mind's eye', Lady Burne-Jones records, 'the long, folded white evening tie which he nailed in loops against his bedroom wall in order to hold his tools.'

Ruskin was another frequent visitor to Red Lion Square. 'To-day we are to go and see Ruskin', Burne-Jones wrote to his friend Miss Sampson. And after their return, he added: 'Just come back from being with our hero for four hours – so happy we've been: he is so kind to us, calls us his dear boys and makes us feel like such old friends. To-night he comes to our rooms to carry off my drawing and show it to lots of people: to-morrow night he comes again, and every Thursday the same – isn't it like a dream?'[4]

But Morris still could not tear himself away from his Oxford friends and on Saturdays often went up to spend a few hours with them. In June 1857 Rossetti, writing to Bell-Scott, mentions that Morris 'is now busily painting his first picture, "Sir Tristram after his illness in the Garden of King Mark's Palace Recognised by the Dog he had given Iseult" from the Morte d'Arthur. It is all being done from nature of course, and I believe will turn out capitally.' If this painting was ever finished, it has since disappeared, though it is the subject of one of the four stained-glass windows Morris designed five years later for the music-room of Harden Grange, Bingley, Yorkshire, and there is a water-colour study for this in the Victoria and Albert Museum which answers to Rossetti's description. He was, however, undoubtedly working at a painting on the subject of Tristram and Iseult, for which there is a sensitive pencil study known as *Tristram and Iseult on the Ship* – though there is no sign of a ship in the drawing, but rather a garden fence and a tree. This may be the study for the painting which Rossetti told Madox Brown in January 1858 had been bought by Plint of Leeds for £75, and William Rossetti in his note on this letter says: 'Topsy's picture was a Tristram and Iseult.'[5] Brown also noted in his diary under 27 January 1858: 'Plint has . . . bought Topsy's (Morris) Tristram and Isult [sic].'[6]

Later in the year we hear of another water-colour, *The Soldan's Daughter in the Palace of Glass*, done when he was on a visit to Dixon in Manchester. This, like Plint's *Tristram and Iseult*, has also disappeared. According to Mackail, the soldan's daughter was seated in a heavy arm-chair, like one of those at Red Lion Square, and the palace was all in shades of bluish glass.

During this visit to Manchester in October to see the Art Treasures Exhibition of 1857, it was the ivories that made the greatest impression on Morris. He wrote there his poem 'Praise of My Lady', included next year in *The Defence of Guenevere*, which begins:

> *My Lady seems of ivory*
> *Forehead, straight nose and cheeks that be*
> *Hollow'd a little mournfully.*
> *Beata mea Domina!*

The poem develops into a description of Jane Burden, whom he had met during the Long Vacation at Oxford.

It was at the Manchester exhibition that Ruskin delivered his first lectures on socialism, 'The Political Economy of Art'. Whether Morris attended the lectures or not, he must have read them when they were published under the title of *A Joy for Ever and its Price in the Market,* as they set the tone of many of those he was to deliver himself. Ruskin firmly believed in mastering the practical details of every craft before producing designs for it. Thus he built an entire brickwork column in the Oxford University Museum, even though it had to be rebuilt later by a professional bricklayer. 'Half my power of ascertaining facts of any kind connected with the arts', he said, 'is my stern habit of doing the thing with my own hands till I know its difficulty.' This principle was to guide all Morris's work in the applied arts for the rest of his life.

When Morris and Rossetti came back from Oxford one day in the summer, they were full of a scheme for painting frescoes on the walls of Woodward's new Union Society. The octagonal hall has large bays above the gallery between the windows and the idea was to fill these blank spaces with scenes from the *Morte d'Arthur.* During the Long Vacation, Rossetti enlisted Arthur Hughes, Hungerford Pollen, Spencer Stanhope, Valentine Prinsep and Alexander Munro to join the scheme, besides Morris, Burne-Jones and himself. Prinsep records how Rossetti came to Little Holland House and persuaded him 'to join him and some other fellows in decorating the Union at Oxford'. When Prinsep urged his inexperience, Rossetti waved aside all objections, saying: 'Nonsense, there's a man I know who has never painted anything – his name is Morris – he has under-taken one of the panels and he will do something very good you may depend – so you had better come!'[7]

By the middle of August they were all at work amid shouts of laughter and the popping and fizzing of soda-water bottles. Unfor-tunately the preparation of the surface to be painted had not been considered and the paint was applied direct to the damp plaster. Moreover, each bay was pierced by two windows, which dazzled the sight and made everything painted on the wall surface between almost invisible when looked at from below. Woodward's building was so new that the mortar was scarcely dry and the rough brickwork was only whitewashed over. The artists were to give their work, but the Union was to pay the cost of their lodging and the materials, though no specification was ever drawn up and, as the work dragged on from week to week, there were complaints about the expense.

With his usual impetuosity, Morris began his picture first, finished it first, and set about painting flowers and foliage on the beams of the roof, which, with his decorative genius, turned out to be the most successful part of the whole undertaking. The subject he chose for his wall-painting was 'How Sir Palomydes loved La Belle Iseult with exceeding great love out of measure, and how she loved not him but rather Sir Tristram', a subject curiously prophetic of the future emotional pattern of his own life. It was, however, one that he had already treated in his story 'Frank's Sealed Letter', and was to return to again and again, not only in his uncompleted novel, but in many of his poems.

The profusion of sunflowers in the foreground of Morris's paint-ing caused general amusement and Rossetti suggested that he might help another of the painters out of difficulties by filling the foreground of his bay with scarlet runners. But Morris's design for the decoration of the roof, Burne-Jones says, 'was a wonder to us for its originality and fitness, for he had never before designed anything of the kind. . . . All the autumn through he worked upon the roof high above our heads, and Faulkner, in afternoons when his work was over at the University, would come to help, having always clever hands for drawing.'[8] Burne-Jones wrote home in October that 'Charley comes out tremendously strong on the roof with all kinds of quaint beasts and birds'. Others, Webb, Swan (a friend of Rossetti), and St John Tyrwhitt of Christ Church, all helped and their names were inscribed on one of the rafters. In the dark angles of the roof, they sometimes painted, instead of flowers or animals, little figures of Morris in the attitude of Holbein's Henry VIII, for Morris was already growing somewhat stout and square. The day's work began at eight o'clock and went on as long as the light lasted. 'If they needed models, they sat to each other. Morris had a head always fit for Lancelot or Tristram.' Rossetti, in fact, drew him as Lancelot for his illustration to 'The Lady of Shalott' in the Moxon Tennyson, which appeared that year. Jones, too, appears as Lancelot in Rossetti's sketch for his Union Society painting of *Lancelot's Vision of the Sancgrael*.

But for the purposes of their drawing, they also needed armour of a date so remote that no examples of it existed. So Morris, who always seemed to know everything about the Middle Ages by a kind of second sight, produced designs for a basinet and a surcoat of ringed mail and had them made under his own direction by a local black-smith. But the first time he tried on the basinet, he could not lift the visor and, to the delight of the others, was seen 'embedded in iron, dancing with rage and roaring inside'. When the mail coat arrived, Morris was so delighted with it that he wore it that evening for dinner. It proved to be so well-designed that, though when it lay on the ground one could hardly lift it, 'once put on the body,' Burne-Jones told Mackail, 'its weight was so evenly ordered that it was less uncomfortable than any top coat I ever wore'.[9] The coat of mail, the basinet and a great sword, made at the same time, are now at Walthamstow.

Rossetti's picture remained unfinished, as he stopped work on it when called to London by the dangerous illness of Lizzie Siddal, and never resumed. He also designed two other pictures which were never even begun, 'Lancelot found in Guenevere's Chamber' and 'The three Knights of the Sangrail'. The water-colour study for the latter, painted several years afterwards, gives a good idea of the method used in the Union paintings, which were all done with small water-colour brushes, and also of the brilliance of their radiant greens and reds and blues. Burne-Jones's subject was 'Nimuë luring Merlin' and Arthur Hughes painted 'The Death of Arthur'. But before long much of the paintwork had flaked off; the smoke and heat of the naked gas-flames lighting the hall did still further damage. Bell-Scott, who went to see the frescoes in June of the following year, reported that little was to be seen of Morris's picture but the head of Tristram over a row of sunflowers. In 1875 Morris redecorated the roof. Since then all the paintings, in spite of restoration by Professor Tristram, have once more become almost indecipherable.

It is possible that both Morris and Rossetti worked on the capitals of the University Museum, whose decoration was also under way at this time. W. R. Lethaby records a meeting with Dr Eddison at Leeds in 1900 at which Eddison said that he remembered seeing Rossetti carving one of these capitals at the time of the redecoration of the Oxford Union. 'It had ivy and bryony on it and I believe I could find it now. I perfectly remember the look of intent interest on his face.'[10] Mackail also says of Morris: 'During these months, too, he was feeling his way in other arts and handicrafts: carving a block of freestone into a capital of foliage and birds, done with great spirit and life, Mr Arthur Hughes says; drawing and colouring designs for stained-glass windows: and modelling from the life in clay. . . . In carving the stone block he struck a splinter into his own eyes: and his language to Dr Acland, who was called in to look after the injury, was even for him unequalled in its force and copiousness.'[11]

The University Museum is of great interest as being the only building in England in which the principles enunciated in *The Seven Lamps of Architecture* and *The Stones of Venice* were put into practice under the direction of Ruskin himself, even though it remained unfinished. Built for the study of natural history, its cast-iron columns burst, near the lofty glass roof, into a riot of leaves and foliage that anticipates Art Nouveau by some twenty-five years. Besides housing the head and claw of a dodo (a bird introduced a few years later by another Oxford man, Lewis Carroll, into *Alice in Wonderland*) and a rather grisly collection of skeletons and stones, the chemical laboratory is copied from the abbot's kitchen at Glastonbury. The headless bodies of O'Shea's carved parrots and owls ('Members of Convocation', as he called them) may still be seen decorating the porch.

During the work at the Union, Morris and Burne-Jones lived together in George Street. When the autumn term began in October, Morris once more found himself among his old Oxford friends and, Mackail tells us, 'regained something of the old light-heartedness which life in London and the imperious domination of Rossetti had begun to impair'.[12] But then, at that time, Morris still admired Rossetti above all men, saying to Burne-Jones on one occasion: 'I want to imitate Gabriel as much as I can.'[13] From Cormell Price's diary of 1857 we get a clear picture of the kind of life he was leading:

Oct. 17. Breakfasted with Top at Johnson's in George St. Rossetti, Hughes, Prinsep, Ted, and Coventry Patmore there. To Union to see the frescoes.

Oct. 18. To Rossetti's. R. painting the Marriage of St George. Stood for Top for two hours in a dalmatic.

Oct. 24. Spent afternoon in daubing in black lines on the Union roof for Topsy. Whist in the evening as usual (at Rossetti's).

Oct. 30. Evening at George St. Rossetti, Ted, Topsy, Hughes, Swan, Faulkner, Bowen of Balliol, Bennet of Univ, Munro, Hill, Prinsep and Stanhope there. Topsy read his grind on Lance-lot and Guenevere – very grand.

Oct. 31. Stippled and blacklined at Union. Evening at George St. Rossetti and I versus Top and Faulkner at whist. Madox

Brown turned up. Rossetti said that Topsy had the greatest capacity for producing and annexing dirt of any man he ever met with.

Nov. 11. To Hill's, where were Topsy, Ted, Swan, Hatch, Swinburne of Balliol (introduced I think by Hatch), and Faulkner.[14]

Swinburne had come up to Balliol the year before, in 1856, and was already an ardent admirer of Rossetti and Morris. Rossetti's remark about Morris's capacity for annexing dirt recalls an entry in Miss Price's diary recording the fact that when Morris called on them one evening, the parlour maid was afraid to let him in, thinking that he was either a tramp or a burglar.

To Val Prinsep we are indebted for a vivid account of an evening spent with Morris, Rossetti and Burne-Jones on his arrival in Oxford that autumn.

There I found Rossetti in a plum-coloured frockcoat, and a short square man with spectacles and a vast mop of dark hair. I was cordially received. 'Top', cried Rossetti, 'let me introduce Val Prinsep.'

'Glad, I'm sure,' answered the man in spectacles, nodding his head, and then he resumed his reading of a large quarto. This was William Morris. Soon after, the door opened, and before it was half opened in glided Burne-Jones. 'Ned,' said Rossetti, who had been absently humming to himself, 'I think you know Prinsep.' The shy figure darted forward, the shy face lit up, and I was received with the kindly effusion which was natural to him.

When dinner was over, Rossetti, humming to himself as was his wont, rose from the table and proceeded to curl himself up on the sofa. 'Top,' he said, 'read us one of your grinds.' 'No, Gabriel,' answered Morris, 'you have heard them all.' 'Never mind,' said Rossetti, 'here's Prinsep who has never heard them, and besides, they are devilish good.' 'Very well, old chap,' growled Morris, and having got his book he began to read in a sing-song chant some of the poems afterwards published in his first volume. All the time, he was jigging about nervously with his watch chain. I was then a very young man and my experience of life was therefore limited, but the effect produced on my mind was so strong that to this day, forty years after, I can still recall the scene: Rossetti on the sofa with large melancholy eyes fixed on Morris, the poet at the table reading and ever fidgetting with his watch chain, and Burne-Jones working at a pen-and-ink drawing.

> *Gold on her head, and gold on her feet,*
> *And gold where the hems of her kirtle meet,*
> *And a golden girdle round my sweet;*
> Ah! qu'elle est belle La Marguerite

still seems to haunt me, and this other stanza:

> *Swerve to left, son Roger, he said,*
> *When you catch his eyes through the helmet slit*
> *Swerve to the left, then out at his head,*
> *And the Lord God give you joy of it!*

I confess I returned to the Mitre with my brain in a whirl.[15]

Whether Morris met Jane Burden at the theatre in Oxford with Rossetti, Burne-Jones and Arthur Hughes, as we are told in the *Memorials*, or whether it was, as Mackail says, Rossetti and Burne-Jones who first saw her sitting with her sister in the row behind them, is not very clear. Certainly it was Rossetti who first introduced himself and asked her to sit for them. Jane was a tall, large-boned girl with a pale ivory face, thick eyebrows, a neck like a tower and an abundance of black crinkly hair, the daughter of Robert Burden of 65 Holywell Street. Mr Burden is sometimes described as a livery stable keeper, but W.H.Bliss, Morris's contemporary at Oxford, told Mackail that Jane was 'a daughter of one of Simmonds' men at the stables in Holywell' – a fact which he was prevailed upon to suppress.[16] From her swarthy complexion, it has been supposed that Jane must have had gipsy blood, but we are told that she came of Cotswold stock, though there may still have been a gipsy strain. Morris made a sensitive pencil study of her head and drew her as *Iseult on the Ship*. She also became the subject of his one surviving oil painting, *Queen Guenevere*.

Morris worked hard at this painting at Red Lion Square for months, 'hating the brute', and finally threw it up, says Webb, who told Lethaby that 'Rossetti took it to finish, and then Madox Brown'.[17] Later, Morris gave it to Oliver Brown, who, in turn, passed it on to Rossetti, who had offered him £20 for it in 1874. Nolly Brown then suggested that he gave the money to Morris, who was 'hard up'.[18] Morris had apparently lost all interest in it, and after Rossetti's death, it was catalogued among his works as *La Belle Iseult* until it was finally returned to Mrs Morris by W. M. Rossetti and hung at Kelmscott. How much 'touching up' this picture underwent at the hands of Madox Brown and Rossetti, it is impossible to say. Morris seems to have found it difficult to finish his paintings. In April 1861, Brown wrote to Plint to say: 'His picture is now in my house, and at my suggestion he has so altered it that it is quite a fresh work.' This is presumably the *Tristram and Iseult* referred to by William Rossetti and Brown.

Morris is said to have scrawled on the back of his study of Jane Burden as Guenevere 'I cannot paint you, but I love you.' Rossetti's first pencil study of her is inscribed: 'J. B. Aetat. xvii, D. G. R. Oxoniae primo delt. Oct. 1857.' Next year Morris and Jane Burden became engaged. Shy and awkward with women, he used to sit with her, according to Prinsep, reading for hours from *Barnaby Rudge*. It is doubtful whether Miss Burden found this form of courtship particularly stimulating. But Sir Sydney Cockerell, who, of course, only came to know her much later on, says that 'she had a charming, unaffected nature and was as responsive to fun as any child'.[19] In Morris's 'Praise of My Lady', which takes the form of a medieval hymn to the Virgin, she already appears passive and abstracted and cast for the role of a mournful blessed damozel.

> *Her great eyes, standing far apart,*
> *Draw up some memory from her heart*
> *And gaze out very mournfully;*
>   ⁄Beata mea Domina!⁄

> *So beautiful and kind they are,*
> *But most times looking out afar,*
> *Waiting for something, not for me.*
>   Beata mea Domina! . . .

> *Her full lips being made to kiss,*
> *Curl'd up and pensive each one is;*
> *This makes me faint to stand and see.*
>   Beata mea Domina! . . .

> *God pity me though, if I miss'd*
> *The telling, how along her wrist*
> *The veins creep, dying languidly*
> *Beata mea Domina!*
>
> *Inside her tender palm and thin.*
> *Now give me pardon, dear, wherein,*
> *My voice is weak and vexes thee.*
> Beata mea Domina!

Morris is the humble supplicant, though he cannot help noticing already that his lady appears to be 'Waiting for something, not for me.' He concludes, in the medieval manner, by charging all men to kneel before her. The attitude of the group is shown in Swinburne's comment in his letter of 17 February 1858 to Edwin Hatch, when he says that he likes to think of Morris 'having that wonderful and most perfect stunner of his to – look at or speak to. The idea of his marrying her is insane. To kiss her feet is the utmost men should dream of doing.'

Rossetti had still to marry the dying Lizzie Siddal, though it seems that it was he who persuaded Jane Burden to marry the in-fatuated Morris, not only for his friend's sake, but in order to keep her within the group as a model. Where his friends' interests were concerned, Rossetti was notoriously the most generous of men. Writing years later, when she was editing her father's works, May Morris said: 'It seems to me that the duty of anyone who ever came into contact with Rossetti (even as I did only in childhood) is to lose no opportunity in passing of stressing the fineness of his character.' And she goes on to quote W. J. Stillmann as saying: 'Mr Mackail's recent life of Morris does great injustice to Rossetti without in any way exalting his friend.' It may be, as Professor Oswald Doughty argues,[20] that the story Rossetti wrote fifteen years later, when he was living at Kelmscott, 'The Cup of Cold Water', gives the essence of the situation (though it is transposed, as usual, into the Middle Ages) as it developed at Oxford at this time. On the other hand, it is evident that in 1871–2 Rossetti was looking back at that time in the light of his present infatuation with Jane and persuaded himself that he had already been in love with her at Oxford.

The young King of a country is hunting one day with a young Knight, his friend; when, feeling thirsty, he stops at a Forester's cottage, and the Forester's daughter brings him a cup of water to drink. Both of them are equally enamoured at once of her un, equalled beauty. The King, however, has been affianced from boyhood to a Princess, worthy of all love, and whom he had always believed he loved until undeceived by his new absorbing passion; but the Knight resolved to sacrifice all other considera, tions to his love, goes again to the Forester's cottage and asks his daughter's hand. He finds the girl has fixed her thoughts on the King, whose rank she does not know. On hearing it she tells her suitor humbly that she must die if such be her fate, but cannot love another. The Knight goes to the King to tell him all and beg his help; and the two friends then come to an explanation. Ultimately the King goes to the girl and pleads his friend's cause, not disguising his own passion, but saying that as he sacrificed himself to honour [i.e. in marrying the Princess] so should she, at his prayer, accept a noble man whom he loves better than all men and whom she will love too. This she does at last.

If we read Rossetti for the king, Morris for the knight, Lizzie Siddal for the princess and Jane Burden for the forester's daughter, the parallel is clear enough. Though Morris met Jane Burden in the autumn of 1857, they did not marry until April 1859, and it was only then that Rossetti married Lizzie, as he felt himself in honour bound to do. If Rossetti was writing a substantially true account, in 'The Cup of Cold Water', of what actually occurred at Oxford between 1857 and 1859, it is quite enough to account for the tragic frustration not only in his own life, but also in the lives of Morris and Jane.

The Defence of Guenevere, and Other Poems appeared in March 1858. It was dedicated 'To My Friend, Dante Gabriel Rossetti, Painter'. Shortly before Rossetti had written to William Allingham: 'Morris's facility in poeticizing puts me in a rage. He has only been writing at all for little more than a year, I believe, and has already poetry enough for a big book. You know he is a millionaire and buys pictures. He bought Hughes' *April Love* and lately several water colours of mine. . . . I have three or four more commissions from him. To one of my water colours, called *The Blue Closet*, he has written a stunning poem.' Among the water,colours Morris commissioned at this time was *Burd Ellayne*, the central figure of his ballad 'Welland River', *The Tune of Seven Towers, Arthur's Tomb* and *The Wedding of St George.* 'These chivalric, Froissartian themes are quite a passion of mine', Rossetti wrote to Charles Eliot Norton in 1858. It was a passion that Morris shared, and several of the poems published in *The Defence of Guenevere* were inspired by Rossetti's water-colours. These poems were attacked by reviewers as being affected and effeminate and of 'Rossetti's School'. 'The Blue Closet' is certainly more Pre-Raphaelite than medieval in spirit.

> *Lady Alice, lady Louise,*
> *Between the wash of the tumbling seas*
> *We are ready to sing, if so you please:*
> *So lay your long hands on the keys;*
>   *Sing, 'Laudate pueri.'*
>
> *Alice the Queen, and Louise the Queen,*
> *Two damozels wearing purple and green,*
> *Four lone ladies dwelling here*
> *From day to day and year to year;*
> *And there is none to let us go;*
> *To break the locks of the doors below,*
> *Or shovel away the heaped-up snow;*
> *And when we die no man will know*
> *That we are dead; but they give us leave,*
> *Once every year on Christmas-eve,*
> *To sing in the Closet Blue one song;*
> *And we should be so long, so long,*
> *If we dared, in singing; for dream on dream,*
> *They float on in a happy stream;*
> *Float from the gold strings, float from the keys,*
> *Float from the open'd lips of Louise;*
> *But, alas! the sea-salt oozes through*
> *The chinks of the tiles of the Closet Blue;*
> And ever the great bell overhead
> Booms in the wind a knell for the dead,
> The wind plays on it a knell for the dead.
>   (*They sing all together*)
> *How long ago was it, how long ago,*
> *He came to this tower with hands full of snow?*

One feels that Morris could go on like this indefinitely, building up his dreamy, fairy-tale atmosphere with its sinister undertones.

But this is only one aspect of *The Defence of Guenevere*, the most purely decorative. Such poems suggest not so much Rossetti's water-colours as the free-flowing lines of Art Nouveau compositions; even, at times, the early poems of Edith Sitwell. Today it is usually the violent, dramatic poems derived from Froissart that are more ad-mired – 'The Haystack in the Floods', 'Concerning Geffray Teste Noir', and 'Sir Peter Harpdon's End', itself virtually a short play. These, indeed, have a quite startling air of reality. But the most passionately felt poems in the book are the title poem and 'King Arthur's Tomb', based upon the *Morte d'Arthur*. Technically, all these dramatic poems, with their flat, down-to-earth diction and abrupt, broken rhythms, are quite original, though Morris himself said that they owed much to Browning. (Later they inspired some of the Provençal poems of Ezra Pound – 'Altaforte', for instance.)

'It has always seemed to me', wrote Professor Saintsbury of Morris's first book, 'that not merely the general, but even the critical public, ranks him far below his proper station as a poet. The very *terza* of the Defence itself is one of the most remarkable examples of the metre in English. . . . And the continuous fours of "King Arthur's Tomb" are finer, though the substance is not so good, and the exaggerated archaism of diction (for it *is* sometimes exaggerated) carries quaintness to affectation.' But he concludes: 'I should like to mention every item in a book which has never had justice done to it. . . . It is enough to say that there is in it, prosodically speaking, trumpet, flute, harp, sackbut, psaltery, dulcimer, and all kinds of music, which they that have not ears to hear, let them not hear.'[21] But those whose ears are attuned to Eliot, Auden, and Larkin are unlikely to hear and will find Morris's medievalism antipathetic, except in so far as it influenced Ezra Pound.

Walter Pater also wrote well of *The Defence*:

The poem which gives its name to the volume is a thing tormented and awry with passion, like the body of Guenevere defending herself from the charge of adultery, and the accent falls in strange, unwonted places with the effect of a great cry. . . . He has diffused through 'King Arthur's Tomb' the maddening glare of the sun, the tyranny of the moon, not tender and far-off, but close down – the Sorcerer's moon, large and feverish. The colouring is intricate and delicate, as of 'scarlet lilies'. The influence of summer is like a poison in one's blood, with a sudden bewildered sickening of life and all things. . . . . It is in 'The Blue Closet' that this delirium reaches its height with a singular beauty reserved perhaps for the enjoyment of the few.[22]

Andrew Lang wrote sensitively of the Froissartian part of the volume and Arthur Symons recognized that Morris had introduced the true spirit of medievalism into poetry: 'His first book, which invented a new movement, doing easily, with a certain appropriate quaintness, what Tennyson all this life had been trying to do.' All the same, such a poem as 'Golden Wings' derives from Tennyson's 'Mariana'.

The finest analysis of the dramatic poems in *The Defence* was given by Jack Lindsay in his lecture to the William Morris Society in November 1958. Lindsay made the point that 'from the outset Morris was looking for a way of life through his art. And in his early poems what mattered for him is the degree of intensity to which he enters into the life of his medieval characters. He creates a new form, which is at once the climax of the romantic idiom and its transformation into its opposite. The romantic vision is merged with a sharp emotional realism. The diction is often archaic, yet its effect is of a casual direct speech wrung-out at the height of an experience that reaches to the depths. The words have almost a stammering slow force as if each word is being searched for, all but lost, then brought doggedly out. . . . The inner stress is so acute that the metre gains its organization through a faltering meditative intensity, not by any strong intrusion of beat.' Such poems, he said, 'look, in their essential form, towards the future, not towards the medieval world'.[23]

Before the publication of *The Defence*, Morris had already begun to write a cycle of dramatic poems on the fall of Troy and there are a few surviving fragments of 'The Maying of Guenevere', the opening piece of an Arthurian cycle which would have ended with 'King Arthur's Tomb'. But the first volume of Tennyson's *Idylls of the King* in 1859 stole all the Arthurian laurels. The titles of the Trojan cycle are noted down in a manuscript book on the page following a fragment of 'The Maying of Guenevere':[24]

1. Helen Arming Paris
2. The Defiance of the Greeks
3. Hector's Last Battle
4. Hector Brought Dead to Troy
5. Helen's Chamber

6. Achilles' Love Letter
7. The Wedding of Polyxena
8. The Last Fight Before Troy
9. The Wooden Horse
10. The Descent from the Wooden Horse
11. Helen and Menelaus
12. Aeneas on Shipboard

Of these sections, each running to about two hundred lines, only six were written and there are fragmentary drafts of two more. As they stand, the poems are of very unequal quality, but they have a quiet naturalness of manner without the quaint archaisms and prettiness that debilitate both *Jason* and *The Earthly Paradise*. The 'Helen and Menelaus' section is a good example of this. Helen at night in a silent Troy, after the departure of the Greeks, is alone in the bedchamber with her new husband Deiphobus, who is sleeping.

> *Three hours after midnight, I should think*
> *And I hear nothing but the quiet rain.*
> *The Greeks are gone, think now, the Greeks are gone.*
> *Henceforward a new life of quiet days*
> *In this old town of Troy is now for me,*
> *And I shall note it as it goeth past*
> *Quietly as the rain does, day by day,*
> *Eld creeping on me.*

But Menelaus is in the room before she knows it and commands her to hold Deiphobus' feet while he kills him. He then drags the bloody corpse onto the floor and takes his own rightful place in the bed, saying:

> *I am the Menelaus that you knew*
> *Come back to fetch a thing I left behind.*

This is a return to the more violent mood of 'The Haystack in the Floods' and 'Sir Peter Harpdon's End'. But it was not to last. When Morris began writing poetry again in 1861, it is the decorative element that is in control and his long, spun-out narratives are as cool and remote and passionless as a frieze by Burne-Jones or Walter Crane.

In August Morris went to France again with Webb and Faulkner. They rowed down the Seine from Paris to Rouen in a boat that had previously been sent over from Oxford. They reached Abbeville on the 17th and Amiens the day after. 'At Amiens, on the Tower of the Cathedral, Morris upset his sovereigns from the satchel in which he carried them', says Webb. 'I had to stop them from running out of the gargoyles by putting my foot on them.'[25] After that, Morris settled down to make a drawing in the choir, while the others explored the galleries above. 'Looking down,' Webb continues, 'we saw him have a struggle with himself and suddenly go away – he had upset his ink bottle all over his drawing.'

They went on to Beauvais. By 21 August they were in Paris, where several of the capitals of Notre-Dame were drawn and the rose and ivy panels of the west porch; but they avoided the Sainte Chapelle. Then they went to Chartres. Returning to Paris, they were about to embark from the quai du Louvre, when they found that their boat had arrived with a hole in its bottom. Morris was 'transported' and rasped the skin off his hand on the parapet of the river in his rage. When they finally embarked, the bridge was lined with people. It was a light, keelless boat and Faulkner insisted on sailing when there was any wind. At Mantes they stopped to have the boat tarred, as it was leaking again. In one of the locks Morris annoyed the lock-keeper, who revenged himself by letting the water out and keeping them shut up. At one inn, they had a battle with soda-water siphons, to keep alive the memory of the good old Oxford Union days. On 1 September they were at Richard Cœur de Lion's Château Gaillard, Petit Andelys. Next day they reached Rouen, where they stayed until the 6th. Here the central spire of the cathedral was not yet completed – 'the upper part lying hateful on the ground'.

It was during this trip that Morris discussed with Webb the plans for Red House. It was largely on the strength of this com-mission that Webb left Street's office and began practising on his own. The drawings for Red House, Bexley Heath, were completed by April 1859 and are now in the Victoria and Albert Museum. On the 26th of that month Morris married Jane Burden at St Michael's, Oxford, a church which had recently been restored by Street. They were married by Dixon, then curate of St Mary's, Lambeth, who absent-mindedly joined them as 'William and Mary'. Faulkner acted as best man and Jane's father signed the register as 'Robert Burden, groom'. The wedding was a very quiet affair; Burne-Jones was there, but apparently not Rossetti. The honeymoon was spent on a tour of Paris, Belgium and the Rhine-land.

Morris was now faced with the problem of sharing his life with a young woman who, after all, was neither Iseult nor Guenevere and who was to pass the greater part of her days as a confirmed invalid.

CHAPTER FOUR

1859–1865

Red House: Morris, Marshall, Faulkner & Co. Fine Art Workmen

THE NEXT important event in Morris's life was the building and decoration of Red House. He had already bought an orchard and a meadow close to the village of Upton in Kent, ten miles from London by road and about three miles from Abbey Wood station. It was here that he determined to build his house so that it should have apple and cherry trees round it from the first. At this time the suburban railway network covering this part of Kent had hardly begun to exist, and the plateau of Bexley Heath was still open country. Here Morris enjoyed five years of unclouded happiness.

Philip Webb's Red House, so-called from being built of red brick at a time when stucco was still in fashion, has been generally represented as a revolution in English domestic architecture. But, in fact, as Mr Brandon-Jones remarks, 'it was only a short step from the vicarage houses on which Webb had been working under Street and those details which did not derive from Street's practice were based on precedents set by Butterfield, whose work Webb had studied and sketched'.[1] Nevertheless, it was its originality that struck visitors, when Morris and Jane moved in towards the end of the summer of 1860. Since returning from their honeymoon, they had been living in furnished rooms in Great Ormond Street, where Webb had his office at No. 7.

Red House is designed as an L-shaped building, two-storeyed with high-pitched red-tiled roofs and deeply recessed Gothic porches. The windows are also recessed and topped with pointed brick arches. The irregularity of the roof-line and the well court, with its conical-roofed brick and timber well, also gives the house a medieval flavour, though Webb included quite unmedieval sash-windows painted white, as well as circular windows on the top floor. The tall weather vane rising from the lantern of the staircase roof has Morris's initials and the horse's head from the family coat of arms. It is a romantic house, but, like Webb and Morris himself, eminently sensible, solid and practical, its structure frankly shown. The porch at the back, facing the well court, was used as a small garden room and one of its walls is still decorated by Morris's tiles.

Morris planned the garden on medieval lines. 'In front of the house', writes Lady Burne-Jones, 'it was spaced formally into four little square gardens making a big square together; each of the smaller squares had a wattled fence round it with an opening by which one entered, and all over the fence roses grew thickly. The stable, with stalls for two horses, stood in one corner of the garden, end on to the road, and had a kind of younger-brother look with regard to the house.'[2] Mackail writes of the garden 'with its long grass walks, its mid-summer lilies and autumn sunflowers, its wattled rose-trellises inclosing richly-flowered square garden plots. . . . The building had been planned with such care that hardly a tree in the orchard had to be cut down; apples fell in at the windows as they stood open on hot autumn nights.'[3] A long wall separates the house and garden from the road, Red House Lane, and large red wooden doors open into a short winding drive.

Aymer Vallance writes that the interior of Red House struck the visitor as 'severely simple and grand' with its high ceilings, exposed beams, brick arches and plain brick fireplaces. Its character is established at once by the hall: a dark red tiled, or flagged, floor, a massive oak staircase with pinnacled newel-posts carrying the eye up to the open and boldly patterned roof. Originally it had been planned to cover the walls of the staircase with tempera paintings of the tale of Troy and below them a great warship filled with heroes. Against the wall on the right, as one enters, stands a massive settle-cupboard designed by Webb and painted with scenes from the *Nibelungenlied*. These paintings, variously ascribed to Rossetti and Burne-Jones, but possibly by Morris, are unfinished. To the left is a long gallery leading to the back porch with high windows along one side filled with painted glass, two small figures by Burne-Jones and the quarries by Webb and Morris – light-hearted and amusing designs of animals and birds. To the right of the hall is the dining-room with its enormous red, Gothic dresser. Though less elaborate, this recalls the kind of furniture that was being designed at this time by William Burges and shows how much a part Webb and Morris really were of the High Victorian Gothic tradition.

The main rooms, on the first floor, were the studio and the draw-ing-room, their ceilings originally carried up to the roof, as in Pugin's bishop's palace at Birmingham. Morris said that he would make the drawing-room the most beautiful room in England. It fills the external angle of the L, its great high window originally looking northward over open country. It is consequently extremely cold, the side of the house facing south and east being occupied by passages. This curious arrangement was decided on partly because the house was built during an unusually hot summer – and Morris hated to be hot – and partly because the room was intended as a setting for frescoes and embroideries, which needed to be protected from the sun. Otherwise the drawing-room is lit by a small oriel window facing west to take the softer evening sun.

The decoration of this room was the work of several years, but remained unfinished. The ceiling was covered with floral designs, painted by Morris and Jane; Burne-Jones began to paint the walls with scenes from the romance of *Sire Degrevaunt*, and Morris did a frieze of trees and parrots below, Rossetti mischievously filling the blank spaces between with a parody of Morris's motto – 'As I can't'. Lizzie Siddal also took a hand in the decorations and Ros-setti painted 'The Salutation of Beatrice' on the doors of the great settle-cupboard from Red Lion Square, which still occupies one end of the room. To this Webb now added a parapet to serve as a minstrels' gallery, though the most striking feature of the room is the chimney-piece of patterned bricks, carried straight up to the ceiling. This may, however, derive from the late fifteenth-century fireplace at Stoneacre, Otham, restored by Aymer Vallance. Burne-Jones's three frescoes are still there, protected by glass panels, but Rossetti's painted doors were later removed from the settle and are now in the Victoria and Albert Museum.

There were no wallpapers at Red House, since Morris had not yet begun to design his own, but the principal bedroom was hung with a coarse dark-blue serge worked by Jane Morris with little sprays of flowers in bright wools, very like the 'Daisy' pattern paper designed by Morris in 1864. Soon after their marriage, Jane told Mackail, Morris taught her the first principles of embroidery. 'We studied old pieces,' she said, 'and by unpicking &c., we learnt much – but it was uphill work, fascinating, but only carried through by his enormous energy and perseverance.' For the dining-room, they carried out a more elaborate series of figure embroideries in wool,

silk, and gold thread on woollen twill, designed to imitate tapestry
and based on Chaucer's Illustrious Women, with trees between and
a running band of flowers at their feet. Seven of these splendid
figures out of the original twelve were completed by the time Morris
left Red House in 1865. Three of them were later made into a screen
for Lady Carlisle and are now in the Green Dining Room at the
Victoria and Albert Museum. Elizabeth Burden, Jane's sister, who
became a teacher at the Royal School of Art Needlework in the
1870s, was also enlisted for this work.

The general effect of the decorations at Red House together with
the new red brick, must have been raw and violent and not unlike
Butterfield's work. 'The adornment had a novel, not to say startling
character', wrote William Bell Scott in his *Autobiographical Notes*,
'but if one had been told it was the South Sea Island style of thing
one could have believed such to be the case, so bizarre was the
execution.' But, as he noted, it was a young man's house and 'genius
always rushes to extremes at first.' Writing to Charles Eliot Norton
in 1862, Rossetti said: 'I wish you could see the house which Morris
(who has money) has built for himself in Kent. It is a most noble
work in every way, and more a poem than a house . . . but an
admirable place to live in too.'

Thus, in all ways, Red House became an expression of Morris:
immensely solid, spacious, down to earth, unpretentious, yet with
a romantic and medieval flavour. At week⁄ends he filled it with his
friends, the Burne⁄Joneses (who had married in 1860), the Rossettis,
the Madox Browns, Faulkner, Arthur Hughes, Swinburne. 'First
was the arrival at Abbey Wood Station,' says Lady Burne⁄Jones,
'a country place in those days, where a thin fresh air full of sweet
smells met us as we walked down the platform, and outside was the
wagonette sent from Red House to meet us; then a pull up the hill
and a swinging drive of three miles of winding road on the higher
land until, passing "Hog's Hole" on the left, we stopped at our
friend's gate.'[4] The discovery of Hog's Hole caused Rossetti infinite
delight and thereafter Red House was familiarly known either by
that name or as the Towers of Topsy. The wagonette was also
designed by Webb and built at Bexley. 'It was covered with a tilt
like an old⁄fashioned market⁄cart, made of American cloth lined
with gay chintz hangings: the Morris arms painted on the back',
records May Morris. 'When it was finished, they used to go little
jaunts with their friends, and their appearance caused much joy in

the neighbourhood, where it was thought that they were the advance guard of a travelling show.'[5]

The week-ends were devoted to decorating the house and to riotous fun and games. There were bowls in the garden and 'bear fights' among the young men in the drawing-room. Lady Burne-Jones writes:

Once, in the middle of a scrimmage that had surged up the steps [of the settle] into the 'Minstrel's Gallery', he [Faulkner] suddenly leapt clear over the parapet into the middle of the floor with an astounding noise; another time he stored windfallen apples in the gallery and defended himself with them against all comers until a too well-delivered apple gave Morris a black eye. . . . Oh, how happy we were, Janey and I, busy in the morning with needlework or wood-engraving, and in the afternoon driving to explore the country round by the help of a map of Kent; we went to the Crays one day and to Chislehurst Common another, finding some fresh pleasure everywhere and bringing back tales of our adventures to amuse the men we had left working at home. Sometimes, but not often, they would go with us. . . . It will be taken for granted that the two men visitors had endless jokes together at the expense of their beloved host. The dinner hour, at middle day, was a great time for them because Mrs Morris and I were there, either as eager onlookers at the fun or to take sides for and against. The dining-room was not yet finished, and the drawing-room upstairs, whose beautiful ceiling had been painted by Mr and Mrs Morris, was being decorated in different ways, so Morris's studio, which was on the same floor, was used for living in, and a most cheerful place it was, with windows looking three ways and a little horizontal slip of a window over the door, giving upon the red-tiled roof of the house where we could see birds hopping about all unconscious of our gaze.[6]

They used to send Morris to Coventry at his own dinner table and refuse to speak to him, all becoming helpless with laughter. After dark there were games of hide-and-seek all over the house, or they sang old English songs round the piano. Good cheer flowed in abundance. 'It was the most beautiful sight', says one of his friends, 'to see Morris coming up from the cellar before dinner, beaming with joy, with his hands full of bottles of wine and others tucked under his arms.' Janey at Red House became a regular tomboy. There is a story of Morris sitting on a stool in front of the fire and someone coming up and slapping him hard behind. 'Don't do it, Janey!' he said, without looking round.[7] Or they would play upon Morris's fear of getting fat and put a tuck in his waistcoat during the night. 'You fellows have been at it again', he would remark good humouredly next morning.

In fact, all the undergraduate fun and horse-play continued un- abated from the Oxford days. But it only took place in the intervals of work. Moreover, Morris's income, derived from Devon Great Consols, was beginning to diminish rapidly, 'and the idea came to him', Burne-Jones tells us, 'of beginning a manufactory of all things necessary for the decoration of a house. Webb had already designed some beautiful table glass, made by Powell of Whitefriars, metal candlesticks, and tables for Red House, and I had already designed several windows for churches, so the idea grew of putting our ex- periences together for the service of the public.'[8] Burne-Jones had also done some painted tiles for the fireplaces, though his frescoes were already beginning to fade. As in the case of the Oxford Union, the walls at Red House were new and had not been properly prepared for painting.

The whole idea of the firm was in origin delightfully casual. Theodore Watts-Dunton records Rossetti as saying:

> One evening, a lot of us were together, and we got talking about the way in which artists did all kinds of things in olden times, designed every kind of decoration and most kinds of furniture, and someone suggested – as a joke more than anything else – that we should each put down five pounds and form a company. Fivers were blossoms of a rare growth among us in those days, and I won't swear that the table bristled with fivers. Anyhow the firm was formed, but of course there was no deed or anything of that kind. In fact, it was a mere playing at business, and Morris was elected manager, not because we ever dreamed he would turn out to be a man of business, but because he was the only one of us who had time and money to spare. We had no idea whatever of commercial success, but it succeeded almost in our own despite.[9]

On the other hand, Mackail states that 'the finance of the company began with a call of £1 per share. On this, and on an unsecured loan of £100 from Mrs Morris of Leyton, the first year's trading was done.' To Morris, however, he adds, 'the firm probably meant little more than a definite agreement for co-operation and common work among friends who were also artists'.[10]

The idea of a revival of useful and decorative arts was not in itself new. It had already been put forward by Henry Cole and the architects Owen Jones and Matthew Digby Wyatt, and the painter Richard Redgrave. As early as 1847 Cole (under the pseudonym Felix Summerly) had founded Summerly's Art Manufactures, which lasted for about three years until his preoccupation with the Great Exhibition of 1851 brought it to an end. The greater part of the 'industrial art' so proudly exhibited there was hideous in the extreme, and Cole believed that it would 'promote public taste' if well-known painters and sculptors could be persuaded to produce designs for manufactured articles of everyday use. The main principle underlying Morris & Co. was that the artists concerned need not be well known, that in fact everyone is a different sort of artist whose innate skill can be developed, and that the same hand that produced the designs should carry them out in whatever the media. In practice, however, as business expanded, Morris found it impossible to adhere to this principle, though at the beginning he himself was careful to master every medium for which he produced designs. In his view, an artist was (or should be) simply a workman, as in the Middle Ages. The peculiar deadness of much Victorian work, Morris maintained, was directly attributable to one man's design being mechanically copied by another hand. His ideal was, of course, handicraft, whereas Cole and his associates accepted the machine unquestioningly.

The South Kensington Museum was founded by Henry Cole after the Great Exhibition of 1851 in order to exhibit 'examples of fine workmanship in the applied arts of all times and peoples'. His schools of design, founded in 1857, were attached to the museum and, as a result, English manufacture soon became independent of French designers and their 'Louis' styles which had hitherto dominated the market. Among the teachers at South Kensington was Christopher Dresser, author of *The Art of Decorative Design* (1862), whose designs for furniture, ceramics, glass, metalware, wallpapers and fabrics ranged from the functional to the eccentric.

Owen Jones, Superintendent of the Works of the Great Exhibition and joint Director of Decoration of the Crystal Palace, for which he designed the Egyptian, Greek, Roman and Alhambra

Courts, when it was removed to Sydenham, had published (with Sir Matthew Digby Wyatt) in 1856 the monumental *Grammar of Ornament*. In his designs for wallpapers and textiles, Owen Jones advocated abstract and formal as against naturalistic patterns, and insisted that all pattern designs should be flat.

It was the exhibition of Victorian and Edwardian Decorative Arts organized by Peter Floud in 1952, which included examples of Dresser's, Bruce Talbert's and Owen Jones's work, together with furniture designed by Burges, Butterfield, E. W. Godwin and others, which finally exploded the myth that the Morris movement was alone responsible for the regeneration of Victorian design.[11] Never/theless, one has only to compare the best of Morris's designs for wallpapers and textiles with those produced by Owen Jones and Christopher Dresser to see at once how stiff and formal the latter really are. With Morris there is nearly always an exciting sense of growth and the abundance and freshness of nature, however tra/ditional his initial inspiration. Indeed, as Dr Pevsner remarks, Morris was 'so far from inventing decorative forms for invention's sake, that if he found models however remote in space and time which met his purpose, he made use of them or at least came under their spell, even if this happened against his own will'.[12]

Both he and Webb, as they readily admitted, found many of their models among the exhibits collected together by Sir Henry Cole, and later J. H. Middleton, at South Kensington. 'They talk of building museums for the public,' Lethaby reports Morris as saying once, 'but South Kensington Museum was really got together for about six people – I am one, and another is a comrade [Philip Webb] in the room.'[13] Nevertheless, Morris's personality comes through so powerfully in most of his designs that this dependence on tradition seldom detracts from their freshness and spontaneity – largely because he combined a genius for pattern designing with an enthusiasm for nature.

Early in January 1861, Morris's eldest daughter Jane Alice ('Jenny') was born. A laconic note to Ford Madox Brown of the 18th from Red House announces the fact: 'Kid having appeared, Mrs Brown says she will stay till Monday, when you are to come to fetch her, please. I send a list of trains in the evening to Abbey Wood met by bus, viz: from London Bridge, 2.20 p.m., 6.0 p.m., and 7.15 p.m. Janey and kid (girl) are both very well.' Many friends, including

Rossetti, Madox Brown and Swinburne, attended the christening and beds were made up in the drawing-room for the men. At dinner Rossetti was noticeably absent-minded and silent; he drank only water and sat eating raisins out of a large bowl. Arthur Hughes told Mackail that he remembered 'D. G. R. quite cowed by Lizzie who snarled at him'.[14] Four months later she gave birth to a dead child.

With growing responsibilities, Morris was now forced to take his duties as a citizen more seriously, and during the invasion scare of the winter of 1859–60 occasioned by Napoleon III's naval programme, he had, like many of his friends, joined the Artists' Corps of Volunteers. The summer of 1861, therefore, found him in camp on Wimbledon Common. He is said to have regularly attended drills and to have been conscientious in the performance of his military duties, whereas Rossetti, in reply to the sergeant major's 'Right about face!' was heard to ask 'Why?'

On 11 April the firm of Morris, Marshall, Faulkner & Co. was founded and a prospectus drawn up. The members described themselves as 'Fine Art Workmen in Painting, Carving, Furniture, and the Metals'. At the head of the prospectus stood the names of: Ford Madox Brown, Edward Burne-Jones, C. J. Faulkner, Arthur Hughes, P. P. Marshall, William Morris, D. G. Rossetti and Philip Webb. Marshall was a friend of Brown, a surveyor and sanitary engineer; though his name was included, Arthur Hughes was never a member of the firm. Morris was to receive a salary of £150 a year as manager and Faulkner the same sum as book-keeper. The prospectus reads:

The growth of Decorative Art in this country, owing to the efforts of English Architects, has now reached a point at which it seems desirable that Artists of reputation should devote their time to it. Although no doubt particular instances of success may be cited, still it must be generally felt that attempts of this kind hitherto have been crude and fragmentary. Up to this time, the want of that artistic supervision, which can alone bring about harmony between the various parts of a successful work, has been increased by the necessarily excessive outlay, consequent on taking one individual artist from his pictorial labours.

The Artists whose names appear above hope by association to do away with this difficulty. Having among their number men of varied qualifications, they will be able to undertake any species of decoration, mural or otherwise, from pictures, properly so-called, down to the consideration of the smallest work susceptible of art beauty. It is anticipated that by such co-operation, the largest amount of what is essentially the artist's work, along with his constant supervision, will be secured at the smallest possible expense, while the work done must necessarily be of a much more complete order, than if any single artist were incidentally employed in the usual manner.

These Artists having for many years been deeply attached to the study of the Decorative Arts of all times and countries, have felt more than most people the want of some one place, where they could either obtain or get produced work of a genuine and beautiful character. They have therefore now established themselves as a firm, for the production, by themselves and under their supervision of –

I. Mural Decoration, either in Pictures or in Pattern Work, or merely in the arrangement of Colours, as applied to dwelling-houses, churches, or public buildings.

II. Carving generally, as applied to Architecture.

III. Stained Glass, especially with reference to its harmony with Mural Decoration.

IV. Metal Work in all its branches, including Jewellery.

V. Furniture, either depending for its beauty on its own design, on the application of materials hitherto overlooked, or on its conjunction with Figure and Pattern Painting. Under this head is included Embroidery of all kinds, Stamped Leather, and ornamental work in other such materials, besides every article necessary for domestic use.

It is only necessary to state further, that work of all the above classes will be estimated for, and executed in a business-like manner; and it is believed that good decoration, involving rather the luxury of taste than the luxury of costliness, will be found to be much less expensive than is generally supposed.

Of this document, Mackail states rather unfairly: 'it is not difficult to trace the slashing hand and imperious accent of Rossetti, now as always contemptuous of all difficulties and not over-scrupulous in accuracy of statement'.[15]

It will be noticed that there is no mention of wallpapers in the prospectus, though there is in the one issued a year later, for by that time Morris had already begun to design the 'Trellis', the 'Daisy', and the 'Fruit' or 'Pomegranate'. The 'Trellis' was the first wallpaper to be designed and has birds by Webb. It probably derived from the rose trellises in the garden at Red House. The delightful and somewhat naïve 'Daisy', for long the most popular of all Morris's wallpapers, was the first to be issued in 1864. The 'Pomegranate' is a more sophisticated design than either of the others, but is equally untypical of the complex, flowing lines and masses of Morris's later work.

The designs were cut on pearwood blocks and printed in distemper colours by Jeffreys of Islington, who continued to produce all Morris and Co. wallpapers until the firm closed down in 1940 and the blocks were taken over by Messrs Sanderson. The success of the printing depended very largely upon the care of Metford Warner, the managing director of Jeffreys. After this first batch, Morris did not design any further wallpapers until 1872, when his style had completely changed. In all, he designed only forty-one wallpapers, and five ceiling papers; the firm produced over the years forty-one others, ten of these by J.H. Dearle, May Morris and Kate Faulkner appeared during Morris's lifetime. The remaining thirty-one were almost all designed by Dearle, though many of them have since been attributed to Morris himself.[16]

At this time, with the revival of the Anglo-Catholic movement in the Church of England, there was a great demand for ecclesiastical art, stained-glass windows, altar-cloths and painted screens. Accordingly Morris wrote on 18 April to his old tutor the Rev. Guy asking for a list of clergymen 'to whom it *might* be of any use to send a circular'.

> You see we are, or consider ourselves to be, the only really artistic firm of the kind, the others being glass painters in point of fact (like Clayton & Bell) or else that curious nondescript mixture of clerical tailor and decorator that flourishes in Southampton Street, Strand, whereas we shall do – most things. However, what we are most anxious to get at present is wall-decoration. . . . In about a month we shall have some things to show in these rooms, painted cabinets, embroidery and all the rest of it. . . .

At 8 Red Lion Square, a few doors from Morris's and Burne-Jones's old rooms, the firm rented the first floor for an office and showroom and the third floor, with part of the basement for workshops. A small kiln was built in the basement for firing glass and tiles. As the work grew, about a dozen men and boys were employed. The boys came from a Boys' Home in the Euston Road and the men chiefly from Camden Town. The foreman, George Campfield, was a glass-painter Morris had met at F. D. Maurice's Workingman's College in Great Ormond Street. Regular business meetings of the firm took place on Wednesday evenings, but apart from that Morris and Faulkner were the only members who worked regularly at Red Lion Square. Marshall did some remarkably spirited designs of St George and the Dragon for stained glass; Albert Moore, William de Morgan and Simeon Solomon did occasional designs for glass and tiles, and Faulkner's two sisters joined him in the painting of tiles and pottery. Faulkner himself, who seems to have been able to turn his hand to anything, also helped to fire the glass in the basement. Jane Morris and her sister, Elizabeth Burden, and Mrs Wardle, with several women working under them, executed embroidery on cloth and silk. Georgie Burne-Jones also did embroidery and painted tiles, and Mrs Campfield helped with altar-cloths. Otherwise the designs for stained glass were produced by Morris, Burne-Jones, Rossetti, Webb and Madox Brown. Morris, of course, worked at everything, including coarse serge hangings in quiet dull colours with figures and floral designs in coloured wool. Each partner was paid for what he did, but the payments to Morris in 1862 were more than those to all the others put together.

In January 1862, Mackail tells us:

a further call of £19 a share was made on the partners, raising the paid up capital to £140. A few hundred pounds of further capital was supplied by loans, which bore, or were supposed to bear, interest at five per cent, from Morris himself and from his mother. . . . In the course of the first three or four years, Morris had, bit by bit, advanced all he could to the concern, and was not yet beginning to receive any appreciable returns. This was an anxious time for him, and perhaps the only time in his life when he was really in trouble about money. Once or twice in these years the accounts showed an actual loss on the year's working. . . . Morris had yet to learn by unpleasant experiences of more kinds than one the principles on which sound business can be conducted. That he did so, and that while he was doing so he carried the business almost unaided through so crucial a period, was due to a persistency, a sagacity, an unweariable industry, for which he has seldom received adequate credit.[17]

The fortunes of the firm really date from the success of their exhibits in the Mediaeval Court of the International Exhibition at South Kensington in 1862, which 'came as the apogee of the High Victorian Style of elaborated pastiche'.[18] Among these were a wall cabinet designed by Webb in 1861 and made by a local cabinet, maker. It has quite admirably painted doors by Morris of the legend of St George. Parts of the painting were done in transparent colour over gold and silver; the interior of the cabinet was deep crimson – 'dragon's blood'. The firm also exhibited a gilded bookcase with painted panels representing seven stages in the life of an English family, quite in mid-Victorian taste.

On the other hand, Rossetti's seven stained-glass panels of 'The Parable of the Vineyard', afterwards incorporated in a window at Scarborough, were judged so much in the medieval spirit that some of the other exhibitors complained that they were actually medieval glass touched up, and tried to have them disqualified! It was this glass which gained the firm their first commissions to decorate Bodley's new churches at Brighton, Scarborough and Selsley. A large cabinet by J. P. Seddon was also painted by Ford Madox Brown, Burne-Jones and Rossetti, with backgrounds by Morris, to illustrate imaginary incidents in the honeymoon of King René of Anjou, as recounted in Walter Scott's *Anna von Geierstein*. There was also another very flamboyant cabinet in the same exhibition designed by William Burges and painted by Edward Poynter with scenes illustrating the legend of Cadmus. Both cabinets are on view at the Victoria and Albert Museum, South Kensington.

Compared to these, the Morris & Co. exhibits appear sober and simple. The jury, who awarded them two medals, observed: 'Messrs Morris & Company have exhibited several pieces of furniture, tapestries &c. in the style of the Middle Ages. The general forms of the furniture, the arrangement of the tapestry, and the character of the details are satisfying to the archaeologist from the exactness of the imitation, at the same time that the general effect is excellent.' The 'tapestry' mentioned here was, of course, embroidery, for Morris did not embark on woven tapestry, as such, until a good many years later. It was described by Christopher Dresser as 'a series of quaint fabrics that have the pattern wrought upon them in thick worsted thread of many colours which is sewn to the surface'. The jurors praised these fabrics highly and awarded them a medal. They were evidently of the same kind as those that decorated the dining-room at Red House.

The furniture which Webb designed for the firm at this time 'was usually of plain oak (often stained green or black) or of oak decorated on the surface by painting, gessowork, and lacquered leather'.[19] Among these was the high-backed settle (the 'Red House Settle'), the upper part of which leans over in a slight curve, with panels of embossed leather painted with sunflowers by Morris. In general design these settles seem to have followed an earlier design by Pugin. Madox Brown had, of course, been designing furniture for some time. In 1860 he had made a very pleasant rush-seated chair of stained oak and he is credited with having originated the green stain so generally used for what was known as Art Furniture. His dressing-table was so much ahead of its time that commercial copies were profitably made fifty years after it was designed.[20] But in general, the furniture produced and sold by the firm (apart again from the elegant rush-seated chair designed by Rossetti) was of the kind des-cribed in the catalogue of the exhibition as 'of solid construction and joiner made' – that is, it had an honest, straightforward appearance, in contrast both to the debased Rococo and Empire styles then in vogue and the more flamboyant Gothic of Burges.

After his first experiments at Red Lion Square, Morris did not design any more furniture. The adjustable-back chair, adapted by Webb from an old Sussex chair, was made by Morris & Co. from about 1866. They also revived the traditional Sussex elbow-chair, with a rush-bottomed seat. In later years, however, one finds the firm's catalogues full of imitations of Queen Anne period tables and cabinets – in spite of Morris's detestation of the eighteenth century.

The firm also exhibited in 1862 an iron bedstead, a sideboard and a washstand by Webb, copper candlesticks (which Rossetti laughed at as being too heavy to carry), jewellery designed by Webb, tiles painted by Rossetti, Burne-Jones, Webb and Morris, and a sofa by Rossetti. But the main business of their first years was the decora-tion of Bodley's new churches: St Martin's, Scarborough; St Michael's, Brighton; All Saints, Cambridge; and All Saints, Selsley in Gloucestershire. In 1869, Morris and Webb also painted the organ screen at Beddington, Surrey. An alphabetical index by Marillier of the firm's cartoons for stained glass, now at the City of Birmingham Museum and Art Gallery, attributes 129 of these to Morris, not counting a few which, on the evidence of Webb's account-book with the firm for the years 1861–76, were in fact also by Morris.

After the first years, Rossetti and Brown dropped out as designers and the vast majority of the figures for stained glass came from Burne-Jones and are in a more lyrical and less dramatic style. They are usually large, single figures done in pale colours, like the 'St Cecilia' of Christ Church, Oxford. A. C. Sewter calculates that Morris must have designed, over the years, at least 150 windows, besides the designs he did for background quarries used in other windows.[21] On the other hand, Webb was responsible for the general arrange-ment of a great many window schemes. His account-book entries make this clear. The very first entry, undated but presumably 1861, reads: 'Glass (stained) for King's Stanley Church. Designs for. [This is actually All Saints, Selsley, built to serve an area formerly in the parish of King's Stanley.] Scale drawings of arrangements have windows with scheme for whole church . . . £3.'

The same method was followed at St Martin's, Scarborough; Christ Church, Southgate; Dedworth parish church. At South-gate there are figures by Morris of the Evangelists with canopy work by Webb. Morris was also responsible for the little 'Three Marys at the Sepulchre' at St Michael's, Brighton (1862), 'St Paul Preaching' and the 'Ascension' window at Selsley (1861), the 'Resurrection' for the chancel east window at Dedworth, near Windsor (1863) – the other two lights were a 'Crucifixion' by Rossetti and a 'Nativity' by Burne-Jones. Ten years later Morris also designed the 'St Catherine' in the right-hand light of the central window of the south aisle at Dedworth. It is unquestionably the finest window in a church now due for demolition, the earlier windows being somewhat amateurish and disappointing, when judged beside the great quantity of admirable Victorian glass produced by other firms.

At St Martin's, Scarborough, the windows are by Rossetti, Burne-Jones, Madox Brown, Webb and Morris, who did the 'St John the Baptist' in the north chapel. Brown's splendid 'Adam and Eve in Paradise' at the west end are portraits of Brown himself and his wife 'in attitudes of indolent content'. Brown's window of 'St

Martin in Heaven' has the ground spotted over with little flowering plants by Morris like those of the 'Daisy' wallpaper. The pulpit was painted by Campfield with designs by Morris, Rossetti and Brown. At All Saints, Selsley, the youthful Morris appears in profile as Christ in Rossetti's window of the 'Sermon on the Mount' (repeated in Christ Church, Albany Street, London in 1867–8) 'and below in front of the listening Apostles lie the Virgin and Mary Magdalen; the former with a look of Christina Rossetti, and the Magdalen with my Mother's head', writes May Morris.[22] In Morris's window of 'St Paul Preaching at Athens', the woman in green crowned with a wreath and lying down in front is again Jane Morris.

In Bodley's opinion, according to May Morris, the firm's glass for St Michael's, Brighton, his rather ugly red brick hillside church of striped Gothic, was their finest achievement. This is certainly not the case, though Madox Brown's 'Archangels' window is indeed splendid, with a strange Celtic flavour. There is also at the same end of the church, a rose window of 'The Creation' by Burne-Jones similar to the one at Selsley. Morris's small two-light window of 'The Three Marys at the Sepulchre' is over the altar in the old vestry at the end of the south transept. The subject is repeated in the east window of St Edmund's Hall chapel, Oxford. The posture of the angel sitting on the tomb is similar to that of a little figure on a shield in the left-hand corner of Samuel Harsnett's memorial brass at Chigwell, Essex, of which Morris had doubtless already taken a rubbing. The chancel roof of St Michael's, Brighton, was also painted by Morris, Faulkner and Webb.

The great east window of Bodley's All Saints, Jesus Lane, Cambridge, is all Morris & Co. glass of 1863–6. It is composed of individual figures in small panels of clear glass. According to J. R. Holliday's notes of 1915 in the Fitzwilliam Museum, Morris designed four of these – 'Elias', 'St Peter' and 'St John the Baptist' in the third tier, and 'St Catherine' in the fourth. The pulpit was painted by Arthur Hughes, and Morris stencilled the walls in sombre patterns, though these are now much faded and yellowed. Morris and Webb also decorated Bodley's new ceilings at Jesus College Chapel at this time, Morris designing a frieze of angels. He also painted the ceiling of the hall of Queens' College, though here his work has recently been restored. The magnificent windows by Burne-Jones at Jesus Chapel were mostly done in the 1870s and show him at the height of his powers, though the 'St Cecilia' had been done for St Saviour's, Leeds, in 1866 and the 'St Ursula' for Liverpool in 1869. To the early 1870s, too, belong the windows in the hall at Peterhouse, where Madox Brown's sturdy figures are in particularly marked contrast to the more feminine work of Burne-Jones. The ornamental work in the bay window is by Morris, the heraldry by Webb, and the figures by Madox Brown. Morris's 'Daisy' tiles decorate the fireplace.

The freshness and unconventionality of the firm's early glass may be seen in Rossetti's small panels of 'The Parable of the Vineyard', beneath his great east window of the 'Crucifixion' at Scarborough, in which both Morris (dropping a stone on the head of a bailiff) and Swinburne appear. A replica of these panels is at the Victoria and Albert Museum, together with one of Morris's charming music angels on lightly drawn quarries of daisies and sunflowers. Perhaps the best example of the firm's early domestic stained glass is the Tristram series done in 1862 for Harden Grange, and now at the Cartwright Memorial Hall, Bradford. There is also Rossetti's admirable 'Music' of 1864 – nearly the same design as he did for the 'King René's Honeymoon' cabinet – the four beautiful 'Morte d'Arthur' panels of Burne-Jones (one of which is now at Walthamstow), and the series he did in 1864 for Birkett Foster's house at Witley (later used for windows in the Combination Room at Peterhouse, Cambridge) of Dido and Cleopatra, the god of Love and Alcestis. 'The figures are standing among tall-growing flowers against a homely wooden fence', writes May Morris. 'The flowers, not coloured, show all the delicate invention of the young artists: they are vividly drawn, against a light ground, with the careful accuracy and rhythmic line of the early herbals – a cyclamen, sweet-william, Indian pink, and other delights, among which the exquisite dog-tooth violet, always a favourite with Morris. It is either his hand one sees here or that of Webb: it is hard to say which.'[23]

None of Morris's figures proved as popular with clients, however, as those designed by Burne-Jones. But Mr Sewter has shown that, apart from the small angels and minstrel figures, Morris's 'St Peter', done in the first instance for All Saints, Cambridge, was repeated at least ten times elsewhere. 'This may be significant,' says Mr Sewter, 'for all his figures have certain qualities of strength, weight and stiff dignity, appropriate to their particular subject, which distinguished them from Madox Brown's more dramatic and Burne-Jones's more elegant designs.' The parish church of St Giles,

Camberwell, formerly had a window of St Paul by Morris, but this was destroyed during the last war. Butterfield's St Alban's, Holborn, was also one of the firm's earliest customers, but this was gutted during the war and has since been rebuilt.

When the cartoons for stained glass came to Morris, they were uncoloured and he it was who worked out the colour schemes and, with Webb, added the details of ornaments and put in the lead lines. Morris gave particular attention to the use of yellow stain. 'He used it with tremendous effect not only as a major element in colour-schemes', writes Mr Sewter,

> for draperies, hair and other details of figures, but especially for rendering on glass an equivalent of embroidered and damask designs on costumes. . . . In time the Morris workshop attained an unrivalled mastery in the use of this stain, and was able to produce a range of tints and tones of gold from the palest yellow to the most intense reddish bronze. It was only when experience with this technique had been acquired that some of the glories of the firm's output, like the Cheddleston [near Leek, Stafford-shire] Angels window of 1869, and the St Cecilia window of 1880, could be produced. But the window which shows most perfectly this minor-pattern aspect of Morris's glass is the Arch-angels window at King's Walden, Herts (*c.* 1869) where all the figures are from his designs. The figures are covered from head to foot with intricate decorative ornament, and the backgrounds also; but so broad and simple are the main lines of the designs that there can be no question of over-ornamentation. The window is among the greatest successes of modern stained glass: and the credit for it belongs entirely to Morris himself.[24]

One can see how closely Morris followed medieval tradition in his designs by comparing them with George Wardle's drawings and water-colours of the figures and details of painted decoration from the rood screens and roofs of Norfolk and Suffolk churches made for the firm in 1865–6, with notes on colouring and technique.[25] The green and red stencilling from the roof of the south transept (originally the Lady chapel) of Aylsham Church was reproduced by Morris on the roof of Jesus College Chapel, Cambridge – that is, the crowned M and the black-and-white diaper work on the beams. He carried out the same sort of stencilling on the walls of the hall at Queens' College shortly after. Again, something very like the pattern on the alb of St Apollonia at Barton Turf Church appears later in one of Morris's fabric designs. It is clear, too, that he studied the drapery of the figures of saints from Wardle's drawings very carefully for his own glass window designs. When Wardle went to Red Lion Square with his drawings, he found Morris 'anxious and over-worked for business was in reality not too good and Morris had to make up all deficits'. Faulkner, who was painting tiles, also struck Wardle as harassed.[26]

The weekly meetings of the firm were, however, still carried on in the same old happy-go-lucky manner. Faulkner, writing to Cormell Price in April 1862, says that they

have rather the character of a meeting of the 'Jolly Masons' or the jolly something elses than of a meeting to discuss business. Beginning at 8 or 9 p.m. they open with the relation of anecdotes which have been culled by members of the firm since the last meeting – this store exhausted, Topsy and Brown will perhaps discuss the relative merits of the art of the thirteenth and fifteenth century, and then perhaps after a few more anecdotes business matters will come up about 10 or 11 o'clock and be furiously discussed till 12, 1, or 2.

There was, too, the usual practical joking. On one occasion, when Morris had to leave the meeting for a few minutes, Faulkner lodged the *London Directory* and two large copper candlesticks on top of the door. When Morris returned, they all fell down on to his head. He let out a yell of rage, and showed signs of becoming really angry; but when Faulkner reproved him for his bad temper, he looked at him for a second and then burst into a fit of laughter.[27] Faulkner also records that the getting ready of their goods for the 1862 Exhibition 'has cost more tribulation and swearing to Topsy than three exhibitions will be worth'. In the year in which they won their medals at the Exhibition, Mary ('May') Morris was born.

William Michael Rossetti, writing in *The Studio* in 1917, described the atmosphere of these early days of the firm:

Light or boisterous chaff among themselves and something like dictatorial irony towards the customers. . . . Mr Morris, as the managing partner, laid down the law and all his clients had to bend or break. . . . The goods were first rate, the art and workmanship excellent, the prices high. No concession was made to individual tastes or want of taste, no question of abatement was entertained. You could have the things such as the firm chose they should be, or you could do without them.

Prospective clients, visiting Red Lion Square, would be confronted with Morris in his round hat and blue workman's blouse, his hands covered with paint, and apparently not caring overmuch whether he secured their orders or not. But, of course, it was this very un-conventionality of the whole thing which made it so intriguing. For here was an educated man, a poet, who actually worked with his hands and did not care tuppence how he looked. It is recorded that on one occasion when someone described as 'a person of importance' visited the Oxford Street showroom and exclaimed: 'Oh but, Mr Morris, I thought your colours were subdued!' Morris brusquely remarked: 'If you want dirt, you can get in the street!'

As orders increased at Red Lion Square, the premises became too small and in 1864 the idea of moving the works to Upton and building a new wing to Red House to accommodate the Burne-Joneses was seriously discussed. But Georgie had been seriously ill with scarlet fever and Ned, always delicate in any case, became ill with worry and anxiety. Moreover, Morris himself had, on a cold journey down from London, caught a chill which developed into rheumatic fever, and when he recovered he felt that he could no longer make the daily journey to town. Evidently Burne-Jones had written about this time to say that they could not after all consider moving from London, for in a letter headed 'Bed, Red House' Morris replied in a very shaky hand in November:

As to our palace of Art, I confess your letter was a blow to me at first, though hardly an unexpected one – in short I cried; but I have got over it now. As to our being a miserable lot, old chap, speaking for myself I don't know, I refuse to make myself really unhappy for anything short of the loss of friends one can't do without. Suppose in all these troubles you had given us the slip what the devil should I have done? I am sure I couldn't have had the heart to have gone on with the firm: all our jolly subjects would have gone to pot – it frightens me to think of, Ned. But now I am only 30 years old, I shan't always have the rheumatism, and we shall have a lot of jolly years of invention and lustre plates together I hope. I need hardly tell you how I have suffered for you in the worst of your troubles; on the Saturday I had begun a letter to you but it read so dismal (as indeed I felt little hope) that I burnt it. . . .

There is only one other thing I can think of, which is when you come back from Hastings come and stay with me for a month or two, there is plenty of room for everybody and everything: you can do your work quietly and uninterruptedly; I shall have a good horse by then and Georgie and J. will be able to drive about with the kids jollily, meantime you need not be hurried in taking your new crib. Janey is exceedingly anxious that you should come and it is in her opinion the best thing you could do. I would give £5 to see you, old chap. . . .[28]

At the end of 1864, while Georgie was recovering, Burne-Jones, with the help of Cormell Price, moved into 41 Kensington Square. Here they lived for the next three years – 'a quiet old square'. Lady Burne-Jones describes it as it then was, 'lying back undisturbed by the world, with nothing except gardens between it and the narrow High Street'. Morris was also gradually becoming reconciled to the idea of giving up Red House and moving back to London. He did not leave it until the autumn of 1865, but after that he never visited it again, saying that the sight of it would be more than he could bear.

'The last visit we paid to Upton was in September 1865,' writes Lady Burne-Jones, 'when on a lovely afternoon Morris and Janey, and Edward and I, took a farewell drive through some of the beautiful little out-of-the-way places that were still to be found in the neighbourhood. Indoors the talk of the men was much about The Earthly Paradise, which was to be illustrated by two or three hundred woodcuts, many of them already designed and some even drawn on the block.' As he wrote the long, soporific tales of his *Earthly Paradise*, Morris would read them aloud to Ned and Georgie, who 'remembers, with shame, often falling asleep to the steady rhythm of the reading voice, or biting my fingers and stabbing myself with pins in order to keep awake'.[29] Later generations are unlikely to take such drastic measures, and there are probably few readers of *The Earthly Paradise* today. But finally, the plan for an illustrated edition had to be abandoned as too costly.

Red House was vacated in November. Much of the furniture was judged too heavy to move.

CHAPTER FIVE

1865–1871

Queen Square: of Utter Love Defeated Utterly

A LEASE of twenty-one years of 26 Queen Square, at a rental of £52 10s. a year, was granted from Midsummer 1865 to Ford Madox Brown, Charles Joseph Faulkner, Edward Burne-Jones, Peter Paul Marshall, William Morris, Dante Gabriel Rossetti and Philip Webb. The Queen Square house was thus taken from the first not as a private residence, but as business premises above which Morris and his family lived.

'Queen Square, in which Morris himself and the firm of Morris & Co. took up house together in the autumn of 1865,' wrote Mackail in the late 1890s, 'is a backwater of older Bloomsbury, which then retained some traces of its original dignity as a suburb of the London of Queen Anne. Put out of fashion half a century before by the more modern splendours of Russell Square, it had lingered on as a residential neighbourhood. . . . The residential was now becoming mingled with an industrial element.'[1] When Morris moved into the square, with its mouldering statue of Queen Anne in the central garden, it must have had considerable charm, though to an eye which could only see virtue in Gothic it probably appeared dull and monotonous. On the north side the square was open to the heights of Hampstead and the small seventeenth-century houses of Devon-shire and Old Gloucester Streets had doubtless, even then, become a slum. No. 26 was on the east side and, when Mackail was writing, had already been pulled down to make room for an extension of the National Hospital for the Paralysed and Epileptic – now Great Ormond Street Children's Hospital. A drawing of it by A. Forestier is preserved in Lady Warwick's *Homes and Haunts of William Morris* of 1912.

The ground floor was turned into an office and showroom and the large ballroom, built at the end of the paved back yard and con-nected with the house by a long corridor where the glass-painters sat, became the principal workshop. Other workshops were accommodated at the back of the house and these in time overflowed into Ormond Yard. The long panelled drawing-room with its five windows on the first floor when Morris moved in was painted white. 'In this particular spot the dinginess of the neighbourhood was conquered, and it had been made to shine with whitewash and white paint,' says Lady Burne-Jones, 'a background that showed better than any other the beautiful fabrics with which the house was furnished.'[2] The Faulkners also had a house a few doors away; by this time Charles Faulkner had returned to Oxford, though he often came down to stay with his mother in Queen Square.

Faulkner's place as business manager of the firm had been taken by Warington Taylor, introduced by Rossetti somewhat earlier at Red House. A tall, thin man with a large Roman nose and an excitable way of speaking, Warington Taylor was the son of a Devonshire squire and a Roman Catholic. He had been briefly at Eton with Swinburne, but was then sent to Germany for his education. After losing all his money, he had joined the army, and, at the time he met Morris, had been working as a check-taker at Her Majesty's Theatre, then an opera house. One reason for taking this job was his passion for music. 'Within a few weeks of his appoint-ment,' writes Lady Burne-Jones, 'the rumour spread that he was keeping the accounts of the firm like a dragon, attending to the orders of customers, and actually getting Morris to work at one thing at a time.' In fact, the business affairs of the firm ('still very infirm', says Lethaby) can best be followed in the series of highly emotional and bullying letters with which Taylor began to bombard Webb and Rossetti.[3] Soon after his engagement, however, his health broke down and he went to live at Hastings. On 13 November 1866 he wrote to Webb, when the firm had received their important com-mission to redecorate the Armoury and Tapestry Room at St James's Palace:

Come down as soon as you can report real visible progress at the palace, so as to give me some cheering news, but do come down soon and bring Morris. Do see that Morris starts those angels for Cambridge roof now [that is, for the roof of Jesus College Chapel]; he will never have them in time, and at the last moment will want others to do the work. How is he looking? I trust well and rosy with good wine. And how is she? . . . Polit. econ.

teaches the doctrine get rich – well, you get rich and you become a blackguard; where is the gain? Human reason, what bosh it is! Progress, what rot it is! Do come down and bring the Squire.

Taylor was an attractive character and no wonder the others took his bullying in good part. His inquiry about Jane reminds one that at this time she was already ailing. We read in the *Memorials* that the weekly dinners of the members of the firm at Queen Square, when 'the merriment of our youth was revived for a time', were 'more fatigue than pleasure' to her and that, as a consequence, they had to be abandoned. Jane probably found it fatiguing to live in a work-shop, dominated by the loud and boisterous manners of her over-whelming husband. For Morris's manners also were medieval. He would fling his dinner out of the window, if it was badly cooked, or, if a door did not open at once, he was liable to wrench its handle off or kick out one of its panels. He could never sit still a moment, even at table, continually getting up and pacing the room. Friends speak of his tempestuous and exacting company, or describe him pacing the room like a caged lion. He was liable to get up and begin work at five o'clock in the morning, or continue, if he felt like it, most of the night. This sort of behaviour, combined as it was by fairly frequent fits of uncontrollable rage, epileptic in origin, could not have been easy to live with.

It is not known what was the matter with Jane Morris, but it is probable that her symptoms were basically neurotic. That, however, did not make them any the easier to bear. She may even have suffered from what is now called a slipped disk, for her malady seems to have been partly a spinal one. Of rude and robust health himself, Morris was inclined to be somewhat impatient of the ail-ments of others – until his daughter Jenny's breakdown – though he could be tender and sympathetic with a friend in trouble.

Another letter of Warington Taylor's of November 1866 to Webb is about the decorations to the Green Dining Room at the South Kensington Museum, another of the firm's big commissions and mainly Webb's work.

What has been settled about the execution of the South Ken-sington windows? Who is to do them now Campfield is ill? This must be settled at once. *See it done.* E.B.-J. ought to have sent in first design by to-day at least. *See to it.* Is the Cambridge window going to hang fire? *See to it.* It ought to go off this week. . . .

You ought to be designing the panelling for South Kensington at once: it is such nonsense to say they don't want it. E. B./J. is to get all the South Kens. window designs done by Xmas. By that time the necessary panels ought to be made and in his house, so that he may go on with them at his leisure. . . . See this panelling designed and executed at once, at any rate get good pieces of wood for E. B./J. forthwith.

Climate here very delightful; population loathsome. . . . I am very queer and frightfully feverish, but don't care now because I am content that MacShane [the firm's clerk] can keep the books in order. According to his last report everything is now started, i.e. all the important jobs.

How such a young firm as Morris, Marshall & Co. received two such important commissions as those at St James's Palace and the South Kensington Museum, is something of a mystery. Henry Cole, the Director at South Kensington, must have been sufficiently im/pressed by their exhibits at the Exhibition of 1862 to have recom/mended them in both cases. (In 1868 he commissioned Poynter, the representative with Leighton of the classical school, to decorate the Grill Room at South Kensington.) The work at St James's evi/dently began at the end of September 1866 and was finished by the middle of the following January. The general decorative plan was Webb's, as in the case of South Kensington, but that does not mean that Morris did not have a hand in every stage of the design and execution.[4] On 27 January Warington Taylor wrote to Webb urging him to charge proper prices for the work: 'Remember we are embezzling public money now – what business has any palace to be decorated at all?'

Webb's accounts with the firm from August 1866 to January 1867 include such items as: '3 visits to St James's Palace, measuring; Pattern panels; Enlarging pattern for ceiling of Armoury; do cornice; Redrawing reticulated pattern of panels, Armoury; Designs full size &c. for ceiling Tapestry Room.' At present the painted dados, doors, window/cases and stone fireplaces of both these rooms at St James's remain virtually in their original state. As for the Green Dining Room at South Kensington, Burne/Jones seems to have had some assistance with the figure panels. But when they were finished, Morris was dissatisfied with them and, according to Aymer Vallance, had Fairfax Murray do the painting all over again.[5] Thus, although the South Kensington authorities grumbled at the cost, from the point of view of the firm the work hardly paid for itself, except in its immense prestige value.

Then MacShane, the firm's book-keeper, died, and Warington Taylor is worried again:

> Who is going to replace him ? There must be a decision or within 6 months you are in a muck. *Summa*, it is your business to call a meeting and settle at once what you are going to do – and just see that you don't talk rot but decide definitely because generally the time would be better employed in a comic song. Of all things British muddle is the worst. Morris confesses he is a Celt, and we know what that means in the practical line. . . . You may be quite certain that you will charge £9 for that which costs you £10. I *know* your ways of calculating profits.

Next autumn Taylor is writing to Rossetti that the firm's affairs are 'consolatory', though there was still a tendency to undercharge:

> The profits represent I think about 28 per cent on the work done, a little over £3000 worth of work during the year. After two years experience I conceive the matter stands thus –
>
> 1. We do about £2300 worth of windows a year roughly stated, twenty windows, all sizes.
> 2. Considering this to be the quantity of work done, nothing but the highest prices can pay.
> 3. This amount of work we shall always get, therefore it is only loss of time to do cheap work. Morris and I never get hot with one another save on the subject of price. He is always for a low price; seeing the amount of work we do it is absurd, we must have a long price: and it must be considered not so much per foot but as so much for painting in glass. Another point is this: Morris and Ned will do no work except by driving, and you must keep up the supply of designs. . . .

> Have you been to see Webb's *chef d'œuvre*, the decoration of the Palace ? It must be stirring.

On second thoughts, however, Taylor is far from satisfied:

> Having commented on the Firm's affairs from the *couleur-de-rose*, I must give you better satisfaction than you have had yet. If Webb's

report to me of yesterday's meeting is correct, all I can say is that the whole question has never been looked at at all in a business-like point of view. . . . The large profit you had put before you was not made on stained glass, but on the Palace decorations. The whole of that work was done by Webb; if Webb had been busy with architecture, it could not have been done. You could never depend upon such work again. Moreover, Webb was miserably paid for his designs. This is no fault of the firm's, but Webb would not have more. He never will charge above a third of what he ought to charge. It was settled, I believe, to divide profits, but you apparently settled no amount to be divided. Then there was no sum settled for working capital. As to increasing salaries, it won't bear what it pays now. I know the tendency at Queen Square to make life comfortable; anything rather than face death or a fact: hence the prosperous appearance of everything. Morris won't have many of the sours of life – can't get him to face that at all.

Again, in another letter:

As to Morris having his capital, keep him without it, he will only spend it on books. In about three years' time it will be of use to him for publishing purposes: at present it would go in wine and books!!! For the present I should advise you not to be too sanguine.

Again:

A business of £2000 a year may give sufficient profit to one person, but it is not large enough for a company; and, in a business doing so small an amount of work, the proprietor should be clerk, manager, and all himself. But with us two large salaries are taken out of the £500 profit that ought to be: Morris takes £150, Taylor £120; and since my unfortunate illness, six months of MacShane £37 10s. Our annual expenditure, roughly stated, comes to quite £1500 out of £2000.

'Poor Taylor,' wrote one of his friends, 'tall with hatchet-face – is ghastly thin but full of mental energy.' But, by his efforts, May Morris records, 'he probably saved the firm from going to pieces through the unpractical ways of its members'. He was particularly worried by Morris's extravagance. Two years later in 1869, he is writing to Rossetti:

The personal extravagance of the members used to be spasmodic: it is now confirmed and habitual. W. M. has grown worse and worse. . . . There is not one of us now who has not got grey hairs in his head – it is very odd that we must still try to play boy – it is only playing at it.

And of Morris in particular:

Remember how I have watched him, how I know his habits. What he will probably do is this – he will draw small cheques for himself – these he will pretend to take no notice of – and at the end of the quarter, he will express surprise when he is told he is perhaps overdrawn £100 – he will have no means of paying it and the firm will be the loser – so he will gradually ruin it. The only remedy is for *one member to inspect the books weekly* to see what he is doing. . . . Every kind of thing has been done to try to save W. M. for the last 3 years – now the only thing is for members to take him in hand.

Taylor followed this up with a broadside to Morris on household expenses, concluding:

It is no good your screaming and saying you will shut the bloody shop up. You can't afford to do it any longer. I told you some years ago that it would become indispensable to you. It is evident that you must give up entertaining. You have not the means to do it. . . . It is no good your blasting anybody's eyes – you must haul in. What does that £60 owing by Ned mean? He never had £60 to pay anybody. You knew all about this. You must have been signing the cheques.

I am not dead yet. How can any man dream of entertaining and going out on £700 a year out of which he pays £100 for rent and taxes nearly. You must reduce your wine consumption down to 2½ bottles a day – this at 1/6 is somewhere about £68 a year.

Taylor's letters give us not only an indication of how Morris lived, they also provide a valuable insight into his unbusiness-like habits and unsystematic way of working, an aspect that Mackail could hardly stress. 'Morris is very nervous about work,' Taylor wrote to Rossetti, 'and consequently often suddenly takes men off one job and puts them onto another. There is in this great loss of time. When I was there, I was able in some way to counteract this: I used to quiet him. Morris will start half a dozen jobs; he has only designs for perhaps half of them, and therefore in a week or two they have to be given up. They are put away, bits get lost, have to be done over again: Hence great loss of time and money.'

It seems that twelve men were employed and Taylor objected that they were 'made to do one day one thing one another'. He would like to have confined the firm to one class of work – stained glass. In a memo he noted: 'Considering the few interested in decoration and limited sale of our papers there will not be any increase of sale of papers by the addition of a few more patterns: in fact, you will probably sell fewer of the present old patterns. Two new patterns would for all business purposes be abundant – Townsend's "Bird" and Scott's "Indian".' It was largely due to Warington Taylor's constant nagging that Morris gradually learned more business-like methods and that the firm began to prosper.

But Taylor died in February 1870, before reaching the age of thirty-three. He was buried at St Thomas's, Fulham, at the firm's expense, under a tombstone designed by Webb. His place as manager was taken by George Wardle.

While the decorations to St James's Palace and the Green Dining Room were in progress, Morris was filling notebook after notebook with hundreds of lines of easily flowing, facile verse. The illustrated edition of *The Earthly Paradise*, or 'The Big Book', was being planned. In 1866 William Allingham noted in his diary:

Monday July 30. Kensington Square. Studio, Psyche drawings. Book planned. Morris and lots of stories and pictures.

Wednesday Aug. 1. At dinner William Morris, pleasant, learned about wines and distilling. The Big Story Book, product of Olympus by Ned Jones. Morris and friends intend to engrave the wood-blocks themselves – & M. will publish the book at his own expense. I like Morris much. He is plain-spoken and em-phatic, often boisterously, without an atom of irritating matter. He goes about 12.

But though a large number of plates were cut on wood (five hundred were projected) by both Morris and Burne-Jones, the project came to nothing. Many of Burne-Jones's *Earthly Paradise* blocks were later used by the Gregynog Press to illustrate an edition of Robert Bridges's *Eros and Psyche*.

Morris, however, continued to produce tales in verse at an astonishing speed. Faulkner records that he wrote seven hundred lines of
Jason in a day. Indeed, this particular story grew to such proportions
that it had to be published separately in 1867. By the spring of 1868,
Mackail tells us, at least seventeen of the twenty-four tales which
were proposed for the complete design of *The Earthly Paradise* had
been written. 'If you had seen and handled those seven great folio
volumes of *The Earthly Paradise*, fair copy and drafts,' says May
Morris,

> you would be particularly impressed by this fact. You would have
> to remember, also, that some twenty or so other MSS of the single
> stories exist in one form or another; that the writer was at this time
> cutting on wood, designing and busy over the hundred and one
> matters that the head of a personally-conducted business has to
> attend to; that he kept no amanuensis and did all the writing of
> notes and drafts and fair scripts in his own hand. It is not sur-
> prising that these endless activities made him a rather careless man
> of business – careless in detail and in housekeeping.[6]

Most of Morris's writing was done at night, or in the small hours of
the morning, and Rossetti used to say that there was a Blue Closet
at Queen Square 'full from top to bottom with Morris's poems'.

'Morris always had a yearning for illustrations to his poems', his
daughter tells us: 'he saw the stories as brilliantly-defined pictures,
and desired that other people should do so, too. "There is nobody but
Burne-Jones who can do them", he often said.'[7] All the early quarto
drafts of *The Earthly Paradise* have notes on the verso for these
illustrations. The first tale to be written and illustrated was 'Cupid
and Psyche', of which several drafts exist. If Morris was not satisfied
with his first version, rather than painfully revise it, he wrote the
whole thing again. Most of his verse may strike us today as lax and
careless, but that was not due to any want of labour, so much as to
his too rapid method of composition. Unfortunately, as he rewrote
them, his poems lost whatever freshness and vitality they originally
had. But vividness was no part of Morris's intention. In fact, he was
at great pains to distance his subjects and to rob them of all urgency
of emotion: his aim was the cool remoteness of pictures in a frieze
or the figures on a faded tapestry. The verse is always deliberately
decorative and closely resembles in general atmosphere Burne-
Jones's 'Cupid and Psyche' frieze, done for the dining-room of

1 Palace Green and now in the Birmingham City Museum and Art Gallery, but based on the original illustrations for Morris's poem.

For the Victorian paterfamilias, *The Earthly Paradise* was ideal for family reading, being 'adapted', according to *The Saturday Review* of 30 May 1869, 'for conveying to our wives and daughters a refined, although not diluted version of those wonderful creations of Greek fancy which the rougher sex alone is permitted to imbibe at first hand'. But a critic in the *Quarterly Review* of 1872, writing on 'The Latest Development of Literary Poetry', remarked that 'the heroines of the tales . . . are as forward as the heroes are languid. . . . Mr Morris, in fact, seems to think that shame and reserve are qualities incompatible with simplicity.' The same critic also observed: 'Mr Morris writes by sentences, and, as his chief aim is to give each sentence an archaic turn, his verse resembles old prose with incidental rhymes.' Nevertheless, in its own day *The Earthly Paradise* had a tremendous vogue: today the shelves of second-hand booksellers are loaded with unsold sets. To achieve the pale decorative charm of these poems, Morris worked hard to rid his verse of everything that had made *The Defence of Guenevere* so original. His first title for the prologue to *The Earthly Paradise* was, significantly, 'The Fools Paradise', which he subsequently altered to 'The Wanderers'.

As a good medievalist, it was natural that Morris should turn to the tale of Troy and thence to Jason. In its monotony and plain-chant drone, *Jason* is one of the longest narrative poems in the language. One feels, as with a poem by Gower or Lydgate, that there is no reason why it should ever stop. At the opening of Book XVII there is an address to Chaucer, phrased with due medieval humility:

> *Would that I*
> *Had but some portion of that mastery*
> *That from the rose-hung lanes of woody Kent*
> *Through these five hundred years such songs have sent*
> *To us, who, meshed within this smoky net*
> *Of unrejoicing labour, love them yet.*
> *And thou, O Master! – Yea, my Master still,*
> *Whatever feet have scaled Parnassus' hill,*
> *Since like thy measures, clear and sweet and strong,*
> *Thames' stream scarce fettered drave the dace along*
> *Unto the bastioned bridge, his only chain. –*
> *O Master, pardon me, if yet in vain*

Thou art my Master, and I fail to bring
Before men's eyes the image of the thing
My heart is filled with: thou whose dreamy eyes
Beheld the flush to Cressid's cheeks arise,
When Troilus rode up the praising street,
As clearly as they saw thy townsmen meet
Those who in vineyards of Poictou withstood
The glittering horror of the steel-topped wood.

This has undeniable charm. Morris is always at his best with pictures elaborated in Pre-Raphaelite detail:

So still she stood, that the quick water-hen
Noted her not, as through the blue mouse-ear
He made his way; the conies drew anear,
Nibbling the grass; and from an oak-twig nigh
A thrush poured forth his song unceasingly.

Morris has a sharp, precise eye for the physical beauty of the world, a craftsman's eye for comely and well-wrought objects, but it is all turned to favour and to prettiness.

The first volume of *The Earthly Paradise* was published only a year after *Jason*, in 1868, ten years after *The Defence of Guenevere*. The title page carried a charming woodcut by Morris of three female musicians in a garden playing on medieval instruments, and the reader is invited in the Prologue to

Forget six counties overhung with smoke,
Forget the snorting steam and piston stroke,
Forget the spreading of the hideous town;
Think rather of the pack-horse on the down,
And dream of London, small, and white, and clean,
The clear Thames bordered by its gardens green.

There follow the stories of the months, from March to the following February, with two stories for each month. Twelve are taken from Greek sources, the other twelve are stories current in Western Europe in French and German romances, in Norse and Icelandic sagas, as well as stories from the East. Taken as a whole, the three volumes of *The Earthly Paradise* (the second and third volumes appeared in 1870) run to 42,000 lines of rhymed verse. The scheme of the work is set forth in the Argument: 'Certain gentlemen and mariners of Norway, having considered all they had heard of the

Earthly Paradise, set sail to find it, and after many troubles and the lapse of many years came old men to some western land, of which they had never before heard: there they died, when they had dwelt there certain years, much honoured of the strange people' – who turn out to be a surviving outpost of ancient Greek civilization. The time is that of the Black Death in Europe and the voyagers are of Norse, Breton and Germanic origin. Each month for a year they entertain their hosts with a story and are entertained in the same manner in return. The idea is, of course, much the same as Chaucer employed in *The Canterbury Tales*, but the resemblance to Chaucer is only superficial, since the emotion underlying Morris's poem is a sense of the emptiness of life. This is evident at the beginning when he writes of himself in the Apology (in medieval rhyme royal) as

> *Dreamer of dreams, born out of my due time,*
> *Why should I strive to set the crooked straight?*
> *Let it suffice me that my murmuring rhyme*
> *Beats with light wing against the ivory gate,*
> *Telling a tale not too importunate*
> *To those who in the sleepy region stay,*
> *Lulled by the singer of an empty day.*

> *Folk say, a wizard to a northern king*
> *At Christmas-tide such wondrous things did show,*
> *That through one window men beheld the spring,*
> *And through another saw the summer glow,*
> *And through a third the fruited-vines a-row,*
> *While still, unheard, but in its wonted way,*
> *Piped the drear wind of that December day.*

> *So with this Earthly Paradise it is,*
> *If ye will read aright, and pardon me,*
> *Who strive to build a shadowy isle of bliss*
> *Midmost the beating of the steely sea,*
> *Where tossed about all hearts of men must be;*
> *Whose ravening monsters mighty men shall slay,*
> *Not the idle singer of an empty day.*

Morris is writing of the condition of the poet in the nineteenth century. The Earthly Paradise, the dream that has haunted the imagination of men since the earliest times, is shown to be an illusion: the reality is the drear December wind, the beating of the steely sea and the ravening monsters, not the pictures conjured up by the wizard. The poet is always

> *waking from delight*
> *Unto the real day void and white.*

Even the delight itself, while it lasts, is shadowy and unsubstantial.

As E. P. Thompson observes: 'A close reading of every poem in the sequence reveals that Morris is not really interested in either the characters or in the action – in the sense that the action is in itself either significant or purposeful.' And he goes on to show that the basic movement of the whole work is 'an almost mechanical oscillation between sensuous luxury and horror, melancholy and despair'.[8] Thus 'The Lady of the Land' appears as a Burne-Jones figure:

> *Naked she was, the kisses of her feet*
> *Upon the floor a dying path had made*
> *From the full bath unto her ivory seat;*
> *In her right hand, upon her bosom laid,*
> *She held a golden comb, a mirror weighed*
> *Her left hand down, aback her fair head lay*
> *Dreaming awake of some long vanished day.*

But at the end of the poem she is transformed into a dragon. The underlying motive of *The Earthly Paradise* becomes explicit in 'The Hill of Venus':

> *As though a cold and hopeless tune he heard,*
> *Sung by grey mouths amidst a dull-eyed dream;*
> *Time and again across his heart would stream*
> *The pain of fierce desire whose aim was gone,*
> *Of baffled yearning, loveless and alone.*

This motive is repeated in the poems on the different months in which, Mackail tells us, 'there is an autobiography so delicate and so outspoken that it must needs be left to speak for itself'.[9] Thus in the lines on September we read:

> *Look long, O longing eyes, and look in vain!*
> *Strain idly, aching heart, and yet be wise*
> *And hope no more for things to come again*
> *That thou beholdest once with careless eyes!*
> *Like a new-wakened man thou art, who tries*

> *To dream again the dream that made him glad*
> *When in his arms his loving love he had.*

'December' is still more explicit:

> *Out break the bells above the year foredone,*
> *Change, kindness lost, love left unloved alone;*
> *Till their despairing sweetness makes thee deem*
> *Thou once wert loved, if but amidst a dream.*

As Thompson remarks, Morris seldom turns to look his fear in the face; when he does, his verse leaps to life, as in 'November' and 'December'. 'But whenever he took refuge from his fear in the world of romance, we meet, not life, but the constant undertow back towards death.'[10] In several of the poems the image occurs of the living struck dead in the postures of life. It is clear that this deadness, this helplessness, was in Morris's own heart. It is as if he now wrote, as he put it in 'Pygmalion and the Image', to 'soothe his heart and dull thought's poisonous stings'. In the late 1860s Morris's private life seems to have foundered in disaster.

From a collection of manuscript poems in the British Museum, inscribed 'Short Poems and Sonnets',[11] several of which appeared in revised forms in Volume XXIV of the *Collected Works* as 'Poems of the *Earthly Paradise* Time about 1865–1870' and in Volume I of the two supplementary volumes as 'Poems of the Earthly Paradise Period', it would appear that while Morris was still passionately attached to his wife, he met with little or no response. The theme of all these poems is, once again, lost love. There can be no doubt that Morris is writing about his own loneliness and despair. May Morris printed 'Near but Far Away', a poem obviously addressed to Jane and inscribed 'May 11th', without the lines that immediately follow it in the manuscript:

> *She wavered, stopped and turned, methought her eyes,*
> *The deep grey windows of her heart, were wet,*
> *Methought they softened with a near regret*
> *To note in mine unspoken miseries:*
> *And as a prayer from out my heart did rise*
> *And struggle on my lips in shame's strong net,*
> *She stayed me, and cried 'Brother!' Our lips met.*
> *Her hands drew me into Paradise.*
> *Sweet seemed that kiss till thence her feet were gone,*

Sweet seemed the word she spake, while it might be
As wordless music – But truth fell on me
And kiss and word I knew, and, left alone,
Face to face seemed I to a wall of stone,
While at my back there beat a boundless sea.

Nay what is this and wherefore lingerest thou?
Why say'st thou the thrushes sob and moan
And that the sky is hard and grey as stone?
Why say'st thou the east tears bloom and bough?
Why seem the sons of men so hopeless now?
Thy love is gone, poor wretch, thou art alone.[12]

This is the same situation as appears in the verses on January and April in *The Earthly Paradise*, written in 1869. Among *Short Poems and Sonnets* are some anguished lines which point quite clearly to the tragic triangular situation which had developed between Morris, Jane and Rossetti. They appear to belong to what Mackail, in an unpublished letter to Mrs Coronio of 12 May 1899, refers to as 'those stormy years of *The Earthly Paradise* time and the time following it', his account of which, he fears, 'must be excessively flat owing to the amount of tact that had to be exercised right and left'. Mackail added that tact 'is a quality unpleasantly near untruthfulness often!'[13] These lines, written hurriedly in pencil, are as follows:

Hearken: nigher still and nigher
Had we grown, methought my fire
Woke in her some hidden flame
And the rags of pride and shame
She seemed casting from her heart,
And the dull days seemed to part;
Then I cried out, 'Ah I move thee
And thou knowest that I love thee.'
Half-forgotten, unforgiven and alone!
Alone, unhappy by the fire I sat . . .

We meet we laugh and talk, but still is set
A seal over things I never can forget
But must not speak of still. I count the hours
That bring my friend to me – with hungry eyes
I watch him as his feet the staircase mount.

> *Then face to face we sit, a wall of lies*
> *Made hard by fear and faint anxieties*
> *Is drawn between us and he goes away*
> *And leaves me wishing it were yesterday.*[14]

These lines are annotated: 'poets' unrealities – tears can come with verse we two are in the same box and need conceal nothing – don't cast me away – scold me but pardon me. What is all this to me (say you) Shame in confessing one's real feelings.' One can only wonder what Jane was being asked to pardon *him* for, unless it was his inability to accept the situation. Evidently Morris seems to have felt that he had failed Jane in some way. Again, in another poem, 'Why Dost Thou Struggle?', he imagines her speaking:

> *Unto deaf ears or unto such as know*
> *The hearts of dead and living wilt thou say:*
> *'A childish heart there loved me once and lo*
> *I took his love and cast his love away.*
>
> *'A childish greedy heart! yet still he clung*
> *So close to me that much he pleased my pride*
> *And soothed a sorrow that about me hung*
> *With glimpses of his love unsatisfied . . .*
>
> *'But now my heart grown silent of its grief*
> *Saw more than kindness in his hungry eyes*
> *But I must wear a mask of false belief*
> *And feign that nought I know his miseries.*
>
> *'I wore a mask because though certainly*
> *I loved him not yet was there something soft*
> *And sweet to have him ever loving me*
> *Belike it is I well nigh loved him oft—*
>
> *'Nigh loved him oft and needs must grant to him*
> *Some kindness out of all he asked of me*
> *And hoped his love would still hang vague, dim,*
> *About my life like half-heard melody.*
>
> *'He knew my heart and over-well knew this*
> *And strove poor soul to pleasure me herein;*
> *But yet what might he do? some doubtful kiss,*
> *Some word, some look might give him hope to win.*

'Poor hope, poor soul, for he again would come
Thinking to gain yet one more golden step
Toward love's shrine and lo! the kind speech dumb
The kind look gone, no love upon my lip –

'Yea gone, yet not my fault. I knew of love,
But my love and not his; nor could I tell
That such blind passion in him I should move.
Behold, I have loved faithfully and well!'[15]

The picture drawn here is clear enough. It is a situation that appears again and again in Morris's published work and it leaves no doubt of his bitterness at this time.

Meanwhile, Jane and Rossetti were seen frequently together at studio parties, which Morris seldom attended. One such occasion in 1870 is recorded by Edmund Gosse at Madox Brown's house in Fitzroy Square – Jane sitting on the model's throne like a queen in a long ivory velvet dress and Rossetti – 'too stout for elegance' – on a hassock at her feet. A cousin of William de Morgan also remembers seeing them sitting together in a corner at another party, Rossetti feeding Jane on strawberries and both apparently oblivious to anyone else in the room.[16]

From 1865, Rossetti drew and painted Jane increasingly at Cheyne Walk, each painting and drawing filled with a strange, brooding, half-mystical sexuality. In June 1866 he began painting her in a peacock-blue dress seated before a vase of creamy roses; before that was finished, he began another portrait of her as Dante's La Pia de' Tolomei; during the spring and summer of 1869 he painted her as Pandora, opening her casket and letting out 'Powers of the impassioned hours prohibited'. La Pia, it will be recalled, had been imprisoned by a cruel husband in revenge for her love for Dante – and left to die in the exhalations of the pestilential Maremma marshes. When Henry James visited Queen Square in March 1869 he saw there, as he wrote to his sister, 'a large nearly full-length portrait of her [Jane Morris] by Rossetti, so strange and unreal that you'd pronounce it a distempered vision, but in fact an extremely good likeness'.[17] This was probably the *Mrs William Morris*, now at Kelmscott. It is hardly 'a distempered vision', though *La Pia* could certainly be so described.

To say that Morris was too preoccupied with his work, or too self-absorbed to be aware of other people, as is sometimes said, is manifestly untrue. Beneath his mask of bluff, burly manliness, he was of an unusually nervous and excitable temperament. Later in life, it is true, when he had endured years of emotional frustration and disappointed love, he had learnt to school his emotions, and it is not unlikely that he then gave the impression of moving through life 'isolated as in a dream, self-centered, almost empty of love or hatred', as Mackail describes him.[18] But as far as the young and middle-aged Morris was concerned, during 'those stormy years of *The Earthly Paradise* time and the time following it', such a verdict is contradicted by the evidence of his poems and letters. In later life Morris channelled his passion into public causes, but this process had not yet begun.

On the surface, however, life remained 'jolly'. We hear of a dinner party given by Rossetti at Cheyne Walk in April 1868 to celebrate the completion of *La Pia*. 'A grand dinner was given in honour of the Topsies, and we were all warned to appear in *Togs*', Madox Brown writes breezily. 'However, Morris, at the last moment, was dispatched to Queen Square to forcibly bring back his partner, Faulkner, thirteen at table being otherwise the mishap.' It was then discovered that they would have been thirteen *without* Morris. In counting up his guests, Rossetti had unconsciously overlooked La Pia's husband! But, concluded Brown, 'it was all magnificent and jolly'.[19] The Morrises stayed at Cheyne Walk for a week, so that Jane should be available to 'sit' at any time the Master willed. Morris, we are told, tried out new instalments of *The Earthly Paradise* in a loud voice from a back window of Tudor House, while from the studio would come the sound of 'frequent and uproarious laughter'.[20]

Otherwise the atmosphere of Tudor House, as described by Sidney Colvin, sounds rather oppressive. Colvin writes of

the combined gloom and richness of its decorations, the sombre hangings, the doors and panellings painted sombre dark green sparsely picked out with red and lighted here and there by a round convex mirror; the shelves and cupboards laden with brassware and old blue Nankin china . . . the long, green and shady garden at the back, with its uncanny menagerie of wombat, racoon, armadillo, kangaroo. . . .

And of Rossetti himself, Colvin writes:

his sturdy, almost burly figure clad in a dark cloth suit with the square jacket cut extra long and deep-pocketed; his rich brown hair and lighter brown, shortish, square-trimmed beard, the olive complexion betraying Italian blood; the handsome features be-tween spare and fleshy, with full sensual underlip and thoughtful forehead . . . the deep bar above the nose and fine, blue-grey colour of the eyes behind their spectacles, and finally the round, John-Bullish, bluntly cordial manner of speech, with a pre-ference for brief and bluff slang words and phrases, which seemed scarce in keeping with the fame and character of the man as the most quintessentially and romantically poetic of painters and writers. . . .[21]

There were big dinners, too, at Queen Square. Allingham notes:

Wed. May 27 [1868] To Queen Square, to dine with Morris and find just alighting Mrs Ned in a gorgeous yellow gown: it is a full dress party! and I in velveteen jacket. Morris, Ned J. (thin), D.G.R. (looking well), Boyce ('has been ill'), F.M.Brown (oldened), Webb, Howell, Mr Wilfrid Heeley, Publisher Ellis and W.A., Mrs Morris, Miss Burden, Mrs Ned (gay), Mrs Howell, Mrs Madox Brown (looks young with back to the window), Lucy Brown, Miss Faulkner (I between these), Mrs Ellis, Mrs Heeley (ten ladies). Banquet – 'Earthly Paradise' I suggest, and Ned writes this atop of the menu. A storm of talking. I away with D.G.R. about 1; walk first, then cab to Cheyne Walk, in and stay chatting and lounging till 3 in old fashion.[22]

By the end of the year, Burne-Jones was in serious trouble, hotly pursued by one of the Greek beauties cultivated by the Pre-Raphaelites and drawn by Rossetti, Mrs Marie Zambaco. On 23 January 1869, Rossetti wrote to Madox Brown:

Poor Ned's affairs have come to a smash altogether, and he and Topsy, after the most dreadful to-do, started for Rome suddenly, leaving the Greek damsel beating up the quarters of all his friends for him and howling like Cassandra. Georgie stayed behind. I hear to-day however that Top and Ned got no further than Dover, Ned being now so dreadfully ill that they will probably have to return to London.

The 'Greek damsel' had insisted on a suicide pact in Holland Walk, Kensington; then she tried to drown herself in the Paddington canal outside Browning's house – 'bobbies collaring Ned who was rolling on the stones with her to prevent it, and God knows what else', comments Rossetti.[23]

Unfortunately, Howell, the evil genius of the Pre-Raphaelites, introduced her to Georgie at the Grange, and when Ned came into the room and saw her he fainted and fell against the mantelpiece, giving his forehead a permanent scar. The affair continued for some years; Luke Ionides was also infatuated with her. Writing to Mrs Coronio on 7 December 1897, Mackail, referring to a letter she had lent him when he was writing his life of Morris, says:

> I am very much obliged indeed for the letter. I will bring it back to you, and should like to do so at a time when I should find you at home. . . . I see the letter is dated Nov. 1872: I had thought M. Z. was all over by that time, but my chronology is very con-fused about that very confused & complicated business. How extraordinarily interesting one could make the story, if one were going to die the day before it was published.[24]

At this time Morris and Georgie must have drawn particularly close together in understanding and sympathy.

In March, Henry James wrote his magnificent description of Jane Morris to his sister:

> Oh, *ma chère*, such a wife! *Je n'en reviens pas* – she haunts me still. A figure cut out of a missal – out of one of Rossetti's or Hunt's pictures – to say this gives but a faint idea of her, because when such a shape puts on flesh and blood, it is an apparition of fearful and wonderful intensity. It's hard to say whether she's a grand synthesis of all the Pre-Raphaelite pictures ever made – or they a 'keen analysis' of her – whether she's an original or a copy. In either case she is a wonder. Imagine a tall lean woman in a long dress of some dead purple stuff, guiltless of hoops (or of anything else, I should say), with a mass of crisp black hair heaped into great wavy projections on each side of her temples, a thin pale face, a pair of strange, sad, deep, dark, Swinburnian eyes, with great thick black oblique brows, joined in the middle and tucking themselves away under her hair, a mouth like the 'Oriana' in our illustrated Tennyson, a long neck, without any collar, and in lieu thereof some dozen strings of outlandish beads. On the wall was a large and nearly full-length portrait of her by Rossetti. . . .

After dinner, James goes on, Morris read from the second series of his 'un-Earthly Paradise' and Jane, having toothache, lay on the sofa, with a handkerchief over her face. There was something very quaint and remote from actual life, it seemed to me, in the whole scene: Morris reading in his flowing antique numbers a legend of prodigies and terrors (the story of Bellerophon, it was), around us all the picturesque bric-à-brac of the apartment (every article of furniture literally a 'specimen' of something or other) and in the corner this dark silent medieval woman with her medieval toothache. Morris himself is extremely pleasant and quite different from his wife. He impressed me most agreeably. He is short, burly, corpulent, very careless and unfinished in his dress. . . . He has a very loud voice and a nervous restless manner and a perfectly unaffected and business-like address. His talk indeed is wonderfully to the point and remarkable for clear good sense. . . . He's an extraordinary example, in short, of a delicate sensitive genius and taste, saved by a perfectly healthy body and temper.

'Morris's poetry, you see,' James adds acutely, 'is only his sub-trade. To begin with, he is a manufacturer of stained glass windows, tiles, ecclesiastical and medieval tapestry, altar-cloths, and in fine everything quaint, archaic, Pre-Raphaelite. . . .'[25]

By July 1869, Jane was in such a poor state that Morris had to take her to the spa at Bad-Ems in Hesse-Nassau for a cure. He resented the loss of time this entailed, though he took his notebook with him and continued writing *The Earthly Paradise*. On 31 July he wrote to Webb from the Hotel Fortuna:

Dearest Friend,
This is really my address though it looks like chaff, and I am not likely to move now during the time of our captivity: I am so jolly glad to have got over the journey on no worse terms, once or twice I felt quite inclined to give in, but here we are. . . . I paddled her about the river in a machine like a butter-boat with a knife and fork for oars; this they call a gondola here: it is all very well for a mile or two while the river artificially deepened and widened is without stream . . . but presently the unlocked river was like a mill-race; I tried it the first day, and made about twenty yards in half an hour and then began to get back way; so I gave it up with hands blistered: however there is a nice green bank in shadow after 5 p.m., just this side of the rapids, and I suppose I shall paddle Janey there pretty often; till she gets better it is like to be her

principal enjoyment as this carriage business shakes her up too much; if ('when' I hope) she gets better there are splendid mokes and mules here, whereon she may climb the hills: bating the company, which is not to my taste, though I've no doubt better than I am, the place is well enough, and ½ mile out of Ems is quite unsophisticate, except for the woods which look sus
piciously like preserves: it is in fact a very lovely valley, though I think not the kind of place I should like to live in, one is so boxed in. . . . At the top of the gorge-side you come upon bold uplands of the Rhine country, all covered with grain and oilseed crops; but it is a strong pull up to the top and till J. is better I am not like to be able to get fairly up; I had a try yesterday morning and was a sight for a tallow-boiler. . . . This morning I managed to scramble through Acontius and Cydippe; I have now got to knock it into shape; I am not sanguine about it.

The tone of Rossetti's letter to Jane of 30 July, sent Post Restante, Cologne, is very different from Morris's bored, exasperated and rather self-pitying letter to Webb. It is, indeed, the letter of a devoted lover, rather than that of a man in 'rude and offensive health' tied un
willingly to an invalid, though that invalid happened to be his wife.

All that concerns you is the all-absorbing question with me, as dear Top will not mind my telling you at this anxious time. The more he loves you, the more he knows that you are too lovely and noble not to be loved: and, dear Janey, there are too few things that seem worth expressing as life goes on, for one friend to deny another the poor expression of what is most at his heart. . . . I can never tell you how much I am with you at all times. Absence from your sight is what I have long been used to: and no absence can ever make me so far from you again as your presence did for years. For this long inconceivable change, you know now what my thanks must be. But I have no right to talk to you in a way that may make you sad on my account, when in reality the balance of joy and sorrow is now so much more in my favour than it has been or could have been hoped to become, for years past.[26]

This can only mean that Jane had now responded, to some extent, to Rossetti's passion for her, though evidently the strain had proved too great and her health had given way. Morris, as we have seen, was not unaware of this, so that the impatient tone of his letters from Ems is understandable.

1

William Morris aged twenty-three.
A photograph taken at Oxford (1).

A sensitive pencil study of Morris
drawn in 1856 by Dante Gabriel
Rossetti, destined to be one of his
closest friends. This drawing was a
study for the head of David in
Rossetti's Llandaff Cathedral
triptych (2).

2

For nine months in 1856 Morris worked as a draughtsman in the Oxford office of G. E. Street, the eminent Gothic Revival architect and designer of the Law Courts in London. St James the Less in Westminster (4) shows a more delicate side of his work with wrought-iron railings which strangely anticipate Art Nouveau.

4

3

Nineteenth-century Oxford was still outwardly a medieval city, 'A vision of grey roofed houses and a long winding street and the sound of many bells'. *Above:* The tower of Merton College chapel seen from Mob Quad (3).

'Unapproachable in its dignity, as beautiful as a cathedral, yet with no ostentation of the builder's art.' Morris's description of the massive tithe barn at Great Coxwell, Berkshire (5).

The critic and writer John Ruskin (6) was probably the most influential figure in nineteenth-century English art. He became, for Morris and his friends, both a hero and a prophet. Ruskin's perceptive analysis of medieval art and his preoccupation with its sociological background inspired much of Morris's later thinking.

7

6

With seven friends, including Rossetti and Burne-Jones, Morris decorated the walls of the newly built Oxford Union with scenes from the *Morte d'Arthur*. Morris soon finished his wall and went on to decorate the ceiling with bold floral patterns (repainted in 1875 after the original had faded) (7). Woodward, the architect of the Union, also designed the University Museum (8) on strictly Ruskinian principles.

8

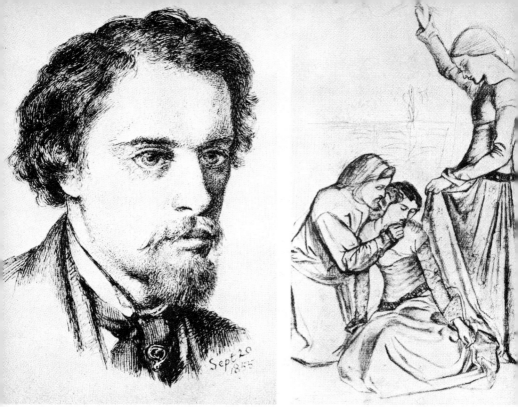

9, 10

Dante Gabriel Rossetti (9). A self-portrait made in 1855. His wife, Elizabeth Siddal, died in 1862 and Rossetti never re-married although he became an intimate friend of Morris's wife Jane. His last years were clouded by drugs and quarrels. Morris dedicated his first book of poems, *The Defence of Guenevere* (1858), to Rossetti and commissioned several water-colours from him on Arthurian themes, including 'Arthur's Tomb' (11) and 'The Blue Closet' (12). Morris himself had begun to paint, and his pencil study of 'Iseult on the ship' (10) reflects Rossetti's Pre-Raphaelite manner.

11

12

Jane Burden – who became Jane Morris in 1859. Her romantic beauty was an inspiration to Rossetti and to Morris himself. Rossetti painted her in 'The Blue Dress' in 1868 (13) and posed her for a photograph taken in 1865 (14). 'Janey Morris and the Wombat', by Rossetti (17), humorously symbolizes his fascination for animals – and for Jane herself. Jane's features often appear in Morris's own work, as in the drawing (16) made a year before their marriage. Another photograph shows her towards the end of her life at Kelmscott Manor (15).

13, 14

15

16

17

Red House, Bexleyheath, where Morris spent five happy years from 1860 to 1865, was designed for him by Philip Webb (20), a fellow pupil of Street, and the two men worked in close collaboration. The informal lay-out, picturesque roof line and barn-like appearance give the house a strongly medieval character (21).

20

The inside of Red House struck visitors as 'severely simple and grand'. The treatment of the stair-case hall (18) and the drawing-room (22) seen here in their present condition, is typical of the whole house. Note the monumental settle in the drawing-room with its 'minstrels' gallery', designed by Morris for his rooms in Red Lion Square.

Left: 'Si je puis' ('if I can', adapted from Van Eyck's 'Als ich Kanne'), taken by Morris for his own motto and painted on tiles in the garden porch (19).

18

19

21, 22

23, 24, 25

Morris, Marshall, Faulkner & Co., 'Fine art workmen in Painting, Carving, Furni-
ture and the Metals', was founded in 1861. Three of the partners are seen above,
Morris himself in a smock (in which he often greeted prospective customers), Edward
Burne-Jones and C.J.Faulkner. After five years at Red Lion Square the firm moved
to 26 Queen Square, Bloomsbury (26), with the Morris family living above the shop.
At this time Morris began to design wallpapers. 'Daisy' (27) was one of the earliest.
Its rather naïve charm contrasts with the later, more elaborate style of 'Wreath',
designed in 1876 (29). Early commissions included the 'St George' cabinet (28),
designed by Webb with painted panels by Morris, for the International Exhibition
of 1862, and (30) stained glass panels for Harden Grange, Bingley, Yorkshire.

26   27

28

How Sir Tristram slew a giant who would have slain King Mark and how King Mark not knowing him brought him to Tintagel, and how he got his wit again and how Isoude knew him again by cause of the brachet which Tristram had given her which leaped upon him and licked him

29   30

31

By 1877 the firm was well established and had
new showrooms at 499 Oxford Street. Samples of
fabrics, furniture and pottery can be seen in the
window (31). The decoration of the Tapestry
Rooms and Armoury (33) at St James's Palace
had been among their most important early commissions. The general scheme was by Webb.

32, 33

From the first Morris & Co. specialized in church decoration. The figure of St Catherine at All Saints, Dedworth (32) is by Morris himself. Stencilled patterns on the walls of All Saints, Jesus Lane, Cambridge, by Morris and Bodley (34), and Morris's cartoon for a window in St Michael and All Angels, Brighton, illustrate a bold handling of traditional motifs (36). In Rossetti's window at Christ Church, Albany Street, London (35) Christina Rossetti, his sister, appears as the Virgin, Jane Morris as Mary Magdalene and Morris as Christ in *The Sermon on the Mount*.

The Story of Cupid and Psyche, in the dining-room at 1 Palace Green, by Burne-Jones, based on his illustrations to Morris's poem from *The Earthly Paradise*. The scheme, supervised by Morris throughout, was an ambitious one and took several years to complete (37). *Pilgrim in the Garden* (39), an embroidered hanging, has figures by Burne-Jones and a decorative background by Morris. (*on facing page*)

37

38

'Woodpecker', a tapestry designed by Morris and incorporating one of his own verses, which was woven in 1885, shows his mastery of natural forms (39).

Webb's green dining-room, designed for the South Kensington Museum (40), contains windows and painted wall-panels by Burne-Jones, an embroidered screen by Morris and his wife illustrating Chaucer's *Illustrious Women*, and a grand piano with gesso work by Kate Faulkner. The walls, with raised gesso decoration, frieze and ceiling, are by Webb himself. The 'St George' cabinet stands under the window.

40

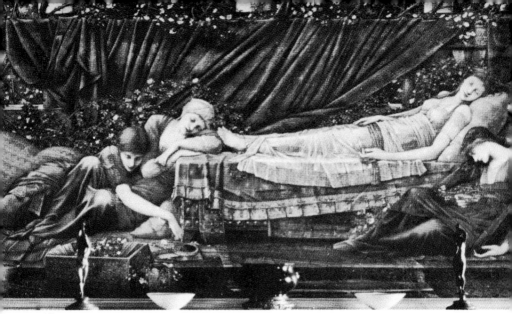

41

The Sleeping Princess from the *Briar Rose* panels painted by Burne-Jones for Buscot Park, Berkshire (41). The 'Clouds' carpet (42) was woven at Hammersmith in 1887 for Clouds House in Wiltshire, built by Webb for the Hon. Percy Wyndham.

42

By this time, however, Rossetti was on the verge of a nervous breakdown himself. His letter of 30 July should be read in the context of such poems as 'Willow-wood' and 'The Stream's Secret', in which we find:

> *For then at last we spoke*
> *What eyes so oft had told to eyes*
> *Through that long-lingering silence whose half-sighs*
> *Alone the buried secret broke,*
> *Which with snatched hands and lips' reverberate stroke*
> *Then from the heart did rise.*
>
> *But she is far away*
> *Now; nor the hours of night grown hoar*
> *Bring yet to me, long gazing from the door,*
> *The wind-stirred robe of roseate grey*
> *And rose-crown of the hour that leads the day*
> *When we shall meet once more.*
>
> *Oh sweet her bending grace*
> *Then when I kneel beside her feet;*
> *And sweet her eyes' o'erhanging heaven; and sweet*
> *The gathering folds of her embrace;*
> *And her fall'n hair at last shed round my face*
> *When breaths and tears shall meet.*
>
> *Beneath her sheltering hair,*
> *In the warm silence near her breast,*
> *Our kisses and our sobs shall sink to rest;*
> *As in some still trance made aware*
> *That day and night have wrought to fulness there*
> *And Love has built our nest.*

The tortured 'Willow-wood' sonnets also celebrate the admission of a long-suppressed, mutual passion. The poet is looking down into a well, Love sits beside him and as their eyes meet in the water 'his eyes beneath grew hers' –

> *Then the dark ripples spread to waving hair,*
> *And as I stooped, her own lips rising there*
> *Bubbled with brimming kisses at my mouth.*

– an unfortunate image, to say the least. But as Love sits singing beside him, the poet sees among the trees 'a dumb throng' –

That stood aloof, one form by every tree,
All mournful forms, for each was I or she,
The shades of those our days that had no tongue.

They looked on us, and knew us and were known;
   While fast together, alive from the abyss,
   Clung the soul-wrung implacable close kiss;
And pity of self through all made broken moan
Which said, 'For once, for once, for once alone!'
   And still Love sang, and what he sang was this:—

III

'O ye, all ye that walk in Willowwood,
   That walk with hollow faces burning white;
What fathom-depth of soul-struck widowhood,
   What long, what longer hours, one lifelong night,
Ere ye again, who so in vain have wooed
   Your last hope lost, who so in vain invite
Your lips to that their unforgotten food,
   Ere ye, ere ye again shall see the light!
Alas! the bitter banks in Willowwood,
   With tear-spurge wan, with blood-wort burning red;
Alas! if ever such a pillow could
   Steep deep the soul in sleep till she were dead.—
Better all life forget her than this thing,
That Willowwood should hold her wandering!'

IV

So when the song died did the kiss unclose;
   And her face fell back drowned, and was as grey
   As its grey eyes; and if it ever may
Meet mine again I know not if Love knows.

Only I know that I leaned low and drank
A long draught from the water where she sank,
   Her breath and all her tears and all her soul:
And as I leaned, I know I felt Love's face
Pressed on my neck with moan of pity and grace,
   Till both our heads were in his aureole.

Rossetti was staying at Miss Boyd's Victorian-baronial Ayrshire castle, Penkill, at this time, and several of the sonnets he wrote there,

'Nuptial Sleep', 'Supreme Surrender' and 'At Last' appear to cele/
brate the consummation of his love for Jane.

All these poems, as Professor Doughty has remarked, have very
much the same atmosphere of secrecy and suspense. Though there
was nothing secret about Jane's visits to Rossetti at Cheyne Walk,
any overt admission of their love could only have brought disaster
and social ostracism. At the same time, Rossetti was tormented by
guilt/feelings about Lizzie, and when a chaffinch settled on his
hand during a walk at Penkill, he was convinced that it was her
soul revisiting him. He was confirmed in this belief when, on his
return to the castle, he was told that the great bell had begun to toll
during his absence for apparently no cause. His only comfort was
the frequency of Janey's letters from Ems. But, as he worked on his
new poems, he thought of the notebook he had buried in Lizzie's
grave at Highgate in 1862, as an act of contrition, containing drafts of
all his earlier poems, and soon plans were under way to retrieve it.
The *Poems* of 1870, therefore, when they appeared, contained many
inspired by Jane as well as earlier ones to Lizzie.

In spite of everything, however, Rossetti did not lose his sense of
humour and in one of his letters to Jane he enclosed a cartoon
endorsed 'The Ms at Ems'. This drawing, now in the British
Museum, shows Jane in her bath, looking very like *La Pia*, keeping
pace with glasses of spa water, numbered 1 to 7, while Morris, in
the background, reads from *The Earthly Paradise*, Volume II. On a
shelf behind stand seven manuscript books of *The Earthly Paradise*.
'The accompanying cartoon', he wrote, 'will prepare you for the
worst – whichever that may be, the 7 tumblers or the 7 volumes.'

Meanwhile Morris was reading *Wilhelm Meister* in Carlyle's
translation. 'I think Goethe must have been asleep when he wrote
it,' he writes to Webb on 9 August, 'but 'tis a great work some/
how . . . Janey excuses herself for not writing to you, saying that it
makes her back ache to sit up to it.' On the 15th he wrote again:

Dearest Friend,
. . . A month yesterday we left London, and 3 weeks to/morrow
we came here: I have some hopes that we shall be at home again
in 3 weeks from to/day, but don't like to think too much about it
though I catch myself now and then looking up the time/tables
and considering which train we shall go to Cologne by. I go out
for a walk every morning now, and if the weather looks well

stretch my legs a bit, but always take a pocket book with me and do a little work. This morning I walked to Nassau and back, 12 miles in all. . . . I also brought Paris's Death to an end roughly; again I'm not very sanguine about the merit of it; but I shall get through the work I set myself to do here in some way, and have a month to turn over the first of the tales before I go to press when I come home.

Written under such circumstances it is hardly surprising if so much of *The Earthly Paradise* makes such depressing reading.

Morris found the warm, moist woods round Nassau 'lonely and dismal' and full of enormous ants and slugs 'like bad veal' and adders as long as his umbrella. To his letter to Webb of the 15th Jane managed to add a note:

My finger-tips are sound – as you see by this – and fit for much more hard labour – I feel that I have not much else about me that is good for anything – but I have a sort of presentiment (though of course you don't believe in such things) that I may make a rapid turn – and feel myself well all of a sudden – and then I have another presentiment that should this change come all those I now call my friends would also change – and would not be able to stand me.[27]

From this, one might be justified in concluding that her trouble was, after all, basically a neurotic one. But presentiments and dreams played as great a part in Janey's life as they had done in Lizzie Siddal's, and this was a great bond of sympathy between her and Rossetti.

Letters continued to arrive from Penkill. Rossetti tells Jane that on one of his walks he has found a little cave above a stream – 'the very place for Topsy to spin endless poetry in, and for you to sit in and listen to the curious urgent whisper of the stream'. Was it here that he wrote 'The Stream's Secret'? This letter of 30 August concludes: 'Give my love to the dear old thing [Morris] & bear in mind how much you are loved by your affectionate D. Gabriel R.' He adds that he feels very feverish and unwell, but has now begun a new poem, 'The Orchard Pit', which may be the best thing he has done.[28]

As for Jane 'not being strong enough to get out', Morris tells Webb, 'there is nothing to interest her in a foreign country & she misses a great many little occupations that wear away the day at home'. The doctor now advised taking her to Switzerland, to try the effect of a more invigorating climate. But they have both had enough, he says, and are coming home.

F. S. Ellis had sent out to Ems a copy of the *Temple Bar* containing an article on Morris's and Arnold's poetry. Austin wrote of Morris as 'the singer of, perhaps, the most unvarying sweetness and sus' tained tenderness of soul that ever caressed the chords of the lyre. . . . Even the critic, accustomed to grasp frail things firmly, almost shrinks from handling these exquisite poems with any but the lightest touch.' He goes on to write of 'the honeyed rhythms of this melodious storier . . . this dulcet client of Apollo'. Morris's poems remind Austin of pressed flowers and he concludes by taking him at his own valuation as 'the idle singer of an empty day'.

Morris replied to Ellis on 18 August:

> Many thanks for your letter again, and the Temple Bar, which did not excoriate my thin hide in spite of the tender contempt with which Mr Austin seemed to regard me. Commercially I suppose I ought to be grateful to him and am so; from the critical point of view I think there is so much truth as this in his article, as that we poets of to'day have been a good deal made by those of the Byron and Shelley time – however, in another sixty years or so, when it won't matter three skips of a louse to us (as it don't matter much more now), I suppose we shall quietly fall into our places.

Eleven days later he wrote to Webb to tell him that he has got the fidgets: 'However, to'day much against the grain I wrote 120 lines but have still got the fidgets.' Morris and his wife returned to London early in September, and later the same month Volume III of *The Earthly Paradise* was ready for publication. On its appearance, Swinburne wrote to Rossetti on 10 December 1869:

> I have just received Topsy's book; the Gudrun story is excellently told, I can see, and of keen interest; but I find generally no change in the *trailing* style of work; his Muse is like Homer's Trojan women – she drags her robes as she walks; I really think a Muse (when she is neither resting nor flying) ought to tighten her girdle, tuck up her skirts, and step out. It is better than Tennyson's short'winded and artificial concision – but there is such a thing

as a swift and spontaneous style. Top's is spontaneous and slow; and, especially my ear hungers for more force and variety of sound in the verse. It looks as if he purposely avoided all strenuous emotion or strength of music in thought and word; and so when set by other work as good his seems hardly done in earnest. The verses on the months are exquisite – November I think especially.

Rossetti replied on the 12th: 'The fact is Topsy writes too much both for his own sake and for that of his appreciators.' Swinburne also wrote to Morris about *The Earthly Paradise*, because on 21 December Morris replied:

Many thanks for your kind letter and the criticisms therein. I am delighted to have pleased you with the Gudrun. For the rest I am rather painfully conscious myself that the book would have done me more credit if there had been nothing in it but the Gudrun, though I don't think the others quite the worst things I have done. Yet they are all too long and flabby, damn it! . . . I am hard at work now, but I am making blunder on blunder, and if I could find anything else that really amused me except writing verses I would give up that art for the present, for I am doing no good.

After writing about *The Egils Saga*, he goes on:

I am about an Icelandic translation now, which quite throws all the other stories into the shade. . . . This is the Volsunga, the story of the Nibelungen in fact. . . . I should very much like to show you the translation, which is nearly finished now, you couldn't fail to be moved by it I'm sure.

On the same day he wrote to Charles Eliot Norton:

I have begun a translation of the 'Nibelungen' which I find very amusing; I have also another translation in hand, the Volsunga Saga viz. which is the Ice: version of the Nibelungen, older I suppose, and, to my mind, without measure nobler and grander . . . the scene of the last interview between Sigurd and the despair, ing and terrible Brynhild touches me more than anything I have ever met with in literature; there is nothing wanting in it, nothing forgotten, nothing repeated, nothing overstrained; all tenderness is shown without the use of a tender word, all misery and despair without a word of raving, complete beauty without an ornament, and all this in two pages of moderate print. . . . I am not getting on well with my work, for in fact I believe the Volsunga has rather swallowed me up for some time past, I mean thinking about it, for it hasn't taken me long to do. I had it in my head to write an epic of it, but though I still hanker after it, I see clearly it would be foolish, for no verse could render the best parts of it, and it would only be a flatter and tamer version of a thing already existing. . . .

Six years later, however, Morris changed his mind and, after his two visits to Iceland itself in 1871 and 1873, he could not resist attempting his epic in *Sigurd the Volsung*. His translation of the saga is, however, quite remarkable for its fidelity to the original and its restraint.

Morris began to study Icelandic, his daughter tells us, in the autumn of 1868, when Warington Taylor introduced him to Eirikr Mag-nusson, who, curiously enough, looked like his double. Magnusson has described their meeting in a letter to May Morris: 'I made my appearance at the appointed hour at 26 Queen Square. I met your father in the hall. With a manly shake of the hand he said: "I'm glad to see you, come upstairs!" And with a bound he was upstairs and I after him until his study and the second floor was reached. . . He proposed to read Icelandic with me three times a week. He asked me what Saga he should begin with me, and I recommended the story of "Gunnlaug the Wormtongue".' The lessons arranged for at this meeting were established by October, though 'lessons' is perhaps not quite the word for them, for, says Magnusson: 'Morris decided from the beginning to leave alone the irksome task of taking regular grammatical exercises. "You be my grammar as we go along" was the rule laid down by himself from the beginning.' In fact, Morris began translating at once. 'We went together over every day's task as carefully as the eager-mindedness of the pupil to acquire the story would allow. I afterwards wrote out at home a literal translation of it and handed it to him at our next lesson. With this before him Morris wrote down at his leisure his own version in his own style, which ultimately did service as printer's copy when the Saga was published. His style is a subject on which', concludes Magnusson, 'there exists considerable diversity of opinion.'[29]

Morris's style was, in fact, a deliberate attempt to get away as far as possible from the literary dialect of the day – 'English newspaper language', as he called it. Its difficulty consists in its very closeness to the original and the use of an obsolete Anglo-Saxon, Germanic vocabulary. In the saga translations there is certainly none of the gentle expansiveness and thin romantic sentiment of *Jason* and *The Earthly Paradise*, where the terrible figure of Gudrun becomes a pretty Burne-Jones damsel.

> *Gold were the locks wherewith the wind did play,*
> *Finer than silk . . .*
> *Bluer than grey her eyes were; somewhat thin*
> *Her marvelous red lips; round was her chin,*
> *Cloven and clear-wrought; like an ivory tower*
> *Rose up her neck from love's white-veiléd bower . . .*

Again:

> *Beneath the new-risen sun she lay at rest,*
> *The bed-gear fallen away from her white breast,*
> *One arm deep buried in her hair, one spread*
> *Abroad, across the 'broideries of the bed,*
> *A smile upon her lips, and yet a tear,*
> *Scarce dry, but stayed anigh her dainty ear—*
> *How fair, how soft; how kind she seemed that morn . . .*

Whatever may be thought of this, and it has a certain thin charm, it is certainly very far in spirit from *The Laxdaela Saga*. A note of self-pity is even introduced – the very thing that, as Morris says himself elsewhere, is most foreign to the sagas. When Kiartan hears that Bodli has married Gudrun he cries:

> *O blind! O blind! O blind!*
> *Where is the world I used to deem so kind,*
> *So loving to me? O Gudrun, Gudrun . . .*
> > *yea, and even now,*
> *How shall I learn to hate thee, friend, though thou*
> *Art changed into a shadow and a lie?*
> *O ill day of my birth, ill earth and sky,*
> *Why was I then bemocked with days of bliss*
> *If still the ending of them must be this?*
> *O wretch that once was happy, days agone,*
> *Before thou wert so wretched and alone . . .*

In the Saga we are told curtly: 'He now heard of the marriage of Gudrun, but did not trouble himself at all over it' – unlike Morris when he came to know of Jane's betrayal of him. And when Bodli kills Kiartan, he behaves like a knight in a chivalrous romance:

Alas! what have I done to thee? . . .
Where was thy noble sword I looked to take
Here in my breast, and die for Gudrun's sake,
And for thy sake – O friend, am I forgot?

Morris finished the translation of 'Gunnlaug the Wormtongue' in a fortnight and immediately published it in *The Fortnightly Review* for January 1869. By then his translation of *The Grettis Saga* was in the press. *The Laxdaela Saga* had been translated in the early part of 1869 and 'The Lovers of Gudrun' was finished by June. As usual, he worked at breakneck speed.

We can see how Morris arrived at the prose style of his renderings (a style which became that of the late prose romances) from his revision of Magnusson's literal translation of *The Saga of St Olaf*, the second part of the *Heimskringla*, published as Volume IV of the Saga Library. Magnusson's manuscript is in the Brotherton Library of Leeds University and was first made use of by J. N. Swannell in his lecture to the Morris Society, in December 1958, on 'William Morris and Old Norse Literature', from which the following quotations are taken. Morris's emendations of what his daughter called Magnusson's 'unconsidered journalese' are printed in italics between brackets.

and for the vikings an onset there was awkward (*it was unhandy to lay them aboard*); that many places be flooded (*that wide about be floods*); he lost many (*he lost a many*); it happened (*it betid*); King Ethelred was sorely bewildered (*King Ethelred was mickle mind-sick*).

Morris is here writing in close imitation of Norse vocabulary and syntax. 'This is the great Story of the North', he wrote in the preface to *The Volsunga Saga*, 'which should be to all our race what the Tale of Troy was to the Greeks.' Indeed, his personal life being so painful at this time, Morris seems to have drawn from the sagas the courage to go on living.

The failure of his marriage Morris regarded as his own personal failure, though one would hardly associate failure in any form with the Jovian head of the Watts' portrait of this year. On Good Friday, 15 April 1870, he wrote to his wife, who was staying with Rossetti at Scalands, near Robertsbridge, Sussex,

Dearest Janey,
Many thanks for note: I was glad to hear from you: I thought
the wine would be useful. . . . I am going to sit to Watts this
afternoon, though I have got a devil of a cold-in-the-head, which
don't make it very suitable. It will be so precious dull here till
after Monday: how I do hate Easter, second only to Christmas:
however I'm going down to Leyton [to visit his mother] on
Monday: I make no doubt I shall come down to you on Wednesday afternoon but will write again meantime. My cold makes
me stupid to-day so I will shut up.

The letter is headed 'at least Bessy seems to have gone to church' –
that is Jane's sister, Elizabeth Burden, who lived with them and got
on Morris's nerves unbearably. But from the chatty, unemotional
tone of his letters to Jane, one would never suspect that anything was
wrong with their relationship at all. Morris went down to Scalands
and the three of them visited churches and collected wild flowers.
'Janey Morris is here,' Rossetti wrote his mother on the 18th, 'and
benefitting greatly. Top comes from time to time.'
    And yet he had written to Jane on 31 January this year, after
one of her visits to Cheyne Walk:

The sight of you going down the dark steps to the cab all alone
has plagued me ever since – you looked so lonely. I hope you got
home safe and well. Now everything will be dark for me till I
can see you again. . . . For the last two years I have felt distinctly
the clearing away of the chilling numbness that surrounded me
in the utter want of you; but since then other obstacles have kept
steadily on the increase, and it comes too late.[30]

On 4 February the same year, he had written out of his loneliness
and yearning:

Funny Sweet Janey,
. . . I feel so badly the want of speaking to you. No one else seems
alive at all to me now, and places that are empty of you are empty
of all life. And it is so seldom that the dead hours breathe a little
and yield your dear voice to me again. I seem to hear it while I
write, and to see your eyes speaking as clearly as your voice; and
so I would write to you for ever if it were not too bad to keep
reminding you of my troubles who have so many of your own. . . .
I always reproach myself with the comfort I feel despite all in the

thought of you, when that thought never fails to present me also with the recollection of your pain and suffering. But more than all for me, dear Janey, is the fact that you exist, that I can yet look forward to seeing you again, and know for certain that at that moment I shall forget all my own troubles nor even be able to remember yours. You are the noblest and dearest thing that the world has had to show me: and if no loss than the loss of you could have brought me so much bitterness, I would still rather have had this to endure than have missed the fullness of wonder and worship which nothing else could have made known to me. . . .[31]

On 18 February he wrote again:

To be with you and wait on you and read to you is absolutely the only happiness I can find or conceive in this world, dearest Janey; and when this cannot be, I can hardly now exert myself to move hand or foot for anything. If I ever wish still to do any work, it is that I may not sink into utter unworthiness of you and deserve nothing but your contempt. . . .

As to the *Academy* question, I do not see that I can suggest anything. I suppose all Top has to do is to signify that he wants my book as soon as it appears.[32]

Meanwhile his *Poems* were about to appear and Morris was to review them for *The Academy*. It was surely the crowning irony of this ambiguous situation that Morris should have to welcome a book which, he must have realized when he came to read it, contained passionate love poems to his own wife. However, in the true tradition of courtly love, he was doubtless prepared for that too, and wrote breezily from Queen Square on 15 March next year to his wife at Hastings:

Dearest Janey,
I am glad to hear from Bessy that you are better. I hope (rather against hope) that you are not deadly dull. I have been hard at work, but have not done much except the translations as they are rather pressing now, and I want to get my Volsung work done this week: then I shall set about Gabriel's review, which I must say rather terrifies me. . . . I send you a *Spectator* with a review [of Volumes I and II, of *The Earthly Paradise*], not bad as things go. It's awfully cold here but sunny – to my comfort, as I suppose it

must be tolerably pleasant in the sun on the parade down there. I shall write to the littles [his daughters, Jenny and May] in a day or two and try to find something pretty to send them: why haven't the little rascals written to me? I hope you find the lodgings pretty comfortable. Please write and tell me how you are and if you want books or anything.

Your loving
W.M.

What could be more typical of a letter from a happily married family man? But then Morris's letters always have something of the bracing quality of a sea-breeze. On 25 April Jane is still away and he writes:

I am so rejoiced that you keep well. I scarcely dared hope you would get so much better. On Sunday I did a good day's work at the Venusberg [that is, 'The Hill of Venus'] and sat up till 3½ last night writing it all out. I think I may finish this last part this week, but then I have to rewrite a good deal of the earlier part. I had a pleasant evening on Friday with Brown and Hueffer: Ellis came in later and quite distinguished himself in the way of talk. I have just parted from Gabriel (and oysters) at Rules: he is pleased with his binding and so am I, the book seems selling well 250 copies. . . . I have sent in my review: I read it to Brown on Friday and he thought it good: the editor has asked me to write on the Academy pictures this year, but I refused, as there wouldn't be ½ a dozen pictures I could speak of without using more forcible words than people expect to see in print. I don't suppose the Volsungs will be out till the end of the week. . . .

At the end of April, Rossetti had made a brief visit to London to autograph copies of his *Poems*, returning to Scalands and Janey the same day.

Morris adds that he is going to see Mrs Aglaia Coronio, one of the daughters of Constantine Ionides, the wealthy Greek merchant and art patron. It was Aleco Ionides' house in Holland Park that the firm decorated.

I am going to receive Aglaia's bland flatteries on my way to Ned's this afternoon – I do rather wish she wouldn't butter me so, if that isn't ungrateful, so you needn't chaff me as one who can't see the fun of it. I shall certainly come down for a day or two next week and fetch you up when you are ready to be fetched – do you want any more wine?

Writing to Ellis on 7 May, Rossetti says: 'Dear old Top is here – not very well', which is, perhaps, not altogether surprising!

Rossetti's *Poems*, when they appeared this month, were greeted by a general chorus of praise, since he had already arranged to have them reviewed by his friends in all the leading journals of the day. Swinburne, in *The Fortnightly Review* wrote of *The House of Life*: 'There has been no work of the same pitch since Dante sealed up his youth in the sacred leaves of the *Vita Nuova*' – though even Rossetti thought that that was going a bit too far. Morris in *The Academy* of 14 May compared these sonnets to Shakespeare's 'for depth of thought, and skill and felicity of execution', though he found many of them 'not free from obscurity, the besetting vice of sonnets'.

His long and careful review bears witness to his continuing admiration for Rossetti as poet and artist.

Ten years ago, with the publication of his beautiful and scholarly volume of translations from the early Italian poets, Mr Rossetti announced the preparation of a volume of original poems. This book, so eagerly looked for by those who knew the author by his great works in painting, has now been given to the public; nor is it easy to exaggerate the value and importance of that gift, for the book is complete and satisfactory from end to end. . . . An original and subtle beauty of execution expresses the deep mysticism of thought, which in some form and degree is not wanting certainly to any poets of the modern school, but which in Mr Rossetti's work is both great in degree and passionate in kind.

Some of the other poems, such as 'Love's Nocturne' and 'The Stream's Secret', he finds obscure and laboured, though the latter, he says, 'is wonderfully finished, and has very high musical qualities, and a certain stateliness of movement about it which makes it very telling and impressive.' Of 'Jenny' he said: 'It is so strong, unforced, and full of nature, that I think it the poem of the whole book that would be missed if it were taken away.' He concluded with a panegyric of the lyrics: 'Nor do I know what lyrics of any time are to be called great if we are to deny that title to these.' He could hardly have said more. Indeed, most readers of today will think that, in his anxiety to do justice to his friend's work, he said too much. Knowing all we know now, one can only admire the generosity and objective tone of a review which Morris confessed was most distasteful to him to write. 'I have done my review, just this moment – ugh!', he had written to Mrs Coronio in April.

It is difficult now, perhaps, to realize the extent to which Rossetti dominated his friends. W. J. Stillman, the American artist and journalist, and lately American consul in Crete, who was sharing Scalands with him and upon whom Rossetti's lavish hospitality fell somewhat heavily, wrote:

> His was a sublime and childlike egotism which simply ignored obligations, until, by chance, they were made legal, at which, when it happened, he protested like a spoilt child. And he had been so spoilt by his friends and exercised such a fascination on all around him, that no one rebelled at being treated in this princely way, for it was only with his friends that he used it. He dominated all who had the least sympathy with him or his genius.[33]

Stillman's remarkable summing up of Morris is in sharp contrast to this:

> On the whole, I consider Morris to have been the largest allround man of the group, not merely on account of the diversity of his faculties . . . but because he had, in addition to these, a largeness and nobility of nature, a magnanimity and generosity which rarely enter into the character of the artist; and perhaps the reason why his gifts were not more highly developed was that his estimation of them was so modest. . . . He remained, owing to the late discovery of himself and his poor opinion of his abilities, only a large sketch of what his completed self would have been.[34]

Stillman later married a Greek beauty, Marie Spartali, another of Rossetti's models, who became Jane Morris's closest friend. Graham Robertson, the painter, amusingly describes her in his book *Time Was* as

> so to speak, Mrs Morris for Beginners. The two marvels had many points in common: the same lofty stature, the same long sweep of limb, the 'neck like a tower', the nightdark tresses and the eyes of mystery, yet Mrs Stillman's loveliness conformed to the standard of ancient Greece and could at once be appreciated, while study of her trained the eye to understand the more esoteric beauty of Mrs Morris and 'trace in Venus' eyes the gaze of Proserpine'.

Jane Morris seems to have been away 'resting' or recuperating for most of 1870. Possibly she found the factory-workshop atmosphere of Queen Square intolerable. Morris, writing to her at Torquay on 3 October, says: 'It was a great relief to know that you are better . . . I shall be so glad of you, dear, when you come home.' But not long after reaching home, in November, she had an attack of sciatica and lumbago and left London again. Morris was 'still hard at work' over the proofs of *The Earthly Paradise*, Volume IV, as he tells her in a letter of 26 November: 'but 'twill soon be all done. . . . I feel rather lost at having done my book: I find I liked working at it better than I thought. I must try and get something serious to do as soon as may be.' Tristan and Iseult presented itself to him as a possible subject for a narrative poem, but he never began work on it.

Instead he turned to illumination and produced, with Burne-Jones, George Wardle and Fairfax Murray the exquisite *Book of Verse*, as a token of his love for Georgiana Burne-Jones. The freshness, delicacy and charm of the book foreshadows the 'Jasmine' wallpaper of some two years later. At the same time he bound the first draft of 'The Lovers of Gudrun' in leather with a spray of pomegranate at the four corners on each side, and inscribed it 'Georgie from W.M. April 15th 1870. This is the first copy of the poem with some alterations inserted: I wrote it in June 1869. William Morris.' This is now in the Fitzwilliam Museum, Cambridge. He thought also of taking up painting again and, for a time, drew from the model in Fairfax Murray's studio. The year 1870 seems to have been one of particular emotional stress and indecision for Morris and this feeling of tension is evident in the drawing of him by Fairfax Murray done at the time. It was during this year, too, that Rossetti painted Jane as Tennyson's Mariana. On the frame he inscribed: 'Take, O take those lips away.'

After finishing the *Book of Verse*, Morris wrote out and illuminated his translation of the first book he had read with Magnusson, *The Eyrbyggja Saga. The Story of the Dwellers at Eyr* is a paper folio of 239 pages. 'I wrote it all out myself, and did all the ornament throughout the book myself except the laying on of the gold leaf on pp. 280, and 239, which was done by a man named Wilday, a workman of ours', Morris notes on the 'spare' final page.[35] The treatment is similar to the *Book of Verse* and has a Blake-like delicacy.

Before this was finished in April, Morris had begun work on the illumination of the *Rubaiyat of Omar Khayyam*. This is on vellum with continuous and elaborate ornament and was not finished until October 1872, when he gave it to Georgie. It is on a smaller scale than the *Book of Verse* – a manuscript of twenty-three pages measuring six inches by three and a half and is an example of even greater labour and even more careful workmanship, with its running ornament of fruit and flowers and its minute figures. 'The raspberries on page 14 and the honeysuckles on page 21', Mackail notes, 'may be specially instanced as unsurpassable in their truth to nature and their decorative effect.' But before it was finished he had begun another copy for Burne-Jones on paper. To this Burne-Jones himself contributed six paintings, each in a different colour scheme, and Morris did the floral decoration in pale colours. As a result of his practice of illumination, Morris began to study handwriting as a fine art and it is from this period that his hitherto careless hand becomes so graceful and distinguished.

In a letter of 6 September 1910 to May Morris, Lady Burne-Jones included some lines from the original envoi to *The Eyrbyggja Saga*, which give a clearer picture of Morris's state of mind at the time of writing than the impersonal lines finally printed:

> *And though this seems so far from me*
> *Though sunk in dreams I still must be*
> *Self-made about myself – yet now*
> *Who knows what out of all may grow;*
> *Who knows but I myself at last*
> *May face the truth, with all fear cast*
> *Clean forth of me; real Love and I*
> *Set side by side before I die.*[36]

CHAPTER SIX

1871–1875
Kelmscott and Iceland

'I HAVE BEEN LOOKING about for a house for the wife and kids, and whither do you guess my eye is turned now? Kelmscott, a little village about two miles above Radcott Bridge – a heaven on earth; an old stone Elizabethan house like Water Eaton, and such a garden! close down by the river, a boathouse and all things handy', Morris wrote to Faulkner on 17 May 1871. 'I am going down there again on Saturday with Rossetti and my wife: Rossetti because he thinks of sharing it with us if the thing seems likely.'

Morris had seen an advertisement for Kelmscott Manor in a house-agent's list, and at once took the train to Faringdon and drove over to see it. Originally quite a small farm-house, it had been enlarged in the seventeenth century by the addition of another block at right angles to it. Philip Webb also went to look at the house and reported it sound and Faulkner joined them from Oxford. Thereupon Rossetti and Morris decided to take it jointly, sharing the rent of £60 a year.

This rather curious arrangement has been thought by some to point to a definite *ménage à trois* – except that when Rossetti was living there with Jane during the first years of their tenancy, Morris seems to have kept out of the way as much as possible. The primary consideration was Rossetti's health. He was now in a highly nervous and disturbed condition and 'it was hoped', Mackail writes, 'that quiet life in a remote country house might do much to restore him'.

Rossetti moved into Kelmscott in the middle of July, taking over the best rooms of the house, and turning the Tapestry Room on the first floor into his studio. Since Morris would, in any case, have to spend most of his time in London, this would appear to be only reasonable. He acquired a gig and three dogs – Morris disliked animals about the place – imported furniture from Cheyne Walk, and was for a time happier than he had ever been in his life.

As for Morris, he said that he had dreamed of Kelmscott before he saw it in actuality, for it is a part of that 'sad lowland country' he had always loved, with its river-meadows, lines of silvery willows and long blue distances. The house stands at the end of the village, among a group of grey stone barns; one enters the front garden through a door in the high wall; a magnificent group of elms flanks it on the river side, and a little field path leads through a grove of willows to the river itself. Nothing seems changed since Morris lived there. When he came to write his Utopian romance, *News from Nowhere*, he could think of no better setting for its final chapters.

In the company of Rossetti, her husband mainly absent, Jane revived as always, 'taking five or six mile walks without the least difficulty', as Rossetti observed. Jenny and May, he found, were 'the most darling little self-amusing machines that ever existed' (evidently they had to be) and he was soon hard at work, making a replica of the *Beata Beatrix* – 'a beastly job,' he said, 'but lucre is lucre'. He did endless drawings of Jane, including one of her asleep over a copy of *The Defence of Guenevere*, and he painted her against a Kelmscott background in *The Water Lily*. He was writing poetry again, too, and by August had thirty new sonnets ready for *The House of Life*, many of which mirror his daily life with Jane.

But it was the loneliness and weariness of Rossetti at this time which struck May Morris as a child, as she saw him returning from his solitary walks across the meadows or sitting alone over his studio fire, in one of her mother's absences from Kelmscott. 'Indeed, we youngsters', she says, 'were more conscious of this element of solitariness in our family life than our elders knew.' At one time, she adds, Rossetti had even wanted to adopt her.[1]

In reality, Rossetti was as much out of place at Kelmscott as Morris was in his element there. He was never, to say the least, a countryman, whereas Morris was indifferent to the fact that the house was cold, damp and draughty, with all the rooms on the upper floor opening out of each other in the most inconvenient manner. After all, people in the Middle Ages did not bother about comfort or privacy and he himself had the capacity of working on, wrapped away in a world of his own, completely oblivious of others.

But as winter approached, Rossetti began to complain of the draughts which, he said, set the tapestries in his studio waving about 'like a house attacked by vertigo'. The subject of the tapestries, too, one of which represents the blinding of Sampson, he found barbarous and repellent and finally covered them up altogether with additional hangings. To Morris, they gave the room an air of romance. 'Another charm this room has,' Morris wrote in 1895 in 'Gossip About an Old House on the Upper Thames', 'that through its south window you not only catch a glimpse of the Thames clover meadows and the pretty little elm-crowned hill over in Berk-shire, but if you sit in the proper place, you can see not only the barn aforesaid with its beautiful sharp gable, the grey stone sheds, and the dove-cot, but also the flank of the earlier house and its little gables and grey scaled roofs. . . .' After Rossetti's departure, when he at last had the house to himself, he would sit in the Tapestry Room writing or designing, and look up and see the yellow harvest moon rising over the barn.

Early in July, Morris set off for Iceland. The journey was both a catharsis and an initiation into a new world. Besides Morris, the party consisted of Faulkner, Magnusson and W. H. Evans, an army officer who joined the others for the fishing and shooting. With the exception of Evans, who had gone on to Leith by sea, they started from London on 6 July to pick up the fortnightly Danish mail boat from Granton. 'That morning', Morris records in the diary that became the first Iceland journal, 'my heart failed me, and I felt as if I should have been glad of any accident that had kept me at home; yet now it would have seemed unbearable to sleep in London another night.'[2] What a relief it is to find Morris writing straight-forward modern English after the fancy-dress prose of the Saga translations! In these journals reality breaks through into his writing for the first time.

His first sight of this strange, new country, so full of waiting menace, is recorded in the journal entry for 13 July, written on board the *Diana*:

a terrible shore indeed: a great mass of dark grey mountains worked into pyramids and shelves, looking as if they had been built and half-ruined: they were striped with snow high up, and wreaths of cloud dragged across them here and there, and above them were two peaks and a jagged ridge of pure white snow. . . . The sea was perfectly calm, and was clear of mist right up to the shore, and then dense clouds hid the low shore, but rose no higher than the mountains' feet; and as I looked the sun overtopped the east hills and the great pyramid grew red halfway down, and the lower clouds began to clear away; the east side of the firth which was clearer of them showed the regular Icelandic hillside: a great slip of black shale and sand, striped with the green of the pastures, that gradually sloped into a wide grass-grown flat between hill and sea, on which we could see the home-meads of several steads: we rounded a low ragged headland presently and were in the firth and off a narrow bight, at the end of which was the trading station of Djúpivogre (Deepbay): half a dozen wooden roofs, a flagstaff and two schooners lying at anchor.

Later, Morris embodied some of this description in one of his best poems, 'Iceland First Seen', published in *Poems By the Way*. From Reykjavik he wrote to Jane on 16 July about leaving the Faroes: 'I have seen nothing out of a dream so strange as our coming out of the last narrow sound into the Atlantic, and leaving the huge wall of rocks astern in the shadowless midnight twilight: nothing I have ever seen has impressed me so much. . . .' At three o'clock on a wild morning he saw Iceland from the deck of the *Diana* – 'very black out to sea, and very bright sun under a sort of black canopy over Iceland'. It is a high-spirited, newsy letter and concludes:

Please dear Janey be happy & don't forget the date of letter to me. The boat starts back for England Sept 1st so I hope to be home about the 8th (in London I mean) if you are still at Kelmscott I will come at once to see you. Be happy. I am with all love.
Your most affectionate
William Morris.

Next day they set off on ponies with their guides to Bergthorsknoll and Lithend. 'Most strange and awful the country looked to me as we passed through, in spite of all my anticipations,' Morris records, 'a doleful land at first with its great rubbish heaps of sand, striped scantily with grass sometimes; varied though by a bank of sweet grass here and there full of flowers, and little willowy grey-leaved plants I can't name.' At Holmr they dismounted and the Icelanders brought out champagne and glasses to drink the stirrup-cup.

So in half an hour's time we said good-bye for six weeks, and they mounted and turned back west, and we rode away east into a barren plain, where the road had vanished into the scantiest of tracks, and which was on the edge of the lava: soon we came on to the lava itself, grown over here with thick soft moss, grey like hoar-frost: this ended suddenly in a deep gully, on the other side of which all was changed as if by magic, for we were on a plain of short flowery grass as smooth as a lawn.

But this soon changed again to

a waste of loose large-grained black sand without a blade of grass on it, that changed in its turn into a grass plain again but not smooth this time: all ridged and thrown up into hummocks . . . this got worse and worse till at last it grew boggy as it got near another spur of the lava-field, and then we were off it on to the naked lava, which was here like the cooled eddies of a molten stream: it was dreadful riding to me unused. . . .

When they had pitched their tents in the grassy plain, Morris went off and shot two golden plovers for their supper, which, he says, he did not like doing at all. The first night in camp, he was too excited to sleep much, disturbed by queer noises: 'the wild song of the plovers, the horses cropping the grass near one, the flapping of the tent canvas'. In the morning Morris fried bacon and plover for breakfast, as usual taking great pride in his cooking. Afterwards, they rode into the hills and were soon riding across a huge waste of black sand all powdered over with sea-pink and bladder campion at regular intervals, 'like a Persian carpet'.

Coming down from the hills again towards the sea, the Westman Isles lying far to the east, they rode across 'utterly barren shaly slopes populous with ravens: the plain before us shows to the west nothing but an awful dead grey waste of lava. . . . So we rode down the shaly hillsides, I with my heart in my mouth the while, for they were as steep as the side of a house. . . .' Next there was a milky white river full of seals to ford, the horses swimming 'with their noses up, snorting and blowing furiously as the ice-cold water washed right over their heads every instant; we were swept a long way down by the tide, so far as to be quite close to the rocky bar, on which we could see the breakers dashing, while we ourselves seemed almost level with the cold grey sea outside'.

They rode eastwards for several days towards the Njala country. At Oddi, the spit of land between the Western and Eastern Rang-rivers, they found that the great guardians of the body of Icelandic lore, Saemund, Ari and Snorri Sturluson, who once lived there, were still in people's minds as the writers of the sagas and the eddas. They crossed Thvera (Thwart-river): 'a dismal white stream running

through a waste of black sand'. Then, as they approached Bergthors´
knoll, riding over 'the deadest of dead flats', they 'saw the dust . . .
over there amid the dreadful wastes whirled up into red and grey
columns'. But they rode in high spirits, racing their horses across the
turf beside the Lithe. At Bergthorsknoll, the site of Njal's house,
they were welcomed by the bonder, 'a black´haired bushy´bearded
carle of about forty; not very clean, but very contented and smiling',
who seemed to enjoy the horse´play between Morris and Faulkner.
But there was not much to be seen, only three mounds in the middle
of the ploughed´up marshes: 'the longest of the three mounds, which
lay west from the house, rightly or wrongly, gave one strongly the
impression of having been the site of Njal's house . . . from its top
one looked south across grey flats with a thin greyer line of the sea
and the Westman Isles rising out of it.' The next morning the bonder
showed them Flosi's Hollow, where he and the other Burners
tethered their horses and lay in ambush before they set fire to Njal's
house.

Riding back along the pastures towards Lithend, Morris found
them thick with a bright blue gentian and other flowers, principally
white clover. At Lithend they were shown Gunnar's Howe, a big
mound rising up from a hollow on the hillside – 'most dramatically
situated to remind one of the beautiful passage in the Njala where
Gunnar sings in his tomb'. It is not surprising that the landscape of
Iceland should sometimes have suggested to Morris that of Hell, or
Purgatory, and this feeling is strong in the journal entry for 22 July,
one of the longest and best written, which records their journey up
the valley of the Markfleet, which he found both terrible and
inspiring:

> . . . the cliffs were much higher especially on this side, and most
> unimaginably strange: they overhung in some places much more
> than seemed possible; they had caves in them just like the hell´
> mouths in thirteenth´century illuminations; or great straight pillars
> were rent from them with quite flat tops of grass and a sheep or
> two feeding on it, however the devil they got there: two or three
> tail´ends of glacier too dribbled over them hereabout, and we
> turned out of our way to go up to one: it seemed to fill up a kind
> of cleft in the rock wall, which indeed I suppose it had broken
> down; one could see its spiky white waves against the blue sky as
> we came up to it: but ugh! what a horrid sight it was when we

were close, and on it: for we dismounted and scrambled about it: its great blocks cleft into dismal caves, half blocked up with sand and dirt it had ground up, and dribbling wretched white streams into the plain below. . . . The great mountain wall which closes up the valley, with its jagged outlying teeth, was right before us now, looking quite impassable, though the map marks a pass, leading up into one of the main roads north and east . . . and, on the other side of the river, a great spherical ball stuck somehow in a steep slope of black rock: more often the wall would be cleft, and you would see a horrible winding street with stupendous straight rocks for houses on either side. . . .

Morris confesses to feeling tired and a little down-hearted at the savagery of the place. As he climbed up slowly through a birch wood, the others outstripped him. As soon as he was clear of the wood, he sat down on the bare shale of the steep slope that over-looked the valley and turned to the mountain that rose over the bounding wall of rocks:

I could see its whole dismal length now, crowned with over-hanging glaciers from which the water dripped in numberless falls that seemed to go nowhere . . . at right angles to this mountain was the still higher wall that closed the valley, which as aforesaid had never changed or opened out as such places generally do; below was the flat black plain space of the valley, and all about it every kind of distortion and disruption, and the labyrinth of the furious brimstone-laden Markfleet winding amidst it lay between us and anything like smoothness: surely it was what I 'came out for to see', and yet for the moment I felt cowed, and as if I should never get back again: yet with that came a feeling of exultation too, and I seemed to understand how people under all dis-advantages should find their imagination kindle amid such scenes.

After discussing the Njala Saga with another bonder, 'a grave black-bearded intelligent-looking carle of about fifty', Morris tried mount-ing his horse *more Islandico*, on the wrong side, and measured his length on the turf. The bonder, without a ghost of a smile on his face, said that he hoped he wasn't hurt and remarked to Magnusson: 'The skald is not quite used to riding, then.' This incident, among others, Morris told against himself, when he got back to Kelmscott, much to the delight of Rossetti and Burne-Jones, who could not understand his Icelandic enthusiasm, and for some time afterwards he was invariably spoken of as 'the skald'.

Next day, they bought about half a dozen more horses, making their number up to thirty, and their guide Jón, on leaving them, presented Morris with a book by an eighteenth-century Icelandic poet. Camping by the Geysir, Morris was disgusted by the refuse left by previous tourists, who only came to Iceland to see geysirs and who 'had never heard the names of Sigurd and Brynhild, of Njal, or Gunnar, or Grettir, or Gisli, or Gudrun'. A south wind drove the stinking steam of the geysir into their faces. 'Let's go home to Haukadal,' said Morris, 'we can't camp in this beastly place.' But the guide, to tease him, insisted that all Englishmen camped there. 'Blast all Englishmen', said Morris in Icelandic. But they had to stay there, after all, for four days, because Faulkner suddenly became very unwell and the weather had grown too bad for riding.

That night they pitched their tent in the rain, and Morris says:

My spirits rose considerably with the warmth and dryness of the tent, and the opening of the beef-tin, and brewing of chocolate; but we had scarcely taken three mouthfuls before there came a noise like muffled thunder, and a feeling as though someone had struck the hollow earth underneath us some half dozen times; we run out, and hear the boiling water running over the sides of the great Kettle, and see the steam rising up from the hot stream, but that was all . . . I confess I went back to my dinner with my heart beating rather. . . .

On the bright, cold morning of 29 July, they started again, with their guide Sigurd, riding northward through the wilderness towards Waterdale and the firths of the North Sea. They had six cold days of rain and bitter wind among 'the horrible black moun-tains of the waste'. Morris notes at the beginning of the climb in the direction of Thorisdale, the site of *The Grettis Saga*: 'On our right is a mass of jagged bare mountains, all beset with clouds, that, drifting away now and then show dreadful inaccessible ravines and closed-up valleys with no trace of grass about them among the toothed peaks and rent walls: I think it was the most horrible sight of mountains I had the whole journey long.'

They explored the cave of Surtshellir, having squeezed unwilling permission from Faulkner to have a candle-end apiece, though the drip from the roof often put the candle out. Morris notes:

In spite of ice and all, I dripped too – with sweat, and got quite done up, especially as the others in their enthusiasm kept well ahead of me, they all being tolerably good climbers: at last after about three quarters of an hour I asked our guide how far we were, and he said encouragingly, 'More than half way', and a little after we came to another broken bubble, and there I must confess I gave in, and Faulkner kept me company; so we hauled ourselves out on to the moss-covered lava, and sitting down fell to a most agreeable pipe, I for one quite dead beat. . . .

When the others came back, Morris felt quite ashamed of not having gone on with them.

But there were quite enough ordeals ahead, as they pressed on through hail and sleet, to find pasturage for the horses, over Erne-waterheath, a dismal highland of bogs and pools where Grettir had lived as an outlaw; then, in 'a cold grey drift of rain', down to Ernewater, where Grettir slew Thorir Red-beard – 'a most mournful desolate looking place, with no signs of life as we rode up but for a swan that rose up trumpeting from the lakeside' – until they came on 6 August to Herdholt and Laxdale, the site of *The Laxdaela Saga*. Here Morris confided his feelings to his journal:

Evans and Faulkner went off to pitch the tent, while I spent my time alone in trying to regain my spirits, which had suddenly fallen very low almost ever since we came into Laxdale. Just think, though, what a mournful place this is – Iceland, I mean – setting aside the pleasure of one's animal life, and feeling of adventure; how every place and name marks the death of its short-lived eagerness and glory. . . . But Lord! what littleness and helplessness has taken the place of the old passion and violence that had place here once – and all is unforgotten . . . yet it is an awful place: set aside the hope that the unseen sea gives you here, and the strange threatening change of the spiky mountains beyond the firth, and the rest seems emptiness and nothing else: a piece of turf under your feet, and the sky overhead, that's all: whatever solace your life is to have here must come out of yourself or these old stories, not over-hopeful themselves.

Perhaps, as John Purkis conjectures, Morris felt at that moment, that he had romanticized the 'old stories' too much after all.[3]

They spent two days at Herdholt. It was to be the farthest point of their journey. Thereafter their faces were set for home as they skirted the northern coast. 'Every little tarn we passed', Evans told Mackail later, 'was occupied by a pair of wild swans, where they scatter to breed; but the first fiord we reached on the north coast was filled with hundreds, and they looked such splendid marks shining in the sun that I said how I wished I had a rifle, which brought down on me the most severe reproof from Morris: he called me a British officer – which was his most severe term of contempt.'⁴

At Stykkisholme, on Broadfirth, there was a Danish brigantine on her way from Icefirth to Liverpool. The captain offered to take letters, and Morris wrote to Jane on 11 August giving her a short account of their travels. He concluded:

> Give dear love to the little ones and tell them I am going to try to bring them my pretty grey pony home; but if I don't they must not be disappointed for there may be many difficulties or he may not turn out well: his name is Falcon, and when he is in good condition he ambles beautifully; fast and deliciously soft; he is about 13 hands high. I wish you could see us to understand how jolly it is when we have got a good piece of road, and the whole train of 28 horses is going a good round trot, the tin cups tinkling and the boxes rattling. . . . I must 'premise' however that I am dirtier than you might like·to see me: my breeches are a triumph of blackness, but not my boots, by Jove! I may mention in passing that an Icelandic bog is not good riding, and that the loose stones on the edge of a lava-field is like my idea of a half-ruined Paris barricade. . . .
>
> Good-bye, my dear, I have often thought of the sweet fresh garden at Kelmscott and you and the little ones in it, and wished you happy – Please write to mother with my best love. . . .

A week later they reached Grettir's-lair on the Fairwood-fells – 'such a dreadful savage place', Morris notes, 'that it gave quite a new turn in my mind to the whole story, and transfigured Grettir into an awful and monstrous being, like one of the early giants of the world'.

In camp at Stafholt on 21 August, Morris was maddened by Faulkner's snoring. He bore it for a time, he says, 'till it rose to a roaring snuffling climax, and I thought I should go mad, and shouted out "damn". This woke C.J.F. who said, as if he had never been to sleep in his life, and in a most disagreeable tone of voice, just as if he were seeking a quarrel, "What's the matter now?"'

'You were snoring like the devil', said Morris. They argued with increasing acrimony for a time, then Faulkner said: 'It was you who were snoring, and dreamed it was I.' In the morning, when they remembered the incident, they both 'fell a-roaring with laughter, so small a joke moving our little minds in those waste places'.

Next day they crossed White-water, riding along White-water-side – 'A monotonous and dreary valley it seemed to me that day. . . . The wind blows strong and cold from the ice to-day too, and no winding of the valley seems to stop it.' Thingvellir, which they reached on 24 August, marked the end of their pilgrimage. Here the Hill of Laws, the great open-air parliament, was most exciting to Morris and they spent two days exploring it. There remained now only the day's ride back to Reykjavik, which they did in the pouring rain. Morris records his excitement on arrival:

I, heeding not other people, galloped my best to Mistress Maria's house, jumping off my horse (Mouse to wit) just six weeks to the minute since I had mounted him before, by the paling of the queer little weedy-looking garden before the black, white-windowed cottage that I have seen in night-dreams and day-dreams so often since. Well, Miss Sæmundson, who met me presently, told me that there were no letters for me there, so I galloped for the post-office. Why doesn't one drop down, or faint, or do something of that sort when it comes to the uttermost in such matters? I walked in quite coolly in appearance and gave Mr Finsen my name scribbled big on a piece of paper; he shuffled the letters and gave me eleven: I opened one from Ellis there and then, thinking that from him I should hear any bad news in the simplest form: though indeed the eleven letters at first glance did somewhat cure my terror, for there was no one dead at least.

Morris read his letters, 'with not more than the usual amount of disappointment, wondering at people's calmness'. They spent three days in Reykjavik in the pouring rain, seeing the museum and dining with the Governor, and then sailed for home on the *Diana*.

On 2 October Rossetti wrote to Bell Scott from Kelmscott:

Morris has been here twice since his return, for a few days at first and just now for a week again. He is now back in London, and this place will be empty of inmates by the end of this week, I guess. Morris has set to work with a will on a sort of masque called 'Love is Enough', which he means to print as a moderate quarto, with woodcuts by Ned Jones and borders by himself, some of which he has already done really beautifully. The poem is, I think, at a higher point of execution perhaps than anything that he has done, having a passionate lyric quality such as one found in his earliest work and of course much more mature balance in carrying out. It will be a very fine work.[5]

Alas, the passionate lyric quality such as one found in his earliest work is not to be found in *Love is Enough*, unless heartache and despair be accounted such. Nor is there the least evidence of the bracing airs of Iceland. Indeed, this is one of Morris's most enervated works. One would think the title ironic, except that Morris was not given to irony. The best thing about it is the design he did for the cover, which, in its delicacy and fineness, recalls the 'Jasmine' wall-paper. It is an interlude in the late medieval manner, written for the most part in a four-stressed unrhymed line reminiscent of Middle English. The theme is the search for a dream mistress. King Pharamond has seen a vision of a beautiful girl singing in a garden and decides to devote the rest of his life to looking for her.

> *Through the world will I wander*
> *Till either I find her, or find the world empty.*

He finds her, only to lose her again at once. He has become, in effect, another idle singer of an empty day, returning to his kingdom at last to find his throne usurped and his people disaffected – much as Morris had returned from Iceland to find Rossetti in his place.

Love is Enough is as rarefied as the illuminated manuscripts of this period. Morris put an enormous amount of work into his interlude and it is, as Rossetti said, 'at a higher point of execution perhaps than anything that he had done' in poetry till then, but the whole thing seems curiously pointless. Morris gives to each character (or, rather, sets of characters) a different verse measure and intersperses the 'action' with choruses, reflecting on the nature of love itself. In his use of receding planes of action, 'he approximates dramatic poetry to the manner of treatment of those late medieval tapestries, the finest of which were his ideal of decorative arrangement', comments Mackail.[6] Unfortunately, *Love is Enough* has none of the vigour and liveliness of medieval tapestry. It is even more pale and wan than

The Earthly Paradise. As in the case of that poem, the projected illustrated edition was never realized, though one of the borders Morris designed for it was used to decorate the spine of the 1901 edition of Mackail's *Life of William Morris*. It is a closely wrought design of leaves and flowers that look like heartsease.

Theodore Watts-Dunton gives an amusing description of a visit to Kelmscott at this time. Morris was coming down for a few days' fishing and Mouse, the Icelandic pony, was to be sent to Lechlade railway station to meet him. 'You must mind your p's and q's with him; he is a wonderfully stand-off chap', Rossetti warned Watts, 'and generally manages to take against people.' The account continues: 'And then I saw coming towards us on a rough pony so diminutive that he well deserved the name of "Mouse", the figure of a man in a wideawake – a figure so broad and square that the breeze at his back, soft and balmy as it was, seemed to be using him as a sail, and blowing both him and the pony towards us.' When Rossetti introduced them, Morris, ignoring Watts, said: 'H'm! I thought you were alone.' But Rossetti, adds Watts, 'was irresistible to everybody, and especially to Morris, who saw that he was expected to be agreeable to me, and most agreeable he was, though for at least an hour I could still see the shy look in the corner of his eyes'. But not one word passed Morris's lips which had not some relation to fish and baits, for Rossetti had warned Watts beforehand against mentioning his poetry.[7]

One of the nicest things about Rossetti was his irreverent sense of fun, and he could not help seeing the funny side of Morris's Icelandic travels. It was at this time that he wrote the memorable lines:

Enter Skald moored in punt,
Jacks and Tenches exeunt.

He was disappointed that Morris did not have more funny stories to tell of his northern exploits, though he roared with laughter when he heard about an Icelandic hostess who had made Faulkner and Magnusson remove their breeches as a ceremonial preparation for dinner. Most of Morris's friends seem to have found it difficult to sympathize with his enthusiasm for Iceland, its hail and sleet and its gloomy savage literature. To Morris, however, it represented a challenge, in the meeting of which he lost his self-pity, writing in a poem he contributed to *The Academy* for March 1871:

> *Ah! shall Winter mend your case?*
> *Set your teeth the wind to face.*
> *Beat the snow, tread down the frost!*
> *All is gained when all is lost.*

But Kelmscott was to become more and more a part of his life as the years passed, his one refuge from London. Next February we find him writing:

> I have come down here for a fortnight to see spring beginning, a sight I have seen little of for years, and am writing among the grey gables and rook-haunted trees, with a sense of the place being almost too beautiful to live in. I have been in trouble with my own work, which I couldn't make to march for a long time; but I think I have now brought it out of the maze of re-writing and despondency, though it is not exactly finished. . . .

This was evidently *Love is Enough*, which was finally not published until the end of 1872. He was also working at a novel of contemporary life, which significantly remained unfinished.[8] It dealt with the love of two brothers for the same woman. In June he sent the manuscript to Georgie's sister, Louisa, the wife of Alfred Baldwin, the ironmaster, who had become a confirmed invalid after giving birth to Stanley Baldwin, the future Prime Minister.

> Herewith I send by book-post my abortive novel: it is just a specimen of how not to do it, and there is no more to be said thereof: 'tis nothing but landscape and sentiment: which thing won't do. Since you wish to read it, I am sorry 'tis such a rough copy, which roughness sufficiently indicates my impatience at having to deal with prose. . . . So here's an end of my novel-writing, I fancy, unless the world turns topsides under some day. Health and merry days to you. . . .

Morris had already sent part of it to Georgie, 'to see if she could give me any hope', he wrote. 'She gave me none, and I have never looked at it since.'

In the middle of May, the minor poet and critic Robert Buchanan had republished in pamphlet form his notorious article, 'The Fleshly School of Poetry', originally contributed the previous October to *The Contemporary Review* under a pseudonym, in which he had viciously attacked not only Rossetti's poetry but his character. The attack was a particularly dangerous one and calculated to arouse that obsessional fear of sex so characteristic of the Victorians. In the previous December, Rossetti had sent a dignified reply, 'The Stealthy School of Criticism', to the *Athenaeum*. Seizing upon the sonnet 'Nuptial Sleep', Buchanan declared Rossetti to be a sensualist – a sin that was making London 'a great Sodom and Gomorrah waiting for doom'. It was plain, however, that Buchanan's hypo⁄critical fulminations were nourished by a private relish of every form of pornography. Of 'Parted Love' he remarked, for instance, 'the lady has retired to get breath and arrange her clothes'. Again of *The House of Life*: 'We get nothing very spicy till we come to Sonnet XXXIX', concluding that the House of Life itself was 'probably the identical one where the writer found Jenny' – that is, a brothel.

The effect of this insulting nastiness on Rossetti was disastrous, particularly as there had been other attacks on his poetry earlier in the year in the *Quarterly Review* and *The Saturday Review*, also on moral grounds. The attack was continued in a leading article in *The Saturday Review* on 1 June.[9] By now he was on the verge of collapse. Insomnia, and the large nightly doses of chloral washed down with whisky that he took to counteract it, fear that these attacks upon his character would interfere with his relations with Janey, guilt⁄feelings about Lizzie and the desecration of her grave, all contributed to the deterioration of his mental condition. He was convinced that there was an organized conspiracy against him and on the night of 2 June he attempted to commit suicide by taking an overdose of chloral, just as Lizzie had done ten years earlier. He lay in a trance for two days at Dr Hake's house and the possibility of sending him to an asylum was discussed. When he had recovered sufficiently, he went to Fitzroy Square to stay with Madox Brown.

As soon as news of this reached Kelmscott, Jane wrote a dis⁄tracted letter to Brown and hurried up to London.[10] From Brown's Rossetti was taken to Scotland on 20 June by Hake, to a house put at his disposal by William Graham, and there his condition gradually improved, though he still suffered from delusions of persecution. Watching seine fishing on the coast, he remarked: 'It is an allegory of my state. My persecutors are gradually narrowing the net round me until at last it will be drawn tight.' Even a civil 'good⁄night' by a passing countryman, Hake wrote to William Rossetti in July, appeared to him as an insult. If a dog barked at him, it was his enemies again setting the brute on. He now talked of returning to Kelmscott.

On 13 July Treffry Dunn, who had gone up to Scotland to help him begin drawing and painting again, wrote to Madox Brown: 'Of course both you, I and all else will think this move to Kelmscott the worst that could be made, but I don't see what can be done to prevent it. . . .'[11] Nevertheless, the first letter Rossetti wrote after his breakdown was to Jane in August. Hake wrote an anxious covering letter: 'As a medical man and viewing you and Mr Morris as among Rossetti's dearest friends, an anxiety arises in my mind to learn whether his letter exhibits any sign of delusion. . . .' Jane replied to William Michael on 15 August to say that his brother's letter to her 'showed no sign whatever of his late distressing illness', and that she believed he would now get perfectly well, provided he remained long enough in Scotland and away from his work.[12]

By the end of September 1872 Rossetti was back at Kelmscott. 'But all, I now find by experience,' he wrote to his brother, 'depends primarily on my not being deprived of the prospect of the society of the one necessary person.' He was soon at work making studies of Jane as Proserpine – 'which I have begun and rebegun, time after time,' he wrote, 'being resolved to make it the best I could do. I think I have struck out into clear waters at last'. But Jane he found 'very delicate and appallingly unable to walk out compared with her condition last year'.

After a visit to Kelmscott this month, Webb wrote to Jane: 'The last visit on arriving did give my soul a twist which I hope my face did not express, as it was quite unavoidable (in the unfortunate circumstance).' What was 'the unfortunate circumstance'? Jane's state of health? Or that she appeared more married to Rossetti than to Morris? Five days later he writes again to thank her for her 'simple and straightforward letter', adding:

I had no idea that you would think it worth while to tell me a lie. I have always taken a great interest in you, and none the less that time has tossed us all about and made us play other parts than we set out upon – I see you play yours well and truly under the changes, and I feel deeply sympathetic on that account – for my own troubles are not so absorbing that I cannot attend to the troubles of those who are wrapt about with the pains of life that are not ignoble. Please believe that I in no·way wish to penetrate into sorrows which I can in no way relieve. . . .[13]

From this one can only conclude that Webb had been puzzled and hurt by what he saw at Kelmscott and had written to Jane for confirmation one way or the other and that she had replied simply and without prevarication.

Rossetti usually managed to have Jane to himself at Kelmscott, even though she brought the children with her. But during her absence in London, he filled the house with his friends and relations, the Hueffers, Watts-Dunton, Bell Scott, Marie Stillman, Alexa Wilding, his mother and his sisters, William and his wife May. He wrote limericks, looked extraordinarily well, and was once more in the best of spirits. Although Morris paid frequent visits, too, his feelings are sufficiently clear from a letter to Aglaia Coronio of 8 October, written from Queen Square:

> I have been backwards and forwards to Kelmscott a good deal this summer and autumn; but shall not go there so often now as Gabriel has come there, and talks of staying there permanently: of course he won't do that, but I suppose he will stay some time: he is quite well and seems very happy.
>
> The weather has been lovely here this autumn, but doesn't seem to have suited me very well, I have been queer several times, and am not very brilliant to-day. As to my mental health – I have had ups and downs as you may very easily imagine: but on the whole I suppose I am getting less restless and worried, if at the same time less hopeful, still there is life in me yet I hope. I am sorry you seem to find Athens a disappointment; but I can imagine how revolting the contrast must be between modern smartness and the ancient glory. I suppose too there are little or no remains of any medieval buildings or few even of the earlier Byzantine, that history has to take a jump from the Acropolis to the stock exchange. . . .

Earlier in the same letter he mentions that he has been house-hunting with Burne-Jones at Hammersmith, further rooms being needed at Queen Square for the expansion of the business. Three weeks later, on 24 October, he is writing to Mrs Coronio again to say how much he misses her. He is still working at his *Northern Love Stories*.

> I suppose you see that Tennyson is publishing another little lot of Arthurian legend. We all know pretty well what it will be; and I confess I don't look forward to it. I went down to Kelmscott

on Saturday last till Tuesday, and spent most of the time on the river: it ought to cool you in dusty Athens there to hear of my Sunday on the Thames: a bitter north-east wind and pouring rain almost all day long: however I enjoyed it on the whole, and Monday was fine and warm, so the *days* went well enough: but Lord how dull the evenings were! with William Rossetti also to help us. Janey was looking and feeling much better. It was such a beautiful morning when I came away, with a faint blue sky and thin far away white clouds about it: the robins hopping and singing all about the garden. The fieldfares, which are a winter bird and come from Norway are chattering all about the berry trees now, and the starlings, as they have done for two months past, collect in great flocks about sunset, and make such a noise before they go off to roost. The place looks as beautiful as ever though somewhat melancholy in its flowerless autumn gardens. I shall not be much there now I suppose. We are looking for a house in the west of London still; but a tolerable one after my wishes seems hard to find. I am going to stay a day or two with the Neds next week I fancy. I have had a hardish time of it here all alone with Bessy; with whom I seldom exchange any word that is not necessary. What a wearing business it is to live with a person with whom you have nothing whatever to do!

Jane was still at Kelmscott with Rossetti and the children, leaving Morris to be looked after by her sister, but by the end of November she was back at Queen Square.

In what is the most revealing of all his letters to survive, that of 25 November 1872 to Mrs Coronio, Morris writes:

Janey has just come back from Kelmscott last Saturday, and is very well apparently, and in good spirits certainly. . . . We must, it seems, turn out of this house next spring for Wardle wants it all for the business. I confess I don't look with pleasure at the prospect of moving; one gets a bit used to a house, even when as with me one feels as if living in a furnished lodging. However I shall keep my old study with the little bedroom still.

When I said there was no cause for my feeling low, I meant that my friends had not changed at all towards me in any way and that there had been no quarrelling: and indeed I am afraid it comes from some cowardice or unmanliness in me. One thing wanting ought not to go for so much: nor indeed does it spoil

my enjoyment of life always, as I have often told you: to have
real friends and some sort of an aim in life is so much, that I
ought still to think myself lucky: and often in my better moods
I wonder what it is in me that throws me into such rage and
despair at other times. I suspect, do you know, that some such
moods would have come upon me at times even without this
failure of mine. However that may be, though I must confess that
this autumn has been a specially dismal time with me. I have been
a good deal in the house here – not alone, that would have been
pretty well – but alone with poor Bessy. I must say it is a shame,
she is quite harmless and even good, and one ought not to be
irritated with her – but O my God what I have suffered from
finding [her] always there at meals and the like! . . . I am so glad
to have Janey back again: her company is always pleasant and
she is very kind and good to me – furthermore my intercourse
with G. [Georgiana Burne-Jones] has been a good deal interrupted; not from any coldness of hers, or violence of mine; but
from so many untoward nothings: then you have been away so
that I have had nobody to talk to about things that bothered
me: which I repeat I have felt more than I, in my ingratitude,
expected to.

Another quite selfish business is that Rossetti has set himself
down at Kelmscott as if he never meant to go away; and not
only does that keep me from that harbour of refuge (because it is
really a farce our meeting when we can help it) but also he has
all sorts of ways so unsympathetic with the sweet simple old place,
that I feel his presence there as a kind of slur on it: this is very
unreasonable though when one thinks why one took the place,
and how this year it has really answered that purpose: nor do I
think I should feel this about it if he had not been so unromantic-
ally discontented with it and the whole thing which made me
very angry and disappointed. There, dear Aglaia, see how I am
showing you my pettinesses! *please* don't encourage me in them;
but you have always been so kind to me that they will come out.
O how I long to keep the world from narrowing on me, and to
look at things bigly and kindly!

I am going to try to get to Iceland next year, hard as it will be
to drag myself away from two or three people in England: but I
know there will be a kind of rest in it, let alone the help it will
bring me from physical reasons. I know clearer now perhaps than

then what a blessing and help last year's journey was to me; what horrors it saved me from.

One does not need to speculate overmuch about the nature of these horrors. In any case, Morris had a healthy man's impatience with the sort of nervous complaints that afflicted both Rossetti and Jane. One of his old friend's ways, to which he was so unsympathetic, was Rossetti's habit of not going to bed until three or four in the morning. Next day, when Morris had been astir and busy since five or six o'clock, Rossetti would lie in a drugged sleep, rising at last to a late breakfast and to deliver himself of witticisms about the discomforts of the house. He would then retire to his studio for the rest of the day, emerging at dusk for a walk for his health's sake and to take dinner with the family, after which, says May Morris, 'we all sat in the studio with him'.[14]

As for Rossetti's passion for Jane, Morris was forced to accept that as good-humouredly as he could. About this time he wrote 'Love's Gleaning Tide', which evidently sums up his feelings about the situation. The last two verses run:

> *Ah when the summer comes again*
> *How shall we say, we sowed in vain?*
> *The root was joy, the stem was pain,*
> *The ear a nameless blending.*
>
> *The root is dead and gone, my love,*
> *The stem's a rod our truth to prove;*
> *The ear is stored for nought to move*
> *Till heaven and earth have ending.*

Next year, 1873, was spent by Rossetti entirely at Kelmscott. In fact, he remained there until another breakdown in the summer of 1874, only paying occasional visits to London, to stave off threatened visits from Fanny Cornforth, though his other model, Alexa Wilding, was asked to stay. At Cheyne Walk, Fanny's 'ways' were amusing, but they would never do at Kelmscott. Rossetti had a very Victorian sense of propriety and would never have dreamed of offending the susceptibilities of either his mother or Jane. Indeed there were occasions, as his letters to her show, when Jane professed herself offended by the warmth of feeling of some of his sonnets to her, complaining that he only cared for her looks and Rossetti would hasten to reassure her that it was her soul that he really loved, asking her how she could think so badly of him! No wonder he sometimes found the frankly vulgar Fanny a relief – not that Jane's origins were far removed from Fanny's, though she had since become the lady of the manor.

Towards the end of 1872 Jane and the children moved out of Queen Square into Horrington House, on the highroad between Turnham Green and Hammersmith, near Chiswick Lane, then a rambling suburb of orchards and market gardens, with a few large old houses scattered about – such as Beavor Lodge, where Sir W. B. Richmond, the painter, lived. Jane described Horrington House as 'a very good sort of house for one person to live in, or perhaps two'.

At Queen Square, the long drawing-room on the first floor was turned into a showroom and the upper floors into additional workshops. Morris wrote to Mrs Coronio on 23 January 1873:

We have cleared out of Queen Sq. as far as our domesticity is concerned: I keep my study and little bedroom here, and I daresay as time goes on shall live here a good deal: for the rest we have taken a little house on the Turnham Green road, about 20 minutes from the Hammersmith station; and otherwise easy to get at because of the omnibuses: it is a *very* little house with a pretty garden, and I think will suit Janey and the children; it is some ½ hour's walk from the Grange which makes it quite a little way for me; on the other hand I can always see anyone I want at Queen Sq: quite safe from interruption: so in all ways it seems an advantage – does it not? Withal I never have had any sentiment of affection for this house, though so much has happened to me while I have lived here: I have always felt myself like nothing but a lodger here.

Next day he continued his letter:

I am going to have the little ones home to Turnham Green today: 'tis a month since I have seen them. Jenny is 12 years old now: bless us, how old I am getting.

Except the work for the firm, in which I am rather busy, I am doing nothing now but translations: I should be glad to have some poem on hand, but it's no use trying to force the thing: and though the translating lacks the hope and fear that makes writing original things so absorbing, yet at any rate it is amusing and in places even exciting.

He was now translating the *Heimskringla*. Sometimes he began to fear that, as he grew older, he would fall off in enthusiasm and imagination, and that he might already have outlived his powers as a poet. This fear he expressed in his next letter to Mrs Coronio of 11 February. He also began to fear lest his business might fail. 'I have so many serious troubles, pleasures, hopes and fears,' he wrote, 'that I have not time on my hands to be ruined and get really poor: above all things it would destroy my freedom of work, which is a dear delight to me.' Nevertheless, this letter is considerably more cheerful in tone:

> We are quite settled in our new house, and I find it very pleasant: my own room is particularly cheerful and pretty, and I can work in it with a much better heart than in the dingy room at Queen Square. I go most days to the Square though, and come back when I feel inclined, or not at all when I feel inclined: all this involves a good deal of walking, which, no doubt, is good for me . . . I really have had a hard time of it: but I hope things have taken a long turn now, and that I shall be something worth as a companion when I see you again. . . .

In April Morris went to Italy with Burne-Jones, but he was already preoccupied with his coming visit to Iceland in the summer. There was little in Italy he wanted to see. When his friend Bliss, who was doing research in the Vatican archives, pressed him to go with him to Rome, Morris answered (as Dr Johnson might have done): 'Do you suppose that I should see anything in Rome that I can't see in Whitechapel?' With such an attitude, it is not surprising if his visit to Italy was hardly a success. For Burne-Jones this must have been a great disappointment. Morris enjoyed the landscape, though, as he wrote to Jane from Florence on 9 April:

> One gets a bit tired of the eternal mulberry trees between Turin & Bologna but the passing of the Apennines thence to Florence is a wonderful journey; especially where you come out of a tunnel and see from the edge of the mountains the plain of Florence lying below you, with the beautiful old town of Pistoija within its square walls at the mountains' feet: it was something also to remember coming down into the plain of Piedmont out of the Alps on the most beautiful of all evenings, and going (still be-tween snowcapped mountains) through a country like a garden:

green grass and feathery poplars, and abundance of pink blossomed leafless peach and almond trees. The Duomo here [is] certainly the most beautiful church in the world outside; and inside I suppose would be if it had not been made as bare as the palm of my hand. The cloisters of S. Maria Novella though is what I have seen most to my mind here. We went through a market this morning and that was the greatest game: the lemons and oranges for sale with the leaves still on them: miraculous frying going on, and all sorts of queer vegetables and cheeses to be sold. . . . The monks of S. Maria Novella make scents: I must bring you home a bottle, also I must, if cash holds out, buy a toy for the littles from the jewellers' shops on the Ponte Vecchio . . . I suppose I shall stay here till Friday, so don't write here again but write to the Hotel Lille & Albion, Rue St. Honoré, Paris. Best love to you & the littles; don't tell them I think of bringing them home a toy though. I hope you are much better.

Next day he wrote to Philip Webb from Florence, to tell him that he has been 'merchandizing for the Firm here, rather to Ned's disgust I am afraid; but can't be helped'. He has, he says, bought 'a lot of queer pots they use for hand-warmers (*scaldini*) of lead glazed ware; also I have ordered a lot of flasks wickered of all sorts of pretty shapes. . . . I bought some things for the Firm in Paris also: so I hope my journey won't be quite unfruitful even if I don't find any-thing in Thun.' For the rest, Morris was depressed by the amount of bad restoration evident on all hands. He continued:

I ought to say a great deal about works of art here, but I had rather wait till I see you and we can talk it over. I am not at all dis-appointed with Italy, but a good deal with myself: I am happy enough, but as a pig is, and cannot bring my mind up to the proper pitch and tune for taking in these marvels; I can only hope that I shall remember them hereafter. I daren't whisper this to Ned who is horribly jealous of the least sign of depression in me here, thinking that Florence ought to make a sick man well, or a stupid one bright. I venture to think though that there is another side to it which may at least make one sad; change and ruin and recklessness and folly and forgetfulness of 'great men and our fathers who begat us' – it is only in such places as this that one can see the signs of them to the full. Well you remember my ways at Troyes, don't you? and they are scarce likely to be better in

Florence: Ned already complains of me that I seem to pay more attention to an olive-tree or a pot than I do to a picture – mind you, though, an olive-tree is worthy of a great deal of attention, and I understand more of pots than of pictures; and he is a painter professed; so it isn't quite fair. This is a dull letter to come from Florence; though by the way Florence seems to me, not dull certainly, but melancholy enough. . . . This is a nice little inn that we are quartered in, and 'tis a great comfort not to form part of the furniture of a gigantic Yankee-hutch.

Morris spent only a fortnight in Italy altogether, with a week in Florence, during which time it rained and was as cold as England. Even Sienna failed to move him: he remarked that he would rather the cathedral library had been painted by someone a century earlier than Pinturicchio. Altogether Burne-Jones found him 'rather exacting' and 'a little disposed to make the worst of things'. On his return he revised his first Iceland journal, and gave a transcript of it to Georgie.

At last the time arrived for the second visit to Iceland with Faulkner in July. They were away for a little over two months. This time Morris felt 'quite at home . . . as if there had been no break between the old journey and this'. However, he wrote to Jane when he arrived at Reykjavik on 18 July:

It is all like a kind of dream to me, and my real life seems set aside till it is over.

Kiss my dear little ones for me and tell them I positively have no time to write to them, as you would easily know if you saw me now amid the boxes with C.J.F. and another man in the room. . . .

My dear how I wish I was back, and how wild and strange everything here is. I am so anxious for you too, it was a grievous parting for us the other day – and this shabby letter! but how can I help it, not knowing whether I am on my head or my heels?

Indeed, he need not have been anxious about her, for on the very day he wrote, Jane had rejoined Rossetti at Kelmscott, 'looking wonderfully well'. Rossetti was busy re-arranging the rooms at the manor-house, shared his meals with a baby owl, 'Mossy', and began a poem with the line

My world, my work, my woman, all my own.

On the boat to Reykjavik Morris had met John Henry Middleton, whose knowledge of medieval art was equal to his own and whose knowledge of Greek and Persian art was considerably greater. The friendship formed at this time was a lasting one. Meanwhile, Morris and Faulkner were preparing to set off for the desolate interior of Iceland. The first ten days were spent going over more familiar ground in the southwest, and then, on 1 August, they set out for the central wilderness. There is nothing in the Iceland journal of 1873 as striking as the best descriptions of the journal of 1871. It does not begin until 24 July and breaks off altogether on 19 August, probably because there was neither the initial shock of the first visit nor so much opportunity for writing. This time there is more about farming and the actual life of the country, and less about the romance of the saga sites. But Morris went to Lithend again and wandered about the site of Gunnar's hall by himself on 29 July.

> It was the same melancholy sort of day as yesterday and all looked somewhat drearier than before, two years ago on a bright evening, and it was not till I got back from the howe and wandered by myself about the site of Gunnar's hall and looked out thence over the great grey plain that I could answer to the echoes of the beautiful story. . . .

Other entries, like that for 6 August, show Morris's sharp eye for wild flowers and birds:

> We passed over two little brooks on the sides of which were a few stalks of angelica; and I noticed a tuft or two of cranesbill, and tried my horse at some dandelions that grew in the black sand. Over the first of these brooks, by the way, hung a few terns looking after worms, and a little past the second a stone bunting flew up into the air, and that was the last living thing except ourselves and horses that I saw for many hours, and after that we were in the wilderness indeed.

The rivers provided them with plenty of fish. Morris used to get up early to catch their breakfast and on one occasion caught a trout big enough to last them two days. But cooking, he confesses, made him feel homesick and depressed. The farthest point reached was Dettifoss and from there they made their way across the northern mountains to the little seaport of Akreyri, and then rode back over the wilderness in a more westerly direction, reaching Reykjavik early in September. One day they were fifteen hours in the saddle.

On his return, Morris wrote to Mrs Coronio from Horrington House:

> The journey was very successful, & has deepened the impression I had of Iceland, & increased my love for it, though I don't suppose I shall ever see it again: nevertheless I was very full of longing to be back, and to say the truth was more unhappy on the voyage out and before I got into the saddle than I liked to confess in my letters from Reykjavik, but the glorious simplicity of the terrible and tragic, but beautiful land with its well remembered stories of brave men, killed all querulous feeling in me, and have made all the dear faces of wife & children, and love, & friends dearer than ever to me: I hope I shall not miss your face from among them for long. . . .
>
> You wrote a very kind letter to me at Reykjavik: you won't want to be thanked for it I know, but you will like to hear that it answered its kind purpose and made me happier – What a terrible thing it is to bear that moment before one gets one's letters after those weeks of absence and longing!

One would very much like to know who Morris had in mind when he wrote of 'All the dear faces of wife and children, *and love*, and friends. . . .' Was this Georgie Burne-Jones, after all?

It seems likely that a number of the poems he had illuminated in *A Book of Verse* in 1870, which bears Georgie's initials on the cover, were actually addressed to her. Like the ironically named 'Love Fulfilled', several of them are poignant with heartache and the pain of separation. They are quite obviously the poems of a man in love, and in 'Thunder in the Garden' that love is fulfilled. There is also a reference to Georgie's clear grey eyes 'truer than truth', of which Graham Robertson writes in *Time Was*: 'Eyes like those of Georgiana Burne-Jones I have never seen before or since, and, through all our long friendship, their direct gaze would always cost me little sub-conscious heart-searchings, not from fear of criticism or censure, but lest those eyes in their grave wisdom, their crystal purity, should rest upon anything unworthy.' Since Georgie was the wife of his best friend, such a situation, if it existed – and many things point to it – would have been peculiarly tormenting for Morris, a source of guilt and misery such as finds expression in the poem 'Hope Dieth: Love Liveth'.

This, however, is little more than speculation, because the originals of all Morris's letters to Georgie were destroyed, either by Georgie herself or by Mrs Mackail, after her husband had used extracts from them in his biography. All we can say is that Morris, who peopled his late romances with idealized young girls, and whose *Story of the Glittering Plain* is of a land of eternal youth spent in the delights of free love, gives one the impression, as F.L.Lucas has said, of a man 'with an intense capacity of feeling starved by circum⁄stance'. When Lucas wrote of Morris so perceptively in his *Ten Victorian Poets*, there was, as he says, no biographical evidence to support this impression. Yet few men had more devoted friends. Moreover, it has long been recognized that Morris is virtually the hero of Lady Burne⁄Jones's *Memorials* of her husband – a book which withholds as much of Burne⁄Jones's emotional life as Mackail was compelled to withhold of Morris's.

Soon after his return from Iceland, Jane fell ill again. In fact, she only seems to have been well in her husband's absence. Webb, writing to her from Kelmscott, where he was convalescing, on 28 September, says: 'I shall ask Morris, who is expected to eat some of a duck of Mr Hobb's here this evening, who & what your new doctor is. I hope he will try to help you.'[15] Nevertheless, she had told him in her letter, she was enjoying Goethe's *Conversations with Eckermann*.

Masochism is one product of frustration and there was a good deal of the masochist in Morris. On 22 October 1873 he wrote to 'Louie' Baldwin:

I have had a good deal to do of a trivial kind & to say the truth have been busy enough over such things: but it seems that I must needs try to make myself unhappy with doing what I find difficult – or impossible – so I am going to take to drawing from models again, for my soul's sake chiefly, for little hope can I have ever to do anything serious in the thing. It must be six years now since I made a habit of drawing and I never, if you can under⁄stand that, had the *painter's memory* which makes it easy to put down on paper what you think you see; nor indeed can I see any scene with a frame as it were round it, though in my own way I can realize things vividly enough to myself – also I am getting old, hard on 40 Louie. . . .

At this time Morris was always harping on his age and seems a little undecided what to do next. 'My dear Louie,' he writes from Queen Square on 26 March 1874:

> Many thanks for your kind and friendly letter: it was very nice of you to remember my birthday, which was solemnized by my staying at home all day and looking very hard at illuminations, now my chief joy. Yesterday, however, was May's birthday, mine was on Tuesday, on which sad occasion I was forty. Yet in spite of that round number I don't feel any older than I did in that ancient time of the sunflowers. [That is, when he was painting the Oxford Union.] I very much long to have a spell of the country this spring, but suppose I hardly shall. I have so many things to do in London. Monday was a day here to set one longing to get away: as warm as June: yet the air heavy as often is in England: though town looks rather shocking on such days, and then instead of the sweet scents one gets an extra smell of dirt. Surely if people lived five hundred years instead of three-score and ten they would find some better way of living than in such a sordid loathsome place, but now it seems to be nobody's business to try to better things – isn't mine you see in spite of all my grumbling – but look, suppose people lived in little communities among gardens and green fields, so that you could be in the country in five minutes' walk, and had few wants, almost no furniture for instance, and no servants and studied the (difficult) arts of enjoying life, and finding out what they really wanted: then I think one might hope civilization had really begun. But as it is, the best thing one can wish for this country at least is, meseems, some great and tragical circumstances, so that if they cannot have pleasant life, which is what one means by civilization, they may at least have a history and something to think of – all of which won't happen in our time.

In this letter Morris outlines the whole Garden City idea, to be developed later by Ebenezer Howard, Cadbury's, the Levers and others, and realized at Letchworth, Bournville, Port Sunlight, Welwyn and Hampstead Garden Suburb. We have also had our fill of 'tragical circumstances', but are no nearer the good life than when Morris wrote. Cities have spread, ruining the country, and what is left of it is rapidly being taken over by electricity pylons, the motor car and other forms of traffic. Meanwhile, thanks to advertising, our material wants have increased and the simple life is the very last thing people desire. 'Sad grumbling,' Morris adds, 'but do you know, I have got to go to a wedding next Tuesday: and it enrages me to think that I lack the courage to say, I don't care for either of you, and you neither of you care for me, and I won't waste a day of my precious life in grinning a company grin at you two.'

The wedding that provoked this rather churlish remark was that of William Rossetti and Lucy Brown, the daughter of Morris's old friend Madox Brown. It was, however, a very quiet affair, though by this time, it seems, Morris had had about enough of the Rossettis, one way and another. He evidently felt that, as Gabriel and his family were monopolizing Kelmscott, he might just as well give up his own share of the tenancy. He therefore wrote on 16 April 1874:

My dear Gabriel,
    I send herewith the £17 to you not knowing where else to send it since Kinch is dead. As to the future though I will ask you to look upon me as off my share, and not to look upon me as shabby for that, since you have fairly taken to living at Kelmscott, which I suppose neither of us thought the other would do when we first began the joint possession of the house; for the rest I am both too poor and, by compulsion of poverty, too busy to be able to use it much in any case, and am very glad if you find it useful and pleasant to use.

Yrs. affectly,
William Morris[16]

It is hard to believe that Morris really intended to give up Kelmscott, though he may have hoped in this way to get Rossetti to give up *his* share. He clearly felt that the situation, as it stood at present, had become quite intolerable and that either he or Rossetti would have to leave the house. But nothing was to be finally settled before the autumn quarter, and, as it happened, events played into Morris's hands.

As the summer of 1874 advanced, Rossetti's condition grew steadily worse. Cheerful as he often appeared to be, as long as he had Janey with him, he had never been the same since his breakdown of two years before. In June, William and Lucy Rossetti, visiting Kelmscott, were alarmed to notice the suspicions of the servants and others. Perhaps Jane herself was becoming rather frightened of him and his obsession with her.

At the end of July Morris, in spite of his 'poverty', took Jane and the children for a tour of Belgium. From Bruges, on 24 July, he wrote to Mrs Coronio, who had sent him some jasmine blossoms from her window:

I am very sorry to have disappointed you about your letter, but I find it very difficult to get time to write, being always with the children and really having no time to myself to think at all: even now they are all here as I write while we are waiting to go out. We have only had 2 railway journeys, from Calais to Tournay last Saturday, and from Tournay to Ghent on Sunday: I must say I had no idea what heat was before, it was like being in a Turkish bath: after the 2nd one we by common consent determined to have no more of them than was positively necessary, & so gave up going to Antwerp and Mechlin, and hired a charabanc at Ghent to drive us to Bruges by road on Tuesday: that was really a very pleasant drive, all among the pretty orchards, the ripening wheat & oats, & the rye that they are already cutting, and so at last into Bruges by the ancient Gate of the Holy Cross: it took all day, about 29 miles it is. We shall stay here till over Sunday, & then go to Ypres & then to Calais, & cross next Wednesday or Thursday night: I devoutly hope the first, for I most earnestly wish to be at home again: not that anything has gone wrong: on the contrary all is well & the children are very good: but travelling without time or space for musing is dreary work to me. We are all very much gnatbitten, my right wrist is so stiff thereby that I really find it difficult to write so you must excuse a short letter. Bruges is a very beautiful place certainly, & I think I shall come over here one of these days when I have some literary work to do, and stay here working for a few days by myself. Janey seems pretty well on the whole, and none the worse for the travelling for the present.

. . . I feel my imagination rather dull & torpid in spite of all the change & beauty: I think 'tis the children being about, & the difference of age between us, & not knowing what they are thinking of. I am in the same room now as Janey & I were in when we came [to] Bruges on our weddingtrip: this morning we went to the Hospital of St John (where the Memling pictures are) and I looked in the book for my name and Murray's & found them October 3rd 1870, & all the while I had been thinking it was only two years ago since I had been here. I will write you another line before I come back to say exactly when we shall be in London.

It will be noticed that Morris says that at Bruges *he* was occupying the same room as he and Janey were in when they came to Bruges on their honeymoon. Very likely the sad change in their relationship since that time depressed him, although he seems to have found the children a nuisance and was daily dreading the effects of travelling upon Jane. Morris was one of those who are bored and restless when separated from their work and had little use for holidays, so-called. He may even have arranged the trip to Belgium to get Jane away from Rossetti at this critical time.

Meanwhile, at Kelmscott, things were going from bad to worse. Strolling one day by the river with Dr George Hake, Rossetti over-heard, or thought he overheard, an insulting remark about himself from a party of fishermen and turned back to overwhelm them with abuse. Hake apologized and explained matters as best he could and hurried Rossetti away. But, as a matter of fact, there was a good deal of local gossip about the peculiar ménage at the manor-house, which doubtless lost nothing by Rossetti's outburst. After that it was felt to be advisable for him to leave the neighbourhood for good.

On his return from Belgium, Morris went with Burne-Jones early in August to stay with the Howards at Naworth Castle, Cumber-land. Canon Dixon was their fellow guest. 'I saw Ted and Morris at the abode of splendour,' Dixon wrote to Cormell Price, 'slept there, and we were most jolly. Ned is in poor health I grieve to find, and a little quieter in manner, otherwise unaltered: Topsy genial, gentle, delightful, both full of affection: it was a most happy meeting.' Rosalind Howard, though clearly apprehensive, also found Morris more urbane. 'Morris arrived early this morning', she wrote,

with such a diminutive carpet bag. He was rather shy – and so was I – I felt he was taking an experimental plunge amongst 'barbarians', and I was not sure what would be the resulting opinion in his mind. However, he has grown more urbane – and even three hours has worked off much of our mutual shyness. . . . He talks so clearly and seems to think so clearly that what seems paradox in Webb's mouth, in his seems convincing sense. He lacks sympathy and humanity though – and this is a fearful lack to me – only his character is so fine and massive that one must admire. He is agreeable also – and does not snub one. Not that I think he will like me – but he puts up with me. We shall jog along all right.[17]

From Naworth, Morris wrote to Mrs Coronio to say how much he was enjoying himself. 'Ned and I pass our mornings in a most delightful room in one of the towers that has never been touched since William Howard of Queen Elizabeth's time lived there. . . . We had a long drive yesterday all along the border, & I sniffed the smell of the moors & felt in Iceland again.' On his return to London, he wrote to Rosalind Howard:

I would like you to understand, as well as my clumsy letter-writing will let you, how very happy I was these few days in the north. I hope you will let me come again some time: and that then you will think me less arrogant on the – what shall I say? – Wesleyan-tradesman-unsympathetic-with-art subjects than you seemed to think me the other day: though indeed I don't accuse myself of it either: but I think to shut one's eyes to ugliness and vulgarity is wrong, even when they show themselves in people not un-human. Do you know, when I see a poor devil drunk and brutal I always feel, quite apart from my aesthetic perceptions, a sort of shame, as if I myself had some hand in it. Neither do I grudge the triumph that the modern mind finds in having made the world (or a small corner of it) quieter and less violent, but I think that this blindness to beauty will draw down a kind of revenge one day: who knows? Years ago men's minds were full of art and the dignified shows of life, and they had but little time for justice and peace; and the vengeance on them was not increase of the violence they did not heed, but destruction of the art they heeded. So perhaps the gods are preparing troubles and terrors for the world (or our small corner of it) again, that it may once again become beautiful and dramatic withal: for I do not believe they will have it dull and ugly for ever. Meantime, what is good enough for them must content us: though sometimes I should like to know why the story of the earth gets so unworthy. . . .

He was to make up his mind about this when, a few years later, he became a socialist and read Marx. Then this unworthiness appeared to him to have its roots in economic causes, and social revolution the only thing worth working for. The Howards, of course, were Liberals with aesthetic leanings, George Howard himself being a water-colour painter in the Pre-Raphaelite manner. Later in life, as president of the Women's Liberal Federation and the National British Women's Temperance Association, Rosalind Howard became a very formidable lady indeed, a tartar to her six sons and two daughters.

Morris now set about the reconstruction of the firm under his sole management. In any case, the others, Rossetti, Brown, Marshall, Faulkner, were at best sleeping partners, all the work of organization having for some time past fallen to Wardle and Morris, who, with Burne-Jones and Webb, produced most of the designs as well. Morris now proposed, or rather, announced, that the original firm should be wound up and that the non-producing partners should retire. This proposal was reasonable enough, though rather tact-lessly put forward, and it caused much resentment among those, like Madox Brown, whose work and influence had launched the busi-ness in the first instance. Brown, in particular, did not see why he should be shouldered out of the firm just when it was beginning to prosper, and took legal advice. Rossetti stood by Brown (his brother-in-law). Marshall took the same stand as Brown and to Rossetti's suggestion that there should be a friendly meeting to discuss the situation with Morris, Brown replied: 'As to Morris, I could never meet him again with the least pleasure – but even if I could, at the present juncture it would disturb all our negotiations, which are going on satisfactorily in Watts' hands – for I only wish to be clear of the whole affair, which I now blush at having ever belonged to. I wish to be quit of it as soon as I can – without ridicule – for I am not inclined to go at Morris's dictation.'[18]

This ill-feeling was not shared by Rossetti, who although he felt he ought to support Brown, was all for coming to a friendly arrange-ment and proposed that his own share of the assets should be set aside for the benefit of Jane. In October Morris wrote:

My dear Gabriel,

Thanks for letter. I have no objection to make, but we must settle how the thing can be done, as the money must be vested in trustees.

For the rest, your views of the meeting I think are not likely to be correct in any one point (except that Marshall will certainly be drunk) for I don't think *he* will venture to face the indignant members, I will tell you why tomorrow, which will be worth at least one grin to you, I flatter myself: Webb, Ned and Faulkner have all promised to come: and though Brown refuses, I have asked Watts to attend (which he has promised to do) so as to report what we have to say to Brown. In short, I consider it an important meeting, even if Brown doesn't come. Watts said he would press him to do so. I expect to see Watts to-day, & he *may* bring news of Brown's being a little more reasonable though I confess I don't expect so.

We will talk the matter over to-morrow if you don't object.

Brown's position, as put by his solicitor at the meeting on 4 November was 'that as in the inception of the firm no member invested money, nor gave any time or labour without being paid at an agreed rate, the position of the several members ought to be considered as equal in respect of their claims on the assets of the firm; and further, that he, Mr Brown, considers that the goodwill ought to be taken at three years purchase and ought to be included in the said assets'. Of course, this was most unreasonable because it meant, as Mackail comments, 'that each of the partners, who had confessedly contributed nothing beyond a trifling sum towards the capital, and who had been paid at the time for any assistance they gave towards the conduct of the business, was entitled to an equal share of the value of the business which had been built up by the energy, the labour, and the money of Morris alone'. If such claims had been pressed, they would have amounted to some seven or eight thousand pounds. In the event, three of the partners, Burne-Jones, Faulkner and Webb, waived their claims: the other three stood fast on their legal rights. In the end it was arranged that Brown, Marshall and Rossetti should be compensated for the loss of interest at the rate of one thousand pounds each, and the firm was thereupon reconstituted under Morris's sole management as Morris & Co., with Burne-Jones and Webb continuing to supply designs for stained glass and furniture. Negotiations, however, were troublesome and protracted, and the affair was not finally settled until March 1875.

After this, we are told by Mackail; the estrangement between Morris and Rossetti was final, even though Rossetti had acted most generously towards Jane. But perhaps it was just this that Morris resented. At any rate, later in the year, we hear of her staying with

Rossetti at Aldwick Lodge, Bognor, where he was putting the finishing touches to his *Astarte Syriaca*. In November, Rossetti wrote to his mother somewhat sharply about the selection of books she had sent to Bognor, adding, however, that the amusement Jane had derived from *Evelina* 'is very beneficial in giving her strength for the sittings'. Jane continued to visit Rossetti at Bognor the following year as well.

Morris apparently raised no objections. His chivalrous attitude to the whole thing is summed up by Luke Ionides' story of how he once heard him consoling a friend who had been left by the woman he loved.

'Think, old fellow,' Morris had said to him, 'how much better it is that she should have left you, than that you should have tired of her, and left her.' I really think he saved his friend's life through his companionship and his help. Though he was a strong man he had the delicate feelings of a tender woman. . . . I would go to him in the depths of misery and after being with him for an hour or two I would leave him feeling absolutely happy. I always compared him with a sea-breeze, which seemed to blow away all one's black vapours.

This power of healing and sympathy in Morris did not, apparently, extend to his own wife. 'Women did not seem to count with him', concludes Ionides.[19]

CHAPTER SEVEN

Wallpapers: Textiles: Embroidery: Sigurd the Volsung

WHEN WILLIAM MORRIS began designing wallpapers in the early 1860s, what we think of as typical Victorian designs – the vulgarly coloured bouquets of cabbage roses and other over-blown flowers done in high relief and often linked with festoons of ribbons or bulbous, Rococo scrolls – had largely given place to geometric or highly conventionalized patterns, printed flatly in light, bright colours. As Peter Floud was the first to point out, in his two now famous broadcast talks of 1954, this revolution in mid-Victorian taste had nothing to do with Morris, but was due mainly to the writings and example of Pugin and Owen Jones, whereas Morris, with his return to naturalistic floral patterns, which some-times even incorporated birds and animals, 'far from continuing and reinforcing this revolutionary movement . . . actually reacted against it, and, to some extent, turned the wheel backwards'.[1] This view, reinforced by the great exhibition of Victorian and Edwardian Decorative Arts, organized by Floud at the Victoria and Albert Museum in 1952, has completely upset the conventional view of Morris as more or less the sole instigator of the campaign against mid-Victorian bad taste.

Startling as this view appeared to be when it was first put forward, it is in reality no belittlement of Morris's genius as a designer, for, as Floud went on to emphasize, 'while others searched for more novel and unorthodox solutions to the problems of design, [he] could exert his influence through the sheer beauty and mastery of his patterns. . . . Morris's best papers demonstrate an instinctive mastery of the art of pattern designing hardly reached by the cleverest of his contemporaries.' However, as Floud had to admit, there was 'some peculiar contradiction between the writings and designs which Morris was producing simultaneously during his later years'.

There was, indeed! For at the height of his socialist campaign in 1887 we find him producing a wallpaper for Balmoral Castle which is in many ways similar to Pugin's heraldic design of about 1848 done for the Houses of Parliament. This contradiction Morris attempted to solve by brusquely asserting on several occasions that, though he had spent so much time designing wallpapers 'and so forth', for his part he would be quite content with white-washed walls and plain deal furniture. Such sentiments went with the Viking aspect of Morris, the 'Man of the North', that became increasingly evident during the second half of his life, when he was reacting against 'the more maundering side of medievalism'. It was a sort of berserk rage that flamed out periodically, as when he and Burne-Jones were decorating Rounton Grange in 1876 – that is some time before he became a professed socialist – for the ironmaster Sir Lowthian Bell. Bell heard Morris talking to himself and walking about excitedly, and went to ask if anything was the matter. 'He turned upon me like a mad animal', Bell told Alfred Powell, ' "It's only that I spend my life in ministering to the swinish luxury of the rich." '² In 1880, nevertheless, we find him decorating the Throne Room and staircase of St James's Palace.

But inevitably it was only the rich who could afford the large-scale decorative schemes produced by Morris & Co. Hence the compensatory attraction for Morris of Iceland and the comparatively primitive conditions of life at Kelmscott. Repeatedly in his lectures Morris asserts that luxury is the enemy of art and that the only hope for a rebirth of the arts of design is a return to unaffected simplicity of life – though, in a complicated and eclectic age, a too deliberate simplicity can also be an affectation. Yet Morris's designs are by no means simple, while the more ambitious products of the firm were the last word in luxury. Curiously enough, Morris had no objection to what he called 'the luxury of taste'.

The years 1876 and 1883 were Morris's most prolific in design-ing wallpaper and textiles, with eleven wallpapers and twenty-two chintzes and twenty-four designs for machine-made carpets, as well as designs for the 'Hammersmith' hand-woven carpets and rugs and for splendid damasks, embroideries and wall-hangings. The wallpapers were printed by Jeffreys of Islington from the pear-wood blocks now used by Messrs Sanderson; the textiles, which became the most important products of the firm, were printed and dyed by Thomas Wardle of Leek, Staffordshire, until the establishment of the Morris print works at Merton Abbey on the waters of the river Wandle in 1881. In 1875 Morris produced his first designs for the machine-made carpets, woven by the Royal Wilton Carpet Works and the Heckmondwike Manufacturing Co. in Yorkshire. To the same year belongs his first design for a machine-woven silk and wool fabric, the 'Anemone'. Two years later he began his experiments in tapestry weaving on a loom set up in his bedroom at Kelmscott House, Hammersmith, where he produced what he familiarly called the 'Cabbage and Vine', similar to a late sixteenth-century English woven table cover, 'Lucretia's Banquet', in the Victoria and Albert Museum. In the following year, 1879, he embarked on the weaving of hand-knotted pile carpets and rugs, much influenced by Persian and Indian work.

Among the embroideries undertaken at this time are some of the very finest of Morris's designs. Such is the silk coverlet, designed about 1876 and worked by Mrs Henry Holiday in brown, pink and yellow threads on indigo-dyed linen. Of this Graeme Shankland has remarked: 'the freedom and flowing line of this astonishing design equals that achieved later by *art nouveau* designers, while retaining the structural pattern Morris always insisted upon'.[3] In fact, as Schmutzler has pointed out: 'Art Nouveau was already contained in Morris's designs and all his disciples had to do was to lift his style out of its intricate weave of small parts in order to transpose it from polyphonic orchestration into a tune for a single voice.'[4]

Until 1876, when they underwent a radical change, Morris's designs were still spontaneous, free-flowing and naturalistic. After that date, as Peter Floud was the first to point out, they become, with a few exceptions, rigid, formal and symmetrical and coincide with his discovery of medieval woven textiles in the South Kensington Museum, where he worked from 1876 onwards as one of the Science and Art Department's examiners. When Morris began designing wallpapers again after his first three experimental designs of 1864, the 'Trellis', the 'Daisy' and the 'Fruit 'or 'Pomegranate', he pro-duced the delicate and intricate 'Jasmine' of 1872, followed by the 'Vine' of 1873, with its naturalistic bunches of grapes; then came the 'Willow' of 1874 – not to be confused with the popular 'Willow Boughs' of 1887 – and the 'Powdered'. The 'Vine' is an example of Morris's skill in keeping that feeling for natural growth, which distinguishes all his designs, within a repeating pattern. But, as Floud remarks, his immediate individual vision was now 'so over-laid with the weight of historical precedent, that he rarely thereafter succeeded in recapturing the spontaneity and freshness which had been the secret of the beauty – and equally of the commercial success – of his earlier creations.'[5]

The first chintz design was the 'Tulip and Willow' of 1873, printed by Thomas Clarkson of Bannister Hall, near Preston, Lancashire, the leading calico printer of the day. The result was so unsatisfactory, in Morris's view, that the design was not put on sale again until some years later, when it was printed at the Merton Abbey works in 1889. The first chintz actually put into production was the 'Tulip', printed by Thomas Wardle of Leek in 1875, a design which combines grandeur with grace. But the most splendid design of this period is undoubtedly the 'Honeysuckle' chintz of 1876, printed at Leek, with its great poppies and fritillaries and honeysuckle sprays. In his lecture 'Making the Best of It' of 1879, Morris said:

> in all patterns which are meant to fill the eye and satisfy the mind, there should be a certain mystery. We should not be able to reach the whole thing at once, nor desire to do so, nor be impelled by that desire to go on tracing line after line to find out how the pattern is made, and I think that the obvious presence of a geo-metrical order, if it be, as it should be, beautiful, tends towards this end, and prevents our feeling restless over a pattern. . . . Everyone who has practised the designing of patterns knows the necessity for covering the ground equally and richly. This is really to a great extent the secret of obtaining the look of satisfying mystery aforesaid, and it is the very test of capacity in a designer. . . . Remember that a pattern is either right or wrong. It cannot be forgiven for blundering. . . . It is with a pattern as with a fortress, it is no stronger than its weakest point. A failure for ever recurring torments the eye too much to allow the mind to take any pleasure in suggestion and intention.

In 'The History of Pattern-Designing' of 1882 he emphasized that 'richness and mystery [are] the most necessary of all the qualities of pattern-work . . . without which, indeed, it must be kept in the strictly subordinate place which the scientific good taste of Greece allotted to it'. Of wallpaper design in 'The Lesser Arts of Life', he said:

> you may be as intricate and elaborate in your pattern as you please; nay, the more and the more mysteriously you interweave your sprays and stems the better for your purpose, as the whole thing has to be pasted flat on a wall, and the cost of all this

intricacy will but come out of your brain and hand. For the rest, the fact that in this art we are so little helped by beautiful and varying material imposes on us the necessity for being specially thoughtful in our designs; every one of them must have a distinct idea in it; some beautiful piece of nature must have pressed itself on our notice so forcibly that we are quite full of it, and can, by submitting ourselves to the rules of art, express our pleasure to others, and give them some of the keen delight that we ourselves have felt. If we cannot do this in some measure our paper design will not be worth much; it will be but a makeshift expedient for covering a wall with something or other; and if we really care about art we shall not put up with something or other, but shall choose honest whitewash instead, on which sun and shadow play so pleasantly, if only our room be well planned and well shaped, and look kindly on us.

We find these principles determining all Morris's most characteristic designs.

The marvellous embroidered panel, 'The Romaunt of the Rose', which Burne-Jones and Morris designed as a frieze for the dining-room at Rounton Grange, belongs to 1874 and was worked in wool, silk and gold thread on linen by Margaret, the wife of Sir Lowthian Bell, and their daughter, Florence Johnson, with as much skill and patience as any two medieval ladies in a bower. It took them eight years to complete, being a frieze three feet deep completely covered by fine stitchery. It may now be seen at the William Morris Gallery, Walthamstow. Another linen panel of four girls with musical instruments in a wood, embroidered in shades of brown silk by Morris and Burne-Jones, is in the Victoria and Albert Museum and was designed in 1875, soon after Burne-Jones had done his series of illustrations for *The Earthly Paradise*. This work has the same lyrical charm as 'The Romaunt of the Rose'. The magnificent coverlets and portières worked by Mrs Henry Holiday were sold by the firm at prices in the region of £120. But the firm also produced small-scale works, such as tea cosies, book-covers, photograph frames, work-bags, cushion covers and so on, as well as billiard-table covers, altar-cloths and a great deal of ecclesiastical work. In all this Jane and May Morris, both very accomplished needlewomen, played their part.

When Morris began to design printed textiles in 1873, he was faced with the whole problem of dyeing as an art. 'In no field', writes Peter Floud, 'was his influence more striking than in that of printed textiles.'⁶ At this time English printed textiles were at a particularly low ebb, both as regards design and colour. The main incentive to the production of cotton goods was the great expanding market of Britain's overseas empire, to exploit which the cotton manufacturers of Lancashire and Scotland turned out millions of yards of cheap prints, while high-class block-printing works, such as Thomas Clarkson of Bannister Hall and Stead McAlpin of Carlisle, merely copied the latest fashions sent over from France. It was these Lancashire firms that ruined the Indian cotton weaver with their cheap debased designs that had already replaced the beautiful native work in the Indian market. Morris's experience with the 'Tulip and Willow' chintz, printed in Prussian blue instead of indigo, so horrified him that he turned to Thomas Wardle of Leek, the leading authority at that time on dyeing and silk cultivation and the brother of George Wardle, the manager at Queen Square. Wardle agreed to let Morris experiment with various printing methods regarded as commercially obsolete.

Characteristically, it was from Gerard's *Herbal*, 'the old favourite of his boyhood', that Morris first learned about certain disused vegetable dyes, and he even went back to Pliny in search of still older methods. As he wrote later in his essay 'Of Dyeing as an Art' for the catalogue of the Arts and Crafts Exhibition Society of 1889:

> Dyeing is a very ancient art; from the earliest times of the ancient civilizations till within about forty years ago, there has been no essential change in it, and not much change of any kind. Up to the time of the discovery of the process of Prussian-blue dyeing in about 1810 (it was known as *pigment* thirty or forty years earlier), the only changes in the art were the result of the introduction of the American insect dye (cochineal) and the American wood-dyes now known as logwood and Brazil wood: the latter differs little from the Asiatic and African Red Saunders, and other red dye-woods; the former has cheapened and worsened black-dyeing, in so far as it has taken the place of the indigo-vat as a basis.

But it was not till the discovery of the aniline dyes, produced from coal tar, that there came about 'an absolute divorce between the *commercial process* and the *art* of dyeing,' Morris continues, 'so that anyone wanting to produce dyed textiles of any artistic quality in them must entirely forego the modern and commercial methods in favour of those which are as old as Pliny, who speaks of them as being old in his time'.

Morris then shows what he has found by his own practice to be the best method of producing the four basic colours needed for dyeing – blue, red, yellow, and brown – green, purple, black and all inter‚ mediate shades being made from a mixture of these colours. He began by obtaining kermes from Greece, through Aglaia Coronio, which yielded a particularly fine shade of red; he then tried boiling some poplar and osier twigs, which gave 'a good strong yellow'; brown he got from the roots of the walnut tree, his blue from indigo. His discussion of the relative quality of the insect dye kermes, and the wood dyes used in the Middle Ages, known by the general name of 'Brazil', shows the care and thoroughness with which he investigated this question.

Some of the wood‚dyes are very beautiful in colour; but unluckily they are none of them permanent, as you may see by examining the beautiful stuffs of the thirteenth and fourteenth centuries at the South Kensington Museum in which you will scarcely find any red but plenty of fawn‚colour, which is in fact the wood red of 500 years ago thus faded. If you will turn from them to the Gothic tapestries [that is, the Brussels tapestries of 1510] and note the reds in them, you will have the measure of the relative permanence of kermes and 'Brazil', the tapestry reds being all dyed with kermes, and still retaining the greater part of their colour. . . . I may also note that no textiles dyed blue or green, otherwise than by indigo, keep an agreeable colour by candle‚light, many bright greens turning into sheer drab.

A series of letters written to Thomas Wardle at this time is evidence of the extraordinary care Morris exercised in getting his colours right.[7] On 26 November 1875 he writes:

I am also as you must know most deeply impressed with the importance of having all our dyes the soundest and best that can be, and am prepared to give up all that part of my business which depends on textiles if I fail in getting them so. However I don't in the least see why I should talk about failing which is after all impossible, as I have no doubt you feel yourself.

Again, he tells Wardle in another letter:

I mean that I can never be contented with getting anything short of the best, and that I should go on trying to improve our goods in all ways, and should consider anything that was only tolerable as a ladder to mount up to the next stage – that is, in fact, my life.

But Morris could never really get results which satisfied his exacting standards at Leek. The printing of the cottons, especially, left much to be desired, so much so that the firm accumulated a good deal of stock which, Morris wrote, was 'only half useful to us', adding:

> you must allow that it is putting us in an awkward position if we have to be the only persons responsible for the pieces, when we have no control over the process of them. . . . It is quite true that you are not likely to get your money back for some time for what you have spent on the dyeing operations, and what I have just said about the printing applies to this just as much or more: for me giving up the dyeing schemes means giving up business altogether, and to give up the printing would be a serious blow to it, especially as last Midsummer our balance showed a loss on that account of £1023.

Throughout 1876 Morris was collecting ancient herbals. In October he went over to Paris to meet Wardle and after his departure searched thirteen shops for old books on dyeing.

> I got Macquer, and a useful looking book rather later in date by one Homasell on dyeing wool, silk and cotton, and printing. . . . I also got another dye book, Teinturier Parfait, that looks rule of thumb. Also a book with detailed description (with good plates) of the carpet making we saw: this is part of the same series as Macquer. Also in the same series a book on cotton-velvet, because it had receipts for printing the velvet. The old chap will send me a Hellot as soon as he can get one; also I told him to buy any old dyeing books.

He found Hellot (Paris 1750) 'very minute about the management of vats'. For Morris, the basis of dyeing was the indigo vat, and while he was experimenting with this at Leek, his hands and arms up to the elbow remained permanently blue.

On 4 February 1875, he wrote to Georgie Burne-Jones from Lichfield, where he was spending the day with Thomas Wardle, it being a Sunday:

I shall be glad enough to get back to the dye-house at Leek to-morrow. I daresay you will notice how bad my writing is; my hand is so shaky with doing journey-man's work the last few days: delightful work, hard for the body and easy for the mind. For a great heap of skein-wool has come for me and more is coming: and yesterday evening we set our blue-vat the last thing before coming here. I should have liked you to see the charm work on it: we dyed a lock of wool bright blue in it, and left the liquor a clear primrose colour, so all will be ready for dyeing to-morrow in it: though, by the way, if you are a dyer, you must call it *her*.

Leek, Monday. I have been dyeing in *her* all the afternoon, and my hands are a woeful spectacle in consequence: *she* appears all that could be wished for, but I must say I should like not to look such a beast, and not to feel as if I wanted pegs to keep my fingers one from the other. I lost my temper in the dye-house for the first time this afternoon: they had been very trying: but I wish I hadn't been such a fool. . . .

As well as experimenting with the dye vat, Morris was busy with illumination work, transcribing the *Odes* of Horace (this manuscript is now at the Bodleian Library, Oxford) and translating the *Aeneid*. He was still in a disturbed state of mind, writing to Aglaia Coronio from Queen Square early in March:

I have missed you very much and never expected that it would be so long between the times of seeing you. I went down to my mother's yesterday and stayed there till noon to-day. I was very dull when I went, and expected that it would make me duller; but somehow I found myself much better this morning, and am quite changed now. I can only hope that it will last. I am ashamed of myself for these strange waves of unreasonable passion: it seems so unmanly: yet indeed I have a good deal to bear considering how hopeful my earlier youth was, & what overweening ideas I had of the joys of life.

Morris ordered special vellum from Rome for his illumination work. 'I enclose a P.O.O. for £5 for further disbursements on vellum', he writes to Fairfax Murray on 11 March. 'I would send more, but for the scraping everything together to pay my partners, who have come to some kind of agreement with me, if they don't cry off before the law business is settled; which drags on confoundedly, and to say the truth bothers me more than I like to confess.' However, the whole thing was settled by the end of the month, leaving Morris in sole control of his business.

Meanwhile, he was racing through Virgil. 'I have got toward the end of the 7th book', he tells Murray in the same letter, 'and shall finish the whole thing and have it out by the beginning of June I hope: so you [can] imagine I have not been idle.' Besides translating Virgil ('it cannot be said that Morris brought to this task any adequate equipment', comments Mackail), he and Burne-Jones were working on their great illuminated manuscript of the *Aeneid*, which was finally laid aside after the completion of the first six books. On 27 May 1875 Morris wrote to Fairfax Murray:

I have somewhat slacked from the Virgil translation, as I found it not possible to get it out this summer and easy enough to get it out by October: also I have begun one of the pictures for the Virgil: I make but a sorry hand of it at first, but shall go on with it till (at the worst) I am wholly discomfited. Whether I succeed or not in the end 'twill be a long job: so I am asking you if you would do some of them and what it would be worth your while to do them for. . . . I am up to the neck and trying out designs for papers, chintzes, and carpets, and trying to get the manufacturers to do them: I think we are doing some good things in that way. . . .

Among wallpapers, the majestic 'Acanthus' was designed this year. Owing to the subtle colour gradations, sixteen blocks were required to print it.

The previous month, Morris had found time to take a holiday in Wales with Faulkner. 'I am going with Charley Faulkner, my inevitable travelling-companion, to look at my fatherland', he writes to Mrs Baldwin on 25 March. 'We are going to Shrewsbury, and thence to a college farm of his on the very head waters of Severn and Wye, where we are to have ponies and go over the hills and far away, only for about a week in all though. . . .' From Bala he wrote to his daughters on 5 April, after riding from Dinas Mawddwy up the valley of the Dyfi,

and then over the mountain-necks into another valley, and so here. . . . To-morrow we go to Dolgelley which is in a shy mountainous country under Cader Idris . . . the next day to Towyn, about a mile from the sea; and on Thursday to Dinas

Mawddwy again by a road that runs on the other side of Cader Idris: on Friday we set off to Oxford and London from that place, so that I shall be back some time on Friday evening probably: and so glad as I shall be to see you and the Mammy. . . . The farmhouse kitchen was such a nice place: there were some pretty children there, but not a word could they talk of anything but Welsh, except one older girl. . . .

From Towyn on 7 April he wrote to Aglaia Coronio. He says that he was glad to find that very little English was spoken in that part of Wales and that the people 'are mostly very polite and much better mannered than the same sort of people would be in England'.

In another letter in April to Mrs Coronio from Queen Square Morris speaks of not feeling very well and that 'an hour or two with you would have helped me to get along'. He has been spending the Easter holidays at Horrington House. Writing on a Monday afternoon, he says that he has not been out of the house 'since Friday morning when I went to the Grange: I have had my nose down on my vellum the rest of the time and am somewhat weary of it though I can't help liking to see the page brighten while I am at it. I think I will try to do violence to my inclination & pound away at a poem good or bad before long. I wonder if I have gone stupid & can't though.' The poem he had in mind was doubtless the immense romantic epic *Sigurd the Volsung*, which appeared next year and which he regarded as his highest achievement in literature.

Whitsun was spent boating at Oxford with Burne-Jones and Faulkner, when the old undergraduate practical joking was resumed, as usual. 'How we teased Mr Morris on the river!' Burne-Jones wrote to his son, Philip.

We took our lunch one day, and it was a fowl and a bottle of wine and some bread and salt – and Mr Faulkner and I managed to hide the fowl away in the sheet of the sail, and when we anchored at a shady part of the river and undid the basket, lo! there was no fowl. And Mr Morris looked like a disappointed little boy and then looked good, and filled his dry mouth with bread and said it didn't matter much, so we drew out the fowl and had great laughter.[8]

The 'chaff' was of an unbelievable simplicity, but part of its charm was that the same kind of practical joke worked on Morris time and again. The greatest joke was to deprive him of his food, for the undisguised gusto with which he partook of his daily luncheon of roast beef and wine was to his friends one of his most endearing characteristics. Moreover, since he was incapable of concealing what he thought or felt, the temptation to tease him was irresistible.

On 21 October Morris wrote to Mrs Coronio from Queen Square:

> We have got a few pieces of printed cloths here, and they are hung up in the big room, where they look so beautiful (really) that I feel inclined to sit and stare at them all day; which however I am far from doing as I am working hard. . . . Item, we have got a pattern of a woolen cloth that pleases me hugely, though I don't know if it would please you, for it looks quite like a mediaeval manufacture.
>
> All this keeps me busy and amuses me very much, so that I may consider myself a lucky man, among so many people who seem to find it hard to be amused.

This can only be a reference to Jane, who was ailing again, and early next month went to stay with Rossetti at Aldwick Lodge, near Bognor. But at least Morris now had Kelmscott to himself and his letter to Jane of 9 November shows his immense pleasure in the house and its surroundings, in spite of pouring rain and floods. Inevitably, he has been fishing.

> My hands are still somewhat stiff with my work on the river. Lord! how cold it blew – wind E. or thereabouts. I am obliged to write by candle-light though 'tis only 4 o'clock. Best love to my one daughter – wouldn't she have liked to have been out on the flooded river with me, the wind right in our teeth and the eddies going like a Japanese tea-tray: I must say it was delightful: almost as good as Iceland on a small scale: please the pigs, I will have a sail on the floods to-morrow.

We may be quite sure that Jane, for one, was thankful to be at Bognor with Rossetti, sitting for *Astarte Syriaca*, rather than en-during the cold and damp of Kelmscott and eating bacon and kangaroo meat, which Morris tells her is all that he has in the house.

She remained at Aldwick Lodge until December, when she left in order to spend Christmas with her family, after which she returned to Bognor with Jenny and May. Morris writes to her on

26 January from Kelmscott: 'I have been muddling about on the river and floods for exercise sake: It is a most beautiful afternoon: there are violets out, and aconites, and the snowdrops are showing all about. Love to the babies.' In March Jane is still at Bognor and Morris writes to her on the 18th:

> I won't press you to come back, then: only let me know by return about when you intend coming: the point is that I have pretty well settled to go to Leek next Wednesday. I intend when I go there to be about a fortnight away: now if you are coming back say this day week, it would not stop my going, as I should ask Bessy to keep Jenny company for those 2 or 3 days: but if you were going to stay much beyond that I should put off my Leek journey till after Easter as I should not like Jenny to be left parentless so long. . . . Give my love to May & thank her for her letter, & tell her that if I were not very busy over my poetry today I would write to her.

Morris went to Leek, working in the dye-house in sabots and blouse. 'I trust I am taking in dyeing at every pore', he wrote to Georgie Burne-Jones on 26 March 1876.

> I have found out and practised the art of weld-dyeing, the ancientest of yellow dyes, and the fastest. We have set a blue vat for cotton, which I hope will turn out all right to-morrow morning: it is nine feet deep and holds 1000 gallons: it would be a week's talk to tell you all the anxieties and possibilities con-nected with this indigo subject, but you must at least imagine all this going on in very nearly the same conditions as those of the shepherd boy that made a watch all by himself.

Two days later he tells Mrs Coronio:

> I am dyeing yellows and reds: the yellows are very easy to get, and so are a lot of shades of salmon and flesh-colour & buff & orange: my chief difficulty is in getting a deep blood-red, but I hope to succeed before I come away: I have not got the proper indigo-vat for wool but I can dye blues in the cotton-vat and get lovely greens with that and the bright yellow that weld gives. This morning I assisted at the dyeing of 20 lbs of silk (for our damask) in the blue-vat; it was very exciting, as the thing is quite unused now, and we ran a good chance of spoiling the silk. There were

4 dyers & Mr Wardle at work, and myself as dyer's mate: the men were encouraged with beer & to it they went, and very pretty it was to see the silk coming green out of the vat & gradually turning blue. . . . To-morrow I am going to Nottingham to see wool dyed blue in the woad-vat as it is called.

From Leek, Morris wrote a somewhat mysterious letter to 'a friend' who, says Mackail, 'was passing through one of those dark-nesses in which the whole substance of life seems to crumble away under our hands'. From its intimate tone one may guess that it was addressed either to Edward or Georgie Burne-Jones. It is couched in the most general terms and there is no other clue to its recipient. But it is further evidence, if that is needed, of the warmth and depth of Morris's feelings for his closest friends and sufficient answer to those who maintain that he lacked humanity. Its tone is both generous and noble.

Wherein you are spiritless, I wish with all my heart that I could help you or amend it, for it is most true that it grieves me; but also, I must confess it, most true that I am living my own life in spite of it, or in spite of anything grievous that may happen in the world. Sometimes I wonder so much at all this, that I wish even that I were once more in trouble of my own, and think of myself that I am really grown callous: but I am sure that though I have many hopes and pleasures, or at least strong ones, and that though my life is dear to me, so much as I seem to have to do, I would give them away, hopes and pleasures, one by one or all together, and my life at last, for you, for my friendship, for my honour, for the world. If it seems boasting I do not mean it; but rather that I claim, so to say it, not to be separated from those that are heavy-hearted only because I am well in health and full of pleasant work and eager about it, and not oppressed by desires so as not to be able to take an interest in it all. I wish I could say something that would serve you, beyond what you know very well, that I love you and long to help you: and indeed I entreat you (however trite the words may be) to think that life is not empty nor made for nothing, and that the parts of it fit one into another in some way; and that the world goes on, beautiful and strange and dreadful and worshipful.

His rash wish to be once more in trouble of his own was granted this summer when Jenny, 'who had been his pride as a child for her intellectual faculties', says Wilfrid Scawen Blunt, at the age of fifteen, became subject to epileptic fits. This was an anxiety that henceforth was never to leave Morris. The worst sorrow of his life, Bernard Shaw tells us, was his realization that Jenny's illness was 'an inheritance from himself. . . . Morris adored Jenny. He could not sit in the same room without his arm round her waist. His voice changed when he spoke to her as it changed to no one else.'[9]

In July, Jane wrote from Deal, where she was staying with the children, sending a good report about Jenny's condition and Morris replied on the 18th:

> I cannot tell you how pleased I am that you think so well of Jenny: you don't say much about May: I suppose it can't fail to do her good: I think it would be a great pity to hurry them away if the place really seems to suit them, and if you can hold out there: I will give you as much of my company as work will let me: to-day week or to-morrow week I hope to come down, and shall stay three days or so at any rate: I am looking forward to it very much.

Earlier in the letter he complains of the heat in London and says that he is

> longing for that tail of the glacier in Thorsmark, or our camp in the wilderness at Eyvindarkofarver under the snow mountains: in fact, though I don't feel unwell (and therefore ought to hold my noise, as you very truly say), I am depressed and languid (say lazy) and don't care for my work, at any rate not the bread and cheese part of it: though for want of finding any amusement in books on Saturday and Sunday I did manage to screw out my tale of verses to the tune of some 250 [lines]. . . .

This was *Sigurd*. He adds that the *Athenaeum* has been 'very civil' about 'that scrap of poem I published in it the other day, though it was not worth publishing, either, and sent me £20; it seems, such is the world's injustice and stupidity, that it was a success – never mind: I shall pay for it when my new poem comes out. . . . I think we had better spend that £20 in carriages at Deal?'

To Mrs Coronio he wrote to say:

> I am getting on with my poem, in quantity at any rate: I have (roughly) done the 3rd part: that is Sigurd and Brynhild are dead, and people are busy forgetting them after the fashion of our

amiable race: all that I have left to do now, if the last written parts turn out successful, is the revenge and death of Gudrun, which will be certainly short, and probably not difficult compared with what I have had to do. I am looking forward to having a rest some day soon: my rebellious inclinations turn towards Iceland, though I know it is impossible, so I suppose it will be Kelmscott and the river. . . .

And Kelmscott and the river it was for much of August and September, except for an interlude with Cormell Price at his tower at Broadway, where he met 'Ned and the children'.

Morris was not over-hopeful about the reception of *Sigurd the Volsung* and when it appeared in November it was, as Mackail says, 'but languidly received'. Its significance to him was, as he wrote in the verse prologue to his translation of *The Volsunga Saga* six years before, that it told

Of utter love defeated utterly,
Of Grief too strong to give Love time to die.

Although Mackail calls *Sigurd* 'the most Homeric poem which has been written since Homer', a later and more severe critic, Dr Dorothy Hoare writes:

> Morris is not quite sure of his grasp on the reality of the feeling; he is interested in sentiment and situation more than in character and passion. . . . Again restraint is turned into looseness and romantic feeling. . . . The completeness and significance of the theme, which the *Volsunga Saga*, in spite of difficulties, presses home, lies in the fact that Gunnar, an honourable and loyal friend, is wrought on by overwhelming passion to slay his friend. It is disastrous, but at the same time it is immense.[10]

Morris – for fairly obvious reasons, arising out of the situation in which he found himself and because of his own essentially chivalrous cast of mind – was unable to accept this. He therefore follows the German version of the epic, the *Nibelungenlied*, in which the principal motive of Gunther's betrayal of Siegfried is, finally, possession of the ring.

Nevertheless, *Sigurd* remains a tremendous work. Of its very nature, as a romantic literary epic of the mid-nineteenth century, it could scarcely have the wildness and savagery of the Icelandic original, any more than Swinburne's *Tristram of Lyonesse*, another elaborately rhetorical work, has the moving simplicity of Béroul or Malory. There is no reason why it should be condemned for not recapturing the original spirit of the saga any more than Wagner's *Der Ring des Nibelungen* can be condemned on the score of its long-windedness and romantic over-emphasis. As Dr J.R. Wahl justly points out:

> Morris's purpose in *Sigurd* is not merely, as Dr Hoare would have her readers assume, to versify the *Volsunga Saga* and provide it with a new ending based on the *Nibelungenlied*. His aim is to write an original English poem having as its theme what he called 'the great Epic of the North' and to do so he drew freely on all the versions of the Volsung and Nibelung story which were available to him. The richness of texture of the poem is, indeed, largely the result of the ease and skill with which he combines and unifies so wide a range of sources.

> Among these were the *Lay of Sigrdrifa* as well as the *First Lay of Gudrun*, the *Snorra Edda*, *Reginsmál*, *Fáfnismál*, the *Short Lay of Sigurd* and the two Atli lays. As the result of his examination of all the existing MSS of *Sigurd*, Dr Wahl has revealed the immense amount of work put into his huge poem, completely exploding the notion that Morris habitually wrote hurriedly and carelessly and was incapable of revision.

> The three episodes that meant most to Morris, are those of Sigurd's birth, his awakening of Brynhild, and his final meeting with her. . . . Of the first of these episodes there are four versions. . . . Sigurd's awakening of Brynhild exists in five versions, of which the first and the third are the most important. . . . The episode which Morris revised most frequently is the crisis and culmination of the poem, Sigurd's last meeting with Brynhild. Of this there are no fewer than seven versions of which four are of distinct importance. . . . After rewriting the scene four times Morris banished from it all trace of plaintive lamentation.[11]

One cannot deny that *Sigurd* bears evidence of this laboriousness, and that it has a certain monotony. At the same time it does carry one forward with the surge and roll of a genuine epic impetus. Both in temper and scale it is heroic. Much of it is Wagnerian in feeling, despite Morris's dislike of Wagner, expressed in his letter of 12 November 1873 to H. Buxton Forman, who had sent him a translation of the libretto of *Die Walküre* in the alliterative verse of the original. Morris wrote that he had not had time to read it yet – and one wonders if he ever did so:

> Nor to say the truth am I much interested in anything Wagner does, as his theories on musical matters seem to me as an artist and non-musical man perfectly abominable: besides I look upon it as nothing short of desecration to bring such a tremendous and world-wide subject under the gaslights of an opera: the most rococo and degraded of all forms of art – the idea of a sandy-haired German tenor tweedledeeing over the unspeakable woes of Sigurd, which even the simplest words are not typical enough to express! Excuse my heat: but I wish to see Wagner uprooted. . . .

In his use of the word 'rococo', Morris was evidently thinking of Italian opera, for it is certainly not applicable to *The Ring*, of which, as 'a non-musical man', he was clearly quite ignorant. There is, as a matter of fact, a distinct parallel between Wagner's theories in *Oper und Drama*, with its emphasis on 'the folk' and myth and its diatribes against the rich and the state, and Morris's lectures on art and socialism. But then Wagner was a revolutionary, whereas Morris was a traditionalist, and though both he and Wagner derived their greatest work from the same sources, Morris had no interest in the drama, except in its medieval form as morality and interlude. Nevertheless, as one reads *Sigurd*, it is the music of *The Ring* which echoes in one's ears. The Burne-Joneses, however, were ardent Wagnerians and Cosima was brought to the Grange by George Eliot, when Wagner was in London in the spring of 1877, conducting concerts at the Albert Hall. She gave Ned a bust of Beethoven and he did a drawing of her.

The Wagners were staying at Orme Square with Dr Edward Dannreuther, the conductor, who was married to Luke Ionides' sister, Chariclea. In his privately printed *Memories*, Luke Ionides records the following incident:

> Madame Wagner told me she much wished to meet Morris, as he treated the same subjects that her husband had treated in his music. So I invited them both to dinner. Morris came, and asked if his bag of gala clothes had arrived. I told him it had not, so he said, 'How can I sit down with all you people dressed as I am!' and then he showed me his hands which were blue from some

experiments in dyeing he had made with indigo. I said it did not matter, and introduced him to Madame Wagner, who was most charming, and delighted to have him next to her at table. I don't think he was equally impressed with her, for he was not a bit susceptible to the charm of women. . . .

In this he differed considerably from Richard Wagner, as he did in almost all other respects. The meeting of these two, the 'Man of the North', who prided himself on his rough manners, and the effusive German, would have been interesting. But Wagner was detained by rehearsals at the Albert Hall.

Bernard Shaw tells us that Morris was fond of reading *Sigurd* aloud, rocking from side to side in time to the rhythm like an elephant.[12] He considered it, says May Morris, the central work of his life, the achievement he 'held most highly and wished to be remembered by'.[13] Indeed, the striking difference in tone between *Sigurd* and the plaintive *Earthly Paradise* shows how much Morris had become master of himself. No longer the 'idle singer of an empty day', he is henceforth committed to what he called 'the religion of courage' in the struggles with his own age that lay ahead.

PART TWO

COMMITMENT

1876–1890

CHAPTER EIGHT

1876–1879
The Anti-Turk Campaign:
Kelmscott House:
Visit to Italy: Experiments in Weaving

SUDDENLY, in October 1876, Morris was shocked by the news that England was on the verge of war with Russia in support of Turkey. Having been appalled by the reports of Turkish atrocities in Bulgaria, this seemed to him, innocent as he was of international diplomacy, utterly shameful. On 24 October he therefore wrote a long letter of protest to the Liberal *Daily News* – his first political utterance.

If, wrote Morris, he had been told that England was going to war with Turkey, 'a gang of thieves and murderers', in order to force them to give their subject peoples 'some chance of existence . . . some security of life, limb and property', he would have understood it. 'And I, a mere sentimentalist, should have rejoiced in such a war, and thought it only good. . . . Yes, I should have thought I had lived for something at last: to have seen England just, and in earnest, the Tories converted and silenced, and our country honoured throughout the world.' But, it now appeared, England was not in earnest when she expressed horror at the impaling of hundreds of Bulgarian men, women and children on stakes, the burning of their villages, the devastation of their countryside, for Disraeli, 'the new-made "brave" Earl, is determined to drag us into a shameful and unjust war – how shameful and unjust no words can say'. Indeed, England, he pointed out, had already waged a great war in the Crimea 'to keep the Turks, their jailors, alive, thinking that we could make them a respectable and even a progressive people -- so sanguine, and, to say the truth, such fools we were!'

However, Disraeli could still be prevented from waging this new shameful war, for 'no Government durst go against the expressed will of the English people, when it has a will and can find time to express it'. But now, 'not even the wretched packed Parliament we have got is sitting . . . the members are too busy shooting in the country, and the nation is dumb.' He concluded:

> I appeal to the Liberal Party, and ask if it is not worth while their making some effort to avoid this shame. I appeal to the working men, and pray them to look to it that if this shame falls upon them they will certainly remember it and be burdened by it when their day clears for them, and they attain all, and more than all, they are now striving for: to the organizers of both these bodies I specially appeal, to set their hands to the work before it is too late, to drop all other watch-words that this at least may be heard – No war on behalf of Turkey: no war on behalf of the thieves and murderers! . . . I who am writing this am one of a large class of men – quiet men, who usually go about their own business, heeding public matters less than they ought, and afraid to speak in such a huge concourse as the English nation, however much they may feel, but who are now stung into bitterness by thinking how helpless they are in a public matter that touches them so closely. . . . If this monstrous shame and disaster – if this curse – has to fall upon us, we cannot make Lord Beaconsfield or Lord Derby, the Tory Party or the House of Commons, our scape-goats; we must, our very selves, bear the curse, and make the best of it, for we put these men where they sit over us, and do their will, such as it is: and we can put them down again if we choose.

And much more to the same purpose, signed 'William Morris, Author of "The Earthly Paradise".'

Morris did not perhaps realize that the real issue, from the point of view of the Government, was not the sufferings of Bulgarian peasants under the Ottoman Empire, but Russia's Slavophile policy, under cover of which she was planning to extend her rule into the Balkans by 'liberating' her Slavonic 'Christian brothers' from the Infidel Turk, just as she has now achieved the same end in Eastern Europe in the name of Communism. What worried England, Disraeli as well as Gladstone, for all what Morris calls 'his noble and generous rhetoric', was the threat to the route to India by Russia's control of the Dardanelles. Hence the support of a bankrupt Turkey as a bulwark against Russian imperialism.

Morris threw himself heart and soul into the Liberal-Radical agitation against Disraeli's war policy. There were mass-meetings of protest in Trafalgar Square and Hyde Park, and a conference, proposed by A.J.Mundella, the Liberal MP, was held at St James's Hall on 8 December 1876. Morris entered enthusiastically into the preparations for this and was elected Treasurer of the Eastern Question Association, which was created at the conference. Throughout the following year the EQA held meetings all over the country. 'At one of these,' George Wardle wrote later in a letter to Sydney Cockerell, 'at Willis's rooms, I think, Morris tried to speak, but was so hoarse from excitement that he could scarce utter a word. I stood by but could only catch "He is a trickster – trickster", meaning Dizzy. This was screamed or hissed with a voice so weakened by his emotion that it was scarce audible. Sir Robert Peel, who stood by, his hat cocked on the side of his head, was highly amused'[1] – as, no doubt, any other professional politician, seasoned in stage-managing the emotions of their audiences, would have been. Even the gentle Ned Burne-Jones was drawn into the fray. 'My soul is a cauldron of mad fury all day and I am thinking of nothing but politics', he wrote to George Howard. 'I've a plan for pulling down Buckingham Palace and the Marble Arch and Burlington House – & to-morrow I speak in the park & on Sunday at a Clerkenwell temperance association, & on Monday at the Spitalfields Vestry Hall.'[2]

War broke out between Russia and Turkey in April 1877 and in May William Morris wrote his pamphlet *Unjust War: To the Working-men of England*, issued by the Eastern Question Association, in which he warned his readers:

Take heed in time and consider it well, for a hard matter it will be for most of us to bear wartime taxes, war-prices, war-losses of wealth and work and friends and kindred: we shall pay heavily, and you, friends of the working-classes, will pay the heaviest. . . .

And who are they who flaunt in our faces the banner inscribed on one side *English Interests*, and on the other *Russian Misdeeds*? Who are they that are leading us into war? Let us look at these saviours of England's honour, these champions of Poland, these scourges of Russia's iniquities! Do you know them? – Greedy gamblers on the Stock Exchange, idle officers of the army and navy (poor fellows!) worn-out mockers of the Clubs, desperate purveyors of exciting war-news for the comfortable breakfast tables of those who have nothing to lose by war, and lastly, in the place of honour, the Tory Rump, that we fools, weary of peace, reason and justice, chose at the last election to 'represent' us: and over all their captain, the ancient place-hunter, who, having at last climbed into an Earl's chair, grins down into the anxious face of England. . . . O shame and double shame, if we march under such a leadership as this in an unjust war against a people who are *not* our enemies, against Europe, against freedom, against nature, against the hope of the world.

Working-men of England, one word of warning yet: I doubt if you know the bitterness of hatred against freedom and progress that lies at the hearts of a certain part of the richer classes of this country: their newspapers veil it in a kind of decent language; but do but hear them talking among themselves, as I have often, and I know not whether scorn or anger would prevail in you at their folly and insolence:– these men cannot speak of your order, of its aims, of its leaders without a sneer or an insult: these men, if they had the power (may England perish rather) would thwart your just aspirations, would silence you, would deliver you bound hand and foot for ever to irresponsible capital – and these men, I say it deliberately, are the heart and soul of the party that is driving us to an unjust war:– can the Russian people be your enemies or mine like these men are, who are the enemies of all justice? They can harm us but little now, but if war comes, *unjust war*, with all its confusion and anger, who shall say what their power may be, what step backward we may make? Fellow citizens, look to it, and if you have any wrongs to be redressed, if you cherish your most worthy hope of raising your whole order peacefully and solidly, if you thirst for leisure and knowledge, if you long to lessen those inequalities which have been our stumbling-block since the beginning of the world, then cast aside sloth and cry out against an UNJUST WAR, and urge us of the Middle Classes to do no less. . . .

In this remarkable document,[3] written to be distributed at meetings, there are premonitions of the position taken up by Morris when he joined the Democratic Federation six years later. But at this time he was still a Liberal, with leanings to Radicalism.

The year 1877, the year of the magnificent 'Chrysanthemum' wallpaper, saw the opening of Morris & Co.'s showrooms at the corner of Oxford Street and North Audley Street, and on 2 May Morris wrote to Jane:

> We are going to have a great anti-Turk meeting next Monday at St James's Hall. . . . There is a great stew in political matters, and our side will be done for and war certain if we don't raise the very devil over it. Picture to yourself 3 years war and the shop in Oxford Street, and poor Smith standing at the door with his hands in his pockets! There is a small meeting tonight at the Cannon Street Hotel: I am going there to swell the crowd. . . .

At the Lord Mayor's Banquet on 9 November 1876, Disraeli had warned the Tsar: 'If England were to go to war in a righteous cause . . . her resources would prove inexhaustible.' This gave rise to the popular music-hall song of the time, the origin of the expression 'Jingoism':

> *We don't want to fight,*
> *But, by Jingo, if we do,*
> *We've got the ships, we've got the men,*
> *We've got the money too!*

It is evidence of the supreme confidence of England in international affairs at that time. But even if England went to war and came out victorious, what could be done about Turkey? Morris asked Faulkner in a letter of 15 November 1876: '" Take it ourselves", says the bold man, "and rule it as we rule India." But the bold man don't live in England at present I think: and I know what the Tory trading stock-jobbing scoundrel that one calls an Englishman today would do with it: he would shut his eyes hard over it, get his widows and orphans to lend it money, and sell it vast quantities of bad cotton.'

Feelings ran high on both sides and on 16 January 1878 the Workmen's Neutrality Demonstration was held in the Exeter Hall. Georgie, who was present with Ned, Faulkner and Cormell Price, wrote a description of the meeting to Rosalind Howard, who, with her husband, Jane Morris and the children, was spending the winter in Italy. Of Morris she says: 'It is such a blessing to hear him put truth into straightforward words as no one else does at present, for he is free from the usual forms of public speaking and in fear of no man. How I wish you had heard his song sung at Exeter Hall by a great part of the 3000 men present to "The Hardy Norsemen". The organ played it and between every verse there was a pause for shouting and clapping which raised the roof.'[4] It began:

> *Wake, London lads, wake, bold and free!*
> *Arise and fall to work,*
> *Lest England's glory come to be*
> *Bond servant to the Turk!*
>
> *Think of your sires! how oft and oft*
> *On freedom's field they bled,*
> *When Cromwell's hand was raised aloft*
> *And kings and scoundrels fled.*

One cannot help feeling that the war party's song was somewhat better than Morris's rather too literary production. But it served its purpose well enough. Afterwards, he wrote to Jane:

The evening meeting was magnificent; orderly and enthusiastic: though mind you, it took some very heavy work to keep the enemy's roughs out; and the noise of them outside was like the sea roaring against a lighthouse and though the overflow meeting in Trafalgar Sq. was in our favour on the whole, yet there was opposition there also: you will have seen about our music: wasn't it a good idea? I think Chesson suggested it first: & then they set me to write the song, wh. I did on the Monday night. It went down very well, & they sang it well together: they struck up when we were just ready to come onto the platform & you may imagine that I felt rather excited when I heard them begin to tune up: they stopped at the end of each verse and cheered lustily: we came onto the platform just about the middle of it. Mundella made a first-rate chairman, & the speaking was much above the average. . . . I send you enclosed 3 'London Lads': I have a bundle of them here & if you want more for the Howards I will send on again. I am very tired with it and shall enjoy a week of dyeing & designing next week if Dizzy will let me have it.

One wonders whether Jane was in the least interested, though she seems to have been concerned for her husband's safety. In his next letter of 1 February, Morris reassures her:

I write you a short line to say that I am all right: safe in wind and limb, and not very likely to risk either at present; though I was at a very noisy meeting last night down at Stepney, where we had a bare majority: I have been writing to Howard today about the 'situation': I must say I feel gloomy enough about it, though I cannot suppose it is hopeless: meantime our people are much dispirited with the defeat at Sheffield, and the row yesterday in the City, at which latter place there were some 7000 people; they behaved very disgracefully, as you will see in the newspapers: they had 400 roughs down in waggons from Woolwich Dockyard, & generally played the gooseberry: people on our side had to hide away in cellars & places & get out anyhow: all of this is very enraging, & I am beginning to say, well if they will have war, let them fill their bellies with it then! . . . I feel very low and muddled about it all: but we have one shot in the locker yet, to wit a big, a real big demonstration in Hyde Park; which however is both expensive & dangerous; especially in England, where it sometimes rains. . . . I am very glad to hear the good news of Jenny: did she get my letter on her birthday? Would she like any book sent to her there do you think? she *hasn't* written to me for ever such a time.

Within three weeks the opposition of the Liberal Party had broken down on a mere report that the Russians had entered Constantinople and Morris complained that 'people go about in a Rule Britannia style that turns one's stomach.' On 25 February he wrote to Jane:

As to my political career, I think it is at an end for the present, & has ended sufficiently disgustingly, after beating about the bush & trying to organize some rags of resistance to the war-party for a fortnight, after spending all one's time in committees & the like: I went to Gladstone with some of the workmen & Chesson, to talk about getting him to a meeting at the Agricultural Hall; he agreed & was quite hot about it, and as brisk as a bee: I went off straight to the Hall, & took it for tomorrow: to work we fell, & everything got into trim: but – on Monday our parliamentarians began to quake, & tease Gladstone, and they have quaked the meeting out now: the E.Q.A. was foremost in the flight, & really I must needs say they behaved ill in the matter. . . . I am that ashamed that I can scarcely look people in the face though I did my best to keep the thing up: the working-men are in a great rage about it, as they may well be . . . there was a stormy meeting of the E.Q.A. yesterday full of wretched little personalities, but

I held my tongue – I am out of it now, I mean as to bothering my head about it: I shall give up reading the papers, and shall stick to my work. . . .

The immediate result on Morris's state of health was a severe attack of gout, which confined him to his room for several days. After that he went to Kelmscott with Ellis and his brother Edgar to fish. Also he was once more house-hunting, Horrington House having been found too small. Morris's first mention of what came to be known as Kelmscott House, Upper Mall, Hammersmith, but was then known as 'The Retreat', occurs in his letter to Jane of 12 March 1878. He says that he has been over it twice, and continues:

if you could be content to live no nearer London than that I cannot help thinking we should do very well there and certainly the open river and the garden at the back are a great advantage: the house is just about big enough for us, and the rooms are mostly pretty: the drawing-room is . . . a great long room facing the river: the drawback to the house is a dreary room at the back: high, darkish, and ugly-windowed: but we should only want it as a subsidiary 'larking-room' and so needn't mind it much when it is duly whitewashed, besides we might keep hens in it; or a pig, or a cow; or let it for a ranters' chapel. The garden is very long and good; it also has a drawback now of being over-looked badly down one half of it, because the wall is lower there; but we might stick up a great high trellis (as the wall would be ours) which would effectively shut out the over-lookers. On the other side there are other gardens and all is quite pretty. If the matter lay with me only I should set about taking the house: for already I have become conscious of the difficulty of getting anything decent: as to such localities as Knightsbridge or Kensington Sq. they are quite beyond our means: a fairish house in such a place means £250 per ann: and they almost always want a premium, which last I cannot pay.

By 18 March Morris has been to see 'The Retreat' for the third time, with Webb, and he writes to Jane to say that this visit had

established the fact that the house was quite dry, and also in very bad repair: there was no smell about; the house could easily be done up at a cost of money, and might be made very beautiful with a touch of my art even the dreary room could be made habitable: You could have a very nice room looking into the garden, and sufficiently to yourself to be comfortable, and there would be a nice room for each of our maidens. The long drawing-room could be made one of the prettiest in London: the garden is really most beautiful and there is a private door at the end leading out into Hog Lane close to the high road.

There is, he says, a walnut tree by the stable, a very fine tulip tree half-way down the lawn, two horse-chestnuts at the end of the lawn and beyond that 'a sort of orchard (many good fruit trees in it) with rough grass (gravel walk all round the garden) then comes the greenhouse & beyond that a kitchen garden with lots of rasp-berries . . . the walls are covered with fruit-trees'. With this letter he enclosed a detailed description of the house, room by room, and a rough plan spread across two pages, showing the newly built Rivercourt Road, with a marginal comment 'those b . . . y new houses'. What would he have said about the arterial motor road that now bisects his garden and makes the back of the house uninhabitable?

Kelmscott House is a plain, three-storeyed, late eighteenth-century building with attics and a lower-ground floor, separated from the river by a tow-path and, until fairly recently, a row of fine elms – now, needless to say, cut down for the sake of the cars. In Morris's time, all the windows facing the river to the south had louvred shutters, giving the house a somewhat French appearance. It was, and still is, a house of considerable charm and character, though not of a character, one would have thought, likely to appeal to Morris. Mackail, in fact, describes it as 'ugly without being mean'. Morris had also looked at a house in Earl's Terrace, Kensington, and considered this a possibility: 'The house is big enough for us,' he says, 'and being not quite modern, is without gross vulgarity; on the other hand it is both scrimpy and dull . . . the garden is just a yard, no more. . . . I don't think either you or I could stand a quite modern house in a district say at Notting Hill: I don't fancy going back among the bugs of Bloomsbury, though 'tis a healthy part & we might do worse: we might as well live at York as at Hampstead for all we should ever see of our friends. . . .' In another letter he says: 'St John's Wood & the Regent's Park I have always hated.'

Meanwhile Rossetti had been making independent inquiries about 'The Retreat' since the previous December. In fact, he had visited it three times in all, and had sent Jane drawings of it by Treffry Dunn. He also reported to her on other possible houses. On 7 December he wrote to say that the garden of 'The Retreat' was 'continually being overflowed by the Thames' – which was certainly untrue. In April he sent her a long list of its disadvantages: the kitchen, he wrote, was so dark that the gas had to be kept on all day, no servants would stay there; the condition of the interior was frightful; the long drawing-room was 'fearful to the eye with blood-red flock paper and a ceiling of blue with gold stars'; the garden was a swamp, and communications were bad.

On 2 April, after much apparent indecision, Morris wrote to Jane to say that he had arranged to take the house, she having reluctantly agreed, on condition that they had three maids. He had also promised her a pony and chaise.

> We can easily house the 3rd maid, and I think 'tis a good idea: the stable could also easily be turned into a gymnasium, and the maidens could have the 2 queer little rooms above for larking rooms. . . . I do think that people will come and see us at the Retreat (fy on the name!) if only for the sake of the garden and river: we will lay ourselves more for company than heretofore. You must remember also that 'tis much nearer the Grange: & I have made Kate Faulkner promise to come & stay with us. So let us hope we shall all grow younger there, my dear.

Rossetti had written again somewhat caustically to say that he hoped Jane would be fit to enjoy the projected visit to Venice and that 'the damps of that sojourn may prepare you somewhat for the Hammer-smith house, which I really do not think a wise choice, if *you* are a person to be at all considered in the matter'.[5]

It had been arranged that Morris should take Jane and his daughters for a tour of the northern Italian cities, but Jane now wrote to say that she felt this would be too much for her. Morris replied on 11 April:

> What is to be said? What would you like best yourself? Will not the babes be dreadfully disappointed not to see Venice? My own feeling about the matter is, that though I should have been glad for work-reasons not to have gone yet now that all arrangements have been made I should indeed like to go.
>
> Nevertheless prudence says that £100 though not nice in itself

is useful: and you know my work cries out for me. Still I should insist on coming out if the Howards are not to bring you home: and once out, why not Venice? and once at Venice, our only way back to Milan will be by the Lombard cities. Summa if the Howards don't come back out I go: if they do you settle it for me yes or no: only don't disappoint my babes too much.

Jenny was at that time seventeen and May sixteen.

Finally Jane agreed to go and Morris went out to Oneglia, only to be crippled by a renewed attack of gout. On reaching Genoa, he had to be lifted and carried from the carriage, but he found himself unable to stand and fainted when they set him down against a wall. He was then carried to a hotel, and looked forward to Venice as 'a hobbler's paradise'. But at Venice he was not much better. Then Jane broke down again – 'a great disappointment to me', as he wrote to Aglaia Coronio. 'We think of staying here about 10 days and then going home by way of Milan, stopping at Padua and Verona at least. I should think Verona right under the mountains would suit us all better than the lagoon – wonderful as the place is in all other respects.' But he was feeling too unwell to get very much out of it. His first view of Garda seems to have moved him more than anything else he saw in Italy. 'What a strange surprise it was', he wrote, 'when it suddenly broke upon me, with such beauty as I never expected to see: for a moment I really thought I had fallen asleep and was dreaming of some strange sea where everything had grown together in perfect accord with wild stories.' At Venice he was so lame that he could only crawl into a few churches and was taken about in a gondola. At Torcello he found it 'a great rest to be among the hedges and the green grass again, and to hear the birds singing; swifts are the only songsters in the city'.

From Verona he wrote to George Howard on 18 May:

As for Verona its general beauty and interest is beyond all praise & I don't know when I have been so moved by any place as I was last night at the look-out from the Arena, but perhaps I am a little disappointed with the architecture as architecture – everything is elegant rather than solemn or poetical. St Marks, Torcello, Fiesole, St Miniato, the Baptistry at Florence: these (but the first above all) are what I have seen in Italy that really move me: the rest that I have seen I must say seem to me very inferior to good French & English Gothic.[6]

At Verona, Santa Anastasia disappointed him, because, as he wrote to Georgie, 'altho' 'tis meant to be exceedingly Gothic & pointed, it is strangely neo-classical in feeling. S. Zeno is not quite what I expected: 'tis a round-arched Gothic church, just as S. Anastasia is a pointed-arched Renaissance one.' He protests that he is 'more alive again, and really very much excited by all I have seen and am seeing'. But one has the feeling that he is preoccupied and only half there.

> Sometimes it all tumbles into a dream and I do not know where I am. Many times I think of the first time I ever went abroad, and to Rouen, and what a wonder of glory that was to me when I first came upon the front of the Cathedral rising above the flower-market. It scarcely happens to me like that now, at least not with man's work, though whiles it does with bits of the great world, like the Garda lake the other day, or unexpected sudden sights of the mountains. Even the inside of St Mark's gave one rather deep satisfaction, and rest for the eyes, than that strange exultation of spirits, which I remember of old in France, and which the mountains give me yet.
>
> I don't think this is wholly because I am grown older, but because I have really had more sympathy with the North from the first in spite of all the faults of its work. Let me confess and be hanged: with the later work of Southern Europe I am quite out of sympathy. In spite of its magnificent power and energy I feel it as an enemy: and this much more in Italy, where there is such a mass of it, than elsewhere. Yes, and even in these magnificent and wonderful towns I rather long for the heap of grey stones with a grey roof that we call a house north-away.

'The infernal furnace-heat' of Italy brought on another attack of gout, and he was only too glad to get away. 'It was such a relief', he writes, 'when the cool mountain breezes woke me out of a doze as the train laboured up the last slopes before the great tunnel; and going through the merry Burgundy country with a fine windy sunny day I got quite merry myself.'

On her return to Turnham Green, Jane wrote to Rosalind Howard on 5 June:

> I shall never forget the pleasant winter we spent with you all. I miss you very much and wish I could have passed another month

in Venice, pray have me sometimes in your thoughts, you are frequently in mine. . . . I dreamt of myself as a monster in many forms, and hated myself whenever I woke up, my dullness and ill-manners seemed unpardonable, pray forgive me and remember me only as someone who loves you. . . . I really do think I owe Jenny's restoration to health to our going to Italy: we consider her quite well now.[7]

Originally, in the previous August, Jane had accepted an invitation to stay with the Howards in Venice for four or five months; this had evidently proved unworkable and she had, in September, taken a house for six months at Oneglia instead, where the Howards evidently joined her with their family.

Morris gained possession of 'The Retreat' at midsummer 1878 and moved in at the end of October. Rossetti gave Jane most of the furniture he had left at Kelmscott: 'all will come in in the new big house', he wrote. Jane replied complaining of all the work to be done and said that she was doing nothing except feeling tired and lying awake at nights, disturbed by the noise of the river steamers.[8] Clearly Morris's patience must have been sorely tried, though the tapestry loom he installed in his bedroom next year and at which he was often at work from half-past five or six in the morning, could not have improved her slumbers. When, in August 1879, Jane went up to Cumberland to stay with the Howards at Naworth, she wrote to Rossetti to say that Kelmscott was out of the question for her that year, as she felt too ill to cope with an extra house and entertain visitors, and that when she saw the doctor again she very much feared that he would send her abroad for the winter. 'Best love to mother, my dear, who I hope is keeping well, or better, I should say', Morris wrote to May on 15 September. As a matter of fact, she was suffering from fainting fits, which occurred whenever she sat up.

Meanwhile, Morris had been to Salisbury with Webb and together they visited Stonehenge and drove up the Avon valley and over to Marlborough, climbing the downs to Oare Hill, 'to a place', Morris wrote to Georgie, 'I remembered coming on as a boy with wonder and pleasure'. However, it rained most of the time and, after visiting Avebury and Silbury, they turned back towards Swindon, Lechlade and Kelmscott. But the roads were flooded and near Inglesham the driver nearly upset them into the ditch, the water coming right over the axles of their wheels. 'We just saved the carriage,' says Morris, 'and after some trouble got into the highroad by Buscot Parsonage . . . so over St John's Bridge and safe to Kelms- cott. But opening the gate there, lo, the water all over the little front garden. . . . The next day was bright and clear between strong showers with a stiff south-west gale: of course we could do nothing but sail and paddle about the floods.' But Morris was in his element. 'Ellis, I hear, is gone to Kelmscott, so I suppose Top is bugging and blaspheming in a boat with him, while he indulges in sonorous British guffaws', Rossetti wrote sourly to Jane at Naworth.[9]

Burne-Jones gives a picture of Morris at this time, at the age of forty-seven, in a letter to Charles Eliot Norton:

> Towards evening Morris came – for it was Georgie's birthday – and you would have found him just as if no time had gone by, only the best talk with him is while he is hungry, for meat makes him sad. So it is wise to delay dinner, and get out of him all you can in walks round the garden. He is unchanged – little grey tips to his curly wig – no more; not quite so stout; not one hair less on his head, buttons more off than formerly, never any necktie – more eager if anything than ever, but about just the same things; a rock of defence to us all, and a castle on the top of it, and a banner on the top of that – before meat – but the banner lowered after that.

But as for Rossetti:

> He has given it all up, and will try no more, nor care much more how it all goes. It's nine years since he came to the Grange – now he goes nowhere and will scarcely see anyone. Four or five times a year I go to spend a ghostly evening with him, and come back heavy-hearted always, sometimes worse than that – it's all past hope or remedy, I think, and his best work has been done – and I don't know how it has all come about.[10]

The decoration of 1 Palace Green was slowly going forward. The series of letters to Rosalind Howard, in which its progress is recorded, are valuable as being among the few examples we have showing Morris actually at work on one of the most important of his decorative schemes.[11] The most elaborate of these was the dining- room, with its 'Cupid and Psyche' panels by Burne-Jones and Walter Crane. On 13 December 1879, Morris writes:

I am bound to ask your pardon for having neglected this job. . . . I am now going to set to work to design ornaments for the mouldings round the pictures, the curved braces of ceiling, and the upper part of the panelling.

Two days later he writes:

Ned and I duly went to Palace Green yesterday and our joint conclusion was that the best hangings for the walls of the boudoir would be the enclosed madder-printed cotton: it brings out the greys of the picture better than anything else: also I think it would make a pretty room with the woodwork painted a light blue-green colour like a starling's egg: and if you wanted drapery about it, we have beautiful stuffs of shades of red that would brighten all up without fighting with the wall-hangings.

Two years later the dining-room is still not finished:

Ned has been doing a great deal to the dining-room pictures and very much improving them: so that the room will be light and pleasant after all, and the pictures very beautiful.

As to the red dove and rose, for a curtain, it will last as long as need be, since the cloth is very strong: I can't answer so decidedly as to the colour; but the colours in it when looked at by themselves you will find rather full than not, 'tis the mixture that makes them look delicate. . . . As to the other version of the dove and rose, if 'tis a smaller sized pattern in green and yellow, you can use it without hesitation; but if it be of the same size as the red, I should scarcely advise it, if the settees are to have heavy wear: you see we made this stuff for curtains and hangings. . . . As to the red silk for curtains, what I am doing (for St James's) is a very fine colour; but you must not forget that I can do pretty well any colour you want, and of sober reds the resources are great. Item, I can do the most ravishing yellows, rather what people call amber: what would you say to a dullish pink shot with amber; like some of these chrysanthemums we see just now ? . . .

The gold and red sunflower is in my board room at Queen Square and I will do my best to hit the due colour.

It was on the site of Kelmscott House at Hammersmith that Morris set the opening chapters of *News from Nowhere*, though there it has become the Gothic house he would doubtless have much preferred.

It was a longish building with its great gable ends turned away from the road and long traceried windows coming rather low down set in the wall that faced us. It was very handsomely built of red brick with a lead roof; and high up above the windows there ran a frieze of figure subjects in baked clay. Everything about the place was handsome and generously solid as to material: and though it was not very large (somewhat smaller than Crosby Hall perhaps), one felt in it that liberating sense of space and freedom which satisfactory architecture always gives to an unanxious man who is in the habit of using his eyes.

Entering Kelmscott House through a generously proportioned front door, set between two Ionic pilasters and with a fanlight above it, one is confronted by the staircase and a rather narrow hall and passage leading through to the garden at the back. There are rooms opening out on each side of the hall. Morris occupied the one on the right as a bedroom and the room on the opposite side as a study and designing room. A small staircase leads up from this room to the first floor of the coach house, where Sydney Cockerell worked when he became Morris's secretary. Morris's study, May Morris tells us, was 'almost frugally bare; no carpets, and no curtains: his writing table in earlier times a plain deal board with trestles, the wall nearly lined with books; just a fine inlaid Italian cabinet in the corner of the study'.[12]

The glory of the house was (and is) the great drawingroom on the first floor, forty feet long, its five windows fronting the river, alive with reflections of the water on sunny days playing across the ceiling. The colour of this room, when Morris had redecorated it, was dusky blue, the cloudy greyblue that he made fashionable. The walls were hung with the 'Bird' fabric, designed this year – 'a perfect blue with pale gleams of colour in the birds and foliage'. There was a blue carpet on the floor and some 'flowerlike' Eastern rugs; the painted cabinet from Red House stood at the west end of the room and on the open hearth was the massive pillared grate Philip Webb had designed for Queen Square, 'while lustre plates above the chimneypiece suggested flushed sunsets and dim moonlit nights beyond the elms'. At right angles to the hearth stood the Red Lion Square settle.

It must have been a room with a peculiar magic of its own, 'a mass of subdued yet glowing colour,' says Mackail, 'into which the eye sank with a sort of active sense of rest'.[13] 'There were no occasional tables, no chairs like featherbeds, no litter of any sort' – Morris used to say that if you wanted to be comfortable, you could go to bed – but, adds May Morris, 'plenty of "quarter-deck" in which to march up and down when discussions got animated and ideas needed exercise.' There was a massive Webb table, covered with a carpet, brass and copper and wrought iron, William de Morgan pots and Damascus plates and bowls, but no pictures.

The staircase and bedrooms, however, were full of Rossetti photographs and sketches. In the lofty dining-room at the back of the house – which Morris had called 'a dreary room' – hung the *Proserpine* and some of Rossetti's large chalk drawings of Jane. One wall was entirely occupied by a white dresser filled with blue china and pewter plates; opposite the fireplace stood a great Italian cypress-wood chest and thereon several pieces of Oriental metalwork and a pair of brass peacocks with jewelled necks. Behind this, says May Morris, 'rose up a carpet spread like a canopy across the ceiling, a specially enchanting piece of South Persian art. Across the lofty window which occupied the whole of the North Wall was placed a long oaken table where we sat at meals as at a dais, each member of the family in his or her own carved chair.'[14]

Morris never succeeded in banishing the eighteenth-century flavour from this room, and though its 'fine cold proportions', his daughter tells us, 'were miles away from his taste and sympathies', he came to recognize its handsomeness. The Eastern influence in its decoration was in strong contrast to the traditionally English fur-nishings at Kelmscott Manor and may have been due to the Persian influence evident in the carpets Morris was beginning to design at this time. But then he had always had the greatest admiration for the textiles of India and, through William de Morgan, for Persian, Syrian and Turkish ceramics. The Middle Eastern Collection of the South Kensington Museum played its part too.

It was, Mackail remarks, a great consolation to Morris, living in London by necessity, 'to think that the water which ran under his windows at Hammersmith had passed the meadows and grey gables of Kelmscott'. Two years later he was to make the journey of 130 miles by water from Hammersmith to Kelmscott with his friends. Even Jane made the trip, not rowing, of course, but gracing the expedition with her presence. It does not seem, however, that she ever got the promised pony and chaise. Morris needed the coach house for his carpet looms and, after their removal to Merton Abbey, for his Sunday evening lectures.

As already mentioned, soon after moving into Kelmscott House, Morris installed a tapestry loom in his bedroom. His diary records his progress on the piece of tapestry he wove there, the 'Cabbage and Vine', as he called it, begun 10 May 1879.[15] (This design is actually a vine and acanthus and includes roses and birds.) On some days he put in as many as nine or ten hours at the loom. A note in the diary reads: 'weather very bad, all this time often dark.' So that on some days he only did two or three hours. But altogether, up to 17 September, he had put in 516½ hours at the loom.

During the winter of 1878–9 weaving in its various forms – on the Jacquard loom at Ormond Yard for figured silks, on the carpet loom for pile carpets, on the tapestry loom for Arras tapestries – took the place of dyeing as Morris's chief interest. At this time, too, he was working regularly as an examiner (of drawings sent in for competition) at the South Kensington Museum's Science and Art Department, where he studied the recently acquired Burgundian and Flemish tapestries and the collection of Persian carpets, textiles and ceramics. 'To us pattern designers,' he said in his lecture 'The History of Pattern-Designing', 'Persia has become a holy land, for there in the process of time our art was perfected, and thence it spread to cover for a while the world, east and west.' Of the great Persian designers he said in another lecture of November 1880, 'Making the Best of It':

In their own way they meant to tell us how the flowers grew in the gardens of Damascus, or how the hunt was up on the plains of Kirman, or how the tulips shone among the grass in the mid-Persian valley, and how their eyes delighted in it all, and what joy they had in life. . . .

But, he goes on, there was little hope for the East now, when Indian carpets were manufactured under the direction of the Government – in prison.

In this case the Government . . . has determined that it will make its wares cheap, whether it makes them nasty or not. Cheap and nasty they are, I assure you; but though they are not the worst of their kind, they would not be made thus if everything did not tend the same way. And it is the same everywhere with all Indian manufactures. . . . In short, their art is dead and the commerce of modern civilization has slain it. What is going on in India is also going on, more or less, all over the East. . . . One thing is certain, that if we don't get to work making our own carpets it will not be very long before we shall find the East fails us: for that last gift, the gift of the sense of harmonious colour, is speedily dying out in the East before the conquests of European rifles and money-bags.

On 13 April 1877 he had written to George Wardle: 'I saw yester-day a piece of *ancient* Persian, time of Shah Abbas (our Elizabeth's time) that fairly threw me on my back. I had no idea such wonders could be done in carpets.'

Morris made an intensive study of Persian work, until he felt that he could begin weaving carpets in the same manner himself. He thereupon set about producing some pile carpet squares on a loom set up in a back attic of Queen Square. But, as production grew, it was transferred to the coach house at Hammersmith, where a number of women were employed as weavers. The 'Hammersmith' carpets produced here had, in some cases, the device of a hammer, a large M, and a waving line for the river woven into their borders. With such examples before him as Persian and Indian work, one can only be astonished at Morris's temerity. Yet in several of his larger carpets, notably the 'Bullerswood' of 1889, commissioned for the Sandersons' house of that name at Chislehurst, Kent, and the 'Clouds', for the Hon. Percy Wyndham of East Knoyle, Morris's natural genius as a designer comes near to rivalling his Persian models.

To begin with, in 1879, he produced a number of hand-knotted woollen pile 'Hammersmith' carpets and rugs of a simpler, less sophisticated design. In May next year he held an exhibition of them and issued a circular in which he said that his aim was 'to make England independent of the East for carpets which may claim to be considered as works of art'. At the same time he produced twenty-four different designs for machine production by the Wilton Royal Carpet Works and the Heckmondwike Manufacturing Co., Yorkshire.

The weaving of figured silk and wool fabrics was continuing at Ormond Yard. The Jacquard loom had been installed there in

1877 and M. Bazin, a Lyons silk weaver, had been engaged to operate it, with the assistance of an old Spitalfields silk weaver. The 'Willow' brocade and a number of furnishing silks, including the 'Flower Garden', and the 'Dove and Rose' silk and wool double cloth, both of 1879, were woven under Morris's supervision, though some damasks and the heavier woollen fabrics continued to be woven by outside firms. 'It was always somewhat pathetic', writes May Morris, 'to watch the weavers at work here on their hand-looms – old men from Spitalfields who had been prosperous once and had been through bad times, saddened by the changes in industrial life that with its scurry and thrusting aside had passed them by.'

It was characteristic of Morris to have engaged such men, just as he had taught himself the lost art of tapestry weaving from an old French book in the *Arts et Métiers* series published before the Revolution. But, of course, he had no choice, hand-weaving having become obsolete in England since the Industrial Revolution and Cartwright's power-loom, patented in the same year as Watt's steam-engine. As for tapestry, the art had been lost in England since the closing of the Mortlake Royal Tapestry Works early in the eighteenth century, and there was no working model at hand to which he could refer.

Morris had, indeed, seen the vertical loom, the *hautelisse*, at work at the Gobelins factory but he abominated the sort of work being produced there, with its copying of oil paintings. This, as he had said in his lecture 'The Lesser Arts of Life' (to be distinguished from the earlier lecture on 'The Lesser Arts') changed tapestry weaving from a fine art to a mere 'upholsterer's toy', for 'it would be a mild word to say that what they make is worthless; it is more than that; it has a corrupting and deadening influence upon all the Lesser Arts of France . . . a more idiotic waste of human labour and skill it is impossible to conceive. There is another branch of the same stupidity, differing slightly in technique, at Beauvais; and the little town of Aubusson in mid-France has a decaying commercial industry of the like rubbish.' Thus tapestry was another art that 'must be spoken of in the past tense', for when the Royal Tapestry Works at Windsor opened they produced work in imitation of Gobelins.

But, with the examples of Burgundy and Flanders in the late fifteenth century before him, Morris was determined that this lost art should be revived. There was nothing to prevent anyone from doing it, he said, 'since the technique is easy to the last degree'. A few small verdure pieces were woven at Queen Square, but tapestry weaving, as the firm's most ambitious activity, was not fully developed until the move to Merton Abbey in 1881.

CHAPTER NINE

Architecture and the Arts of Life

As HE WAS driving a party of friends from Kelmscott to stay with Cormell Price in his tower at Broadway in the Cotswolds on 4 September 1876, the sight of Burford Church being pulled down, writes May Morris, 'set my father to making notes for a letter of appeal for some united action' – that is, to preserve what was still left of English medieval ecclesiastical architecture. Two years before, however, one finds Morris's signature among others, including Webb, Gilbert Scott, Basil Champneys, Rossetti, Madox Brown, Holman Hunt, Charles Keene etc., protesting against the proposed demolition and rebuilding of the tower and the east end of Hamp/stead parish church.

During the Victorian age, the strange practice had grown up of rebuilding cathedrals and parish churches all over England in order to make them uniform in style. This practice was known as restoration. Its instigators were the Cambridge Camden Society, who believed that no building should remain a collection of different styles, which our cathedrals and parish churches, as they had grown up over the centuries, obviously were, but should all be restored to one style of Gothic – preferably Early English, as being the most pure. Gilbert Scott, who undertook the lion's share of this work, with an energy and thoroughness typical of his age, did not proceed by conjecture; when doing away with a Perpendicular window, for instance, he followed the style of the fragments of Early English fabric he found embedded in the wall. 'That', he would say, 'is what the church originally looked like.' The result was, of course, in most cases, no more than a lifeless copy of the original style. But it was done conscientiously and with the highest principles.

At Oxford, with sublime self/confidence, Scott pulled down the whole of the east end of the cathedral and rebuilt it in the Norman style, because he knew that it must have once been Norman. The wonder is that he did not pull down Westminster Abbey and rebuild it in the Norman style, too. Nevertheless, Scott worshipped Pugin and loved Gothic. Unfortunately his love was heavy/handed and often vulgar in expression – not always, however, as witness the magnificent roof of the chapter/house at Westminster.

Most people would take this for genuine medieval work, though they might well be puzzled and disappointed by the lifeless and anaemic quality of the north porch, which is Scott and Pearson at their very worst. The trouble was, as usual, the Victorian vice of over-production: Scott undertook far too much. A list published in *The Builder* in 1878, gives the names of over 730 buildings with which he was concerned after 1847. It includes 39 cathedrals and minsters, 476 churches, 25 schools, 23 parsonages, 43 mansions, 26 public buildings, 58 monumental works and 25 colleges or college chapels; but the list is said to be incomplete.[1]

Nevertheless it should be recognized that had it not been for Scott and his like, disastrous as their efforts often were, there would have been little enough medieval architecture left in England for Morris and his Society for the Protection of Ancient Buildings to protect. In many cases medieval churches, neglected for centuries, were in an advanced state of decay and would literally have fallen down. But this, of course, does not justify the wholesale destruction of perfectly sound late medieval work, and there are less drastic ways of restoring, or preserving, an ancient building.

It was not till his visit to Tewkesbury in the spring of 1877, where he witnessed with indignation the same destruction going on as he had seen at Burford, that Morris wrote the vigorous letter to the *Athenaeum* of 5 March that led to the formation of SPAB – or, as it came to be familiarly known, Anti-Scrape, from the current practice of scraping all the weathering off the stonework of churches and leaving them characterless and smooth, a practice on a par with denuding their interiors of the original fittings in favour of shiny pitch-pine pews, encaustic tiles and glass in hard, glaring colours. Since that time, of course, many Victorian churches have mellowed and have a period charm of their own, though they tend on the whole to be extremely depressing. Morris wrote:

My eye just now caught the word 'restoration' in the morning paper, and, on looking closer, I saw that this time it is nothing less than the minster of Tewkesbury that is to be destroyed by Sir Gilbert Scott. Is it altogether too late to do something to save it – it and whatever else of beautiful or historical is still left us on the sites of the ancient buildings we were once so famous for? Would it not be of some use once for all, and with the least possible delay, to set on foot an association for the purposes of watching

195

over and protecting these relics, which, scanty as they are now become, are still wonderful treasures, all the more priceless in this age of the world, when the newly-invented study of living history is the chief joy of so many of our lives?

Your paper has so steadily and courageously opposed itself to those acts of barbarism which the modern architect, parson, and squire call 'restoration', that it would be waste of words to enlarge here on the ruin that has been wrought by their hands; but, for the saving of what is left, I think I may write a word of encourage-ment, and say that you by no means stand alone in the matter, and that there are many thoughtful people who would be glad to sacrifice time, money, and comfort in defence of those ancient monuments: besides, though I admit that the architects are, with very few exceptions, hopeless, because interest, habit, and ignorance blind them, and that the clergy are hopeless, because their order, habit, and an ignorance yet grosser, blind them; still there must be many people whose ignorance is accidental rather than inveterate, whose good sense could surely be touched if it were clearly put to them that they were destroying what they, or, more surely still, their sons and sons' sons, would one day fervently long for, and which no wealth or energy could ever buy for them.

In this letter, except for the gratuitous insult to the clergy in general, may perhaps be seen the moderating influence of Webb and Faulkner.

Morris followed this up with a letter in reply to Sir Edmund Lachmere, who had written to say that the purpose of the work going on at Tewkesbury was to restore it to 'its former state' – that is, to pull down later additions and rebuild them in the style of the earlier parts of the minster. Morris pointed out in the manifesto he wrote for SPAB that this was simply forgery, and stripped the building so treated of its life. Other ages had altered and added to our cathedrals and larger churches, but the effect was never disastrous, as it was with the Victorians, since every age up to the nineteenth century had had its own architectural style, as an expression of its needs and way of life. The Victorian age alone had no style of its own. So he concluded his second letter to the *Athenaeum* on 4 April 1877 by saying:

Prudence, we submit, should enlist the public on our side, for architecture is at present in a wholly experimental condition, as I suppose I need scarcely call on London streets to witness; and yet, such is the headlong rashness of our architects, that they have for the last thirty years made the priceless relics of medieval art and history mere blocks for their experiments; experiments which some of them must regret heartily, and sorely wish to 'restore'.

In my belief there is no remedy for the spreading of this disease but for the public to make up its mind to put up with 'compara-tively recent' incongruities in old churches and other public buildings, and to be content with keeping them weather-tight; and if they have any doubts about the stability of the fabric, to call in an engineer to see to it, and let iron ties, and the like, do what they can. For my part, I cannot help thinking that they will soon find it easy to bear the absence of stained glass, and shiny tiles, and varnished deal roofs, and all the various upholsteries with the help of which our architects and clergy have striven so hard to 'replace' our ancient buildings in their 'former state', or at any rate, in some 'former state' imagined by themselves to be super-excellent.

On the face of it this is a somewhat surprising letter coming from the head of a firm itself specializing in stained glass and ecclesiastical upholstery, but from this time on Morris made it a principle not to accept commissions for stained-glass windows in the case of ancient churches. Burne-Jones's windows of 1878 for Salisbury Cathedral were, in fact, the last order of this nature accepted by Morris & Co. The windows for Birmingham Cathedral done ten years later, were undertaken on the grounds that St Philip's is an eighteenth-century church; the same argument applied to the St Peter's, Vere Street, windows of 1880. But from its earliest days, the firm's decorations had mostly been confined to modern churches.

The first annual meeting of SPAB was held on 21 June 1878. The report of the meeting may be found in the first volume of May Morris's *William Morris: Artist, Writer, Socialist*. Among the original members of the committee were Thomas Carlyle, James Bryce, Sir John Lubbock, Lord Houghton, Aldis Wright, Leslie Stephen, Mark Pattison, Coventry Patmore, Charles Keene, Holman Hunt and Edward Burne-Jones. The committee meetings were held at first in the Oxford Street showrooms of Morris & Co, with Morris himself as secretary. His annual address to the society, however, was given at Queen Square. By November 1878 the society had an office at 9 Buckingham Street, in the Strand, and Newman Marks became secretary for a few years. It was left to Morris himself to visit the churches and other buildings due for restoration, which was, as Lethaby observes, 'perhaps hardly tactful'. At one cathedral, having been shown some commercial work in the choir stalls, he remarked: 'Why, I could carve them better with my teeth!' On another occasion, when a canon of another cathedral was pointing out the 'improvements' he wanted done, Morris remarked cuttingly: 'The place is not good enough for you.' At other times he was known to shake his fist in the faces of astonished vicars, whose great pride was their newly decorated and restored parish church.

When Carlyle accepted membership in the society, he made a special allusion to Wren's City churches, whose existence was threatened, as 'marvellous works, the like of which we shall never see again'. Morris had to read this out at the first public meeting. 'You may imagine that he didn't relish it,' comments William de Morgan, who recounts the incident, 'and one heard it in the way he read it – I fancy he added mentally, "And a good job too!"' Never theless, with all his dislike of Renaissance architecture, the letter Morris wrote to *The Times* of 17 April 1878, is a fair and balanced estimate of the beauty and uniqueness of Wren's churches, though he managed to combine it with a disparaging remark about St Paul's, which, he says,

is only one of a class of buildings common on the Continent – imitations of St Peter's, Rome. . . . The Continent possesses nothing in the least resembling our City churches, and the fact that they are all found in such close proximity to one another only serves to make them the more valuable for purposes of study. . . . Surely an opulent city, the capital of the commercial world, can afford some small sacrifice to spare these beautiful buildings the little plots of ground upon which they stand. Is it absolutely necessary that every scrap of space in the City should be devoted to money-making, and are religion, sacred memories, recollections of the great dead, memorials of the past, works of England's greatest architect, to be banished from this wealthy City?

Since then what Morris called in an earlier passage of this letter 'the Mammonworship and want of taste of this great city' has allowed another characterless office-block to be erected which partially obscures the west front of St Paul's itself!

In his address to the twelfth annual meeting of the society on 3 July 1889, Morris reminded them that: 'the greatest side of art is the art of daily life which historical buildings represent . . . what romance means is the capacity for a true conception of history, for making the past part of the present'. One can see the force of this in Morris's sensitive and loving treatment of the little church of Inglesham, standing by the river not far from Lechlade, where the ancient stonework has been treated with respect and the old oak box pews and screen retained. One sees it again at Blythburgh, a splendid Suffolk church Morris visited for S P A B, and, indeed, in the more recent restoration of the stonework at Norwich Cathedral, Westminster Abbey and the Divinity Schools at Oxford. The battle is now engaged to preserve the best of Victorian architecture, which, beside the self-effacing monotony of the modern style, often appears boldly self-confident and imaginative.

Morris gave his first public lecture on 4 December 1877 to the Trades' Guild of Learning, 'in a dismal hole near Oxford Street', as he wrote to Jane. This was 'The Decorative Arts: Their Relation to Modern Life and Progress', published in *Hopes and Fears for Art* (1882) as 'The Lesser Arts'. At the end of November he had written to Jenny: 'I went with Wardle to the place, & read Robinson Crusoe to him to see if I could make my voice heard: which I found easy to be done: yet I can't help feeling a little nervous at having to face my fellow beings in public. . . .'

'The Lesser Arts' contains the essence of all that Morris was to say in his later lectures and is an important statement of his standpoint in general. It is the love of luxury and show that has ruined the arts since the Renaissance, he says. We must return, therefore, to the traditional yeoman's house and the humble village church for the best of English decorative art, which is

never coarse, though often rude enough, sweet, natural, and un-affected, an art of peasants rather than of merchant princes or courtiers, it must be a hard heart, I think, that does not love it. . . . A peasant art, I say, and it clung fast to the life of the people, and still lived among the cottagers and yeomen in many parts of the country while the big houses were being built 'French and fine': still lived also in many a quaint pattern of loom and printing-block, and embroiderer's needle, while overseas stupid pomp had extinguished all nature and freedom, and art was become, in France especially, the mere expression of that successful and exultant rascality which in the flesh no long time afterwards went down into the pit for ever.

It is just this emphasis on peasant crafts that determined the whole direction of the later Arts and Crafts movement, though there is certainly nothing primitive or peasant-like in Morris's own designs, nor in the sumptuous fabrics produced by his firm. But basically, it was a call for a return to functional simplicity in 'the arts of life', a desire to get back to such fundamentals as fitness for use, to a respect for materials, and Morris thought that this would follow from substituting production for use for production for profit.

In order to produce natural, unaffected work, men had once more to begin living natural, unaffected lives.

To my mind it is only here and there (out of the kitchen) that you can find in a well-to-do house things that are of any use at all: as a rule all the decoration (so called) that has got there is there for the sake of show, not because anyone likes it. I repeat, this stupidity goes through all classes of society: the silk curtains in my lord's drawing-room are no more a matter of art to him than the powder in his footman's hair; the kitchen in a country farm-house is most commonly a pleasant and home-like place, the parlour dreary and useless.

Simplicity of life, begetting simplicity of taste, that is, a love for sweet and lofty things, is of all matters most necessary for the birth of the new and better art we crave for: simplicity everywhere, in the palace as well as in the cottage . . .

But with simplicity must go cleanliness and decency everywhere. Instead, what do we get nowadays? Morris continues

in the defacements of our big towns by all that commerce brings with it, who heeds it? who tries to control their squalor and hideousness? there is nothing but thoughtlessness and recklessness in the matter. . . .

Is money to be gathered? cut down the pleasant trees among the houses, pull down ancient and venerable buildings for the money that a few square yards of London dirt will fetch; blacken rivers, hide the sun and poison the air with smoke and worse, and it's nobody's business to see to it or mend it: that is all that modern commerce, the counting-house forgetful of the workshop, will do for us herein. . . . unless people care about carrying on their business without making the world hideous, how can they care about Art ? . . .

Sirs, I believe that art has such sympathy with cheerful freedom, open-heartedness and reality, so much she sickens under selfish-ness and luxury, that she will not live thus isolated and exclusive. I will go further than this and say that on such terms I do not wish her to live. . . .

I do not want art for a few, any more than education for a few, or freedom for a few.

No, rather than art should live this poor thin life among a few exceptional men, despising those beneath them for an ignorance for which they themselves are responsible, for a brutality that they will not struggle with – rather than this, I would that the world should indeed sweep away all art for awhile. . . .

Here, of course, we have the incipient Marxist rather than the director of Morris & Co. whose business it was 'to minister to the swinish luxury of the rich'. But this was to be the burden of all his lectures.

If one thinks of what Morris called, in a subsequent lecture, the 'simply blackguardly' houses being built in his time for wealthy industrialists ('ignorant, purse-proud digesting machines') and, at the other extreme, of the 'sweltering dog-holes' and grim barracks built for the poor, many of which still survive, one can agree with him, even though one is not prepared to sweep away the entire achievement of the eighteenth century, that golden age of English craftsmanship, in favour of cottage crafts, simply because it expressed the classical taste of a dominant aristocracy. But Morris maintained that this was merely an artificial taste taken at second-hand from Greek and Roman civilization and applied mechanically from the pattern books. This he stigmatized as 'barren classicalism'. It is at least a point of view one can respect when we relate it to Morris's aim to take up the tradition of English design before it succumbed to Continental influences under the Tudors.

Even as he wrote, a great new school of painting was flourishing in France. Morris seems to have been unaware of it, and he doubt-less agreed with Rossetti, who referred in a letter of February 1881 to 'a French idiot named Manet, who certainly must be the greatest and most uncritical ass who ever lived'.[2] Nor is there any doubt about the enormous popularity of English subject painting at this time, when long queues of ordinary people waited to see such works as *The Doctor* and *The Casual Ward* by Luke Fildes, or Frith's *Paddington Station* and *Derby Day* – works which can profitably be compared to the officially sponsored art in the Soviet Union today. This, after all, was popular art: there is no question of it being 'art for the few', nor was it an art of escape, like the over-ripe con-temporary paintings of Burne-Jones and Rossetti, for its subject matter was frequently taken from working-class life.

But then Morris's emotional attachment to Ned prevented him from judging his work by the critical standards he so ruthlessly applied to others. In any case, he was more interested in Burne-Jones's more purely decorative work, in which he must be ranked as a master. There is an undeniable grandeur in the *Briar Rose* sequence at Buscot, an absolute mastery of lyrical design in the Rounton Grange 'Romaunt of the Rose' embroidery panel and in the Jesus College Chapel windows – to mention only these – and surely that is enough for one man. Morris gave expression to this in the lecture he delivered on the Pre-Raphaelite collection at Birmingham on 24 October 1891, when he said that Burne-Jones

> added [to the movement] the element of *perfect* ornamentation, the completely decorative side of the Art. In fact, when the pre-Raphaelite School was completed by this representative man, it then became apparent that what pre-Raphaelitism was, was suffici-ently indicated by its name. That is to say, it was the continuation of the art that had been current throughout Europe before Raphael marked the completion of the period when art became academical, i.e., inorganic; the so-called renaissance.

Morris would seldom criticize a contemporary and was impatient of the refinements of art criticism as such. 'What's all the damned fuss about ?' he is reported as saying, 'A picture's either jolly well painted or it's not, and that's all there is to it.' The fact is, he was not really interested in painting for its own sake, and though, his daughter tells us, he loved Van Eyck and Holbein, he would cheer-fully have sacrificed the entire National Gallery collection for the sake of the medieval illuminated manuscripts in the British Museum. As he said in his lecture of 13 November 1880 to the Trades' Guild of Learning, 'Hints on House Decoration', subsequently called 'Making the Best of It': 'I must confess that I should hold my peace on all matters concerned with the arts if I had not a lurking hope to stir up both others and myself to discontent with and rebellion against things as they are.' Impressionism to Morris probably meant Whistler, to whom he seems to be referring when he wrote of 'clever and gifted men of the present day who are prepared to sustain as a theory that art has no function but the display of clever executive qualities, and that one subject is as good as another'. Such pictures, he says, seem 'intended to convey the impression on a very short-sighted person of divers ugly incidents seen through the medium of a London fog'.

Again, in the preface he wrote to *Arts and Crafts Essays* in 1893, he said: 'For the 18th century was quite unconscious of its tendency towards ugliness and nullity, whereas the modern "Impressionists" loudly proclaim their enmity to beauty, and are no more unconscious of their aims than the artists of the revival are of their longing to link themselves to the traditional art of the past.' And yet how affected and artificial Rossetti and Burne-Jones seem today beside such a painting as Whistler's *Little White Girl*! It is astonishing that this should have been painted in 1864, when Pre-Raphaelite medieval-ism was in full flood. But then Whistler had lived and worked in Paris.

Morris's dislike of the Renaissance was not merely irrational pre-judice. He did not deny 'the splendid outburst of genius' it repre-sented, but he regarded this as the climax of centuries of medieval art. In so far as it originated in an attempt to revive the arts of Greece and Rome he said that it was merely 'pedantic imitation'. The same charge might be levelled with some justice against many of his own designs, which largely derived from medieval, Tudor and Persian work. He conveniently disregards the fact that the achievements of the medieval glass-painter, mason, wood-carver and embroiderer were basically an expression of his religious faith and that their beauty was not merely the outcome of pleasure in the work as such. After all, the men who built the cathedrals were not humble, anonymous masons, but great architects with armies of masons working under them. It is true that while the cathedrals were built to the glory of God, the palaces of the Renaissance were built to glorify the wealth and power of individual men. In England particularly the great houses of the sixteenth century were built out of the ruin of the abbeys and priories and, as such, could be regarded as expressions of 'exultant rascality', but then Morris was only con/ cerned with the architectural aspect of the great medieval religious foundations and their embodiment of history. When he spoke of 'exultant rascality' he was not thinking so much of the dissolution of the monasteries under Henry VIII and Thomas Cromwell, and the great houses that rose out of their ruins, in which many of the traditions of medieval craftsmanship were continued, but of the Palladian mansions of the eighteenth century built by the great landowners and merchants, who saw themselves as the inheritors of Roman civilization.

In his lecture 'The Prospects of Architecture', delivered in March 1880, Morris contrasts the Victorian jerry/built house with the average yeoman's cottage built some two hundred years ago in the Cotswold villages. It is these, not the 'so/called Queen Anne ones or the distinctively Georgian' that represented to him the ideal type of small English house. As for the houses of the eighteenth century, he admits in his lecture, 'Making the Best of It', that 'they are built solidly and conscientiously at least, and if they have little or no beauty, yet they have a certain commonsense and convenience about them'. His main objection to them is that they are difficult to decorate, 'especially for those who have any leaning towards romance, because they still have some style left in them which one cannot ignore. . . .' 'Still,' he concludes, 'they are at the worst not aggressively ugly or base, and it is possible to live in them without serious disturbance to our work or thought, so that by force of con/ trast they have become bright spots in the prevailing darkness of ugliness that has covered all modern life.'

The decorative schemes outlined in this lecture point forward to the kind of thing developed by Ambrose Heal in the 1920s – that is, 'simple tints', light oak woodwork, bare floors with a rug or two. For Morris, 'the real meaning of the arts' was always 'the expression of reverence for nature, and the crown of nature, the life of man upon the earth'.

On 10 August 1880 he wrote to Georgie Burne/Jones:

By the way, I give my third lecture to the Trade Guild of Learning in October ['Making the Best of It']; that will be my autumn work, writing it, if I have any quiet time away from home. Also I have promised to lecture next March at the London Institute –

subject, the prospects of Architecture in modern civilization. I will be as serious as I can over them, and when I have these two last done, I think of making a book of the lot, as it will be about what I have to say on the subject, which still seems to me the most serious one that a man can think of; for 'tis no less than the chances of a calm, dignified, and therefore happy life for the mass of mankind.

In 'The Prospects of Architecture in Modern Civilization', Morris once again reminded his audience of what happens when some large old house is pulled down 'to be turned into ready money, and is sold to A, who lets it to B, who is going to build houses on it which he will sell to C, who will let them to D and the other letters of the alphabet'. The first thing that usually happens on this building site is that all the trees are cut down. Morris was one of the first to protest against this indiscriminate destruction. In 'Making the Best of It' he had said: 'in our part of the world few indeed have any mercy upon the one thing necessary for decent life in a town, its trees; till we have come to this, that one trembles at the very sound of an axe as one sits at one's work at home'. He admits that the difficulties involved in dealing with the problem of 'the devouring hideousness and squalor of our great towns, and especially London' is 'one far too huge and wide-spreading to be grappled with by private or semi-private efforts only'. It is in such conclusions that he reached out to the town planning of the twentieth century.

As a rule, when decorating large houses, Morris would use oak wainscotting for the lower walls and Arras tapestry above – wall-paper he regarded as a very poor substitute for tapestry or printed cotton hangings. His name is now chiefly associated with wall-papers because most people cannot afford tapestry and cannot decorate their homes on the scale of Hardwick or Hampton Court. But more and more, Morris came to emphasize the need for the utmost simplicity in decoration, or even no decoration at all, preferring 'a sanded floor and whitewashed walls, and the green trees and flowering meads and living waters outside', as he puts it in 'The Prospects of Architecture'. And when he looked into the future, as in his talk 'Textile Fabrics' of July 1884 at the International Health Exhibition, he said: 'I do not conceive to myself of there being a very great quantity of art of any kind, certainly not of ornament, apart from the purely intellectual arts. . . . Looking forward from out of the farrago of rubbish with which we are now surrounded [I can] chiefly see possible negative virtues in the externals of our household goods; can see them never shabby, never pretentious, or ungenerous, natural and reasonable always: beautiful also, but more because they are natural and reasonable, then because we have set about to make them beautiful' – which is extraordinarily perceptive and anticipates the functionalism of our own time.

As a matter of fact, however, the decorative schemes that were being carried out by Oscar Wilde in 1884, with the assistance of Whistler and E. W. Godwin, in his house in Tite Street, Chelsea, were far more revolutionary, and anticipated modern taste – or what used to be modern taste until the recent Victorian revival – more than anything produced by Morris & Co. In his study the walls were pale primrose and the woodwork red. Another room had a blue ceiling, yellow walls and white furniture. 'The prevailing note of the dining-room', Vyvyan Holland tells us in his *Oscar Wilde: A Pictorial Biography*, 'was white, blending pale yellow with pale blue, the carpet and dining-room chairs being white, the walls white picked out with blue and the sideboard and other furniture yellow.' In such colour schemes one can see a reflection of the simplicity of Japanese taste.

Wilde was lecturing on interior decoration all over the country at the same time as Morris. On 16 May 1885 he wrote to W. A. S. Benson:

I don't at all agree with you about the decorative value of Morris's wallpapers. They seem to me often deficient in real beauty of colour. . . . Then as regards design, he is far more successful with those designs which are meant for textures which hang in folds, than for those which have to be seen flat on a stretched material. . . . I am surprised to find we are at such variance on the question of the value of pure colour on the walls of a room. . . . I have seen far more rooms spoiled by wallpapers than anything else: when everything is covered with a design the room is restless and the eye disturbed. . . . My eye requires in a room a resting-place of pure colour, and I prefer to keep design for more delicate materials than papers . . . and the only papers I use now are the Japanese gold ones . . . with these and with colour in oil and distemper a lovely house can be made. . . . Anybody with a real artistic sense must see the value and repose of pure colour.

He concludes by hoping that wallpapers 'will be used much less frequently than they are, that Morris will devote his time, as I think he is doing, to textile fabrics, their dyes and their designs. . . .'[3]

It is interesting to contrast Morris's expressed views about architecture with the kind of houses Philip Webb was building at this time and which Morris was decorating. These show a distinct leaning towards a Queen Anne or neo-Georgian style. As Mr Brandon-Jones points out, as well as a Gothic mansion like 1 Palace Green, Webb built Smeaton Manor for Sir Lowthian Bell's son-in-law, Major Goodman, in 1877: 'a symmetrical, red brick building with white painted sashes of Georgian proportions', anticipating by more than ten years Norman Shaw's 170 Queen's Gate, which 'set the fashion for the English Renaissance revival'. The main rooms of Smeaton Manor had white-painted panelling and simple fireplaces 'rather like those of an eighteenth-century builder'.[4] Between 1877 and 1886, Webb was building his masterpiece, Clouds, near East Knoyle (where Wren was born), about twenty miles from Salisbury, for the Hon. Percy Wyndham. Mrs Wyndham was one of the great political hostesses of the period. Her house was frequented by the Balfours, the Curzons, the Londonderrys and the Tenants, and among her friends were Morris, Burne-Jones, Leighton, Wilfrid Scawen Blunt and Watts. The interior decoration of Clouds was very different from either 'the rather gloomy richness' of Palace Green of ten years before or Rounton Grange of 1872. 'In the Great Hall the elements of construction formed the basis of the design. Unstained roof-timbers and gallery panelling were supported on Purbeck Marble shafts and combined with elegant white painted joinery and door-casings. Colour was introduced in limited quantities by the use of Morris tapestry and carpets.'[5] The great Clouds carpet, now in the Regent House, Cambridge, is predominantly pale cloudy blue and white. 'The drawing-room was all white with a delicately modelled ceiling and frieze in plaster, the dining-room was also given a fine plaster ceiling, but the walls were panelled in oak and there was an antique marbled fire-place of Italian design.'[6] 'It was,' concludes Brandon-Jones, 'the unusual combination of an extremely fine finish with a completely unconventional approach that made Webb's work unique.'[7]

Like Morris, Webb was drawn to the austere and the gaunt. He admired his friend Bentley's Westminster Cathedral and wished that the interior could be whitewashed and left without the overlay of marble and gilding. He also admired the Ashmolean at Oxford. But Morris appears to have been considerably more flexible in practice than in theory. For the decorations carried out at St James's Palace in 1881, at the time he was delivering the lectures included in *Hopes and Fears for Art*, he used wallpapers by Walter Crane and Bruce Talbert, both of which included *amorini* – that is, a classical motive – as part of their design. But whereas Webb reacted against Street's medievalism, Morris, in 'The Revival of Architecture', included in the posthumous collection *Architecture, Industry and Wealth*, described his Gothic Law Courts in the Strand as 'the last attempt we are likely to see of producing anything reasonable or beautiful for that use'. In this, of course, he followed Pugin and Ruskin, though by this time Ruskin had turned against the Gothic Revival.

In his lecture 'Gothic Architecture' of 1889 Morris states once more that if we are ever to have architecture at all, we must take up the thread of living tradition from where the medieval builders left it, 'because that Gothic Architecture is the most completely organic form of the Art which the world has seen . . . all the former developments tended thitherward, and to ignore this fact and attempt to catch up the thread before that point was reached, would be a mere piece of artificiality, betokening not a new birth, but a corruption into mere whim of the ancient traditions'. He sees Roman building as engineering rather than architecture, though he admits that 'its massive and simple dignity is a wonderful contrast to the horrible and restless nightmare of modern engineering. . . .' He hastens to add, however, that he only mentions Roman architecture 'because of the abuse of it which took place in later times and has even lasted into our own antiarchitectural days; and because it is necessary to point out that it has not got the qualities essential to making it a foundation for any possible new birth of the arts', even though 'the first obscure beginning of Gothic or organic Architecture' can be seen in Diocletian's palace at Spalato, where 'the rebel, Change, first showed in Roman art'.

While no hard and fast distinction can be made between architecture and engineering – the cathedrals themselves were, after all, engineering in stone – Morris shows in this lecture that he is by no means insensitive to Roman art, though he says: 'well as the Roman ornament is executed in all important works, one almost wishes it were less well executed, so that some mystery might be added to its florid handsomeness'. Greek architecture he criticized for its 'pedantic perfection', a perfection that could not be maintained, 'so that as Greek energy began to fall back from its high-water mark, the demand for absolute perfection became rather a de-mand for absolute plausibility, which speedily dragged the architectural arts into mere Academicism'. Here again he is follow-ing Ruskin.

It is in the thirteenth-century Gothic of Salisbury Cathedral that we are invited to see 'a complete and logical style with no longer anything to apologize for, claiming homage from the intellect, as well as the imagination of men; the developed Gothic which has shaken off the trammels of Byzantium as well as of Rome. . . . All over the intelligent world was spread this bright, glittering joyous art, which had now reached its acme of elegance and beauty.' As far as the 'freedom' of the medieval sculptor was concerned, the icono-graphy of thirteenth-century religious art was fairly rigidly controlled. The representation of a sacred image with the wrong attributes could lead to a charge of heresy. The medieval mason or sculptor was only really free to let himself go with the gargoyles, misericords and roof bosses.[8]

Morris relates the development of Gothic in England to the growth of the craft guilds and the free towns. But he omits to add that the beginning of the Hundred Years War in France in 1337 (which appears in the pages of Froissart as a chivalric romance) resulted in a cessation of church and cathedral building in favour of castles and prisons, the virtual closing down of the workshops and the impressment of masons everywhere into military service, while plague, famine and battle all but decimated the population. It was not till the mid-fifteenth century that sculptors and stone-cutters were again free to pursue their art, when the building of churches and cathedrals was resumed.[9]

In England the situation was somewhat different for in spite of the war with France and the Black Death, the reigns of Edward III and Richard II stand out as a golden age of medieval crafts-manship before the chaos and misery of the Wars of the Roses in the fifteenth century. Meanwhile, as Morris points out, commercialism and bureaucracy were steadily growing: 'Society was preparing for a complete recasting of its elements: the Medieval Society of Status was in process of transition into the modern Society of Contract. . . .

Henceforth the past was to be our present, and the blankness of its dead wall was to shut out the future from us.' That is, architects and sculptors had begun to look back to Rome for their models; of St Paul's he says, 'I have found it difficult to put myself in the frame of mind which could accept such a work as a substitute for even the latest and worst Gothic building. Such taste seemed to me like the taste of a man who should prefer his lady-love bald.'

But, though Morris remained loyal to his old master, Street, he was no friend of the Gothic Revival. Writing in this same lecture 'Gothic Architecture', he says, 'The greater part of what we now call architecture is but an imitation of an imitation of an imitation, the result of a tradition of dull respectability, or of foolish whims without root or growth in them.' Morris wanted an architectural style which was 'the growth of our own times, but connected with all history' – vague enough, but the sort of eclecticism, perhaps, that we find in Webb's houses.[10] In fact, he was in something of a quandary, because although he held that modern architecture should be founded on Gothic, he said that it should not imitate it. Although such men as Butterfield, Pearson, Sedding, Waterhouse and Burges were all using Gothic creatively and so, presumably, doing what Morris advocated, he does not mention them. Nor does he mention the pleasant Gothic variations of Voysey; nor, again, that really revolutionary example of domestic architecture in his time, the plain white Japanese-style house that Godwin built for Whistler in Tite Street, Chelsea – infinitely more forward-looking than the outsize 'Queen Anne' fantasies of Norman Shaw.

But when, after 'the ridiculous travesties of Gothic buildings' of the earlier part of the century, Morris says, a genuine study of medieval architecture began, it was realized that the nineteenth century had too little in common with the finest Gothic – that of the early fourteenth century – to make it possible to link one with the other, so architects turned to Perpendicular as a 'more workaday' style, and then even to the late sixteenth and the first half of the seventeenth centuries – 'which in England at least (as in literature so in art) had retained some of the beauty and fitness of the palmy days of Gothic amidst the conceits, artificialities, and euphemism of the time of Elizabeth and James the First . . . but still a new and living style would not come'.

Under the general condemnation of 'the horrible and restless nightmare of modern engineering' Morris included, of course, such revolutionary structures of iron and glass as the railway stations that were being built at this time – Brunel's Paddington Station and Manchester Central of 1876–9, whose iron vault was higher than the vault of Canterbury Cathedral and though weighing 2,400 tons and with a span of 210 feet, appears almost diaphanous. Or, for that matter, the astounding Forth Bridge. While the Victorian architect returned to Gothic and classic forms, the Victorian engineer got on with the job of creating buildings that were an expression of the new age of steam and power – though Gilbert Scott still masked the functional part of St Pancras, the actual train shed, with the vast romantic Gothic pile of his hotel. The same thing occurred at other stations, for example at Liverpool Street, with its 'Romanesque' front. But it was from the daring structures of the Victorian engineers that the architecture of the twentieth century was born – including what contemporary architects contemptuously referred to as Joseph Paxton's conservatory, the Crystal Palace of 1851. Otherwise Paxton was building the Gothic and Italianate villas typical of his time.

If 'Gothic Architecture' is Morris's most reasoned and sub-stantial essay on that style and its development, his last word on the condition of architecture in his own day is to be found in 'The Revival of Architecture':

All we have that approaches architecture, is the result of a quite self-conscious and very laborious eclecticism, and is avowedly imitation of the work of past times. . . . Meanwhile whatever is done without conscious effort, that is to say the work of the true style of the epoch, is an offence to the sense of beauty and fitness. . . . It is no longer passively but actively ugly, since it has added to the dreary utilitarianism of the days of Dr Johnson a vulgarity which is the special invention of the Victorian age. The genuine style of that era is exemplified in the jerry-built houses of our suburbs, the stuccoed marine parades of our watering-places, the flaunting corner public-houses of every town in Great Britain. . . . These form our true Victorian architecture. Such works as Mr Bodley's excellent new buildings at Magdalen College, Mr Norman Shaw's elegantly fantastic Queen Anne houses at Chelsea, or Mr Robson's simple but striking London board schools, are mere eccentricities with which the public in general has no part or lot. . . .

The enthusiasm of the Gothic revivalists died out when they were confronted with the fact that they form part of a society which will not and cannot have a living style, because it is an economical necessity for its existence that the ordinary everyday work of its population shall be mechanical drudgery; and because it is the harmony of the ordinary everyday work of the population which produces Gothic, that is, living architectural art, and mechanical drudgery cannot be harmonized into art.

Morris concludes by saying that the society of the future 'will not need or endure mechanical drudgery' for 'it will not be hag-ridden as we are by the necessity for producing ever more and more market wares for profit, whether anyone needs them or not . . . it will produce to live, and not live to produce, as we do. Under such conditions architecture, as a part of the life of the people in general, will again become possible, and I believe that when it is possible, it will have a real new birth. . . .'

By the mid-twentieth century a new international style of architecture has established itself and has made a clean sweep of all former styles. It is possible, however, that Morris would have regarded it as the expression of what he called the mechanical rather than the human energies of mankind, as engineering rather than architecture. But it is certainly 'a part of the life of the people in general'; as is mechanical drudgery, an inevitable part of the growing complexity of our mechanized society, whose outlook is still as commercial as ever. The interesting thing is that there is now a fairly widespread revival of Morris's designs, prompted by the wish, perhaps, to bring back something of the abundance and freshness of nature into the blank, dehumanized emptiness of our brave new surroundings.

In spite of their confusion, more or less inevitable at that time, Morris's lectures on architecture and the allied arts are important because he saw, as Pugin did, that the sort of art we have is the direct outcome not only of our social organization, but of our whole attitude to life. He realized that no building could be considered as an isolated unit, as the expression of an individual architect's taste. If we are ever to have harmonious architecture, and cities that are not an affront to the eye, a building must be thought of in relation to other buildings, to the countryside, and, above all, to social needs. Architecture could no longer be divorced from town planning. 'We are all waiting', he said, 'for what must be the work, not the leisure and taste of a few scholars, authors, and artists, but of the necessities and aspirations of the workmen throughout the civilized world.'[11] It is such a conclusion as this that makes Morris, for all his medieval-ism, a pioneer.

CHAPTER TEN

1879–1883

Hammersmith, Kelmscott, Merton Abbey

'AS TO POETRY, I don't know, and I don't know', Morris wrote to Georgie Burne-Jones in October 1879. 'The verse would come easy enough if I had only a subject which would fill my heart and mind: but to write verse for the sake of writing is a crime in a man of my years and experience. . . .'

He was, however, as usual, busy in many other ways. As secretary of SPAB, he was speaking at meetings all over the country, in an attempt to arouse a national movement of protest against the proposed rebuilding of the west front of St Mark's, Venice. He drafted a memorial addressed to the Italian Minister of Works, which both Disraeli and Gladstone signed, but was irritated that it had to be handed formally to the Italian Ambassador and could not just be posted 'as to an ordinary mortal. In truth what has really worried me in this matter', he wrote to Georgie in November, 'has been all the ridiculous rigmarole and social hypo-crisy one has to wade through. . . .' There was also a meeting of protest at the Sheldonian Theatre in Oxford at which Morris, and even Burne-Jones, spoke. But the restoration work on the mosaic had been stopped before the memorial reached the Ambassador.

This year Morris also became Treasurer of the National Liberal League, a working-class association formed largely from the radical elements that had organized themselves in opposition to the Eastern policy of the Government in 1876. 'At the meetings of this League he made his first essays in the practice of extempory speech', says Mackail. 'It was a thing which, partly from constitutional shyness and partly from the pressure of thought behind his language, came to him, as far as it did come at all, with great difficulty. "When he spoke off-hand," a colleague of his at this time notes – and the description is highly characteristic – "he had a knack at times of hammering away at his point until he had said exactly what he wanted to say in exactly the words he wished to use, rocking to and fro the while from one foot to the other."'[1] When he lectured, on the other hand, on his own chosen subjects, Morris would read out a carefully prepared talk.

As well as his regular work for the firm and as adviser at the South Kensington Museum and the Royal School of Art Needle⁄ work, Morris was involved in much political work. But when the general election of 1880 brought the Liberal Party to power and he saw that they were not much better than the Tories, he lost his faith in Gladstone and resigned from his treasurership of the Liberal League. 'I think some *raison d'être* might be found for us', he wrote, when handing over his accounts, 'if we had definite work to do: I do so hate – this in spite of my accounts – everything vague in politics as well as in art.'

Meanwhile the firm was carrying out their new decorations for the Throne and Reception Rooms at St James's Palace. Morris designed a silk damask for this purpose, painted the ceiling and cornices and designed a special paper for the main staircase, the 'St James'. But politics preoccupied him. Writing to Jane, who was staying with the Howards at Bordighera, on 10 February 1881, he brusquely tabulated the subjects of his letter:

1st weather: stormy & wild; sometimes disgusting, sometimes beautiful & sunny: to⁄day wettish but very warm.

2nd work: I am still on my lecture which bothers me sorely: I know what I want to say, but the cursed words go to water between my fingers. . . .

3rd Politics – Not pleasant, & yet I suppose, properly speaking not unhopeful: if I say I don't trust the present government, I mean to say that I don't trust it to show as radical; Whig it is & will remain: the Coercion Bill [the Irish Coercion Bill of 1881] will soon be read: it is a very bad bill, but I fancy the Government will give way a little in committee; and anyway Forster don't *intend* to use it tyrannically. . . . But I repeat the Government, i.e. Gladstone, is much stronger in the country than I thought for, and if only he could stop these damned little wars he might stop in till he had carried a regular liberal programme, and we should make a good step forward. But little wars with defeats and inglorious victories dovetailed into one another shake a Government terribly, & especially a Liberal one. . . .

This was Gladstone's second ministry. He had come to power on the wave of popular reaction against Disraeli's Jingoism and by vague democratic aspirations not formulated into any definite policy, but on a platform of 'Peace, Retrenchment and Reform'. The 'little wars' at this time were with the Boers in the Transvaal and there was also fighting in Afghanistan. The defeat at the hands of the Boers at Majuba (which followed the 'pacification' of the Kaffirs and the Zulus) was accepted by Gladstone for fear lest the Dutch of Cape Colony should come to the support of their blood-brothers. Meanwhile Cecil Rhodes was developing new British territories to the north and west of the Transvaal, and next year British troops occupied Egypt, where Turkish rule had broken down.

The same month Morris wrote to Jane about the affairs of the firm:

> Tom Wardle is a heap of trouble to us; nothing will he do right, & he does write the longest winded letters containing lies of various kinds: we shall have to take to chintzes ourselves before long and are now daily looking about for premises. . . . I am starting designing the long carpet for Naworth as Bell's [Sir Lowthian Bell of Rounton Grange] gets on apace: 'tis rather a difficult job, & I am puffing & blowing over it rather: hence and from our manufacture-hunting I suppose, a long dream I had: how we were making carpets by the river side & yet in Red Lion Sq. the rooms very large & desirable. . . .

In his next letter of 27 February he says that he is hard at work for George Howard at Palace Green – 'work at St James's all finished & happily, with good profit: so don't spare to ask for cash if you want it. . . . Good-bye, my dear, take care of yourself: and *please* pay your way duly to Mrs Howard: I can't go owing money to Earl-kin.'

It was at this time that Henry James, also in Italy, met Jane Morris again. 'I didn't fall in love with the strange, pale, livid, gaunt, silent and yet in a manner graceful and picturesque wife of the poet and paper-maker', he writes.[2] Indeed, Jane seems to have been extremely unwell for some time. 'I cannot bear to hear of these fainting fits occurring in your case', Rossetti had written to her in August 1879, when she was staying at Naworth. In January the following year he wrote:

Dear Suffering Janey,

I have just kissed your handwriting, the most welcome thing in the world that I could have seen to-day. I am not so *very* low except on your account just now, but I had got so nervous & frightened about you that I don't know how I should have got through the night if I had not heard.

Later the same month he writes again: 'I was glad to hear that at any rate you are in about your usual state. As for meeting at present, that seems more than ever a dream.'[3] He wonders whether she should go to Hastings or Seaford for the air and sends her a prescription for neuralgia, with instructions to take thirty drops every hour. Has she thought of going to Rome for the winter? he asks, or Florence, where the Stillmans would be delighted to look after her. He is worried lest Morris should get hold of the copy of Calderon's plays he has sent her, 'for then it will be scattered to the winds'. On 2 February 1880 he writes: 'I am desolate enough, as you know – indeed, without my work I should be lost altogether. It is a comfort to me to think that you on your side are not quite so companionless. I often hope that your daughters are worthy of you and devoted to you.' He is consoling himself, however, by working on his favourite painting of her, *The Day Dream*, which he had first called *Vanna Primavera*. But as she is still too weak to sit for him, he has to make do with an earlier drawing of her done at Sealands in 1870 and a silk dress she had left behind her in his studio – 'empty as it is now'. For her part, Jane says that she is grateful for the return of spring so that she can 'breathe without gasping', which sounds as though she suffered from asthma as well.

Those letters of Jane Morris to Rossetti which have survived are mostly kind and sensible, with occasional flashes of humour.[4] They show no signs of a reciprocated passion. 'I almost fancy, Janey,' Rossetti writes to her in February 1880, 'you ought to get away again. Your handwriting looked so firm and hopeful when you were at Hastings.' By April Jane was apparently fit to sit for him again, though 'sit' is perhaps hardly the word for it, for Rossetti assures her that he can draw her hands while she is lying down. When she sat up she felt faint. But she did not go to Cheyne Walk in April after all, having developed 'flu, at which Rossetti comments sadly: 'Truly if you live with open windows in this weather, what but influenza can ensue? Nevertheless, alas! . . .' Open windows and bracing airs were, as he knew all too well, very much a part of Morris's way of life.

Throughout 1881 Rossetti had been preparing his *Ballads and Sonnets* volume and submitting the *House of Life* sonnets to Jane before finally passing them for press. 'I have passed the proofs to send to Hammersmith and hope there may be no adverse view taken', he wrote to Watts-Dunton on 17 July. 'But whatever it is, I must act on it.' Jane, however, objected to several of the new sonnets as compromising her and Rossetti promised to withdraw them. 'Every new piece that is not quite colourless will be with-drawn and the book postponed', he wrote in August.[5]

Nevertheless one cannot help feeling that Jane would have been happier in the claustrophobic atmosphere of Tudor House. Indeed, she continued to visit Rossetti there right up to the time that he went to Cumberland with Hall Caine in September 1881, in a last vain search for health. On his return, he was a broken man. It was during the wretched night journey back to London from the Lakes, according to Hall Caine, that Rossetti confessed to him that 'after engaging himself to one woman in all honour and good faith, he had fallen in love with another, and then gone on to marry the first out of a mistaken sense of loyalty and a fear of giving pain'.

Rossetti died on 9 April 1882, and Morris wrote to Bell Scott on the 27th:

> What can I say about Gabriel's death, but what all his friends, or almost all, must feel? It makes a hole in the world, though I have seen so little of him lately, and might very likely never have seen him again: he was very kind to me when I was a youngster. He had some of the very greatest qualities of genius, most of them indeed; what a great man he would have been but for the arrogant misanthropy that marred his work, and killed him before his time: the grain of humility which makes a great man one of the people and no lord over them, he lacked, and with it lost the enjoyment of life which would have kept him alive, and sweetened all his work for him and us. But I say he has left a hole in the world which will not be filled up in a hurry.[6]

Like most of his other old friends, Morris had been estranged from Rossetti for years, and in his case there were more particular reasons for this estrangement. But this did not prevent him from hanging Gabriel's paintings and drawings of Jane in both his houses, nor from subsequently printing three volumes of his poems at the Kelmscott Press. He never wavered in his appreciation of Rossetti's work, any more than he did in that of Burne-Jones, though he later remarked to James Mavor: 'Sometimes Rossetti was an angel, and sometimes he was a damned scoundrel.'[7]

Nevertheless, some of Morris's friends were just as puzzled about his attitude as we are today. This, at least, would seem to be the implication of F. S. Ellis's letter of 17 July 1887, from Torquay, to Bell Scott. After an account of a visit to Kelmscott, during which, he says, he had managed to keep Morris off socialism, he goes on: 'if I thought his opinions on the relations of the sexes in old days were the same as he *professes* to hold now – why then, you might believe anything – as it is I am quite inclined to forget old histories – whatever fault if any attached to the poor lady in question I fear she has had and has ample room and cause for repentance and regret and has rather a sad time of it now all things considered'.[8]

In February next year, 'the poor lady in question' wrote from Lyme Regis to Theodore Watts to thank him for sending her the notices of the Rossetti Memorial Exhibition. She says that she 'agrees heartily with those who consider the early work the best. . . . That Gabriel *was* mad was but too true. No one knows that better than myself, but that his work after 1868 was worthless (as Gosse has the impudence to assert) I deny. I don't know why I'm writing all this to you,' she concludes pathetically, 'but I feel that I want to talk to someone about him. I am not likely to be in town for a very long time to have any actual talk with you. Jenny is very ill still. I am almost in despair about her.'[9]

It was in August 1880 that the epic voyage of the whole Morris family and their friends up the river from Hammersmith to Kelmscott took place. For the journey, Morris had hired a small houseboat, *The Ark*, from Salter's of Oxford.

He wrote to Georgie on 10 August:

Imagine a biggish company boat with a small omnibus on board, fitted up luxuriously inside with two shelves and a glass-rack, and a sort of boot behind this: room for two rowers in front, and I must say for not many more except in the cabin or omnibus. Still what joy (to a little mind) to see the landscape out of a square pane of glass, and to sleep a-nights with the stream rushing two inches past one's ear. Then after all, there is the romance of the bank, and outside the boat the world is wide: item, we can always hire a skiff for some of the party to row in and stretch their muscles, and in that way I propose to start this afternoon at $2\frac{1}{2}$ after dining here.

Besides the Morrises, the company consisted of William de Morgan, Cormell Price and 'Dick', the Hon. Richard Grosvenor. *The Ark* was rowed at first by Biffin's men; Morris and Crom followed in a skiff, the *Albert*.[10] Farther up the river, May Morris says that they were towed by 'a man and a boy and a pony'. Morris described the whole trip in detail in a long letter to Georgie, as, indeed, he wrote to her about everything he did, felt and thought. The first day he and Crom rowed as far as Kew, where both *The Ark* and the *Albert* were made fast to some barges and towed by 'a mercantile tin kettle' to Twickenham. They did not reach Sunbury, some six miles above Hampton Court, till ten thirty in the evening, Morris and Price sleeping aboard *The Ark*.

The next night was spent at Windsor and the following morning Richard Grosvenor took them up to Eton. 'In spite of drawbacks it is yet a glorious place', Morris writes to Georgie.

Once more the morning was grey and even threatening rain (wind N.N.E.), but very soon cleared up again into the brightest of days: a very pleasant morning we had, and dined just above Bray lock; cook was I, and shut up in the Ark to do the job, appearing like the high priest at the critical moment pot in hand – but O the wasps about the osier bed! We got quite used to them at last and by dint of care did not swallow any with our food, nor were stung.

There was a regatta at Maidenhead and both banks crowded with spectators, so that we had to drop the tow rope before our time, and as the Ark forged slowly along towards the Berkshire side with your servant steering on the roof, and De Morgan labouring at the sculls, you may think that we were chaffed a little. After Maidenhead you go under Cliefden woods, much admired by the world in general; I confess to thinking them rather artificial; also eyeing Mr Dick with reference to their owner I couldn't help thinking of Mr Twemlow and Lord Snigsworthy. But at Cookham Lock how beautiful it was: you get out of the Snigsworthy woods there; the hills fall back from the river, which is very wide there, and you are in the real country, with cows and sheep and farm-houses, the work-a-day world again and not a lacquey's paradise. . . . The sun had set as we cleared Cookham Lock, and we went facing the west, which was cloudless and golden, till it got quite dark: by that same dark we had to get through the Marlow Lock, with no little trouble, as we had to skirt a huge weir which roared so that we couldn't hear each other speak, and so to our night's lodging: Crom and I in the Ark close to the roaring water, Dick and De M. in the inn (a noisy one) and the ladies up town, over the bridge.

On the morning of 12 August they spent an hour looking at Lady Place, Hurley – 'once a monastery, then a Jacobean house, and now there's but a farm-house, somewhat gammoned . . . the Church has been miserably gammoned but kept its old outline'. Morris 'played the cook again a little short of Henley'; and then they went on 'in a burning afternoon through a river fuller and fuller of character as we got higher up: stuck in the mud for 20 minutes at Wargrave; past Shiplake, which is certainly one of the most beautiful parts of the Thames, and so to Sonning for the night: a village prepensely picturesque and somewhat stuffy that hot night'.

The following day they started early, as they had planned to get to Wallingford that evening. 'We had all got well used to the Ark by now, and there was Janey lying down and looking quite at home. . . . But now out of the over-rated half-picturesque reach of Streatley and Goring here we were on the Thames that is the Thames, amidst the down-like country and all Cockneydom left far behind, and it *was* jolly.'

After 'stuffy grubby little Wallingford', they forged ahead through a dull, cool day ('I cooked 'em their dinner just above Culham Lock', says Morris) till they reached Oxford a little after nightfall. At Oxford they left *The Ark* and after spending the night at the King's Arms, Jane went on by train to Lechlade; the others rowed up the river as far as New Bridge. 'One thing was very pleasant', Morris adds:

They were haymaking on the flat flood-washed spits of ground and islets all about Tadpole; and the hay was gathered on punts and the like; odd stuff to look at, mostly sedge, but they told us it was the best for milk.

Night fell on us long before we got to Radcot, and we fastened a lantern to the prow of our boat, after we had with much difficulty got our boats through Radcot Bridge. Charles was waiting for us with a lantern at our bridge by the corner at 10 p.m., and presently the ancient house had me in its arms again: J. had lighted up all brilliantly, and sweet it all looked you may be sure.

This journey up the river in August 1880 forms the basis of Chapters XXII–XXVIII of *News from Nowhere*, written ten years later. They are perhaps the most beautiful chapters in that always charming work.

On his return to London the same month, Morris wrote to Georgie:

You may imagine that coming back to this beastly congregation of smoke-dried swindlers and their slaves (whom one hopes one day to make their rebels) under the present circumstances does not make me much more in love with London, though I must admit to feeling this morning a touch of the 'all by oneself' independence which you wot of as a thing I like. . . . The few days we spent at Kelmscott made a fine time of it for me. . . . Thursday we went to Fairford in the afternoon, and I was pleased to see the glass and the handsome church once more. Though the country that way is not remarkable, every turn of the road and every by-way set me longing to go afoot through the country, never stopping for a day; after all a fine harvest time is the crown of the year in England. . . .

So here I am on the lower Thames, finding it grimy; I have just been over my carpeteers; all going pretty well. The 'Orchard' being finished is a fair success as to manufacture – lies flat on the whole – and as a work of art has points about it, but I can better it next time. . . .

The following August the 130-mile expedition up the river was repeated. This time the party included Faulkner, William de Morgan, De Morgan's sister, and two girls, Bessie Macleod and Lisa Stillman. 'According to my recollection of these voyages,' De Morgan told Mackail, 'we none of us stopped laughing all the way', De Morgan himself contributing to the general hilarity by such witticisms as that Iffley-on-Thames was 'the original birthplace of the hypothesis'. Morris had rather dreaded repeating the trip, in case it should turn out to be a failure. In any case, a visit to Oxford always worried him. 'A kind of terror always falls upon me as I near it', he confessed to Georgie, indignation at wanton or rash changes mingles curiously in me with all that I remember I have lost since I was a lad and dwelling there. Perhaps if one dreads repeating a pleasure at my time of life it is because it marks too clearly how the time has gone since the last time, and certainly I feel more than a year older since I came up the water in 1880. At any rate the younger part of us have enjoyed themselves thoroughly; and indeed so have I.

In an unpublished essay, of which there are three versions,[11] Violet Hunt recalls, as a young girl of sixteen, seeing the party pass under Sonning Bridge early one morning. She remembers Morris standing up in his boat and

shouting indecorously worded advice to the other boat. . . . Behind him, sitting up very stiffly, was the now historic 'Janey' – Venus Verticordia, Aurea Catena, La Ghirlandata, and La Pia of the Purgatorio. Gaunt, ashen-coloured, hair and all, in the sunlight, yet perfectly beautiful, she looked, just now, more like the forlorn lady undone by the miasma of the marshes than the others. In the following boat two persons were standing up and both dressed in blue. The young girl [Lisa Stillman] was the daughter of another of the beautiful women [Marie Spartali, who had married Stillman] who posed for the lucky D.G.R. The man who propelled the boat looked older than William Morris, the hair of his bare, dome-like head was spare, wiry and grey.

This was William de Morgan. One of the other versions of these reminiscences states that this boat was propelled by May Morris and contained Marie Stillman, Crom Price and William de Morgan. Morris, says Miss Hunt, was dressed in 'blue, very blue, serge. . . . His golden beard showed up against the lapis lazuli of his attire' – an obviously romanticized picture, for by 1881 Morris's beard was distinctly grizzled, as can be seen in Hollyer's photographs. When Bernard Shaw met him seven years later, he said that he looked ten years older than his age.

Violet Hunt was at school with Jenny (she calls her by her second name, Alice) and May, and had met Morris face to face in his own house at Hammersmith. She describes Jenny at this time as

tall, stoutish, hefty, with brown hair done in a way we should call 'bobbed' nowadays, very like her father and with his hasty mode of talking, as if she wanted to say her say and have done

223

with it. I asked her once, over our desk at school, very seriously, which of her father's poems she preferred and, after a ruminative pause and while the class mistress's eye was off her, she announced clearly that it was '"Sir Peter Harpdon's End" – and no mistake!' Her younger sister Mary was simply, to my eyes, the most beautiful creature I ever saw, cold and unkind to me who adored her from afar and watched her sailing in and out of the ugly pitch-pine school, looking like Lady Alice De La Barde – Yolande of the Five Towers. She had her mother's famous night-coloured hair but her mouth held no suggestion, even then, of her mother's noble and fulsome curve.

One day Jenny asked Violet back to tea at Kelmscott House.

Rapt, holding my breath with awe, I had tea with her and her father and mother. I can never forget Mrs Morris sitting still, silent, and withdrawn, on the high-backed settle with the painted bend-over roof. Beauty such as hers need not palter with small talk. I cannot remember any word from her lips that day except, 'There's your milk, Jenny.' I believe that she was diffident . . . proudly conscious of a want of mere book-learning, but, like Joan of Arc, who maintained at her trial that where her needle was concerned, she feared neither maid nor wife of Rouen. Mrs Morris was famous for her embroidery, and sitting 'lily-like arow', with Red Lion Mary and Mrs W. [Wardle], who was really Madel[e]ine Smith,[12] laid with her needle the foundations of the firm of Morris, Marshall and Faulkner & Co.

Morris's letters to Georgie Burne-Jones this autumn are full of his delight in Kelmscott, with accounts of expeditions by pony and trap into the beautiful, deserted countryside. In September he writes:

We went a most formal expedition on Saturday by water to Lechlade: then took a trap there and drove to Cirencester, which turned out a pleasant country town, and to us country folk rather splendid and full of shops. There is a grand church there, mostly late Gothic, of the very biggest type of parish church, romantic to the last extent, with its many aisles and chapels: wall-painting there and stained glass and brasses also. . . .

Again, of the harvest at Kelmscott:

It has been a great pleasure to see man and maid so hard at work carrying at last. Hobbs began at it on Wednesday morning, and by the next morning the thatchers were putting on the bright straw cap to the new rick: yesterday they were carrying the wheat in the field along our causeway and stacking it in our yard: pretty as one sat in the tapestry-room to see the loads coming on between the stone walls. . . . I am afraid that last winter has killed us a great many birds here; small ones especially: I don't see the blue tits I look for at this time of the year. I have seen but one moorhen (yesterday) and was glad to see him, as I feared they were all dead: plenty of rooks, however; they have just left off making the parliament-noise they began about six this morning: starlings also, but they haven't begun to gather in our trees yet.

The other morning as I was coming up the river by our island I heard a great squealing of the swallows, and looking up saw a hawk hanging in the wind overhead, and the swallows gathered in a knot near him: presently two or three swallows left their knot and began skirting Mr Hawk, and one swept right down on him and fetched him a crack (or seemed to). He considered for a minute or two, then set his wings slantwise and went down the wind like lightning, and in an instant was hanging over Eaton Hastings. . . .

Another unfailing attraction to Morris was the great thirteenth-century tithe barn at Great Coxwell, four miles from Kelmscott, just inside the Berkshire border. He used to take his friends to see it, declaring that it was 'unapproachable in its dignity, as beautiful as a cathedral, yet with no ostentation of the builder's art', with its great buttresses and its hundred and fifty feet of grey roof raised on a forest of oak timbers. At the other end of the village stands the little parish church of St Giles with the two early Tudor brasses of 'Willm Morys, sutyme fermer of cokyswell' and of 'Johane the wyf of Willm Morys' – a coincidence that was, understandably, a source of delight.

The earlier William Morris was lord of the Manor of Coxwell, originally granted to the Cistercian Abbey of Beaulieu by King John in 1204, and his family were tenants for several generations before he obtained a grant of the manor. On the little brass he appears dressed in a fur-collared, wide-sleeved gown drawn in by a belt, and between his feet springs a small three-stemmed flower, reminiscent of Morris's designs for the wool hangings at Red House and the 'Daisy' wallpaper. 'At the end of the inscription below

Johane's figure is a leaf that fills in the line', observes Mr R. C. H. Briggs. 'The resemblance between the form and employment of this and one of the Kelmscott Press leaf ornaments, as well as between the flower on the brass and the first watermark for Kelmscott Handmade paper, leaves little doubt that Morris, when making his designs, remembered the old brasses at Great Coxwell.'[13]

Sir W. B. Richmond, the painter, a neighbour of Morris at Beavor Lodge, Ravenscourt Park, in a letter of 1881, describes a typical day's fishing at Kelmscott.[14] 'A quarter to six saw us astir, half past at a breakfast of fish and eggs, a little later hard at work for pike and perch, dace, chub, with paternosters and spinning: a few sandwiches and a bottle of claret fed us during our leisure moments until dark – dinner, sleepy talk about poetry and art until 9, and then *such* sleep.' Next day they sculled down the river to Oxford, doing the work of the locks and weirs themselves, dined at University common-room, and were back by midnight.

'Morris is quite splendid company', notes Richmond.

> English to the marrow of his bones, original, energetic, and simple as a boy, delighting in romance, and able at 47 to lead an imagin-ary life and to enjoy the simplest pleasure with childish gusto. . . . When he and I pulled from Kelmscott to Oxford, on arriving I was dead tired, but Morris was as fresh as when we started. He saw new beauties in his delightful house every day. He loved to study the old timbers in the roof, the stone paths of the garden, the lichen-grown stone of its walls. He loved the stone pavement, but confessed to permitting it to be hidden by oriental rugs in the winter. For in his way he liked comfort, if it was not too far removed from what was possible in the fifteenth century, or even earlier. . . . With all his magnificent enthusiasm, with all his prejudices – and he has many – Morris was one of the most sensible men I have known. Folly irritated him. He valued accuracy and spotted a guess in a moment: for fools he had no compassion. . . . It was good, indeed, for us all to be in contact with a man of such power and industry. He was the manliest fellow that ever tried to pull an effete society together. He had the roughness and strength of a Norseman together with the tenderness, nay, even shyness, of a woman.

Naturally, Richmond is thinking of the Victorian ladies of his acquaintance. Both these qualities are evident in his account of a visit with Morris to the offices of the Thames Conservancy Board, in protest against the cutting down by the Board of an avenue of willows along the towpath between Hammersmith Bridge and Barnes – that is, on the opposite side of the river to Kelmscott House.

As they approached Finsbury Square, Morris began to show signs of nervousness, in spite of his previous indignation. 'I say, old chap,' he said, plucking at Richmond's sleeve, 'you do the talking.' Richmond objected, saying that, after all, the protest was Morris's idea. When they actually reached the office, Morris repeated his request, more urgently still. Richmond, probably with some amuse-ment, again refused and they were ushered into a vast empty board-room with an enormous table in the centre of it. Presently, the door was flung open by 'a giant of a man who looked as if he had been fed on rum all his life':

> 'What the hell do you bloody chaps want?' he roared. 'What is your bloody business?'
> Morris's shyness disappeared in a flash. 'We've come to ask you savage, bloody chaps why the hell you have cut down a pleasant grove of willows.'
> 'What the hell's that to you?' asked Captain B.
> 'We mean', said Morris, 'to kick up the devil's own row about this bloody affair, and to demand a very hell of reparation from the bloody Board.'

A dose of his own medicine had a visibly tranquillizing effect on the chairman, and he finally agreed that fresh trees should be planted. 'Not a bad chap, after all, is he?' said Morris, as they left.[15] Richmond claimed to have a score of such stories. In fact, Morris considered their treatment of the river so outrageous that he seldom lost an opportunity of stating his opinion in the most forcible language he could muster to any of the Board's representatives he happened to meet on the quiet reaches of the Upper Thames, in each case his own language matching and over-topping that of the retired seamen the Conservancy Board employed.

Sir Arthur Richmond, too, recalls meeting Morris on several occasions as a boy at Beavor Lodge. On one of these he remembers him arriving at the house soon after Walter Pater. 'In a blue blouse, untidy trousers, and disordered hair and beard, Morris presented a complete contrast to the correct and demure figure of Pater. In each hand he carried a large glass goblet he had just made and now presented to my mother.' As he did so, Morris pointed out their noble proportions, each capable of containing nearly a bottle of champagne –

> goblets, as he declared, fit for Vikings to drink from. He seemed literally bursting with what he wanted to say. He didn't sit down: as he walked about the room he described the wonderful hours he had spent that morning – his inspiration seemed to flow effort-lessly from him. He had written dozens – or was it hundreds? – of verses. There was no hint of boastfulness about what he said: he was just unable to contain the pressure of exuberant vitality and delight in the force that possessed him.[16]

Sir Arthur observes that though Morris was apparently quite oblivious to other people's opinion of him, he was sensitive to criticism of his work. One day at a garden party at Beavor Lodge, at which Oscar Wilde was also present, he had come up to them 'boiling with indignation. "The press ignores me", he angrily exclaimed. "There's a conspiracy of silence about my book." Quickly came the retort from Oscar Wilde: "Why not join it, Morris?" '[17]

If this classic remark really was addressed to William Morris and not to the indefatigable poeticizer Sir Lewis Morris, it may be the occasion to which Morris refers in his letter to Jane of 31 March 1881, when he wrote: 'Did the babes tell you how I met Oscar Wilde at the Richmonds? I must admit that as the devil is painted blacker than he is, so it fares with O.W., not but what he is an ass: but he certainly is and clever too. . . .'

At that time, Wilde, soon to be the subject of *Punch* caricatures and the central figure in Frith's *Private View of the Royal Academy, 1881*, had just published his *Poems*. These were largely a pastiche of everyone else's work, and he was advertising them by his incom-parable wit and peculiar clothes at social gatherings. Ten years later he published 'The Soul of Man Under Socialism' in *The Fortnightly Review*, perhaps written after attending one of Morris's lectures at Kelmscott House. It is astonishing to find Wilde writing in 1891: 'It is to be regretted that a portion of the community should be practically in slavery, but to propose to solve the problem by en-slaving the entire community is childish. . . . If the Socialism is Authoritarian; if there are Governments armed with economic power as they are now with political power; if, in a word, we are to have Industrial Tyrannies, then the last state of man will be worse than the first.' Again: 'High hopes were once formed of democracy; but democracy means simply the bludgeoning of the people by the people for the people.' Wilde's views on crime are also much in advance of his age.

> As one reads history, not in expurgated editions written for schoolboys and passmen, but in the original authorities of each time, one is absolutely sickened, not by the crimes that the wicked have committed, but by the punishments that the good have inflicted; and a community is infinitely more brutalized by the habitual employment of punishment than it is by the occasional occurrence of crime. It obviously follows that the more punish-ment is inflicted the more crime is produced, and most modern legislation has clearly recognized this, and has made it its task to diminish punishment as far as it thinks it can. . . . When there is no punishment at all, crime will either cease to exist, or, if it occurs, will be treated by physicians as a very distressing form of dementia, to be cured by care and kindness.

Morris must have read, or at least known of, 'The Soul of Man Under Socialism', though he may have been put off by its apparently flippant opening sentence 'The chief advantage that would result from the establishment of Socialism is, undoubtedly, the fact that Socialism would relieve us from the sordid necessity of living for others. . . .' Wilde means, of course, that under socialism all personal responsibility for the well-being of others would be taken over by the state. As he goes on to say, private acts of charity merely pro-longed the disease of poverty. 'They try to solve the problem of poverty, for instance, by keeping the poor alive; or, in the case of a very advanced school, by amusing the poor' – just as the Duchess of Berwick's nieces in *Lady Windermere's Fan* devoted their lives to 'making ugly things for the poor, which I think so useful of them in these dreadful socialistic days'. Wilde may even have sent Morris a copy of *The Fortnightly Review*, for in 1891 we find him writing to thank Morris for a copy of one of his books, probably the paper-covered edition of *News from Nowhere*, because Wilde remarks that the binding is not worthy of the contents.[18]

Morris was by no means unappreciative of ironical wit, for his daughter tells us that Samuel Butler's *Erewhon* was 'almost a household word'.[19] It was Shaw who told Hesketh Pearson that 'when Morris was slowly dying he enjoyed a visit from Oscar Wilde more than from anyone else', saying 'that he had never been so entertained in his life'. Shaw told Pearson that he had had this from May Morris. But there is no other reference to Wilde ever having visited Hammersmith. Morris could not properly be said to be dying until 1896 and Wilde was in prison from May 1895 until May 1897. Shaw, when questioned about this by Pearson, said that Morris was already a dying man 'long before Reading Gaol was ever thought of', which is perfectly true, as he never recovered from his serious illness of 1891. If so, Wilde's letter of that year, which begins 'The book has arrived!', could be taken to indicate a meeting at which Morris had promised to send him *News from Nowhere*.[20]

Morris's unpublished diary for 1881[21] gives one a good idea of how he spent his days. At this time he was still experimenting with weaving and also designing and pointing the 'Naworth' carpet for George Howard. This was the largest carpet the firm had so far executed and was nearly a year in hand. It was woven in the coach house at Hammersmith. For his carpets, Morris would first make a one-eighth scale drawing of the design, colouring this very carefully with his own hand. This coloured drawing was then enlarged by a draughtsman on point paper. To begin with, this very laborious work was done by Morris himself, as well as much of the actual weaving. He also did the designing and pointing for all the patterned and woven stuffs produced on his looms at this time.

Turning to the diary, we find an entry for 12 March: 'Up at 7.30, about four hours tapestry.' Next month, as the mornings grew lighter, we read: 'Up at 5.30, three hours tapestry.' Then:

12 May. Up late. Worked on paper hanging in morning. In afternoon to Office of Works about St James. To S.P.A.B. dined Grange. 4 [hours] at Howard's carpet. Wind E. in morning: seemed to change to S. in evening: bright in morning: warm all day but cloudy in afternoon bright night.

17 May. Up at 5½. 3 hours tapestry. Working on paper hanging tulip and anemone. Dined Grange. Leaf border finished another began. Wind SW cloudy & dull warmer trying to rain amidst a gale all day rain in the night but not hard.

20 May. Up at 5. 3½ [hours] tapestry. To Grange. To Queen Square: the green for Peacock [a woven hanging] all wrong – did day books & Friday [that is, Friday's work of signing cheques etc.] besides seeing to all this. Took away model of G.H. carpet from K. Meeting St Mark's Committee. Dined A.Ionides. Wind W.SW. very fine, bright day. Cool in evening.

The expansion of the firm's three principal activities, weaving, dyeing and cotton printing now made spacious workshops an absolute necessity. Hitherto most of this work had been given to outside firms and Morris was becoming increasingly dissatisfied with the results. Experimental work only could be done in the cramped quarters at Queen Square – though the looms at Hammersmith wove carpets up to twelve feet across – and Morris was anxious to bring every stage of the manufacture of his products as far as possible under his own control.

At first he was in favour of moving the works to Blockley, near Chipping Campden, in the Cotswolds, where there was still a tradition of silk weaving. The idea had come to him as early as 1878, when he had driven over with Cormell Price from Broadway. At Blockley he found the old mills still standing, with even the notices of the last reduction of wages made before they finally closed down at the end of the eighteenth century pasted to the walls. Morris fell in love with the place, and even more with the idea of reviving its old traditions. But Blockley was a hundred miles from London and twenty-five miles across country from Kelmscott – a long drive by pony and trap – and Morris reluctantly gave up the idea before the determined opposition of Wardle, his manager, who insisted on finding premises nearer London.

'Edgar went to look at the print-works at Crayford on Monday', Morris wrote to Jane on 23 February 1881. 'They seemed promising: how queer it would be if we were to set up our work there again . . .', Crayford being not far from Bexley Heath. 'I went with De Morgan to Crayford on Monday', he writes a week later, 'the whole country about seems much spoiled since we were there. . . . However, it wouldn't do. . . . I saw Hall Place once more and it made the stomach in me turn round with desire of an old house.' In March he went with De Morgan to look at an old print works at Merton Abbey, only seven miles from Charing Cross. 'Though the suburb as such is woeful beyond conception,' he wrote to Jane, 'yet the place itself is even very pretty: Summa, I think it will come to taking it, if we can get it on fair terms – and then I shall be as aforesaid a London bird. . . .'

The stones of the original Merton Abbey had been used by Henry VIII when building Nonesuch Palace.[22] Early in the eighteenth century it became the site of a silk-weaving factory started by Huguenot refugees, which had been used more recently for printing 'those hideous red and green table-cloths and so forth', Morris observes. The Merton Abbey print works, when Morris took them over, consisted of a collection of old wooden sheds, red-tiled and weather-boarded, standing among willows and poplars on the banks of the river Wandle, then a clear and beautiful stream turning a water-mill and supplying water of the special quality, Morris found after analysis, needed for madder-dyeing. The property was about seven acres and included an orchard and a vegetable garden.

As a factory, Merton Abbey was the realization of a Ruskinian dream. But to get there from Hammersmith (unless he walked or drove, as he sometimes did) meant going by the Metropolitan rail-way to Farringdon Street, crossing the city to Ludgate Hill, and then taking another train to Merton, a journey of about two hours. When work was at high pressure, Morris got into the habit of staying the night at Merton, where he fitted up a couple of rooms for his personal use. Negotiations were practically through by April, but permission had to be got to build kilns for glass and tiles, and the lease was not finally signed until 7 June 1881.

Morris would not pull down any of the old workshops, which were still in quite a reasonable state of repair, but the roofs had to be heightened for the looms and the foundations trenched and puddled to keep out the damp, water at Merton lying four feet below the ground. Pits had to be dug and lined for the indigo vats, carpet looms built and the buildings generally adapted to their new purposes. Morris planted poplars round the meadow on which the grounds of the calico prints had to be cleared by exposure to the air. He at once began designing a whole new batch of chintzes and was chafing at the inevitable delay before they could be put into pro-duction. The actual move to Merton did not take place until November. 'I am in an agony of muddle', he writes early in Novem-ber, 'I now blame myself severely for not having my way and settling at Blockley: I knew I was right; but cowardice prevailed.' The agony was only produced by his impatience to get things started.

By Christmas everything had been cleared out of Queen Square and its annexes, and chintzes were already being printed at Merton. A circular issued at this time gives a list of the different types of work undertaken. These come under no less than twelve headings:

1. Painted glass windows.
2. Arras tapestry woven in the high-warp loom.
3. Carpets.
4. Embroidery.
5. Tiles.
6. Furniture.
7. General house decorations.
8. Printed cotton goods.
9. Paper hangings.
10. Figured woven stuffs.
11. Furniture velvets and cloths.
12. Upholstery.

'We are prepared as heretofore', Morris wrote in the circular, 'to give estimates for windows in churches and other buildings, *except in the case of such as can be considered monuments of Ancient Art*, the glazing of which we cannot conscientiously undertake, as our doing so would seem to sanction the disastrous practice of so-called Restoration.' This meant refusing many commissions on principle. Morris refused to execute a window for Westminster Abbey and when Dean Stanley cited the Vyner Window at Christ Church, Oxford, as a precedent, Morris replied, Mackail tells us, that 'even that window, the excellence of which as a piece of modern work he did not deny, was an intruder where it stood, and alien in character and sentiment from the building in which it was placed'.[23]

In principle, of course, he was right, but this did not prevent cathedrals and churches from being filled with glass of inferior quality – as at Ely, whose roof, Morris said a little unfairly, 'had been daubed over like a music hall'. (The roof of the nave at Ely was the work of Henry Styleman le Strange, who had also worked with Butterfield on the original decorations to St Alban's, Holborn.) Rivals in the trade were not slow to spread the rumour that Morris & Co. had given up glass painting altogether. And since 'Morris glass' was popularly supposed to be medieval in feeling, the firm's refusal of commissions struck most people as incomprehensible.

In December 1882 Morris wrote to Jane, who was at

233

Bournemouth with Jenny: 'As to our printing, we are really not quite straight yet: I am quite ashamed of it: however they are doing Brother Rabbit successfully, & the Anemone will go on now, & when we are once out of this difficulty, I really think we shall have seen the worst of it.' Unfortunately, an attack of gout prevented him from getting about the works, but it did not stop him designing new patterns for chintzes. After the amusing and light-hearted 'Brother Rabbit' and the 'Bird and Anemone', the famous 'Strawberry Thief' was in production by the following Whitsun. For this chintz (also used as a curtain) Morris revived the obsolete and laborious art of indigo-discharge printing, which gave a peculiarly rich effect. This was followed by other designs requiring the same technique, the ever-delightful 'Eyebright', the 'Wandle' and the 'Evenlode'.

In an astonishing burst of creative energy, Morris designed this year (1883) the 'Rose', the 'Wey', the 'Evenlode', the 'Windrush', the 'Cray', the 'Borage', the 'Corncockle', and the 'Kennet' – several being named after his favourite rivers. His designs made an immediate impact.

> Their beautifully controlled colours, the combination of delicacy and boldness in the drawing of the flowers, and the rich and masterly elaboration of their patterning seemed like a breath of fresh air to a generation tired of the stale clichés of the ordinary furnishings, so that already by the early 1880s 'Morris chintzes' were a household word in both England and the United States. Indeed so great was their reputation that many late-Victorian families made it a point of honour to have nothing but Morris papers and fabrics in their houses.[24]

The decade following the move to Merton Abbey, from the age of forty-eight to fifty-eight, was Morris's most prolific period in the design of patterns for wallpapers, printed and woven textiles and carpets. It was also the decade which coincided with his greatest political activity, his years as a militant socialist and a strenuous life of political speaking all over the country.

Of the actual working conditions at Merton Abbey, George Wardle writes in the notes he prepared for Mackail:

> There seems nothing to say except that it was altogether delightful. We had a spacious ground floor, well-lighted, for the carpet looms, and, over it, a 'shop' for the block printers. This was

another advantage gained by the change: we now began to print chintzes. We had a dye house appropriate to them and other necessary 'ageing' rooms etc., etc.; we had also a dye house for silk and wool and blue vats for silk, wool and cotton. There was an abundance of pure water, light and air. The glass painters had also their studio and Mr Morris his own. Mr Morris occasionally slept there, but not latterly. . . . He came down twice or thrice a week in those days. It is noticeable perhaps, in remembering his nervous temperament that, though he disliked the journey (from Hammersmith) intensely . . . he showed no sign of irritation on arriving. The latter part of the journey, perhaps, through the fields, was soothing and then there was the short passage from the station through the garden of the Abbey and the prospect of being soon at work which together may have restored his equilibrium. But there remained a certain impetus in his manner, as if he would go at 20 miles an hour and rather expected everything to keep pace with him. This was, I think, the effect of the railway journey. I had noticed it at Queen Square if he arrived from a journey. His first business on arriving at Merton was to discuss any new matter, then he would visit the workshops and after seeing that all was on time, he settled down to his own easel. There was always a design in progress and often more than one, for it was necessary to break off now and then to have parts repeated, if it was a repeating pattern, and while these repetitions were being made he took up another. He drew as quickly and accurately as he wrote.[25]

Mackail has left an idyllic picture of Merton Abbey.

As one turns out of the dusty high road and passes through the manager's little house, the world seems left in a moment behind. The old-fashioned garden is gay with irises and daffodils in spring, with hollyhocks and sunflowers in autumn, and full, summer by summer, of the fragrant flowering shrubs that make a London suburb into a brief June Paradise. It rambles away towards the mill pond with its fringe of tall poplars; the cottons lie bleaching on grass thickly set with buttercups; the low long buildings with the clear rushing little stream running between them, and the wooden outside staircases leading to their upper storey, have nothing about them to suggest the modern factory; even upon the great sunk dye-vats the sun flickers through leaves, and trout leap outside the windows of the long cheerful room where the carpet-looms are built. 'To Merton Abbey', runs an entry in a visitor's diary on a day at the end of April, 1882, when the new works had settled fairly down to their routine: 'white hawthorn was out in the garden: we had tea with Mr Morris in his room in the house, and left laden with marsh-marigolds, wallflowers, lilac, and hawthorn'.[26]

Morris himself would also sometimes return to Hammersmith with an armful of flowers and wondered why the business men and clerks in the Underground, with their noses in their evening papers, found it amusing.

The first piece of tapestry woven at Merton was a frieze of greenery with birds for George Howard. Months of dogged daily practice had familiarized Morris with the problems and difficulties of the craft, and before the move to Merton he had trained three boys, among them J. H. Dearle, who himself became a first-class designer, in the work. For Morris had found that tapestry weaving, which involved little muscular effort, was best done by small flexible fingers. He therefore set Dearle to work on the first figure piece pro-duced on the high-warp loom, 'The Goose Girl', designed by Walter Crane. 'In about a fortnight we shall have finished the Goose Girl tapestry', Morris writes to Jenny on 28 February 1883, 'Uncle Ned has done me two lovely figures for tapestry, but I have got to design a background for them: I shall probably bring that down next time I come for my holiday task.' This is a reference to the 'Flora' and 'Pomona', which succeeded the 'Goose Girl' in 1885. With their backgrounds of swirling acanthus leaves, these are the most splendid tapestries produced at Merton Abbey, even though they are not on the same scale as the 'Holy Grail' series done for Stanmore Hall, one panel of which took ten years to weave and was practically all executed by three boys. The 'Flora' and 'Pomona' were repeated in the smaller versions of 1896 and 1898, with floral backgrounds by Dearle. The 'Holy Grail' panels were bought by the Duke of Westminster for Eaton Hall for 3,400 guineas at Sotheby's in 1920, at a little less than their original cost. There are also detached panels of this series in Birmingham City Museum and Art Gallery.

There is, it must be admitted, a certain effeteness about Burne-Jones's figures for these large-scale works, which May Morris seems to have felt when she wrote:

Despite the beauty and distinction of his design we may yet again regret that, as in the case of the glass for windows, Morris himself had not put aside his own private feeling of uncertainty in draughtsmanship, and produced more figure pieces himself. The result would have been something in a different atmosphere, with perhaps a certain rough vigour well in accord with the tapestry technique. His handling of draperies in the cartoons for glass, etc. . . . are, in their breadth and crispness, so in touch with English work of the fifteenth century that it makes one feel that Morris was in very truth merely carrying on the tradition of English art. . . .

And she adds in a footnote that she has in mind the paintings in the churches in East Anglia: 'some of them might have been by the hand of William Morris'.[27] Indeed, it was these very paintings of ceilings and rood screens, as copied for him by George Wardle in the mid-1860s, that Morris often followed.

The only figure piece by Morris, the 'Orchard' of 1890, shows the influence of Burne-Jones, though the treatment is rather more vigorous. Had one not been told that the figures were actually designed over twenty years earlier for a frieze in the nave of Jesus College Chapel one would have taken them for studies of May and Jenny. Morris also designed the fruit trees in this piece, but the flowers in the foreground are by Dearle.

Between 1885 and 1887, Morris designed the 'Woodpecker' and the 'Forest' tapestries, the latter for Alexander Ionides, with its lion, hare, fox and peacock by Webb and its flowers once more by Dearle. For all these tapestries Morris wrote delightful verses, woven into the borders in Gothic characters. These are included in *Poems by the Way* as 'Verses for Pictures'. For the 'Pomona' he wrote:

I am the ancient Apple-Queen,
As once I was so am I now.
For evermore a hope unseen,
Betwixt the blossom and the bough.

Ah, where's the river's hidden Gold!
And where the windy grave of Troy?
Yet come I as I came of old,
From out the heart of Summer's joy.

This, as his friends could not help feeling, was a truer expression of Morris than the 'Chants for Socialists' he was writing at this time for the pages of *Justice*. The first large-scale figure subject done at Merton was the sickly and unpleasant 'Star of Bethlehem', presented to Exeter College Chapel, where it still hangs. The enormous Burne-Jones water-colour study for this is at Birmingham Art Gallery. It was during the 1880s that the embroidery section of the firm became increasingly important under the direction of May, who, with Dearle, produced and worked many of the designs.

In 1885 Arthur Lazenby Liberty (whose signature may be seen scratched on a glass panel at Red House) bought Littler's print works at Merton Abbey, a property very near Morris's, where he began printing his 'Paisley' silks and Art Nouveau designs which came to be known on the Continent as 'Stile Liberty'.

'I am hard at work on my Birmingham lecture,' Morris writes to Georgie on 10 January 1882, 'I don't feel as if I had much left to say, but must do all I can to say it decently, so as not to discredit the cause.' This was 'The Lesser Arts', delivered at the Midland Institute, Birmingham, on 23 January. A week later he writes again to say that he is at work on another lecture, which became 'The History of Pattern Designing'.

It now seems that Morris began to be oppressed with a sense of the futility of his work in face of the ever-growing vulgarity and ugliness of his age. But the regeneration of the arts, he felt, was 'not basically a question of art at all'. It was basically a political and economic question and no general improvement in design could be hoped for within society as then constituted. This feeling comes out clearly in the letter to Georgie of 17 January:

> . . . it sometimes seems to me as if my lot was a strange one: you see, I work pretty hard, and on the whole very cheerfully, not altogether I hope for mere pudding, still less for praise; and while I work I have the cause always in mind, and yet I know that the cause for which I specially work is doomed to fail, at least in seeming: I mean that art must go under, where or how ever it may come up again. I don't know if I explain what I'm driving at, but it does sometimes seem to me a strange thing indeed that a man should be driven to work with energy and even with pleasure and enthusiasm at work which he knows will serve no end but amusing himself; am I doing nothing but make-believe then, something like Louis XVI's lock-making?

Yet he admits that the problem has no practical application as far as he is concerned – 'since I shall without doubt go on with my work, useful or useless, till I demit'.

Morris's state of mind at this time comes out still more clearly in his criticism of Swinburne's *Tristram of Lyonesse*, which had just appeared. The letter to Georgie in which he expressed it is one of the very few instances where he allowed himself to criticize a contemporary and should be compared with his review of Rossetti's *Poems* of 1871.

As to the poem, I have made two or three attempts to read it, but have failed, not being in the mood I suppose: nothing would lay hold of me at all. This is doubtless my own fault, since it certainly did seem very fine. But, to confess and be hanged, you know I never could really sympathize with Swinburne's work; it always seemed to me to be founded on literature, not on nature. In saying this I really cannot accuse myself of any jealousy on the subject, as I think also you will not. Now I believe that Swinburne's sympathy with literature is most genuine and complete; and it is a pleasure to hear him talk about it, which he does in the best vein possible; he is most steadily enthusiastic about it. Now time was when the poetry resulting merely from this intense study and love of literature might have been, if not the best, yet at any rate very worthy and enduring: but in these days, when all the arts, even poetry, are like to be overwhelmed under the mass of material riches which civilization has made and is making more and more hastily every day; riches which the world has made indeed, but cannot use to any good purpose: in these days when the issue between art, that is, the godlike part of man, and mere bestiality, is so momentous, and the surroundings of life are so stern and unplayful, that nothing can take serious hold of people, or should do so, but that which is rooted deepest in reality and is quite at first hand: there is no room for anything which is not forced out of a man of deep feeling, because of its innate strength and vision.

In all this I may be quite wrong, and the lack may be in myself: I only state an opinion, I don't defend it: still less do I my own poetry. . . .

Indeed, if such criticism applies to *Tristram of Lyonesse*, it applies with equal force (as Morris himself realized) to *The Earthly Paradise*. Yet much of the greatest poetry, Spenser's or Milton's, could be said

to derive from 'an intense study and love of literature'. And Swinburne's opinion of Morris is playfully expressed in his letter to
Watts of the same year, where he says:

> Let him build – & burn – as many halls or homesteads after the
> pattern of Burnt Njal's as he pleases – but for my sake withhold
> him from more metrification à la Piers Plowman. I always fore-
> saw that he would come to reject Chaucer at last as a modern. It
> is my belief that you encourage all this dashed and blank Vol-
> sungery which will end by eating up the splendid genius it has
> already overgrown and incrusted with Iceland moss.

But Morris was already working towards the extreme position of his
letter to Georgie of 21 August 1883:

> I really don't think anything I have done (when I consider it as I
> should another man's work) of any value except to myself: except
> as showing my sympathy with history and the like. Poetry goes
> with the hand-arts, I think, and like them has now become
> unreal: the arts have got to die, what is left of them, before they
> can be born again. You know my views on the matter: I apply
> them to myself as well as to others. This would not, I admit,
> prevent my writing poetry any more than it prevents my doing
> my pattern work, because the mere personal pleasure of it urges
> one to the work; but it prevents one looking at it as a sacred duty
> and the grief aforesaid [Jenny's epileptic attacks which had
> become worse] is too strong and disquieting to be overcome by a
> mere inclination to do what I *know* is unimportant work.

Early in the previous year work at Merton Abbey had been
threatened by the London and South Western Water Company's
plan to tap the head-springs of the river Wandle at Carshalton and
so to reduce it to a muddy ditch. Morris wrote to George Howard,
now Liberal MP for Cockermouth, for help and his protest, joined
to that of thirty-nine other mill-owners on the Wandle, was
successful.

In January 1882 we find him writing for a platform ticket for the
meeting held at the Mansion House to protest against the persecution
of the Jews in Russia. 'I have the greatest dislike of pushing myself
forward in any matter,' he says, 'but when I remind you that I was
actively engaged in the work of the Eastern Question Association
some years back, I think you will understand why I wish to lose no

opportunity of showing that tyranny and brutality are always hateful to me, whosoever the butchers and whosoever the victims may be.' The year before he had written to Georgie in a fury of indignation at the sentence of sixteen months hard labour passed at Bow Street on Johann Most, the editor of the German socialist paper *Freiheit*, who had extolled the assassination of Alexander II of Russia. But mostly it was the judge's speech, with its 'mixture of tyranny and hypo-crisy', which had disgusted him. 'These are the sort of things', he wrote, 'that make thinking people so sick at heart that they are driven from all interest in politics save revolutionary politics: which I must say seems like to be my case.'

Socialism was in the air in the 1880s. As fifty years later, in the 1930s, London was full of political refugees from Germany, Russia, France and Austria. Ruskin, Marx and Henry George were being widely read. In fact, the moral impetus of Ruskin's *Unto This Last* had more influence in creating the British Labour movement than perhaps anything else. Matthew Arnold had also turned in despair from the Philistine commercial middle class and had addressed him-self explicitly to the workers. Indeed, the 'progressive' movements and sects of the time were legion. There were anarchists, syndicalists, positivists, secularists, anti-vivisectionists, Shelleyan vegetarians, who all spoke on one another's platforms. The various socialist sects were soon quarrelling bitterly among themselves and sometimes appeared to hate one another far more than the common enemy, the capitalist ruling class. But in the Democratic Federation of Henry Myers Hyndman, Morris saw the opportunity of doing something practical at last, though it was thought at first, indeed, that it was only necessary to put the principles of socialism clearly before the numerically superior working class for them to rise up in a body and overthrow the state. The social revolution was fixed, somewhat prematurely as it turned out, for 1889.

Faced with the misery and squalor of the industrial towns and the spectacle of whole areas of London given over to brothels, into which the children of the poor were quite openly herded for the perverted pleasures of the rich, juvenile prostitution being a prevalent Victorian vice, it may seem now that it must have been very difficult for a person of ordinary decent feeling *not* to be a socialist. But, as the starving armies of the unemployed demonstrated ever more angrily in the West End of London during the 1880s and the spectre of revolution raised its head, the more comfortable classes began to fear for their own position and what sympathy they had had for 'the deserving poor' evaporated. In any case, most people saw no practical alternative to the established social order, and the horrors of the Paris Commune, 'the red fool fury of the Seine', as Tennyson called it, were still fresh in their memories. After all, England, as the richest and most powerful nation, still led the world, even though in London streets of large Italianate houses abutted on unspeakable slums and the approach of a 'poor person' could be smelt yards away.

Foreign visitors to London at this time, Taine and Dostoevsky among them, were appalled at the spectacle of the Haymarket at night, where prostitutes gathered in their thousands, where mothers put their little daughters up for sale and children of twelve seized your arm and wanted to follow you. 'The spectacle of debauchery in this country', wrote Taine in his *Notes sur l'Angleterre*, 'leaves one with the impression of nothing but degradation and misery.' Gustave Doré, in his great work *London: A Pilgrimage* (1872) has left a pictorial record of the hell inhabited by the poor, together with magical engravings of the life of the rich. It was in the 1880s that W. T. Stead began his series of articles in the *Pall Mall Gazette*, under the title of 'The Maiden Tribute of Modern Babylon', in which he exposed the worst horrors of juvenile prostitution. It was all a far cry from the innocent peace of Kelmscott and the thirteenth-century barn at Great Coxwell, but it was a cry to which William Morris could no longer stop his ears.

In an address to the School of Science and Art connected with the Wedgwood Institute at Burslem, Morris told his audience on 13 October 1881:

As I sit at my work at home, which is at Hammersmith, close to the river, I often hear some of that ruffianism go past the window of which a good deal has been said in the papers of late, and has been said before at recurring periods. As I hear the yells and shrieks and all the degradation cast on the glorious tongue of Shakespeare and Milton, as I see the brutal reckless faces and figures go past me, it rouses the recklessness and brutality in me also, and fierce wrath takes possession of me, till I remember, as I hope I mostly do, that it was my good luck only of being born respectable and rich, that has put me on this side of the window among delightful books and lovely works of art, and not on the other side, in the empty street, the drink-steeped liquor-shops, the foul and degraded lodgings. I know by my own feelings and desires what these men want, what would have saved them from this lowest depth of savagery: employment which would foster their self-respect and win the praise and sympathy of their fellows, and dwellings which they could come to with pleasure, surround-ings which would soothe and elevate them; reasonable labour, reasonable rest. There is only one thing that can give them this – art.

That is, again, art in its very widest application to our whole material environment – not painting, as such, even the work of the Pre-Raphaelites, which, Mackail tells us, Morris now regarded with a 'mixture of admiration and impatient despair' as being out of touch with 'the general sympathy of simple peoples', a lack which made it, he complains in this lecture, 'feverish and dreamy, or crabbed and perverse'. Morris demanded of art an essential moral quality: the qualities most fatal to it, he says, are 'vagueness, hypo-crisy, and cowardice. . . . It is better to be caught out in going wrong when you have had a definite purpose, than to shuffle and slur so that people can't blame you because they don't know what you are at.'

CHAPTER ELEVEN

1883–1884

The Social Democratic Federation

ALMOST TO THE DAY, 13 January 1883, that he was
elected an Honorary Fellow of his college at Oxford, Morris
enrolled as a member of the Democratic (afterwards Social Democratic) Federation. He was now only two months short of fifty. On
his membership card he described himself as 'designer', basing his
claim to admission to a nominally working-class organization on
his status as a workman. His membership card was signed by
H. H. Champion, the son of General Champion, who had resigned
his army commission because of his disapproval of British intervention in Egypt and the Sudan.

The Democratic Federation had been formed in 1881 from the
various Radical clubs of the time, under the chairmanship of Henry
Myers Hyndman. Hyndman's conversion to socialism dated from a
meeting with Karl Marx, a political émigré from Germany, who
had written his epoch-making work *Das Kapital* in the Reading
Room of the British Museum. Hyndman's pamphlet *England for
All* was a direct outcome of his conversations with Marx, though
he did not acknowledge this in his preface. 'I don't like the man,'
George Wardle reports Morris saying of Hyndman, 'but as he is
trying to do what I think ought to be done, I feel that everyone
who has similar ideas ought to help him.'[1]

Meanwhile Morris began to study *Das Kapital* in its French translation. He very much enjoyed the historical chapters, he says (and,
indeed, made liberal use of them in his lectures and in *The Dream
of John Ball* and *News from Nowhere*) but, being unfamiliar with
general economic theory and Hegelian dialectics, confessed that he
'suffered agonies of confusion of the brain over reading the pure
economics of that great work'.[2] They were, he said, 'stiffer going
than some of Browning's poetry'. Nevertheless, he plugged away
with his usual obstinacy and ten years later produced, with the
English Marxist Belfort Bax, *Socialism: Its Growth and Outcome*.

'I do not think he had read any distinctively socialist books before he joined Hyndman', Wardle wrote to Sydney Cockerell on 24 August 1898.

He would have been sure to speak of it, more especially as just then he was very keen on the various theories or schemes for social change, more particularly the emancipation and education of the workman. This brought him into relation with trades unionists. . . . Morris's aim was to proceed by the social advancement of the workmen and to that end he hoped to organize a strong political party out of the radical elements or out of the trade unions. We had meetings in our showroom in Queen Square (in the evenings) to which he invited leaders of the working-men radicals.

At this time Morris was working out a plan of profit sharing based on Leclaire's experiment. Wardle states:

The plan was clearly no solution of the question which was occupying Morris, but he adopted so much of it as to give some half dozen of us a direct interest in the business. I pointed out that the expansion of the plan to the whole shop would involve endless book-keeping – a thing he hated. . . . The evenings in the showroom could not have been before the removal to Horrington House, they may have been some years later than that. The profit-sharing arrangement could only have been made after Morris was sole owner of the business.

But the more he became involved in socialist propaganda the more acutely aware Morris became of his own anomalous position as a capitalist. Admittedly his position was a difficult one, though none of his own workers at Merton Abbey seems to have felt it, since he always dealt with them on a basis of man-to-man equality.

After his earlier experiences with the Eastern Question Association and his more recent relations with the Liberal Party, Morris had grown completely disillusioned with party politics. Nothing, he felt, could now be done with the old gang: new material was wanted and could only be had, if at all, out of the working class. His efforts were, therefore, directed to forming some kind of political party largely out of that class which would be independent of the accepted Radical leaders. 'He attended many meetings of working men', Wardle continues, 'in hopes, I suppose, of finding some sympathetic minds, but he did not get much encouragement. They were mostly, if not all, occupied with local or trade politics and for my own part I remember nothing of the few I myself attended, with him or alone, but the feeling of disappointment.' Wardle adds that he himself had no time for politics:

my ordinary day's work often leaving me sufficiently tired, and moreover I was very unsympathetic, partly from that feeling of hopelessness which took possession of me, the hopelessness of doing anything effective by organization which was not more methodical than anything Morris would have submitted to – and because I was obliged to discourage Morris from talking politics all day, which he gladly would have done, at that time. . . . In the beginning, when it was rather a question of educating the work, men, more especially the artisan or worker in some of the fine arts, Morris gave his first lectures on Art. They were given for Warr [Professor G. C. W. Warr, a positivist, had founded, with Morris's help, the London Trades Guild of Learning for educat, ing young workers, apprentices and so on, with Lord Rosebery as president] who got up the meetings. I need hardly say there were very few workmen of any kind there, except the men from Queen Square and that the bulk of the audience was formed of Morris's clients.

The education of the workman of course always remained the end and motive of his political action. It was the true root of his socialism. . . . His socialism then had the future of English Art for its justification – if we accept excellence in the fine arts as the test of a nation's moral elevation and of its general happiness.[3]

The Democratic Federation had absorbed by this time many of the former pupils of Mill, Spencer, Comte and Darwin, who under the influence of Henry George's *Progress and Poverty* had left aside evolution and free thought and taken to 'insurrectionary economics'. Other members of the Democratic Federation included – or were to include, when it became the Social Democratic Federation – Marx's brilliant daughter Eleanor, who formed a disastrous liaison with Edward Aveling (the original of Shaw's Dubedat), Annie Besant, who afterwards became a Theosophist, and J. L. Joynes, a former classics master at Eton, who was dismissed after making a tour of Ireland with Henry George. Joynes was married to the daughter of Henry Salt, another Eton master and Shelleyan vegetarian, who had given up his house to live in a workman's cottage in Surrey and to found the Humanitarian League. Among Salt's friends were Bernard Shaw, who used to play piano duets with Salt's wife, and Edward Carpenter, a socialist and pioneer writer on homosexuality, whom they used to call 'the Noble Savage'. Closely associated with this group were Stewart Headlam and other Christian Socialists.

When the Fabian Society was founded in 1884, Shaw persuaded Sidney Webb and Sydney Olivier, both Colonial Office clerks, to join – 'Marx having convinced me', says Shaw, 'that what the movement needed was not Hegelian theorizing but an unveiling of the official facts of Capitalist civilization, which Webb had at his fingers' ends.'⁴ Later, Graham Wallas joined, too. But in the Salt-Joynes-Carpenter circle, Shaw tells us, there was 'no question of Henry George and Karl Marx, but a good deal of Walt Whitman and Thoreau'. Such were the progressives of the 1880s. One finds many of their views expressed in Carpenter's remarkable book *Civilization: Its Cause and Cure*. Most of these men were, at one time or another, associated with Morris. But the 'enormous advantage' the founders of the Fabian Society had over the Democratic Federation, according to Shaw, was 'their homogeneity of class and age. There were no illiterate working-men among them; there were no born poor-men; there was not five years' difference between the eldest and the youngest.'⁵ Again: 'Hyndman's congregation of manual-working pseudo-Marxists could for me be only hindrances.'⁶

When Morris joined the Democratic Federation, he was, says Hyndman, 'even too eager to take his full share in the unpleasant part of our public work and speedily showed that he meant to work in grim earnest on the same level as the rank and file of our party. . . . He was never satisfied unless he was doing things which, to say the truth, he was little fitted for, and others of coarser fibre could do much better than he.' But as a speaker, Hyndman adds, 'his imposing forehead and clear grey eyes, with the powerful nose and slightly florid cheeks, impressed you with the truth and importance of what he was saying, every hair of his head and in his rough shaggy beard appearing to enter into the subject as a living part of himself'.⁷

On 6 March 1883 Morris lectured to the Manchester Royal Institution on 'Art, Wealth, and Riches'. It was his angriest indictment of capitalist civilization so far. 'Why don't we care about art?' he cried. 'Why has civilized society in all that relates to the beauty of man's handiwork degenerated from the time of the barbarous, superstitious, unpeaceful Middle Ages?' It is because, under the system of division of labour, the workman 'is part of a machine, and has but one unvarying set of tasks to do, and when he has once learned these, the more regularly and with the less thought he does them, the more valuable he is'. Hence the dullness and lifelessness of what is produced, though Morris conceded that it will have 'a certain high finish, and what I should call shop-counter look, quite peculiar to the wares of this century'. But the result in human terms of this degradation of the workman was the frightful gulf between the classes. In spite of all 'the shouts of progress that have been raised for many years . . . there are two languages talked in England: gentleman's English and workman's English'. Morris found this 'barbarous and dangerous; and it goes step by step with the lack of art which the same classes are forced into; it is a token, in short, of that vulgarity, to use a hateful word, which was not in existence before modern times and the blossoming of competitive commerce'.

Since Morris's time we have witnessed a considerable levelling of classes, with results in this country rather different from those he expected. For the vulgarity he complained of has become, thanks to the mass media of press, cinema, television and radio, the new popular culture. 'Workman's English' has become literary English and the recklessness and brutality Morris abhorred as disgracing the tongue of Shakespeare and Milton has become the distinguishing mark of our new drama and fiction. We have an affluent society based on competitive commerce in which the standards of life are set by advertising. At the same time, however, this has brought about a widespread reaction in a desire for further education, new universities and university grants. At no time have concert halls, opera houses and picture galleries been so frequented by all classes of people as today. It is an anomalous situation of extremes which have yet to find their level.

Morris concluded his lecture on 'Art, Wealth, and Riches' by a statement of some of the changes he wanted to see. It tells us a good deal about the sort of man he was.

I want, then, all persons to be educated according to their capacity, not according to the amount of money which their parents happen to have. I want all persons to have manners and breeding accord- ing to their innate goodness and kindness, and not according to the amount of money which their parents happen to have. As a consequence of these two things I want to be able to talk to any of my countrymen in his own tongue freely, and feeling sure that he will be able to understand my thoughts according to his innate capacity; and I also want to be able to sit at table with a person of any occupation without a feeling of awkwardness and constraint being present between us. I want no one to have any money except as due wages for work done. . . . I want those who do the rough work of the world, sailors, miners, ploughmen, and the like, to be treated with consideration and respect, to be paid abundant money-wages, and to have plenty of leisure. I want modern science, which I believe to be capable of overcoming all material difficulties, to turn from such preposterous follies as the invention of anthracine colours and monster cannon to the invention of machines for performing such labour as is revolting and destructive of self-respect to the men who now have to do it by hand.

Thus we see that Morris was very much in favour of genuine labour-saving machinery, instead of machinery which saved labour in order, as he said, that it might be spent when saved on tending other machinery. Since his time, however, modern science, through nuclear fission and bacteriological research, has perfected means not only for abolishing the human race altogether, but for rendering the earth itself completely sterile. In a humbler way, by its invention of chemical sprays and insecticides, now widely used in agriculture, it has gone a long way towards getting rid of the wild flowers, the birds and the butterflies of our hedgerows – where, indeed, the hedges themselves have not been rooted up and the trees cut down in the name of scientific farming. Science is thus fast robbing the countryside of its natural beauties – our one solace for the growing nightmare of our towns and cities.

Morris concluded, a voice crying in the wilderness:

I want this . . . that these islands which make the land we love should no longer be treated as here a cinder heap, and there a game preserve, but as the fair green garden of Northern Europe, which no man on any pretence should be allowed to befoul and disfigure. . . . I want all the works of man's hand to be beautiful, rising in fair and honourable gradation from the simplest house-hold goods to the stately public building, adorned with the handiwork of the greatest masters of expression which that real new birth and the day spring of hope come back will bring forth for us.

For the 'change', Morris believed, would certainly come. He is only anxious that it should come gradually and peaceably. 'How, then, can we prevent its coming with violence and injustice that will breed other grievances in time, to be met with fresh discontent? Once again, how good it were to destroy all that must be destroyed gradually and with good grace!'

It was for such sentiments that Engels called Morris 'a settled sentimental Socialist'.[8] Nevertheless, when his lecture was reported in *The Manchester Examiner*, it raised a storm of protest. One indignant reader complained that Morris had 'raised another question than one of mere art'. Morris at once replied that that was precisely his intention.

> I specially wished to point out that the question of popular art was a social question, involving the happiness or misery of the greater part of the community. The absence of popular art from modern times is more disquieting and grievous to bear for this reason than for any other, that it betokens that fatal division of men into the cultivated and the degraded classes which competitive commerce has bred and fosters. . . . What business have we with art at all unless all can share it? . . . I could never forget that in spite of all drawbacks my work is little more than pleasure to me; that under no conceivable circumstances would I give it up even if I could. Over and over again have I asked myself why should not my lot be the common lot.[9]

Morris felt that he had only to project his vision of the good life sufficiently clearly for all men to desire it. But in this he was mistaken, as he came reluctantly to realize because, as a matter of fact, for the average worker the good life was represented by the kind of life led by the average capitalist – the sort of life which Morris himself abhorred.

Meanwhile things were not going too well at Merton Abbey. Morris wrote to Jenny on 14 March:

> We are not getting on so fast with the printing at Merton as we ought: I was away for a fortnight with gout, & Wardle was away more than usual: the colour mixer Kenyon is a good fellow, but rather a muddler, & often in order to be sure that the thing is

properly done either Wardle or I have to stand over him all the time: this is especially the case with the madder dyeing which we are on now. . . . I have just got back my lecture [the Manchester lecture, issued as a leaflet by the Democratic Federation] with the proofs, as they are going to print it: so I shall be able to bring it down & read it to you. . . .

Early in April Morris was lecturing at Hampstead. 'The audience if not large was at least as large as the room would hold', he wrote to Jenny,

> they were very polite, and buttered me, as Mr Jorrocks would say, most plentifully; I didn't think that there were many working men there: the others seemed mostly very 'advanced' as the slang goes, & some very intelligent. It was rather a job getting there & back and I didn't get home till past midnight. By the way among the other *intelligent* people who should I stumble across but C. J. Faulkner who [had] been to call on his Orrin-Smiths. I preach at Clerkenwell on April 15th and shall do my best for them. . . .

The Hampstead lecture also produced irate letters to the press, since Morris made it clear that he was speaking for the Democratic Federation and distributed their leaflet.

On Whit Monday 1883 he writes to Jenny from Hammersmith: 'I hope it won't be long before you are all up here: a *grass bachelor's* life is not very delightful amongst other things. . . . I was a great deal at Merton last week, though I didn't sleep there, anxiously super-intending the first printing of the Strawberry Thief, which I think we shall manage this time.' The previous day, he had entertained a large company at Hammersmith:

> old Dr Bock who is the man who set on foot all the lore of old woven stuffs; he could not talk English: so I had to talk English-French against his German-French; doubtless a concert to make the Gods laugh: also there was another German, Andreas Scheu a Vienna Socialist, who seems a very nice fellow, talks English well: also Middleton, Benson [W. A. S. Benson, architect and designer in metalwork], & De Morgan. I gave and received presents of stuffs with Bock, for which I hope your mother won't scold.

In May he is lecturing at the Irish National League rooms in the Blackfriars Road: 'all or most Irish there; and Parnellites to the backbone, but dear me! such quiet respectable people!' he tells Jenny. 'I was able to please them by assuring them of my sympathy for their views, and also by telling them that I had read and much admired translations of their ancient literature.' At Merton, he continues, 'the marsh marigolds are all out and are splendid. . . . I got my first bundle of sparrow-grass there to-day, but I thought it too small to send to you: so I left it with Kate Faulkner, with whom I teaed this evening, knowing that she liked it. My dear Jenny, good-bye; did you like the flowers I sent you from Axminster by the way? I will pluck a big bunch of wallflowers to-morrow and send them to you somehow.' In his next letter of 19 May he tells her:

> On Tuesday and on Thursday I walked all the way to Merton by Roehampton Lane; really a pleasant walk: I am quite sick of the Underground & I think I shall often walk to or from Merton, it takes a long 2 hours; but you see it is not all pure waste like the sweltering train-business. . . . I went to the meeting of the Demo-cratic Federation on Monday, and I found I was driven into joining its executive: so I am in for more work: however I don't like belonging to a body without knowing what they are doing: without feeling very sanguine about their doings they seem certainly to mean something. . . .

On 28 August he writes to Jenny again: 'I was rather tired yesterday, as besides the walk [to Merton Abbey] I spent the afternoon dyeing tapestry wools, & finished by my usual Monday talk at Hyndman's, however dyeing is a good sport to me still.'

At Hyndman's Morris discussed the theory and practice of socialism, and collaborated in a sixty-four-page pamphlet, *A Summary of the Principles of Socialism*, for which he designed the wrapper. But it was Merton Abbey that provided the main refresh-ment of his life. In comparison the preparation of lectures was very hard work. ' 'Tis to be a short one but will give me a fortnight's work I know', he complains of one lecture.

Burne-Jones had also been elected an Honorary Fellow of Exeter with Morris, but neither of them had as yet formally taken his place as a Fellow. On 2 July 1883, therefore, they both went to Oxford to dine in hall, just as they had entered the university together thirty years before. Soon after Morris joined the Democratic Federation, Burne-Jones completed his *King Cophetua and the Beggar Maid*, which was as far as he ever got towards social commentary in his painting. To his wife, this picture 'contained more of Edward's distinctive qualities than any other that he did'.

But socialism was a subject the two friends left alone when they were together, by tacit agreement – not that Morris had any illusions about Hyndman and the Democratic Federation. As he wrote to Georgie that August:

I am like enough to have some trouble over my propagandist work, let alone that I am in for a many lectures: for small as our body is, we are not without dissensions in it. Some of the more ardent spirits look upon Hyndman as too opportunist, and there is truth in that; he is sanguine of speedy change happening some-how, and is inclined to intrigue and the making of a party; towards which end compromise is needed, and the carrying people who don't really agree with us as far as they will go. As you know, I am not sanguine, and think the aim of Socialists should be the founding of a religion, towards which end com-promise is no use, and we only want to have those with us who will be with us to the end. But then again, if the zealots don't take care they will blow the whole thing to the winds. . . . In the midst of all this, I find myself drifting into the disgraceful position of a moderator and patcher up, which is much against my inclination.

Meantime it is obvious that the support to be looked for for constructive Socialism from the working-class at present is nought. Who can wonder, as things now are, when the lower classes are really lower? Of vague discontent and a spirit of revenge for the degradation in which they are kept there is plenty I think, but that seems all. What we want is real leaders them-selves working men, and content to be so till classes are abolished. But you see when a man has gifts for that kind of thing he finds himself tending to rise out of his class before he has begun to think of class politics as a matter of principle, and too often he is simply 'got at' by the governing classes, not formally, but by circumstances I mean. Education is the word doubtless; but then in comes the commercial system and defends itself against this in a terrible unconscious way with the struggle for bread, and lack of leisure, and squalid housing – and there we go, round and round the circle still.

In this many will recognize a characteristically perceptive outline of the future of the Labour movement in England.

In October, Morris was invited by the Russell Club, a society of Liberal undergraduates with Radical tendencies, to speak in the hall of University College, Oxford. As a member of the Democratic Federation he saw no reason to moderate his views for the sake of his audience and he made this quite clear beforehand in a letter to Faulkner. There was a growing interest in social studies at Oxford at this time, under the stimulus of such men as Arnold Toynbee. The idea of University settlements in the East End of London, in which Toynbee Hall was to lead the way, was already in the air and social reform was the current subject of discussion in college debating societies and filled the pages of the Oxford magazines. Henry George himself had lectured at Oxford on land nationalization, and the studied incivility with which he was treated by the authorities had aroused a strong reaction in his favour. But the university evidently felt that it was probably a good thing to give this alarming new movement a chance to dissipate itself in discussion. In adopting this attitude they proved wiser than their opposite numbers on the Continent, where being repressed, the intellectual movement towards socialism became an explosive force.

Nevertheless, the Master of University College seems to have found it difficult to believe that a Fellow of Exeter, a well-known poet and the head of Morris & Co. could really be a socialist in any militant sense. He was soon to realize his mistake. 'I am tired of being mealy mouthed', Morris had written to Jenny in March. He called his lecture 'Art and Democracy'. It was his first definite public pronouncement as a socialist and one of his main butts was 'Oxford culture, so-called'.

On 14 November, then, under the auspices of the Master of University College, the Warden of Keble, the Warden of Merton, and John Ruskin, the Slade Professor of Fine Art, Morris began his lecture by saying straight away that his real subject was art under plutocracy and that he was not there to criticize any special school of art or artists, or to plead for any special style, but to talk about the hindrances in the way towards making art what it should be. He pointed out that art could not be dealt with in isolation, but that it was closely bound up with the general condition of society – 'especially with the lives of those who live by manual labour and whom we call the working classes'. He went on to say that he could not help thinking that there was a feeling of despair as to what art would be in the future, and by art he said that he meant 'every one of the things that goes to make up the surroundings among which we live'. How does it fare, he asked, with our external surroundings in these days?

> Go through Oxford streets and ponder on what is left us there unscathed by the fury of the thriving shop and the progressive college. . . . Not only are London and our other great commercial cities mere masses of sordidness, filth, and squalor, embroidered with patches of pompous and vulgar hideousness, no less revolt' ing to the eye and the mind when one knows what it means: not only have whole counties of England, and the heavens that hang over them, disappeared beneath a crust of unutterable grime, but the disease, which, to a visitor coming from the times of art, reasons and order, would seem to be a love of dirt and ugliness for its own sake, spreads all over the country, and every little market town seizes the opportunity to imitate, as far as it can, the majesty of the hell of London and Manchester. Need I speak to you of the wretched suburbs that sprawl round our fairest and most ancient cities? Must I speak to you of the degradation that has so speedily befallen this city, still the most beautiful of them all, a city which, with its surroundings, would, if we had a grain of commonsense, have been treated like a most precious jewel, whose beauty was to be preserved at any cost? I say at any cost, for it was a possession which did not belong to us, but which we were trustees of for all posterity. . . . When I remember the con' trast between the Oxford of to'day and the Oxford which I first saw thirty years ago, I wonder I can face the misery (there is no other word for it) of visiting it, even to have the honour of address' ing you to'night . . . in short, our civilization is passing like a blight, daily growing heavier and more poisonous, over the whole face of the country. . . . So it comes to this, that not only are the minds of great artists narrowed and their sympathies frozen by their isolation, not only has co'operative art come to a standstill, but the very food on which both the greater and the lesser art subsists is being destroyed: the well of art is poisoned at its spring.

As he sat listening, Ruskin surely must have felt proud of his pupil: his mantle had fallen upon broader and more vigorous shoulders. But doubtless the other dignitaries on the platform wondered a little uneasily what was coming, when Morris continued:

> I not only admit, but declare, and think it most important to declare, that so long as the system of competition in the production and exchange of the means of life goes on, the degradation of the arts will go on; and if that system is to last for ever, then art is doomed and will surely die; that is to say, civilization will die.

But fortunately, he went on, remembering his Marx, the present system was no more eternal than that of citizen and chattel slave, or feudal lord and serf, and would evolve, as other systems had evolved, through the antagonism of classes, into a classless society. 'For I am "one of the people called Socialists",' Morris declared. 'I hold that the condition of competition between man and man is bestial only, and that of association human.'

'Art and Democracy' is one of Morris's most splendid lectures and in it he puts forward his defence of handiwork as opposed to machine civilization:

> Under this system of handiwork no great pressure of speed was put on a man's work, but he was allowed to carry it through leisurely and thoughtfully; it used the whole of a man for the production of a piece of goods, and not small portions of many men; it developed the workman's whole intelligence according to his capacity, instead of concentrating his energy on one-sided dealing with a trifling piece of work. . . . It was this system, which had not learned the lesson that man was made for commerce, but supposed in its simplicity that commerce was made for men, which produced the art of the Middle Ages, wherein the harmonious co-operation of free intelligence was carried to the furthest point which has yet been attained, and which alone of all art can claim to be called Free. The effect of this freedom, and the widespread or rather universal sense of beauty to which it gave birth, became obvious enough in the outburst of the expression of splendid and copious genius which marks the Italian Renaissance. Nor can it be doubted that this glorious art was the fruit of the five centuries of free popular art which preceded it, and not of the rise of commercialism which was contemporaneous with it; for the glory of the Renaissance faded out with strange rapidity as commercial competition developed, so that about the end of the seventeenth century, both in the intellectual and the decorative

arts, the commonplace or body still existed, but the romance or soul of them was gone.

The present system of production, he thundered, which employed men, women and children, had spread the curse of unhappiness throughout society,

> from the poor wretches, the news of whom we middle-class people are just now receiving with such naïve wonder and horror; from those poor people whom nature forces to strive against hope, and to expend all the divine energy of man in competing for something less than a dog's lodging and a dog's food, from them up to the cultivated and refined person, well lodged, well fed, well clothed, expensively educated, but lacking all interest in life except, it may be, the cultivation of unhappiness as a fine art.

But it may be, he went on, that the mass of the working people in England have no hope, that it may not be hard to keep them down for a while, possibly a long while. But there was plenty of discontent about, and he called upon 'those who think there is something better than making money for the sake of making it, to help in educating that discontent into hope, that is into the demand for the new birth of society.' He concluded:

> I am representing reconstructive Socialism before you; but there are other people who call themselves Socialists whose aim is not reconstruction, but destruction; people who think that the present state of things is horrible and unbearable (as in very truth it is) and that there is nothing for it but to shake society by constant blows given at any sacrifice, so that it may at last totter and fall. May it not be worth while, think you, to combat such a doctrine by supplying discontent with hope of change that involves reconstruction?

But, he warned his audience, the change, however long delayed, would come. Before that time some members of the middle classes will have renounced their class and thrown in their lot with the working men, 'influenced by love of justice and insight into facts'. And it would largely depend on the attitude of the middle classes, he told them, whether the change or the new birth, when it came, would be peaceable or violent.

Since I am a member of a Socialist propaganda I earnestly beg of those of you who agree with me to help us actively, with your time and your talents if you can, but if not, at least with your money, as you can. . . . Art is long and life is short: let us at least do something before we die. We seek perfection, but find no perfect means to bring it about: let it be enough for us if we can unite with those whose aims are right, and their means honest and feasible . . . organized brotherhood is that which must break the spell of anarchical Plutocracy.

It was a noble speech, by any standard, and has since become a classic. But it raised a storm of protest. For a Fellow of an Oxford college to abuse the hospitality of another college by appealing for funds for a socialist organization, was unheard of. The Master, Dr Bright, got up to protest. But Ruskin, as chairman, says H. W. Nevinson, who was present, 'with his usual exquisite tact, quietly insisted that Morris was entirely right'.[10]

To most people, socialism in those days meant either the Paris Commune or anarchist and nihilist bomb outrages and assassination. 'Socialism! Then blow us up, blow us up! There's nothing left for it but that', cried Dr Warne, headmaster of Eton, when he heard of Henry Salt's conversion in 1880. Tennyson, when William Alling-ham told him of Morris's conversion to socialism, cried: 'He's gone crazy!'

From Merton Abbey, Morris wrote to Georgie:

I have been living in a storm of brickbats, to some of which I had to reply: of course I don't mind a bit, nor even think the attack unfair. My own men here are very sympathetic, which pleases me hugely; and I find we shall get on much better for my having spoken my mind about things: seven of them would insist on joining the Democratic Federation, though I preached to them the necessity of really understanding it all. . . .

But Morris's friends observed that he was losing his sense of humour and that it was no longer possible to discuss politics with him with-out the risk of a quarrel. 'When he went into it', Burne-Jones wrote bitterly:

I thought he would have subdued the ignorant, conceited, mis-taken rancour of it all – that he would teach them some humility and give them some sense of obedience, with his splendid bird's-eye view of all that has happened in the world and his genius for History in the abstract. I had hopes he would affect them. But never a bit – he did them absolutely no good – they got complete possession of him. All the nice men that went into it were never listened to, only noisy, rancorous ones got the ear of the movement.

Yet Burne-Jones understood how Morris felt:

How can some men help having an ideal of the world they want, and feeling for it as a religion, and sometimes being fanatical for it and unwise – as men are too for the religion that they love? It must be, and Morris is quite right, only for my sake I wish he could be out of it all and busy only for the things he used to be busy about.[11]

And London was changing for the worse, too. The District Railway had reached Fulham and the speculative builder with it. The old elms had been cut down in North End Lane and the gardens adjoining the Grange were laid waste, then built over. 'The Sleep of Arthur in Avalon is my chief dream now,' Burne-Jones had written the previous autumn, 'and I think I can put into it all I most care for.'

Morris still regularly breakfasted at the Grange on Sundays and after breakfast retired to Ned's studio and read to him as he worked. Mackail quotes from a private diary (perhaps Cormell Price's) which records such an occasion.

Feb. 22 [1883]. At Ned's. Top came in to breakfast: was extremely brilliant as soon as he had shaken off a little drooping of spirits owing to bad news about Jenny. Was very angry against Seddon for replacing old Hammersmith Church ('a harmless silly old thing') by such an excrescence. He was bubbling over with Karl Marx, whom he had just read in French. He praised Robert Owen immensely. He had been giving an address to a Clerkenwell Radical Club and found the members 'eager to learn but dreadfully ignorant'. . . . Finely explosive against railways. Some imitation Morris wallpaper was 'a mangy gherkin on a horse dung ground'. Spent the evening at Top's – a long talk on birds: T's knowledge of them very extensive: can go on for hours about their habits: but especially about their form.

Morris had many opportunities to observe birds as he sat fishing at Kelmscott. His letters are full of their doings. 'In the twilight the stint or summer snipe was crying about us and flitting from under the bank and across the stream,' he writes on one occasion, 'such a clean-made, neat-feathered, light grey little chap he is, with a wild musical note like all the moor-haunting birds.' His observations bore fruit in such designs as the 'Bird and Anemone', the 'Straw-berry Thief', the 'Vine and Acanthus' and 'Woodpecker' tapestries, the 'Bird', the 'Dove and Peacock' hangings, and in endless birds in the hand-made carpets, though it is invariably said that all the birds and wild animals in the Morris & Co. textiles were designed by Webb. Morris used to watch the thrushes at work among the strawberry beds at Kelmscott with wry amusement and told the gardener, who growled 'I'd like to wring their necks', that no bird in the garden must be touched. A notice to this effect hung in the dining-room. 'There were certainly more birds than strawberries', says May Morris.

Shortly before Morris joined the Democratic Federation he sold his library, in order to devote the proceeds to the furtherance of social-ism. Among the books sold at this time was a copy of *De Claris Mulieribus*, his first purchase among the masterpieces of the early printers. He also sold his Skalaholt Press collection of sagas, which he had bought in Iceland. 'If the modern books are unsaleable, per-haps you would let me take them out after your valuation,' he wrote to Ellis, 'as I have no idea what they are worth to sell (though beastly dear to buy), and though I hate them and should be glad to be rid of them as far as pleasure is concerned, they are of some use to me professionally – though by the way I am not a professional man, but a tradesman.'

Morris designed a membership card for the Democratic Federa-tion inscribed Liberty, Equality, Fraternity in block capitals and below, against a background of a widely branching oak tree, scrolls bearing the name of the organization and the exhortation 'Educate, Agitate, Organize'. Meanwhile, a new executive had been elected which included Hyndman, J. L. Joynes, H. H. Champion, James Macdonald, a Scottish tailor who had read Engels, Belfort Bax and Andreas Scheu, an Austrian furniture-designer, who, May Morris says, looked like one of Dürer's bearded warriors. Morris was made treasurer, as he was the only member, except Hyndman, with any money.

In January 1884, the Democratic Federation became the Social

Democratic Federation and launched its weekly paper *Justice*, on funds provided by Edward Carpenter, converted to socialism by Hyndman's *England for All*. The first issue was sold by the members of the executive themselves in Fleet Street. 'It was a curious scene,' Hyndman wrote later in his autobiography, 'Morris in his soft hat and blue suit, Champion, Frost and Joynes in the morning gar﹣ments of the well﹣do﹣do, several working﹣men comrades, and I myself wearing the new frock﹣coat in which Shaw said I was born, with a tall hat and good gloves, all earnestly engaged in selling a penny Socialist paper during the busiest time of the day in London's busiest thoroughfare.' Not many people bought *Justice*, so that when Carpenter's funds ran out, Morris had to finance it. Engels, too, had a poor opinion of it. On 16 February he wrote to Paul and Laura Lafargue: 'Hyndman combines internationalist phraseology with jingo aspirations, Joynes is a muddle﹣headed ignoramus – I saw him a fortnight ago – Morris is all very well as far as he goes, but it is not far.'

A monthly paper called *To﹣Day* had just been taken over by Belfort Bax and Joynes, and Morris wrote to Swinburne saying that 'it would give them a lift if you would undertake to write something for them, verse if possible . . .'. He concluded by inviting Swinburne to join the S D F: 'You ought to write us a song, you know; that's what you ought to do: I mean to be set to music, for singing at meetings of the faithful.' Swinburne replied on 21 November: 'I need not assure you, I should hope, of my sympathy with any who aspire to help in rectifying that state of things which allows the existence of such horrors and iniquities as surround us', and went on: 'there is no one in England with whom I should be so glad or so proud to work as I should be to work with you, yet I am very seriously convinced that I can do better service – if any – as a single and private workman than as a member of any society or federation. I do trust you will not . . . regard me as a dilettante democrat if I say that I would rather not join. . . .'[12]

It was *To﹣Day* which, this year, serialized Shaw's early novel, *An Unsocial Socialist*, after it had been refused by most of the publishing houses in London. But Morris was amused by it and asked to meet the author. In another number, Eleanor Marx reported Morris's address at the opening of an art exhibition in Commercial Street, Whitechapel, under philanthropic auspices, in order to 'bring art to the people'. After paying tribute to the good nature of those who had made the exhibition possible by lending paintings, Morris remarked dryly that the time of the meeting, in the middle of the afternoon, 'shows that we expect to have it to ourselves – the middle-class – and therefore may talk the freer about our own shortcomings'. He went on to say that he intended to talk about the relations of labour to the rest of life and that 'as our life in general depends on the condition of labour, so it is clear that which we call art does more particularly depend upon it'. The foundation of all art being 'manly reverence for the life of man past and present and to come . . . I say once more that those who look upon art as merely a handmaid to the luxury of rich and idle people, do not understand what it means'.[13] Eleanor Marx comments of the well-to-do gathering at the exhibition: 'It was amusing to note the astonishment not unmingled with irritation of these good people when the poet in very plain prose told them they were not so very superior after all.'[14]

In January 1884 Morris had given two lectures to the Hampstead Liberal Club, that on the 16th being the famous 'Useful Work *versus* Useless Toil'. In the course of this he said: 'The first step to be taken then is to abolish a class of men privileged to shirk their duties as men, thus forcing others to do the work which they refuse to do.' He followed this with a clear exposition of Marx's theory of surplus value. The lecture 'Art and Socialism' was given to the Leicester Secular Society on 23 January. In February he was lecturing in Bradford. Afterwards he wrote to Jane on the 25th:

They are mostly a sad set of Philistines there, and it will be a long time before we can do anything with them: you see the workmen are pretty comfortable there because all the spinning and weaving is done by women and children; the latter go to the mill at 10 years old for 5 hours a day as half-timers: I don't think all my vigorous words (of a nature that you may imagine) shook the conviction of my entertainers that this was the way to make an Earthly Paradise. Well, I met Hyndman and our emissaries at Blackburn afterwards and we had a very good meeting in the big hall there, about 1500 people present: and a branch was formed: all likely to do well there.

I don't think I shall get gout, I haven't time for it; but I have a cold and what's more it's got into my throat to make me hoarse for to-night. . . .

The first anniversary of the death of Karl Marx occurred in March 1884 and Morris marched to Highgate Cemetery to do him honour, writing to Jane on the 18th:

> On Sunday afternoon I performed a religious function. I was loth to go, but did not dislike it when I did go: in brief, I trudged all the way from Tottenham Court Rd. up to Highgate Cemetery (with a red ribbon in my button-hole) at the tail of various banners and a very bad band to do honour to the memory of Karl Marx *and* the Commune: the thing didn't look as absurd as it sounds, as we were a tidy number, I should think more than a thousand in the procession, and onlookers to the amount, when we got to the end, of some 2 or 3 thousand more I should say. Of course they wouldn't let us into the cemetery, and honoured us with a heavy guard of policemen; so we adjourned to an un-comfortable piece of waste ground near by and the song [pre-sumably the 'Internationale'] was sung and speeches made; only diversified by a rather feeble attempt by the hobblehoys to interrupt, which our people checked with the loss of one hat (Mr Williams'); after which we marched off the ground triumphant with police-men on each side of us like a royal procession.

Morris seems to have enjoyed the whole thing. Cobden Sanderson joined them at the cemetery and they went back to Hammersmith together, with Hyndman, 'and finished the evening, Dick and Mr Gell and brother being there, with discussion and supper, fairly harmoniously. . . . All well with business: the new blocker is come and seems a good fellow: we are striking off a fend of "Wandle" now: item, we are going to begin our velvet-weaving soon, it will be very grand. . . .'

The 'Cray' and 'Wandle' chintzes, printed at Merton Abbey this year, with the 'Wey' of the previous year, have an emphatic diagonal design which Morris had never used before and which Peter Floud attributes to the influence of the fifteenth-century Italian cut velvet acquired by the South Kensington Museum in 1883. 'Morris', writes Floud, 'followed this model not only in the direction and angle of the diagonal, but more particularly in carefully arranging the flowers which grew out on either side of the diagonal stem so that their repetitions form a subsidiary horizontal and vertical grid, which helps to give stability to what would otherwise be a very restless type of design.'[15]

As well as travelling all over the country to give lectures, Morris did a good deal of writing for *Justice*, including a review of the Royal Academy Summer Exhibition, which he described as 'a wild jumble of inanity'. Otherwise he was writing *Chants for Socialists*. These were fairly elementary, more or less doggerel pieces written to be set to music and sung by choirs, during 'Art Evenings' organized by the SDF, at which Morris and Edward Aveling gave readings and Bernard Shaw played piano duets with Annie Besant and Kathleen Ina. The Hammersmith branch of the SDF also had its choir, which met at Kelmscott House and was trained by Gustav Holst, a neighbour.

By the summer of 1884 Morris was speaking regularly at open-air meetings in Hyde Park, Regent's Park and Victoria Park in the East End together with Hyndman, John Burns, Tom Mann, and Jack Williams. On 23 July a great demonstration of Radical working men was organized in Hyde Park by the London Trades Council, after the House of Lords had thrown out the Third Reform Act which introduced the County Franchise. There was a call for the abolition of the House of Lords and for municipal government for London. John Bright also demanded a severe limitation of the Lords' right of veto. The SDF, however, did not participate in this agitation, but set up their own separate platform to preach socialism from a cart with a red flag and a *Justice* poster, while unemployed East Enders were enrolled to sell the paper itself.

Morris, Hyndman and Champion went to the Park with a dozen or so other members, and took up their position on the top of a mound near the reservoir. Champion, Hyndman and John Burns addressed a crowd of four to five thousand people. All went well till Burns began to abuse John Bright and the crowd rushed the platform. 'Some fellows seemed to be going for Burns,' Morris wrote to Scheu on 26 July,

> and I was afraid he might be hurt: so I bored through the crowd somehow and got up to him and saw a few friends about us, Cooper of Merton Abbey, Champion, Sanderson, Burns' brothers and others. However off the hill we were shoved in spite of our shoulders. But at the bottom of the hill we managed to make a ring again and Burns began again and spoke for 3 or 4 minutes, but we were too near the hill, there was another ugly rush which broke up our ring and we were shoved away again.

The crowd was in an angry mood and wanted to duck Burns in the Serpentine, but fortunately at that moment the police arrived and took charge of the situation, and Burns was marched off under their protection. Morris was furious when a German member of the Marylebone branch of the SDF told him that as 'an old man' he should not be there and tried to get him out of the crowd. But, see-ing that Burns was safe, he left with Sanderson, though Williams and some of the others kept their ground and spoke until nightfall. 'Hyndman and Champion speak in Hyde Park to-morrow,' the letter concludes, 'but I don't suppose there will be a row there, as both last Sunday meetings have been good. So much for that. Shaw gave us a very good lecture last Sunday [at Hammersmith] and we got 3 new members; and I think shall get a good many more soon.'

The following month Morris was invited to lecture to the Edin-burgh Philosophical Society, but they cancelled the engagement when he said he was going to speak about socialism. 'The idiots had the cheek to dictate a subject to me, "Art in the Household", or some such twaddle', he wrote to May, 'didn't see the connection between art and socialism – yah!'

But all was not well within the socialist ranks. In vain Morris tried to get his comrades to put aside their personal grievances for the sake of the larger issue. Nevertheless, he had, with two or three others, come to distrust Hyndman thoroughly. 'I have done my best to trust him, but cannot any longer', he wrote in August.

> Practically it comes to a contest between him and me. If I don't come up to scratch I shall disappoint those who I believe have their hearts in the cause and are quite disinterested, many of them simple and worthy people. I don't think intrigue or ambition are among my many faults; but here I am driven to thrusting myself forward and making a party within a party. However, I say I foresaw it, and 'tis part of the day's work, but I begin to wish the day were over.[16]

The main point at issue was Hyndman's dictatorial attitude. As Engels wrote to Kautsky on 22 June 1884:

> Hyndman is thinking to buy up all the little movement here. . . . Himself a rich man, and in addition having at his disposal resources supplied by the very rich artist-enthusiast but un-talented politician Morris . . . he wants to be the sole master. . . . Hyndman is a skilful and good business man, but a petty and

hard-faced John Bull, possessing a vanity considerably in excess of his talent and natural gifts. . . . Bax and Aveling have most excellent intentions, but everything has gone to pieces and those literateurs alone cannot do anything. The masses still will not follow them.[17]

By the summer two factions were evident within the SDF, and a regular feud developed between Hyndman and Scheu. On one occasion, Hyndman had interrupted a speech by Scheu to point out that everything Marx and Lassalle had said had already been said by English economists. To a devoted Marxist like Scheu, this was a red rag to a bull. In return, Scheu pressed Morris to assume the leadership of the movement. Morris replied that he knew enough of himself to be sure that he was

> unfit for the rudder – at least not yet, but I promise to take my due share in all matters, and steadily to oppose all jingo business; but, if I can with coolness, or I shall be bowled over, since I have not yet got hold of the strings that tie us to the working-class members; nor have I read as I should. Also my habits are quiet and studious and if I am too much worried by 'politics', i.e. intrigue, I shall be no use to the cause as a writer. . . . If in the long run I am pushed into a position of more importance, I will not refuse it from mere laziness or softness.

But Scheu still thought that Morris should assume the leadership and accused him of weakness. 'As to me and my backbone or lack of it,' Morris replied in August, 'you must put up with me, and I will do the best I can. I am behind hand with my ordinary work just now and rather confused in my wits with a multiplicity of business: please to remember that I am getting to be an old man. . . . I am getting very full of lecture engagements now: I don't like to say no to them at present.'

Morris had taken the chair, much against his inclination, at several meetings of the executive, and when in July Hyndman was displaced as president, he nominated Morris. But Morris declined. Opposition to Hyndman had been growing with the election to the executive of Eleanor Marx, Edward Aveling and Joseph Lane. But Hyndman made no secret of the fact that he regarded Eleanor Marx and Aveling as nothing but emissaries of Engels and as representing the foreign element in British socialism. He was also jealous of Aveling's abilities as a theoretician, for Aveling was a brilliant scientist, a Fellow of University College, Vice-President of the National Secular Society, a member of the London School Board for Westminster, and the author of many books on secularism and Darwinism.

However, there were 'irregularities' with regard to the accounts of the Secular Society, and Bradlaugh, the president, demanded Aveling's expulsion, whereupon Hyndman demanded his resigna-tion from the executive of the SDF. Morris, on the contrary, was in favour of his remaining on the executive, as he regarded him as a man of great capacity, even though at meetings he assumed the supercilious air of a dandy and regularly borrowed money not only from Morris but from the poorest members of the Federation. Hyndman also felt, with some justice, that he and Eleanor Marx were doing no good to the socialist movement by openly living together and refusing, as a matter of principle, to regularize their union. May Morris, who evidently disliked Aveling heartily, refers to 'this strange little lizard of a man who . . . was spewed out of every Socialist and Secularist Society because in money matters and sexual relations he was almost incredibly shameless, conscienceless and heartless'.[18] Her opinion seems to be justified, as he finally drove Eleanor to suicide, after getting her to make a will in his favour.

By October, feelings on both sides had become so inflamed that the meetings of the Federation developed into little more than dog-fights, with Morris trying to keep the peace. Hyndman, as editor, insisted on keeping control of *Justice*, in spite of the fact that it was financed by Morris and that other members thought it should be under the control of the executive. Morris's resignation from the Federation came after his discovery of Hyndman's attempts to undermine Scheu's position as secretary of the Edinburgh branch, after Scheu had devoted much hard work to building up a Scottish socialist movement among Secularists and Radicals. The 'clearances' in the Highlands, when the crofters were turned off their land in order that artificial wildernesses might be created for stag-hunting and grouse-shooting, had led to the formation of a Scottish Land Restoration League in Glasgow. It was on the executive of this body that John Bruce Glasier served – a young architectural student and the son of an island crofter, who in his old age put down his memories of Morris in *William Morris and the Early Days of the Socialist Movement*, after he had become a member of the Independent

Labour Party in the 1920s. It was Scheu's intention to form a Scottish Land and Labour League, affiliated to the SDF, but in this Hyndman saw a threat to his authority and Morris warned Scheu in a letter of 18 July that 'it will be looked on here as secession, I am afraid'.

When Morris went up to Edinburgh to lecture in December, he had just written to Scheu excusing Hyndman on the general grounds that 'he could not help it', adding good-humouredly: 'I really begin to think that he *will* be Prime Minister before he dies.' At that time Morris knew nothing of Hyndman's more underhand intrigues in Scotland.

Bruce Glasier gives a vivid account of Morris lecturing in Glasgow:

> He was then fifty-one years of age, and just beginning to look elderly. His splendid crest of dark curly hair and his finely textured beard were brindling into grey. His head was lion-like – not only because of his shaggy mane, but because of the impress of strength of his whole front. . . . I noted the constant restlessness of his hands, and indeed of his whole body, as if overcharged with energy. . . . He read his lecture, or rather recited it, keeping his eyes on the written pages, which he turned over without concealment. . . . Occasionally he paused in his recital, and in a 'man to man' sort of way explained some special point, or turned to those near him on the platform for their assent. . . . As we listened, our minds seemed to gain a new sense of sight, or new way of seeing and understanding why we lived in the world.

It was this wider view of man's destiny that made Morris's lectures so different from the doctrinaire political ranting of the other speakers.

At Glasgow Morris lectured on ' "Art and Labour" – life or the art of living itself' – under the auspices of the Sunday Lecture Society. After the lecture he went to a SDF branch meeting in a room above a warehouse off Gallowgate, where he found the members divided by the London quarrel. He got a frigid reception from the secretary Nairne, who said 'he supposed Comrade Morris would like to say a few words'. Morris was tactful, but it was clear that the bulk of the members sided with Hyndman. It was at this meeting that there occurred the famous incident, often repeated by those anxious to show that Morris was not a Marxist. There was a certain amount of heckling. Then Nairne suddenly asked: 'Does

Comrade Morris accept Marx's theory of value?' At this Morris lost his temper and replied, according to Glasier:

I am asked if I believe in Marx's theory of value. To speak quite frankly, I do not know what Marx's theory of value is, and I'm damned if I want to know. Truth to say, my friends, I have tried to understand Marx's theory, but political economy is not in my line, and much of it appears to me to be dreary rubbish. But I am, I hope, a Socialist none the less. It is enough political economy for me to know that the idle class is rich and the working class is poor, and that the rich are rich because they rob the poor. I need read no books to convince me of it. And it does not matter a rap, it seems to me, whether the robbery is accomplished by what is termed surplus value, or by means of serfage or open brigandage. The whole system is monstrous and intolerable, and what we Socialists have got to do is to work together for its complete over⁄ throw, and for the establishment in its stead of a system of co⁄ operation where there will be no masters or slaves, but where everyone will work jollily together as neighbours and comrades for the equal good of all. That, in a nutshell, is my political economy and my social democracy.[19]

But that, of course, would not do for the more doctrinaire members and only appeared to confirm Hyndman's suspicions. As he left with Glasier and James Mavor, Morris remarked good⁄humouredly: 'Our friend Nairne was putting me through the catechism a bit, after your Scottish kirk⁄session fashion, don't you think? He is, I fancy, one of those comrades who are suspicious of us poetry chaps, and I don't blame him. He is in dead earnest, and will keep things going, I should say.' Naturally, Morris's irritated outburst did not represent his considered view of Marx, though Nairne's question had got him on a sore point, as he was only too conscious of his deficiency in economic theory and had confessed once to Scheu that he was 'only good for sentiment'. The kernel of his reply to Nairne was 'what we Socialists have got to do is to work together', and this was what Hyndman was making it impossible for them to do.

Matters came to a head on Morris's return to London. On 18 December he wrote to Jane, who was 'wintering' at Bordighera:

When I got up north there I found that Hyndman had been behaving so atrociously, that I was determined to stand it no longer. I got our friends together an hour before last Tuesday's meeting, and we agreed to stand by each other: and at the meeting I opposed him in very plain and set terms, so that he could not fail to understand that I would have no more to do with him: the fact is he is a precious rascal . . . he has been back-biting Scheu up there and telling absurd lies about his dealings with Aveling and Glasse[20]: I suppose he thought Glasse wouldn't tell me. There was a motion on Tuesday to expel W. J. Clarke, a stupid but honest opponent of H. who has shown his hand too soon, and whom he was determined to crush in any way foul or fair. I defended poor Clarke, and we outvoted Hyndman by 9 to 7.

The question is now whether I shall get out of the S.D.F. or Hyndman: we are now only fighting for the possession of the name and the adherence of the honest people who don't know the ins and outs of the quarrel. On Tuesday next we move confidence in Scheu, and the paper *Justice* is to be handed over to a joint editorship excluding Hyndman: if these are carried out I don't see how the beggar can stay in the Federation.

All this is foul work: yet it is a pleasure to be able to say what one thinks at last: and if once we get rid of H. I am sure plenty of people will join us who now hang back. . . .

On the same day he wrote to Scheu: 'I believe you may trust me to speak out next Tuesday . . . what a pleasure not to have to shake hands with H. again.'

After the Tuesday debate he wrote to Georgie Burne-Jones on 24 December:

My merry Christmas is like to be enlivened by a scene or two, at all events. Last night came off to the full as damned as I expected, which seldom happens: and the worst of it is that the debate is adjourned till Saturday, as we couldn't sit any later than midnight yesterday. It was a piece of degradation, only illuminated by Scheu's really noble and skilful defence of his character against Hyndman: all the rest was a mere exposition of backbiting, mixed with some melancholy and to me touching examples of faith. However, by Saturday I *will* be out of it. Our lot agreed before-hand, being I must say moved by me, that it is not worth fighting for the name of the S.D.F. and the sad remains of *Justice* at the expense of a month or two of wrangling: so as Hyndman con-siders the S.D.F. his property, let him take it and make what he can of it, and try if he can really make up a bogie of it to frighten the Government, which I really think is about all his scheme; and we will begin again quite clean-handed to try the more humdrum method of quiet propaganda, and start a new paper of our own. The worst of the new body, as far as I am concerned, is that for the present I have to be editor of the paper, which I by no means bargained for, but it seems nobody else will do.

Morris adds that he had been to Chesterfield to see Edward Carpenter and 'found him very sympathetic and sensible at the same time. I listened with longing heart to his account of his patch of ground, seven acres: he says that he and his fellow can almost live on it: they grow their own wheat, and send flowers and fruit to Chesterfield and Sheffield markets: all that sounds very agreeable to me.'

At the four-hour Saturday meeting, Hyndman was out-voted by ten to eight; Morris read out the prepared resignation of the majority. Hyndman made 'a long and clever and lawyer-like speech', Morris wrote to Georgie from Merton Abbey on 28 December: 'all of which, as in the House of Commons, might just as well have been left out, as either side had made up their minds how to vote from the first.' The form of resignation was as follows:

Since discord has arisen in the Council owing to the attempt to substitute arbitrary rule therein for fraternal co-operation, contrary to the principles of Socialism, and since it seems to us impossible to heal this discord, we, the undersigned, think it better in the interests of the cause of Socialism to cease to belong to the Council, and accordingly hand in our resignation.

William Morris	E. Belfort Bax
Edward Aveling	John L. Mahon
Robert Banner	S. Mainwaring
J. Lane	W. J. Clarke
Eleanor Marx-Aveling	J. Cooper

This produced, Morris continues,

what penny-a-liners call 'a revulsion of feeling', and most of the other side came round me and assured me that they had the best opinion of me and didn't mean all those hard things: poor little Williams cried heartily and took a most affectionate farewell of us.... This morning I hired very humble quarters for the Socialist

League, and authorized the purchase of the due amount of Windsor chairs and a kitchen table: so there I am really once more like a young bear with all my troubles before me. We meet to inaugurate the League to-morrow evening. There now, I really don't think I have strength left to say anything more about the matter just now. I find my room here and a view of the winter garden, with the men spreading some pieces of chintz on the bleaching ground, somewhat of a consolation. But I promise myself to work as hard as I can in the new body, which I think will be but a small one for some time to come.

Before the last meeting with the SDF Morris and Aveling had called on Engels at Primrose Hill, at his suggestion, to discuss their new paper *The Commonweal*. Engels told them that they were 'weak in *political* knowledge and journalistic skill', Morris wrote to Scheu on 28 December, and advised that *The Commonweal* should begin as a monthly.

I must confess that though I don't intend to give way to Engels, his advice is valuable; and on this point I am inclined to agree: all the more as I don't see where the money is to come from for a weekly, unless we sell a great many more than *Justice*: and I am sure we could make a 2*d.* or 3*d. paper*, not magazine, very good, and it would be worth doing on the understanding that it was to lead to a weekly one.

It seems that Morris was hoping for some assistance from Edward Carpenter towards starting *The Commonweal*. In the event he himself contributed £300 and Faulkner another £100. But 'paying for *Justice* has somewhat crippled me', he wrote to Scheu, 'and I shall have to find money for other expenses of the League at first'.

CHAPTER TWELVE

1885–1887

The Socialist League

THE FIRST NUMBER of *The Commonweal*, with Morris as editor and Edward Aveling as sub-editor, appeared at the beginning of February 1885, its title printed in bold Roman lettering. For the second number Morris designed a block, cut on wood by George Campfield, with a reassuring background of willow tracery; the third number for April carried a design by Walter Crane of a labourer with a spade and a student with a pen, united by the winged figure of Freedom, wearing a Liberty cap against a background of horns of plenty and sprays of corn. It bore the legend 'Equality, Freedom, Fraternity'.

'*The Commonweal* has one aim – the propagation of Socialism', Morris wrote in the first number.

> We shall not, therefore, make any excuses for what may be thought journalistic shortcomings, if we can but manage to attract attention to the study of our principles from those who have not yet thought of Socialism, or who are, as often happens, bitterly hostile to them through ignorance. . . . To waken the sluggish, to strengthen the waverers, to instruct the seekers after truth: these are high aims, yet not too high for a journal that claims to be Socialistic, and we hope by patience and zeal to accomplish them.

The Commonweal was issued at 1d. and on 1 May 1886 became a weekly with Morris as sole editor. Later he was joined by Henry Halliday Sparling as joint editor. Some of Morris's best writing is to be found in *The Commonweal*, though Mackail dismisses most of it as journalism, and at least two of his major works: *A Dream of John Ball* and *News from Nowhere*. In the issue for 17 July 1886, Morris reviewed Shaw's novel *Cashel Byron's Profession*. A regular front page feature was his 'Notes on Passing Events', which begins in the issue for 8 May 1886. Next year it continued as 'Notes on News'.

In July the League issued its manifesto, written by Morris and

Belfort Bax. This began: 'Fellow Citizens – We come before you as a body advocating the principles of Revolutionary International Socialism: this is, we seek a change in the basis of Society – a change which would destroy the distinctions of classes and nationalities.'[1] The manifesto was signed by the members of the provisional council of the League, which included, besides Morris, Bax, Aveling and Eleanor Marx-Aveling, a railway engineer W. Bridges Adams, W. J. Clarke, J. Cooper, W. Hudson, James Mavor, Edward Watson, an old Chartist E. T. Craig, C. J. Faulkner, Scheu and Maguire. Of these Eleanor Marx was a particularly attractive character, with a passion for Shakespeare, for Ibsen and the 'new drama'. She was described by Edouard Bernstein in 1880 as 'a blooming young maiden of twenty-four with the black hair and black eyes of her father, and an exceptionally musical voice. She was unusually vivacious, and took part, in her sensitive and emotional manner, in our discussions of party matters.'[2] Her love of Shakespeare she had shared with her father, having many a time walked with him from their home in Chalk Farm to Sadler's Wells to stand all the evening in the pit, since they were too poor to afford seats, and then to walk home again. Originally Eleanor had wanted to become an actress.

Morris was now open to attack as an employer and a capitalist. In a long letter to Georgie Burne-Jones of June 1884 he had already gone very carefully and with a laborious conscientiousness into the whole position. 'I am not a capitalist, my friend,' he wrote, 'I am but a hanger-on of that class like all professional men.' At one time, it seems, Morris was seriously considering selling his business and living on a weekly wage in order to join the proletariat. Fortunately, commonsense and a regard for his family prevailed. In any case, as he told Georgie, 'everyone of us therefore, workman and non-workman, is *forced* to support the present competitive system by merely living in the present society, and buying his ordinary daily necessaries: so that an employer by giving up his individual profit of the goods he gets made would not be able to put his workmen in their proper position: they would be exploited by others though not by him.' As far as his own firm is concerned, he continued:

Some of those who work for me share in the profits formally: I suppose I made the last year or two about £1800, Wardle about £1200, the Smiths about £600 each, Denby and West £400.

274

All these share directly in the profits: Kenyon, the colour mixer, & Goodacre, the foreman dyer, have also a kind of bonus on the amount of goods turned out: the rest either work as day-workers, or are paid by the piece, mostly the latter: in both cases they get more than the market price of their labour: two or three people about the place are no use to the business and are kept on the live-and-let-live principle. . . .

Now as you know I work at the business myself and it could not go on without me, or somebody like me: therefore my £1800 are pay for work done, and I should justly claim a maintenance for that work: shall we say £4 a week (about Kenyon's screw) or £200 per annum; that leaves £1600 for distribution among the 100 people I employ besides the profit sharers; £16 a year each therefore: now that would I admit be a very nice thing for them, but it would not alter the position of any one of them, but leave them still members of the working class, with all the disadvantages of that position: further, if I were to die, or be otherwise disabled the business could not get anyone to do my work for £200 a year, and would in short at once take back the extra £16 a year from the workmen. . . .

I have left out 2 matters which complicate the position: 1st I have a small literary income, about £120, and 2nd there are those other partners called my family: Now you know we ought to be able to live on £4 a week, & give the literary income to the revolutionary agitation; but here comes the rub, and I feel the pinch of society, for which society I am only responsible in a very limited degree. And yet if Janey and Jenny were quite well and capable I think they ought not to grumble at living on the said £4, nor do I think they would.

In those days £4 a week was equal to about £20 now, at least. But all the same, had Morris attempted to live on it, it would probably have meant giving up one of his houses, doing without two of the servants at Hammersmith, drinking water or ale instead of the wine he loved, and not buying his tobacco from Frieborg and Trier in the Haymarket. Nor would he have been able to buy medieval illuminated manuscripts at £1000 or £900 a time. But, as he went on to point out, profit sharing, where it had been tried, had only resulted in the workmen becoming small capitalists and then larger ones.

Now, much as I want to see workmen escape from their slavish position, I don't at all want to see a few individuals more creep out of their class into the middle class: this will only make the poor poorer still. . . . Here then is a choice for a manufacturer ashamed of living on surplus value: shall he do his best to further a revolution of the basis of society . . . which would turn all people into workers, as it would give a chance for all workers to become refined and dignified in their life; or shall he ease his conscience by dropping a certain portion of his profits to bestow on his handful of workers – for indeed it is but charity after all, since they don't claim it from *him* but from his class. . . .

But, as it was, May Morris tells us, his work for the party was now doubled: 'the next six years are a long story of lecturing, travelling, office and editorial work, and that most difficult of all tasks, keeping the peace among people of different temperaments: people eager and impetuous and most of them honest in their aims, but possessing a positive genius for misunderstanding each other'. For it was not long before the same sort of quarrelling and intrigue which Morris had fled from in the S D F broke out again in the Socialist League.

Every week-end found him speaking in London or the suburbs, and soon he began campaigning travels through the provinces every two or three months. The mere routine work in London took up most of his leisure hours in the week: a Council meeting of the Socialist League on Monday; Publishing Committee on Wednesday; Ways and Means Committee on Thursday; Hammersmith Branch on Friday.

There was also the selling of *The Commonweal* in the streets, for sometimes, as May Morris puts it,

there would be added to these labours the specially choice one of a Paper-selling Brigade – trying and even humiliating for any-one who has not the talent for that form of martyrdom. . . . As for Sunday, most times there was a street-corner meeting in the morning and a lecture at night – often in some faraway East End club where half the members were chatting and drinking and knocking billiard-balls about in the background. . . . The very announcements in *The Commonweal* remind one of those arid wanderings in train and 'bus through the Desert of London.[3]

It cannot be said that May Morris sounds particularly enthusiastic about the work of 'making Socialists'. Indeed the 'martyrdom' she underwent on the occasions she accompanied her father to the East End, or stood in Hammersmith Broadway trying to sell *The Commonweal*, or patiently held the Socialist League banner, while Morris discoursed at Walham Green or Weltje Road on the iniquities of capitalism, may partly account for the aggrieved and discontented expression noticeable in most of her photographs. As for Jane, she would have nothing to do with the 'comrades' when Morris invited them back to the house. She even disliked Shaw, since she suspected him of egging her husband on in his more undesirable activities. Having come from the working-class herself, her attitude to them was more realistic, and having secured for herself a life of comfort and dignity, she did not see the point of throwing it away for the sake of some very problematical socialist Utopia.

But what made all Morris's work ultimately vain, from his point of view, was that he saw industrialism itself as the source of all the evils that afflicted the world and the mere fact of industry being controlled by public bodies, rather than private enterprise, would not bring the sort of world he wanted any nearer. In fact, socialism actually meant an intensification of industrialism, to meet the increasing needs of the community – not a return to rural communities, handicrafts and the simple life. Morris would hardly have thrown his hat into the air and rejoiced at higher production figures in industry. In fact, he is credited by W.B.Yeats with the antisocial remark, 'If any man puts me into a labour squad, I will lie on my back and kick.'[4] That, however, is not the best way to get on in a People's Democracy.

In fact, Morris's attempt to wed Ruskin to Marx resulted in a basic confusion in his thought, as Engels perceived, when he called him a Utopian rather than a scientific socialist. But, of course, Morris could not see, or admit, this. Had he done so, he would have realized that all his work as a socialist was actually directed against everything he held most dear. He could hardly be expected to see that after the revolution what he called 'the dull squalor of civilization' would spread even farther. The very last thing people wanted (or want) was to reduce their needs to a minimum in order to achieve Morris's ideal of simplicity of life. In fact, they *liked* all the hideous things produced by the capitalist-controlled machines and wanted ever more of them.

On 20 March 1886 Engels wrote to Paul and Laura Lafargue in Paris:

> Fortunately the Socialist League is sleeping for the time being. Our good Bax and Morris, torn by the desire to do something (if they but knew what!) are restrained only by the circumstance that there is absolutely nothing to do. Nevertheless they have far more truck with the anarchists than is desirable. Their fête on the 18th was held in common with the latter, and Kropotkin spoke at it – rubbish so I am told. But with Hyndman, who knows his way about crooked politics and is capable of every folly to push himself forward on the one hand and our two political innocents on the other, the prospects are not brilliant.

By this time almost in spite of himself, Morris had become one of the most notable socialist leaders in the country, though privately he was becoming less and less hopeful about the prospects of socialism in his time, as he wrote to Georgie on 13 May of the previous year:

> I am in low spirits about the prospects of our 'party', if I can dignify a little knot of men by such a word. . . . You see we are such a few, and hard as we work we don't seem to pick up people to take our places when we demit. All this you understand is only said about the petty skirmish of outposts, the fight of a corporal's guard, in which I am immediately concerned: I have [no] more faith than a grain of mustard seed in the future history of 'civilization', which I *know* now is doomed to destruction, and probably before very long: what a joy it is to think of barbarism once more flooding the world, and real feelings and passions, however rudimentary, taking the place of our wretched hypocrisies. . . . I used really to despair once because I thought what the idiots of our day call progress would go perfecting itself: happily I know now that all that will have a sudden check – sudden in appearance I mean – 'as it was in the days of Noë'.

In April he had been lecturing in Scotland and staying with Edward Carpenter at Millthorp. On his way back, he had been entranced with the north – ' 'tis the pick of all England for beauty', he wrote to Georgie, 'I fared to feel as if I must live there, say somewhere near Kirby Stephen, for a year or two before I die: even the building there is not bad; necessitous and rude, but looking like shelter and quiet.' In the train he had read Richard Jefferies's *After*

London, with its picture of an England deserted by most of its former inhabitants, London a poisonous swamp and the country once more covered with vast forests and relapsed into a state of barbarism. 'Absurd hopes curled round my heart as I read it', Morris confesses. Instead there were talks to be delivered in working-men's clubs in the East End. On 27 May he writes to Georgie:

> On Sunday I went a-preaching Stepney way. My visit intensely depressed me, as these Eastward visits always do: the mere stretch of houses, the vast mass of utter shabbiness and uneventfulness, sits upon one like a nightmare: of course what slums there are one doesn't see. You would perhaps have smiled at my congregation; some twenty people in a little room, as dirty as convenient and stinking a good deal. It took the fire out of my fine periods, I can tell you: it is a great drawback that I can't *talk* to them roughly and unaffectedly. Also I would like to know what amount of real feeling underlies their bombastic revolutionary talk when they get to that. I don't seem to have got at them yet – you see this great class gulf lies between us.

This reminds us that Morris read his lectures and that all his 'fine periods' about the arts and crafts and the beauty of the earth, doubtless mystified his audience.

Sometimes, however, Morris enjoyed his lecture trips. One such occasion was when Charley Faulkner invited him up to Oxford with the Avelings in February to speak in the Music Room in Holywell – 'just opposite where Janey used to live', he notes. He wrote to Georgie afterwards:

> Well, we had a fine lot of supporters, town and gown, both, who put on red ribbons and acted as stewards, but the 'enemy' got in in some numbers, and prepared for some enjoyment. Charley was in the chair and led off well, and they heard him with only an average amount of howling . . . the hall was quite full. I had to get up when Charley sat down: I was rather nervous before I began, as it was my first long speech without book, but the noise and the life braced me up, and after all I knew my subject, so I fired off my speech fairly well, I think: if I hadn't our friends the enemy would have found it out and chaffed me with all the mercilessness of boys. Of course they howled and stamped at certain catch-words and our people cheered, so it was all very good fun.

The 'grads' listened to Morris, but they had determined that Aveling should not speak. In the event, he made such a clever speech that they listened to him better than they had listened to Morris. But at question time someone let off a stink bomb and when the two factions converged upon the platform, Faulkner closed the meeting. 'We had some serious talk at our inn after the meeting with the best of the lads,' Morris concludes, 'and then some of them took us into New College cloisters to see their loveliness under the moon.' Morris found the whole thing very amusing, as he wrote to May at Bordighera, where Janey was wintering while Jenny kept house for him at Hammersmith: 'Still some of the young gentlemen were very rude, especially to Faulkner', and at a donkey-race dubbed one of the donkeys 'Socialist' and another 'Comrade Faulkner'. Nevertheless, adds Morris, Faulkner was doing very good service at Oxford, where he had founded a strong branch of the Socialist League.

Scheu gives a rather touching account of his Sunday morning walks with Morris at Hammersmith.

We would stroll early on a Sunday morning in the streets. I would speak to a few youths who came our way. 'Friends! we have come to talk to you and to enlighten you. . . .' They would always stand and listen, gazing with astonishment at the two strange men and soon a dozen or more would be standing there. 'Now,' I would say to Morris, 'now you have an audience that is not critical of you. Speak to your heart's content.' And he did. He spoke of his hatred of the commercial system, and of its 'orderliness' and of its ugliness. He showed how the struggle for daily bread suppressed the feeling for beauty which existed in human beings.

As a rule, however, on a Sunday morning Morris was to be found holding what he said were usually taken for Salvation Army meetings at one of the regular open-air stands of the League at Walham Green or Hammersmith Bridge. These meetings even cut short the pleasant Sunday morning routine of breakfast at the Grange, when Morris would accompany Ned into his studio and read to him from More's *Utopia* or Dumas, while he worked on some dreamy allegory of knights and ladies.

But now the authorities declared war on the socialists, breaking up meetings and arresting the speakers for 'obstruction'. They began operations with a raid on the International Workingmen's Club in Stephen's Mews, Tottenham Court Road, in May 1885, when police, assisted by a gang of roughs who burst in shouting 'bloody foreigners', wrecked the furniture and manhandled and arrested several of the members.[5] A defence committee was at once formed, with Morris as treasurer and a number of delegates from the Radical Clubs. As a result three policemen were committed for trial at the Old Bailey. But the arrests of speakers for 'obstruction' at open-air meetings continued. The SDF and the League thereupon started a campaign for free speech, which suddenly brought Morris into con-flict with the forces of Law and Order.

The principal battleground was a dreary site at the corner of Dod Street and Burdett Road, Whitechapel, which had long been used for public gatherings and open-air meetings by Radical and religious bodies. Socialist meetings, however, were regarded as potentially dangerous and the police gave notice that they were to cease. On the morning of 20 September a large crowd gathered at Dod Street to hear Radical and socialist speakers protesting against the recent sentence of a month's hard labour passed on Jack Williams of the SDF for 'obstruction'. 'The joyful expectation of a disturb-ance', says Mackail, 'drew a crowd estimated at about a thousand people to the place that Sunday. Against this crowd, which was determined not to be dispersed so long as there was the chance of seeing any fun, the dozen or so police who had been drafted to the spot found themselves almost helpless.' The speakers, among them Hyndman in his top hat and frock coat, were in the middle of the crowd and the unfortunate police were jostled and hooted at, till one o'clock struck and the public houses opened and drew off most of the crowd. This gave the police the chance they had been waiting for and they knocked down two banners and arrested eight men.

Next day the men were charged at Thames police court for ob-struction and resisting the police in the execution of their duty. Morris attended the hearing and when Aveling gave evidence for the accused, Saunders, the presiding magistrate, told him that he had broken the law by attending and speaking at the meeting, since any such meeting was an obstruction. Aveling replied that he intended to speak again next Sunday. 'I advise you not to,' said the magistrate, 'or else you will find yourself locked up.' Aveling replied: 'I shall speak there each Sunday till I am locked up.' Eleanor Marx followed Aveling's example. When a tailor, Lewis

Lyons, was sentenced to two months' hard labour and the rest were fined forty shillings each or a month's imprisonment, loud hisses and cries of 'Shame!' were heard. At once the police began to clear the court and Aveling says in his account of the proceedings, 'com/ menced an assault upon all and sundry. William Morris, remon/ strating at this hustling and thumping, became at once the chief thumpee.'[6]

Threatening to summons the police for assault, Morris was at once put under arrest and, after two hours, was brought up before Saunders. Constable Brind K463 declared that after the sentence had been passed, he was 'endeavouring to restore quiet when the prisoner called out "Shame" and hissed, became very violent, and struck him on the chest and broke the strap of his helmet'. A some/ what farcical scene followed.

Mr Morris – I give a direct negative to that. I certainly did not hit him.

Mr Saunders – Have you any witnesses? You must rebut the evidence, or I must act upon it.

Mr Morris – I do not know whether there is anyone here who saw it. I was here listening to the case, in which I have an interest, because I am a member of the Socialist League, to which several of the prisoners belong, and I quite confess that when I heard the sentences passed on the prisoners my feelings got the better of me, and I did call out 'Shame', but not so loud as I am now speaking. As to hissing, that was a mistake. Then this policeman came and distinctly hustled me. When you are pushed you naturally push again, but that is not resisting the police. I turned round and remonstrated with the policeman, but I distinctly assert that I never raised my hands. He was very rough, and I am quite prepared to bring a charge of assault against him.

Mr Saunders – What are you?

Mr Morris – I am an artist and a literary man, pretty well/known I think throughout Europe.

Mr Saunders – I suppose you did not intend to do this?

Prisoner – I never struck him at all.

Mr Saunders – Well, I will let you go.

Prisoner – But I have not done anything.

Mr Saunders – Well, you can stay if you like.

Prisoner – I don't want to stay.

'He was liberated', concludes the *Daily News* report, 'and on getting into the street was loudly cheered by the crowd who had gathered there.'

Next day, writing to Jane at Kelmscott, Morris told her that he did not go to the East End meeting, but felt bound to go to the police court, where 'the behaviour of the police, their bullying and hectoring, was quite beyond belief'. Morris was charged at the police station with breaking the constable's chin strap, which, he says, 'I suppose he had done himself . . . the inspector and the constable gravely discussing whether the damage done to the helmet was 2*d*. or 1½*d*.' Morris also wrote to Wilfrid Scawen Blunt: 'Thanks for your note. I really did not put myself in old Saunders' way: and my puff of myself was done, by no means as a piece of vanity, but to save myself from oakum picking which I should certainly have undergone if I had not bounced to that old fool.' The sentence on Lyons was, however, subsequently quashed on appeal, as the police evidence broke down. The *Pall Mall Gazette* protested against the police action as an outrageous attack on free speech, and the whole affair produced a good deal of sympathy with the socialists.

On the following Sunday far larger crowds of between thirty and fifty thousand, mostly Radicals of the East London Radical Club, gathered at Dod Street. Aveling was as good as his word and spoke, together with Hyndman, Shaw, John Burns and the Rev. Stewart Headlam for the Christian Socialists. All these speakers were deliberately courting arrest and defying the police regulations on principle. But the police had evidently had instructions to keep their distance. On the following Sunday, again, Morris spoke, welcoming Jack Williams on his release from prison.

The police, however, persisted in interfering with smaller meetings, where the risk of rioting was less, and this caused some indignation throughout the country. As the *Daily News* correspondent wrote: 'Police interference has caused more obstruction and disturbance than twelve months of Socialist lecturing.' Actually, the League could not have asked for anything better in the way of advertisement. But for police persecution its existence would have remained un⁄ noticed. As Morris wrote:

All goes well. We Socialists have suddenly become popular, and your humble servant could hardly have received more sympathy if he had been racked by Mr Saunders. All this has its absurd, and even humiliating side, but it is encouraging to see that people were shocked at unfairness and persecution of mere opinion, as I think they really are.

Nevertheless he was suffering from the strain and in October went down with an attack of sciatica and gout. But he wrote reassuringly to Scheu on the 16th:

It's all right, I am to lecture on Sunday next. I suppose we shall try the Park again, and I will go if I am well enough; but I can't get rid of my sciatica and now I have a cold to boot. . . . I have just come back (last night) from Preston where I have been on the stump; the people there were a little better than last year; but very wooden. I think of making some arrangements for a stumping tour in the North in early spring next year – make a fortnight of it.

But ten days later he was writing to Jenny that he was laid up with gout in both feet and had been passing the time

reading trashy novels . . . but having tried Ouida's *Strathmore* I found I really couldn't, not even with the gout to help me. We had a pretty good meeting here last night; of course I couldn't go to it, as I have really not been able to put a foot to the ground. I am wheeled to the dining-room & back here on the sofa. We had also a good meeting in Hyde Park, as we always seem to do now.

Five days later, on 31 October, he writes to Georgie:

it was quite a luxury to lie here in the morning and let the sun creep over me and watch the clouds. . . . I don't think it [sciatica and gout] comes from my knocking about to meetings and the like, but rather from incaution as to diet, which I really must look after. You see, having joined a movement, I must do what I can while I last, that is a matter of duty. Besides, in spite of all the self-denying ordinances of us semi-anarchists, I grieve to say that some sort of leadership is required, and that in our section I unfortunately supply that want; it seems I was missed last Monday, and stupid quarrels about nothing took place, which it was thought I could have stopped. All this work I have pulled upon my head, and though in detail much of it is repulsive to the last degree, I still hold that I did not do so without due considera, tion. Anyhow, it seems to me that I can be of use, therefore I am impelled to make myself useful. . . .

You see, my dear, I can't help it. The ideas which have taken hold of me will not let me rest: nor can I see anything else worth thinking of. How can it be otherwise, when to me society, which to many seems an orderly arrangement for allowing decent people to get through their lives creditably and with some pleasure, seems mere cannibalism; nay worse (for there might be hope in that), is grown so corrupt, so steeped in hypocrisy and lies, that one turns from one stratum of it to another with helpless loathing. One must turn to hope, and only in one direction do I see it – on the road to Revolution: everything else is gone now. And now at last when the corruption of society seems complete, there is arising a definite conception of a new order, with its demands in some sort formulated. . . .

Meantime what a little ruffles me is this, that if I do a little fail in my duty some of my friends will praise me for failing instead of blaming me. I have a pile of worry about the party ahead of me when I am about again, which must excuse me for dwelling on these things so much.

In spite of these worries, he still found time to write to the *Daily News* protesting once more against the vulgarization of Oxford.

. . . I wish to ask if it is too late to appeal to the mercy of the 'Dons' to spare the few specimens of ancient town architecture which they have not yet had time to destroy, such, for example, as the little plaster houses in front of Trinity College or the beautiful houses left on the north side of Holywell Street. These are in their way as important as the more majestic buildings to which all the world makes pilgrimage. Oxford thirty years ago, when I first knew it, was full of these treasures; but Oxford 'culture', cynically contemptuous of the knowledge which it does not know, and steeped to the lips in the commercialism of the day, has made a clean sweep of most of them; but those that are left are of infinite value, and still give some character above that of Victoria Street or Bayswater to modern Oxford. Is it impossible, Sir, to make the authorities of Oxford, town and gown, see this, and stop the destruction ? . . .[7]

It was, indeed, impossible, as the present aspect of Oxford testifies. Morris was still unwell by the end of November and wrote to Jenny from the Burne-Joneses' house at Rottingdean, where he was confined by the rain with his invalidish wife ('Mother seems to have a cold on her which tires her'), filling in the time with games of backgammon, varied by cribbage and draughts.

Meanwhile, distress, due to the trade recession of 1885-6, had been steadily increasing throughout the country. For some time past, Champion, Burns and Tom Mann had been conducting an agitation among the unemployed in the East End. On 'Black Monday', 8 February 1886, the SDF staged a demonstration in Trafalgar Square in opposition to a meeting called by the Tory 'Fair Traders', and Hyndman, Burns, Williams, Champion and Halliday Sparling addressed between eight and ten thousand unemployed. Afterwards the crowd marched to Hyde Park. In Pall Mall, some of the clubmen began to jeer at them and the starving and angry men replied with a volley of stones, smashing the windows of the Carlton and Reform Clubs. Thoroughly roused by this time and full of indignation against the rich, they poured on up St James's, smashing windows, stopping carriages and demanding money, looting the shops in Piccadilly. Morris & Co.'s showrooms at the corner of Oxford Street and North Audley Street escaped being wrecked by only a few minutes; the shutters were put up and the doors locked just as the mob irrupted into Oxford Street. Reaching Hyde Park, they overturned several carriages. Champion addressed them and told them to go home, but on their return down Oxford Street the smashing of shop-windows and looting continued.

This, as far as Morris was concerned, was the first visible result of the propaganda. Next day there was panic in London, the widespread fears of revolution increased by the dark, foggy weather and rumours that the entire East End – that unspeakable plague spot, unvisited by the well-to-do – was on the march. Nothing like it had been seen in London since the Chartist riots of the 1840s, and *The Times* demanded the arrest of Hyndman and Burns. There were demonstrations by the unemployed in other cities as well, in Birmingham and Norwich, with rioting in Leicester. Work schemes were hurriedly organized, charity organizations and benevolent funds set going. At Windsor, Princess Christian, Queen Victoria's daughter, instituted cheap dinners for children and 'invited several ladies to assist in carrying out this benevolent object'. There was also the Mansion House Fund for the unemployed, which suddenly rose from £30,000 to £75,000. But socialists were execrated on all hands. Thomas Hughes, a one-time Christian Socialist, wrote to *The Times* demanding 'a year or two's oakum picking' for those 'notorious ruffians Mann, Hyndman & Co.'. Burns, Hyndman, Champion and Williams were, in fact, charged at Bow Street for inciting to riot and committed for trial at the Old Bailey, but after three days were found not guilty – a remarkable instance of British moderation. One gentleman, however, who had had both his carriage windows and his spectacles smashed wrote to *The Times* to say that, as a result, he was cancelling his subscriptions to various charities and hospitals.

In the next number of *Commonweal*, Morris wrote:

> Apart from what actual plunder there was, the wrecking of shops to carry the contents away, the proceedings of the crowd seemed a sort of gigantic joke against the tyrant – Sham Society – a joke mingled with threatening, embittered by anger and contempt; characterized by the English tendency towards brutality masked by good humour, which is so apt amongst our countrymen to accompany the first stages of a great tragedy.

He added that he had no doubt that the rioting was set off by 'the "truly gentlemanly" behaviour of the fools at the Carlton Club, who took for granted that a crowd of English "lower classes" will stand anything'.

To Dr John Glasse he wrote:

> Well, it is a mistake to try to organize riot; yet I do not agree with you that Monday's affair will hurt the movement. . . . Altogether taken I think we must look upon this affair as an incident of the Revolution, and so far encouraging: the shop wrecking was partly a grotesque practical joke (quite in the English manner) at the expense of the upper classes. At any rate it is a glimpse for them of the bed-rock of our present society, and I hope they like it. Yesterday they were gibbering with terror in spite of the sham calm heroics of the newspapers.

Morris also wrote a long account of the whole incident to John Carruthers, a consulting engineer who was building railways in South America and who had joined the League.

Contemptible as the riot was, as a riot, it no doubt has had a great effect, both here and on the Continent: in fact the surprise of people in finding that the British workman will not stand every, thing is extreme. As for the League, we are out of it at present: but the times seem to me both helpful and rough; I fancy there will be another attempt on our meetings this summer and I rather expect to learn one more new craft – oakum-picking to wit. . . .

The police now attempted to make up for their conspicuous absence from the scene of trouble on 'Black Monday' by attacking and breaking up all socialist meetings on principle. At a large demon, stration organized by the SDF in Hyde Park on 21 February as reported in *The Times*, they 'were compelled to draw their batons and use them without mercy on all who encountered them'. Many people were simply ridden down. Perhaps, after all, the revolution was nearer at hand than anyone realized. Morris wrote to Georgie:

I have often thought that we should be overtaken by the course of events – overtaken unprepared I mean. . . . I myself shall be glad when this ferment sinks down. Things industrial are bad – I wish they would better: their doing so would not interfere with our propaganda, and would give us some chance of getting at working men with intelligence and some share of leisure. Yet if that will not come about and the dominating classes *will* push revolution on us, let it be! – the upshot must be good in the end. If you had suffered as I have from the apathy of the English lower classes (woe's me how low!) you would rejoice at their awakening, however ugly the forms it took. As to my capacity for leadership in this turmoil, believe me, I feel as humble as could be wished, yet after all it is my life, and the work of it, and I must do my best.

After the breaking up of the last Sunday meeting in Hyde Park, the SDF leaders were arrested and this involved Morris in 'a wearisome time before the Bow Street magistrate', where he went bail for Burns and Williams. Another such occasion was the prosecution of Frank Kitz, a very poor member of the League, the son of a German exile. Morris and Carruthers had left a social evening at the League's Farringdon Road quarters to stand as sureties for him at West Ham police station. 'What are you?' the police inspector asked Morris. But before he could answer, Carruthers stepped up to the desk and said somewhat naïvely: 'Don't you know? Why, this is the author of *The Earthly Paradise.*' 'Good heavens, Carruthers,' Morris said to his friend, 'you don't expect a *policeman* to know anything about *The Earthly Paradise*, do you?' Then, turning to the inspector, he said: 'I am a shopkeeper, carrying on business in Oxford Street.'[8] The police were always embarrassed by Morris, as well they might have been, and were uncertain how to deal with him. Knowing this, Morris made a point of putting in an appearance whenever any of his comrades had been arrested, as they now began to be almost daily.

Bell Street, off the Edgware Road, where speakers had been unmolested for years, became the next objective in the campaign to prevent further open-air socialist meetings, and the police persuaded the local shopkeepers to complain of such meetings as a public nuisance. In July 1886, Mainwaring and Jack Williams were both arrested and committed for trial at the Middlesex Sessions. Morris at once stepped into the breach and, writes Mainwaring, 'when we all thought that a long term of imprisonment would be the result, he volunteered to speak in the interval between the committal and trial; and, when reminded of the general impression that imprison-ment would be the result, he simply said: "Well, it will be another experience, and we must not allow fear of consequences to interfere with our duty." '

The next Sunday, therefore, Morris took up his stand at Bell Street, where he announced that he had come to Marylebone to maintain the right of the socialists to speak in the streets in the same way that people holding other opinions were allowed to speak. He refused, he said, to live contentedly under a condition of society which made a perpetual prison for the majority of the community. He was impelled to talk to them that morning because the present condition of things was a bad one. He had been asked by a lady the other day why he did not talk to the middle class. 'Well, the middle class had their books with plenty of leisure to read them: the working class had no leisure, no books.'

At this point Chief Inspector Shepherd made his way into the crowd and requested Morris to desist. As Morris refused he took his name and address, and Morris went on to declare that 'the middle and upper classes were enabled to live in luxury and idleness on the poverty and degradation of the workers. There was only one way in which this state of things could be altered – society must be turned downside up', and he appealed to his audience to prepare for the great social revolution.[9] He was thereupon summoned for obstruction.

Morris and Mainwaring appeared in court on the same day. Turning to Morris, the magistrate said that 'as a gentleman, he would at once see, when it was pointed out to him, that such meet‚ ings were a nuisance, and would desist from taking part in them'. He therefore fined Morris a shilling. Williams and Mainwaring, not being gentlemen, were both fined £20 and bound over with one surety each to keep the peace for twelve months. As they both refused to pay this fine, they were sent to prison for two months. On 14 August Morris wrote to Jenny with an account of the pro‚ ceedings:

> May and I were in court all day yesterday, and a sorry exhibition it was, except for our comrade Mainwaring's speech which was very good: in fact I was proud of his bearing altogether. The Judge was abhominable, really a kind of Judge Jeffries the younger. You would have thought our friends had at least com‚ mitted a murder with aggravated circumstances so bitter an advocate he was against them. It is too disgraceful: being working men they cannot themselves pay so heavy a fine, and though we could find the money, I don't think either of them would agree to this. However, as I told the lads yesterday they mustn't grumble, as all this is the why and the wherefore of their being Socialists.

The Bell Street decision did not prevent Morris or any of the League's Marylebone branch from continuing to speak at open‚air meetings. Later the same month, Morris wrote to Jenny of one of his busy Sundays:

> I had a brisk day yesterday, though tell your mother, no police‚ man's hand touched my sacred collar. I went from the Grange to Walham Green where we had a good little meeting attentive and peaceable, back then to the Grange & dinner and then away Eastward Ho to Victoria Park rather sulky at having to turn out so soon after dinner. Though Victoria Park is rather a pretty place with water (dirty though) and lots of trees. Had a good meeting there also spoke for nearly an hour altogether in a place made noisy by other meetings near, also a band not far off. Whereby I was somewhat hoarse for our evening lecture which was Shaw's not mine, and very good. . . . I have been hard at

work all day long at an article. Did another & lots of Homer all Saturday.

By September, he tells Bell Scott, he is in the middle of the ninth book of the *Odyssey*, which he was busy translating into the metre of *Sigurd*. He was lecturing all over the country, from Edinburgh to Norwich and Reading. On the 16th he writes to Joynes to warn him: 'I shall be away Monday, Tuesday, Wednesday, Thursday and Friday this week.' A fortnight later, on 29 October, he is telling Jenny:

> I am afraid I am too much tossed about by doing many things to have much head for writing a long letter to you, my darling. . . . I go to Lancaster on Tuesday and am at Preston on Wednesday: back again on Thursday and if I possibly can I will come down [to Kelmscott] on Friday evening or Saturday morning. A beautiful bright morning & quite warm to-day. I felt almost inclined to walk to Merton, but am afraid I can't spare the time. I have finished the 10th Book of the Odyssey now & shall certainly do 12 books before the year is out. It really would be rather convenient to me to have a little gout in order to do some literary work. I am going to start getting my *Pilgrims of Hope* in order, so as to make a book of it: I shall add and alter a good deal though. . . .

The *Pilgrims of Hope* had been appearing at intervals in *The Common- weal* since 1885. It may not amount to very much as poetry, but it has considerable biographical interest, for here Morris is writing not only of his work for the socialist cause but also, once again, of his private miseries. It is again a story of intimate 'betrayal', of a man whose wife falls in love with his best friend. It is the only long poem Morris wrote with a contemporary setting, and it leaves no doubt of his baffled love for his wife, or of her unhappiness either.

> *'O Richard, Richard!', she said, and her arms about me came,*
> *And her tears and the lips that I loved were on my face once more.*
> *A while I clung to her body, and longing sweet and sore*
> *Beguiled my heart of its sorrow; then we sundered and sore she wept,*
> *While fair pictures of days departed about my sad heart crept,*
> *And mazed I felt and weary. But we sat apart again,*
> *Not speaking, while between us was the sharp and bitter pain*

As the sword 'twixt the lovers bewildered in the fruitless marriage bed.
Yet a while, and we spoke together, and I scarce knew what I said,
But it was not wrath or reproaching, or the chill of love-born hate;
For belike around and about us, we felt the brooding fate.
We were gentle and kind together, and if any had seen us so,
They had said, 'These two are one in the face of all trouble and woe.'
But indeed as a wedded couple we shrank from the eyes of men,
As we dwelt together and pondered on the days that come not again.

This explains why those who came to Morris's house and saw him with Jane saw them as a united married couple.

Earlier in the poem Morris allows us a rare glimpse of himself speaking at a Radical club.

Dull and dirty the room. Just over the chairman's chair
Was a bust, a Quaker's face with nose cocked up in the air;
There were common prints on the wall of the heads of the party fray,
And Mazzini dark and lean amidst them gone astray.
Some thirty men we were of the kind that I knew full well,
Listless, rubbed down to the type of our easy-going hell.
My heart sank down as I entered, and wearily there I sat
While the chairman strove to end his maunder of this and of that.
And partly shy he seemed, and partly indeed ashamed
Of the grizzled man beside him as his name to us he named.
He rose, thickset and short, and dressed in shabby blue,
And even as he began it seemed as though I knew
The thing he was going to say, though I never heard it before.
He spoke, were it well, were it ill, as though a message he bore,
A word that he could not refrain from many a million men . . .
But they sat and made no sign, and two of the glibber kind
Stood up to jeer and to carp, his fiery words to blind.
*   . . . I rose ere the meeting was done,*
And gave him my name and my faith – and I was the only one.

The passage reflects Morris's discouragement and weariness as he talked, as so often, to an unresponsive audience about things of which they had no conception. This feeling comes out in many of his letters. And it was this feeling, combined with his private unhappiness and frustration, and his ever-present anxiety about Jenny, that wore him out before his time – feelings he did his best to smother by constant over-work.

The futile bickering and intrigue still went on among the 'comrades', not only inside the League, but between the League and the SDF, each accusing the other of trying to break up its local branches by insinuation or open abuse. When the two bodies met on the same platform, there were petty squabbles about precedence. Morris wearily did his best to make peace, but he found Hyndman 'stiff and stately, playing the big man, and complaining of being illtreated by us, which was a wolf and lamb business. . . . Why will people quarrel when they have a serious end in view?' Morris, though a far greater figure than Hyndman, never 'played the big man'. For him no task was too small or undignified to undertake for the common cause. He carried the banner on marches, he handed the hat round at meetings, and even walked in the street as a sandwich man to advertise *The Commonweal*. Nevertheless, the other branches of the League called Morris's Hammersmith branch 'the damned bourgeois branch'.

All through 1887 the campaign of lecturing and public speaking continued unabated. Morris recorded his engagements that year in a diary.[10]

Sunday 2 Jan.	South Place 4 pm Early England
Sunday 23 Jan.	Merton Abbey True and False Society
Tues. 25 Jan.	Hammersmith Club Labour Question
Wed. 2 Feb.	Take chair for Mrs Besant
Wed. 9 Feb.	Lewisham
Sunday 13 Feb.	Here Medieval England
Sunday 6 March.	Hoxton
Sunday 13 March.	Hackney branch Monopoly
Monday 14 March.	Edinburgh
Sunday 20 March.	Chiswick Monopoly
Tues. 22 March.	Club Feudal England
Sunday 27 March.	Boro of Hackney Club Haggerston
Sunday 3 April.	Glasgow
Wed. 27 April.	Xtian Socialists True and false Society
Wed. 1 June.	Farringdon Road
Thurs. 9 June.	Battersea
Wed. 15 June.	102 Brompton Rd.

There is a gap here until 21 August.

Sunday 21 Aug.	Hoxton
Wed. 24 Aug.	Clerkenwell
Sunday 2 Oct.	Lecture at Manchester
Sunday 9 Oct.	Lecture here
Sunday 16 Oct.	S.D.F. Paddington
Sunday 30 Oct.	Nottingham
Sunday 6 Nov.	Fulham Liberal Club. What Socialists Want
Tues. 8 Nov.	Huddersfield

And so it went on. Against 'Sunday 27 Nov.' is written: 'Mrs Besant here mustn't be absent'. Morris also began to keep a more detailed account of his comings and goings this year, but it is fragmentary and comes to an end after three months. It is remarkable as showing, Mackail says, what immense labour he continued to spend in the service of the League, 'and how clearly nevertheless he saw the weakness of their machinery and the futility of the greater part of their efforts, and of his own.' It begins on 25 January:

I went down to lecture at Merton Abbey last Sunday: the little room was pretty full of men, mostly of the labourer class: any⁄ thing attacking the upper classes directly moved their enthusiasm; of their discontent there could be no doubt, or the sincerity of their class hatred: they have been very badly off there this winter, and there is little to wonder at in their discontent; but with a few exceptions they have not yet learned what Socialism means. . . . Jan. 26th. Went to South Kensington Museum yesterday with Jenny to look at the Troy tapestry again since they bought it for £1,250: I chuckled to think that properly speaking it was bought for me, since scarcely anybody will care a damn for it. H. Cole showed us a lot of scraps of woven stuff from the tombs of Upper Egypt; very curious as showing in an unusual material the tran⁄ sition to the pure Byzantine style from the classical; some pieces being nothing but debased classical style, others purely Byzantine, yet I think not much different in date: the contrast between the bald ugliness of the classical pieces and the great beauty of the Byzantine was a pleasing thing to me, who so loathe all classical art and literature. I spoke in the evening at the Hammersmith Radical Club at a meeting to condemn the Glenbeigh evictions . . . the frightful ignorance and want of impressibility of the average English workman floors me at times.

At the Chiswick Club on 7 February he was called upon to open a debate on the class war.

My Socialism was gravely listened to, but taken with no enthusiasm, and in fact however simply one puts the case for Socialism one always rather puzzles an audience: the speakers, except Hogg and a timid member of our branch, were muddled to the last degree. . . . The sum of it all is that the men at present listen respectfully to Socialism, but are perfectly supine and not in the least inclined to move except along the lines of Radicalism and Trades' Unionism.

Of his talk at Mitcham on Sunday 23 February, in 'a tumbledown shed opposite the grand new workhouse . . . amongst the woeful hovels that make up the worse (& newer) part of Mitcham', he notes: 'I doubt if most of them understood anything I said. . . . I wonder if people will remember in times to come to what a depth of degradation the ordinary English workman has been reduced; I felt very downcast among these poor people in their poor hutch whose opening I attended some three months back (and they were rather proud of it).'

'Yesterday all day long with Bax trying to get our second article on Marx together: a very difficult job: I hope it may be worth the trouble.' Morris used to refer to his Marxist sessions with Belfort Bax as 'compulsory Baxination'. Much of the diary is given up to his reflections on party politics, which can have very little interest after this lapse of time. What is of interest is its period flavour and the good straightforward writing, showing us what Morris was doing from day to day.

March 9th . . . Sunday I went to the new premises of the Hoxton Branch (the Labour Emancipation League) to lecture: I rather liked it: a queer little no-shaped slip cut off from some workshop or other, neatly whitewashed, with some innocent decoration obviously by the decorator member of the branch: all very poor but showing signs of sticking to it: the room full of a new audience of the usual type of attenders at such places: all working men except a parson in the front row, and perhaps a clerk or two, the opposition represented by a fool of the debating club type; but our men glad of any opposition at all. . . . I attended the Council

meeting [of the League] on Monday. It was in the end quarrel-
some. . . . We passed a resolution practically bidding our speakers
not to draw on quarrels with the police: though I doubt if they
will heed it often: as some of them are ambitious of figuring as
heroes in this 'free-speech' business. This is a pity; as if the police
stick to it, they can of course beat us in the long run: and we have
more out-a-door stations already than we can man properly.

March 20th. The annual meeting of our Hammersmith Branch
came off: a dead failure, as all our meetings except open-air ones
have been lately.

I lectured in the Chiswick Club Hall and had a scanty
audience and a dull. It was a new lecture, and good, though I
say it, and I really did my best; but they hung on my hands as
heavy as lead.

March 24th. 53 years old to-day – no use grumbling at that.

On 27 April the diary ends, with the note: 'I have been busy about
many things, and so unable to fill up this book.'

Next month he was touring Scotland – 'my regular Scotch tour',
he calls it in a letter to Jenny of 30 March.

I shall be about in several places I scarcely know where: Glasgow,
Edinburgh, Dundee, Paisley, Hamilton, Coatbridge – what
know I ? I shall try to make it as much of an outing as I can and
be jolly and free from anxiety: but it will be good hard work. . . .
The Government has brought in a very ferocious coercion bill
against the Irish; and I fear that there will be 'wigs on the green' if
it is carried. There are to be Radical demonstrations against it;
but I don't know if we shall be allowed to join, as the orthodox
Liberals are taking it up. Uncle Ned is a great friend of Balfour,
the Irish Secretary who has charge of this stupidity, and seems to
be a very headstrong stiff sort of Tory. Of course Uncle Ned
don't agree with him politically. [It was for the dining-room of
Balfour's house at Carlton House Terrace that Burne-Jones did
his *Perseus* series, begun in 1875 but never completed.] I am
sorry poor old Tennyson thought himself bound to write an ode
on our fat Vic's Jubilee: have you seen it ? It is like Martin
Tupper for all the world.

I must tell you, my dear, that I am getting famous or at least
notorious in Hammersmith town. The other day opposite the

Nazareth a covered green grocer's cart hailed me as Socialist & then as Morris! – I don't think it was meant to be complimentary. Also a week ago as I was going down River Court Road, so a small boy chubby about 7 years old sitting swinging on one of the iron gates, very uncomfortably I should think as they have a sort of cabbage ornaments, sings out to me: Have a ride – Morris!

At these two places I was known: but last Sunday it befell me to go to Victoria Park (beyond Bethnal Green) to a meeting. Now I have mounted a cape or cloak grey in colour so that people doubt whether I be a brigand or a parson: this seemed too picturesque for some 'Arrys who were passing by and sung out after me, Shakespeare – Yah!

Morris's letters to Jenny this spring give a detailed account of his Scottish lecture tour. An incident which caused him some amusement is recorded by Bruce Glasier. After speaking from a slag heap at Coatbridge, he was recognized by the cashier of the neighbouring ironworks, who said to the small audience of steelworkers: 'You people don't, I suppose, know who the gentleman is who has been addressing you. He is one of the leading men of literature and art today, and it is one of the greatest surprises of my life to find myself listening to him address a meeting of this kind at Coatbridge.' With a twinkle in his eye, Morris replied: 'After all, my friend, I wish to remind you that this is just the sort of way that Diogenes and Christ, and for all we know, Homer and your own Blind Harry the Minstrel, used to get their audiences; so I am not so far out the high literary convention after all!'

Glasier continues:

With the advance of the evening, the ground now became thronged with people, and a cheapjack and Salvationist band had made their respective appearances in close proximity to our meeting. A lively competition for the favour of the crowd therefore took place between the oratory of the poet of *The Earthly Paradise*, the drumming of the Salvationists and the blatant vociferations of the cheapjack, who, quite unconscious of the grim mockery of his performance was displaying rolls of loudcoloured linoleum and wallpaper which he described as 'the newest and best designs on the market, fit to make the homes of the workingclass vie with the palaces of princes'.[11]

Morris describes this incident in a letter to Jenny of 14 April. He mentions the competition with the Salvation Army and the cheap-jack, but says that they 'had a good meeting only disturbed by a drunken Irishman, who insisted with many oaths on our telling him the difference between a Home-Ruler and a non-Home-Ruler, and swore by Christ that *he* would teach us Socialism *he* would: but the crowd soon put him down. All this we did by star and furnace light, which was strange and even dreadful.'

In the same letter, written after his return to Hammersmith, Morris mentions that 'May has gone with Sparling to exhibit that young man to your Granny' – that is, as her fiancé. In June, Jane wrote to Rosalind Howard: 'May's love affair has not progressed since you saw the lovers. They are as much in love as ever, & no nearer marriage as far as one can see. May rightly insists on employ-ment being found by her fiancé before she marries, and I strongly uphold her.' In another letter of August to the same correspondent, after asking if she might go up to Naworth – 'I want so much to have a little bright life before the dreary winter sets in' – she goes on: 'May is away at Kelmscott Manor alone learning cooking & how to live on a few shillings a week. She is bent on marrying without waiting till her future husband gets employment. I have said & done all I can to dissuade her, but she is a fool, and persists.'[12]

May's marriage to the tall, thin, bird-like Henry Halliday Sparling, one of the most ardent members of the Socialist League, was not of very long duration. When they went to live at 8 Hammersmith Terrace, they invited Shaw to come and stay with them – a situation which seems to be forecast by Burne-Jones in an undated letter to Mrs Coronio in which he says: 'That is funny news of May – but I'm glad she has a pleasant companion and only wish she had two which would suit her state better – & why not – I like people to get what they want. . . .'[13] This, however, seems to have created an impossible situation for Sparling. Shaw felt in honour bound, he says, to leave the house, doubtless having done everything to fascinate May, and when he did so, Sparling also left. 'Of the particulars of the rupture I know nothing,' writes Shaw innocently, 'but in the upshot he fled to the Continent and eventually submitted chivalrously to being divorced. . . . The beautiful one abolished him root and branch, resuming her famous maiden name.'[14] Certainly May never refers to her brief married life, any more than Mackail does in his life of her father, and she went so far as to erase her signature as May

Sparling from the Kelmscott visitors' book, where she had previously written it under the years 1892, 1893 and 1895, after which she signed herself May Morris.[15] Christmas 1892, however was spent by May, Sparling and Shaw together at Kelmscott. That year Sparling had edited *The Recuyell of the Histories of Troy* for the Kelmscott Press and next year he edited *The History of Godefrey of Boloyne*. Presumably he then 'fled to the Continent'.

After her mother's death, May, now a moustached and masculine figure, lived at Kelmscott with Mary Lobb, who moved in after working as a land girl for Mr Hobbs during the 1914–1918 war. Miss Lobb is described by Sir Basil Blackwell as 'large, hearty, crop-headed, and always dressed in a Norfolk jacket and knicker-bockers. A less Pre-Raphaelite figure than the androgynous Miss Lobb could hardly be imagined.' Nevertheless, she was devoted to May, and it was due to her persuasion that Sir Basil finally agreed to publish the two bulky supplementary volumes, *William Morris, Artist Writer Socialist* in 1936. She even offered him her entire savings to this end, not because she admired Morris – 'an awful old bore', she said – but because 'you are worrying May, and I won't have her worried'.[16]

Shaw has written of his 'Mystic Betrothal' in the delightful essay he contributed to the two supplementary volumes. Though from her photographs, May can hardly be described as beautiful, Shaw writes of her as 'then in the flower of her youth. You can see her in Burne-Jones's picture coming down *The Golden Stair* [sic], the central figure.' But he was, he says, at that time far too poor to think of marriage. 'Suddenly, to my utter stupefaction, and I suspect to that of Morris, the beautiful daughter married one of the comrades.' But, of course, Morris was not stupefied as he had long accepted Harry as May's prospective husband and their love affair was common knowledge among Morris's friends.[17] When Shaw went to live at Hammersmith Terrace, May, he says, was glad to have him in the house, 'and he was glad to have me because I kept her in good humour and produced a cuisine that no mere husband could elicit. It was probably the happiest passage in our three lives.' Shaw was at this time, on his own admission, an inveterate philanderer.[18]

At May's death in 1938, Sir Sydney Cockerell wrote: 'I first met her, a beautiful girl of 23, in 1885 . . . with many excellent qualities she combined a dissatisfied attitude on life which interfered greatly with her happiness and with that of others.' Later he added: 'If only she could have married the right man what a different, more effective, and far happier woman she would have been! . . . She was in love with Bernard Shaw before he was famous and he with her. . . . Stanley Baldwin fell in love with her too, and so did Burne-Jones.'[19] The fact is, of course, that for May no man could ever come anywhere near her father in her estimation, though Jenny was his favourite. After his death she devoted the rest of her life to the service of his memory.

Describing a visit early in the 1930s to the 'frozen stillness' of the museum atmosphere at Kelmscott, Sir Basil Blackwell writes of May: 'Hers was a face of noble and austere beauty, somewhat haggard, with eyebrows set at an angle reminiscent of a Greek tragic mask and suggesting some sad and painful happening in her life. . . . Her appearance and her bearing were apt to a sense of dedication which her conversation constantly revealed; for the words "My Father" were ever on her lips.' From the bedroom they passed into 'the chill of the tapestried chamber, where, perished with cold, while a woodfire sent its modest warmth straight up from a huge open hearth, the hieratic May would turn for you with an ivory knife the vellum pages of some manuscript by her father, or sit at her loom, surrounded by grim titanic figures portraying the blinding of Samson'.[20]

CHAPTER THIRTEEN

1887–1890

A Dream of John Ball: the Odyssey: Bloody Sunday and the End of the Socialist League

A DREAM OF JOHN BALL, the romance into which Morris put his deepest thoughts on life and human destiny, had begun to appear in the pages of *The Commonweal* in November 1886. It stands apart from his later prose romances as being set in a recognizable England at the time of the Peasants' Revolt in Kent at the end of the fourteenth century. In the clear brilliance of its pictures of the Middle Ages it recaptures the vividness of his early poems in *The Defence of Guenevere*. Its language is of great purity and simplicity and its deliberate archaisms strike one as a natural part of the subject. Morris put himself into it as the Dreamer, in the likeness and habit of Chaucer. It is extraordinary that such a serene and beautiful work should have been written at a time when Morris was so harassed and 'tossed about by doing so many things'. It is evidence of that deep well of strength and tranquillity within the man that enabled him to combine so many and such disparate activities.

Somewhat earlier, Morris had suggested to another member of the League that he should write a serial story on the theme of Wat Tyler's rebellion and had been met with a refusal on the grounds of a lack of epic faculty. This had annoyed him and, according to Sparling, he had begun to shout in reply: 'Epic faculty be hanged for a yarn! Confound it, man, you've only got to tell a story!' And a few days later he himself turned up with the first instalment of *John Ball*.[1]

It was at this time that Morris threw open his lecture room at Hammersmith to speakers of many different persuasions. The Sunday-evening lecturers in the coach house included such names as Shaw, Scheu, Graham Wallas, Percy Dearmer, Sydney Olivier, Sidney Webb, Herbert Bland, Walter Crane, Annie Besant and

Ernest Rhys. The young W. B. Yeats, then living with his family at Bedford Park, also attended regularly for a time and was among those whom Morris invited to stay for supper after the lecture. 'I met at those suppers', Yeats says in his *Autobiographies*, 'very constantly Walter Crane, Emery Walker . . . and less constantly Bernard Shaw and Cockerell . . . and perhaps but once or twice Hyndman the Socialist and the Anarchist Prince Kropotkin. There, too, one always met certain more or less educated workmen, rough of speech and manner, with a conviction to meet every turn.'

But at one of the lectures, Yeats burst out, saying that all the changes they talked about could only come through 'a change of heart' and only religion could make it. 'What was the use of talking about some new revolution putting all things right, when the change must come, if come it did, with astronomical slowness, like the cooling of the sun, or it may have been like the drying of the moon.' At this point Morris began ringing his chairman's bell for Yeats to sit down, and at supper afterwards he said to him: 'Of course, I know there must be a change of heart, but it will not come as slowly as all that. I rang my bell because you were not being understood.'[2] In fact, one of the 'more or less educated workmen' told Yeats that he had listened to more nonsense from him in half an hour than he had heard in all his life. After that Yeats ceased to attend the lectures, though his elder sister became an embroideress under May, working the hangings for the great four-poster bed at Kelmscott.

No man he had ever known, says Yeats, was so well-loved as Morris. 'You saw him producing everywhere organization and beauty, seeming almost in the same instant helpless and triumphant; and people loved him as children are loved.'[3] And earlier in the same book he remarks: 'To-day I do not set his poetry very high, but for an odd altogether wonderful line, or thought. . . .' For Yeats Morris always remained 'the dreamer of the middle ages', as he appears in the Watts portrait, with eyes 'like the eyes of some dreaming beast', though he adds that Morris's dream world 'was as much the antithesis of daily life as with other men of genius, but he was never conscious of the antithesis and so knew nothing of intellectual suffering. His intellect, unexhausted by speculation or casuistry, was wholly at the service of hand and eye, and whatever he pleased he did with an unheard of ease and simplicity, and if style and vocabulary were at times monotonous, he could not have

made them otherwise without ceasing to be himself.'[4] Yeats remembers Morris at supper dispraising the houses he had decorated,
saying: 'Do you suppose I like that kind of house? I would like a
house like a big barn, where one ate in one corner, cooked in
another corner, slept in the third corner, and in the fourth received
one's friends.'[5] But though Morris himself did not feel the need of
privacy, even in the Middle Ages the lord and lady of the manor
could, and usually did, retire to the solar.

In seeing Morris as 'the one perfectly happy and fortunate poet of
modern times',[6] Yeats was seeing him too much in terms of the late
prose romances, in which he does succeed in recapturing an
innocence and simplicity which had nothing to do with the nineteenth century or, for that matter, with the problems that had
agitated his whole life. Otherwise, Morris was only too conscious of
the antithesis between the sort of world he would have liked to
create, and which he believed socialism would create, and the
loathsome reality created by Victorian industrialism. To say that he
knew nothing of intellectual suffering is manifestly untrue, for it was
this ever-present consciousness of what life might be for the majority
of people and what it actually was that made him a socialist.

Morris still believed in the possibility of changing the world
through revolutionary action, though it is true that his experiences
on 'Bloody Sunday' in the November of this year, and the petty
dissensions in the little socialist body of which he was the leader,
disillusioned him in the prospect of any radical change taking place
in his time. But it is quite wrong to suppose that he ever deserted his
principles. Indeed, he stood, from 1883 until the end of his life, as
Shaw says, with one part of his mind, at least,. 'on the side of Karl
Marx *contra mundum*'.[7] But with the other part, for there was a basic
contradiction, he stood beside Chaucer *contra mundum* and an unchanging English tradition which he endeavoured to project into
the future. His last years were spent writing prose romances in a
strange archaic language, collecting illuminated manuscripts,
designing books on medieval models and, after producing a Chaucer
at the Kelmscott Press, was well on the way to a great edition of
Berners' translation of Froissart. To that extent, Morris never
succeeded in escaping from his medieval dream.

A rather different view, from below stairs, of the Sunday-evening
gatherings at Kelmscott House is given in a recent interview
with Floss Gunner, who went into service with the Morrises as

kitchenmaid at the age of fourteen in 1891.[8] From this it appears that the domestic staff at Hammersmith consisted of the cook and the kitchenmaid, the houseboy and three others – parlourmaid, housemaid and tweeny. Floss says that she was always glad to get away to Kelmscott:

> it was nice to breathe there, because at the London house the kitchen was well down below ground level. It wasn't such a drudgery at Kelmscott Manor. . . . They had a hall which runs down by the side of Kelmscott House, where they used to have Sunday evening meetings. When they held meetings there, any Tom, Dick or Harry would come in and have supper . . . I think that's why they came to the meetings – so they could come in and have a good square meal afterwards. That made us very busy on Saturdays. And if you went out on Sundays you had to be in by 6 o'clock. . . . It did amount to slavery really very often. When they had a party it was nothing to be up till turned 11 o'clock after the dinner party, cleaning the copper with the palm of your hand; with salt, sand and vinegar. You wasn't allowed a rag. . . . Then you've got to be up by 5 o'clock, and I wasn't very old.

Floss remembered Morris as a short man with a beard and a round hat. Of Jane, she said: 'She was a very handsome woman; very handsome and very nice. May Morris . . . used to help her father. And Jenny . . . was always at home, because she had epileptic fits very badly. . . . She was very sweet.'

In April 1887 Morris published the first volume of the *Odyssey*, much of which had been translated on train journeys during his northern lecture tours. Fifty lines were done on the boat returning from Dublin earlier the previous year. 'My translation is a real one so far,' he wrote to F. S. Ellis, 'not a mere periphrase of the original as *all* the others are. . . . I don't think the public will take to it; it is too like Homer.' Some people felt it was too like *Sigurd* and, as Oscar Wilde remarked in his review in the *Pall Mall Gazette* of 26 April, 'rather Norse than Greek, and perhaps, at times, more boisterous than beautiful'. Yet he said of it:

> Of all our English translations this is the most perfect and the most satisfying. It is, in no sense of the word, literary; it seems to deal immediately with life itself, and to take from the reality of

things its own form and colour; it is always direct and simple, and at its best has something of the 'large utterance of the early gods'. . . . . Of all our modern poets, Mr William Morris is the one best qualified by nature and by art to translate for us the marvellous epic of the wanderings of Odysseus. . . . Master as he is of decorative and descriptive verse, he has all the Greek's joy in the visible aspect of things, all the Greek's sense of delicate and delightful detail, all the Greek's pleasure in beautiful textures and exquisite materials and imaginative designs; nor can anyone have a keener sympathy with the Homeric admiration for the workers and the craftsmen in the various arts. . . .

Wilde's review of the second volume in November was equally enthusiastic. 'How really admirable is this whole translation . . . how straightforward it is, how honest and direct! Its fidelity to the original is far beyond that of any other verse-translation in our literature, and yet it is not the fidelity of a pedant to his text but rather the fine loyalty of poet to poet.'

Mackail, however, was far more critical and doubted whether Morris's *Odyssey* was as successful as his earlier translation of the *Aeneid*, remarking: 'Notwithstanding his deep love and admiration for the Icelandic epics, notwithstanding the essentially Homeric tone of his own great Volsung epic, the romantic element in Virgil was perhaps more nearly akin to his own most intimate poetical instincts. . . .' Mackail also criticized the metre chosen as apt to become formless and loose.

Halliday Sparling has left a vivid account of Morris's peculiar working methods:

He would be standing at an easel or sitting with a sketchblock in front of him, charcoal, brush or pencil in hand, and all the while would be grumbling Homer's Greek under his breath . . . the design coming through in clear unhesitating strokes. Then the note of the grumbling changed, for the turn of the English had come. He was translating the *Odyssey* at this time and he would prowl about the room, filling and lighting his pipe, halting to add a touch or two at one or other easel, still grumbling, go to his writing-table, snatch up his pen, and write furiously for a while – twenty, fifty, and hundred or more lines, as the case might be . . . the speed of his hand would gradually slacken, his eye would wander to an easel, a sketchblock, or to some one of the manuscripts in progress, and that would have its turn. There was something well-nigh terrifying to a youthful onlooker in the deliberate ease with which he interchanged so many forms of creative work, taking up each one exactly at the point at which he had laid it aside, and never halting to recapture the thread of his thought. . . .[9]

In October, Morris's interlude *The Tables Turned, or Nupkins Awakened* was produced at the Farringdon Road office of the League, for the benefit of *The Commonweal*. Shaw says he had never been present at such an overwhelmingly successful first night. The scene is 'A Court of Justice', and the case is heard by Mr Justice Nupkins. Morris himself took the part of the Archbishop of Canterbury, called as a witness for the defence in a police prosecu-tion of a member of the League on a charge of obstruction and incitement to riot. The archbishop, needing 'some little refreshment from the toils of ecclesiastical office', as he said in his evidence, had taken a cab to Hammersmith to see for himself what a socialist meeting was really like. But he was disappointed by 'the extreme paucity of the audience' and disgusted by 'the rude and coarse words' of the prisoner, who had complained that it was ' "damned hard lines to have to speak to a lamp-post, a kid, and an old buffer" – by the latter vulgarity indicating myself, as I understand'.

Another witness called was Tennyson, who had attended a meeting at League headquarters in disguise. 'They sat and smoked,' said Tennyson, 'and one fool was in the chair, and another fool read letters; and then they worried till I was sick of it as to where such and such fools should go and spout folly the next week; and now and then an old bald-headed fool and a stumpy little fool in blue made jokes, at which they laughed a good deal; but I couldn't understand the jokes – and came away.'[10] At the time all this must have seemed uproariously funny. May and Sparling also took part, and Ernest Rhys records seeing Jane Morris join the audience before the curtain went up: 'a figure, which might have stepped straight out of a Pre-Raphaelite picture . . . whose superb tall form, long neck, and austere, handsome, pale features looked more queenly than any Guinevere or Cleopatra.'[11]

For *The Tables Turned*, Morris drew upon his own experiences of open-air meetings and attendances at police courts, which had taken up so much of his time in recent years, and in Tennyson's evidence

A Dream of John Ball: Bloody Sunday

probably expressed much of what he felt about the meetings at the League itself. The trial of the comrade is interrupted by the singing of the 'Marseillaise' and the outbreak of the revolution offstage. Part II opens in the fields near a country village after the revolution, with Justice Nupkins alone, fearing arrest as a rogue and vagabond. To him enters May Morris 'prettily dressed' as Mary Pinch. 'How pleasant it is this morning!' she says. 'These hot late summer mornings, when the first pears are ripening, and the wheat is nearly ready for cutting, and the river is low and weedy. . . .' And we are at Kelmscott and already in the world of *News from Nowhere*. 'All that pretty picture of plenty that I told you about on that day when you were so hard upon me has come to pass, and more', she says to Nupkins. 'Come along, and I'll show you the pretty new hall they are building for our parish; it's such a pleasure to stand and watch the lads at work there, as merry as grigs.' And Nupkins, in a world without lawyers, is condemned to dig potatoes as a temporary penance. The play ends with the song:

> *What's this that the days and the days have done?*
> *Man's lordship over man hath gone.*
>
> *How fares it, then, with high and low?*
> *Equal on earth, they thrive and grow.*
>
> *Bright is the sun for everyone;*
> *Dance we, dance we the Carmagnole.*

Attacks on demonstrations of the unemployed continued throughout 1887 and in October Trafalgar Square was on several occasions cleared by mounted police. But, in spite of this, by November large unemployed meetings were being held in the square daily, and at night hundreds of homeless people were sleeping in the streets. On 8 November Sir Charles Warren, the Commissioner of Police, banned all further meetings in the square on the pretext that it was Crown property. In this he was supported by the press, which complained that these continual meetings in the heart of London, and the scuffles with the police into which they developed, were becoming a public nuisance. The Liberal *Daily News*, for instance, stated that they were 'soon like to try the patience of the public' and commended the police in their efforts to maintain order.

But while the greater part of the press denounced the unemployed as idlers and criminals, W.T.Stead in the *Pall Mall Gazette* championed the cause of free speech and blamed the authorities for provocation. There was also great indignation at this time in Radical and socialist circles over the action of the police in the United States in opening fire on a peaceful demonstration of strikers. This action had provoked another protest demonstration at which a bomb was thrown, killing several policemen. As a result, several anarchists were condemned to death and one of them to life imprisonment, sentences which *The Times* of 12 November com﹣ mended. Judges and juries in America, wrote *The Times*, 'draw no distinction between incendiaries of the platform and the Press, and the men who do their dirty work'. As for the American police: 'They carry revolvers, and use them without mercy when they see signs of resistance.' Such firmness, *The Times* concluded, set us an example in the handling of disorders in Ireland and nearer home.

Morris promptly wrote to the *Pall Mall Gazette*, proposing a Law and Liberty League to defend the right of free speech, and the issue was taken up by the Metropolitan Radical Association, and by Mrs Besant, W.T.Stead, Cunninghame Graham and the Rev. Stewart Headlam. The Federation of Radical Clubs and the Irish thereupon called for a demonstration in Trafalgar Square on Sunday 13 November – the day which came to be known as Bloody Sunday – to protest against coercion and the treatment in prison of the Irish M.P. O'Brien. On the 12th Sir Charles Warren issued a further notice that no organized procession would be allowed to approach the square.

On the following day, as contingents of demonstrators converged from north, east, south and west, hundreds of thousands strong, the police attacked and dispersed them. Meanwhile, Trafalgar Square was guarded by cordons of police four deep in addition to mounted police, who at once rode down any incipient gathering, striking out right and left with their batons. The few stragglers that managed to get through were at once surrounded and mercilessly clubbed. Behind the police stood three hundred foot soldiers with fixed bayonets, armed with twenty rounds of ammunition apiece. These again were supported by a battalion of Life Guards. The scene was set for a full﹣scale massacre. But thanks to the generalship of Warren, in dispersing the columns at the approaches to the square, only three people died as a result of injuries, though two hundred were treated in hospital for wounds. Doubtless many other wounded people were afraid to go to hospital for fear of arrest.

Morris marched with the Socialist League contingent from Clerkenwell Green. Before starting, he and Annie Besant, according to *The Times* report, addressed their 'respectable artisans' from a cart, saying that 'whenever free speech was attempted to be put down, it was their bounden duty to resist the attempt by every means in their power. He thought their business was to get to the Square by some means or other, and he intended to do his best to get there whatever the consequences might be. They must press on into the Square like orderly people and good citizens.'

The Clerkenwell contingent, composed of members of the Socialist League, the Patriotic Club, some East End workmen's clubs and a branch of the SDF, were some five thousand strong. But they only got as far as Seven Dials. Suddenly, police, irrupting from the side-streets, attacked the procession on both sides and in the rear. Morris had been marching in the middle of the column with Shaw, but, anticipating trouble, had moved to its head. As he wrote in the next number of *The Commonweal*:

It was all over in a few minutes: our comrades fought valiantly, but they had not learned how to stand and turn their column into a line, or to march on to the front. . . . The police struck right and left like what they were, soldiers attacking an enemy, amid wild shrieks of hatred from the women who came from the slums on our left. The band-instruments were captured, the banners and flags destroyed, there was no rallying point and no possibility of rallying, and all the people composing our strong column could do was to struggle into the Square as helpless units. I confess I was astounded at the rapidity of the thing and the ease with which military organization got its victory. I could see that numbers were of no avail unless led by a band of men acting in concert and each knowing his part.

What happened to us happened, as I hear, to the other pro-cessions with more or less fighting. An eye-witness who marched up with the western column told me that they were suddenly attacked as they came opposite the Haymarket Theatre, by the police rushing out on them from the side streets and immediately batoning everybody they could reach, whether they resisted or not. The column, he said, was destroyed in two minutes, though certainly not quite without fighting: one brave man wrapping his banner torn from the pole round his arm and facing the police till he was hammered down with repeated blows.

Once in the Square we were, as I said, helpless units, especially as there were undoubtedly a good many mere spectators, many of them gentlemen and other members of the class which employs Warren.

In fact, the police were so much masters of the situation that Morris says he was surprised to see the Life Guards form at the south of the square and march up to St Martin-in-the-Fields with the magistrate at their head ('a sort of country-gentleman-looking imbecile') to read the Riot Act. The soldiers were cheered, as well as hooted, by the crowd, 'I think under the impression', says Morris, 'that they would not act as brutally against the people as the police: a mistaken impression, I think, as these gorgeous gentry are just the helmeted flunkies of the rich and would act on their orders just as their butlers and footmen would do. . . . Sir Charles Warren has thus given us a lesson in street fighting. . . . We Socialists should thank our master for his lesson.'

One wonders if the police had had instructions to respect the person of the author of *The Earthly Paradise*, for they clubbed Cunninghame Graham mercilessly when he reached the square with John Burns and Hyndman. The police, Graham wrote to *The Commonweal*, actually dragged him *into* the square by the hair. Nevertheless, he says that he had ample time to observe a good deal:

I saw repeated charges made at a perfectly unarmed and helpless crowd: I saw policemen not of their own accord, but under the orders of their superiors, repeatedly strike women and children; I saw them invariably choose those for assault who seemed least able to retaliate. One incident struck me with considerable force and disgust. As I was being led out of the crowd a poor woman asked a police inspector (I think) or a sergeant if he had seen a child she had lost. His answer was to tell her she was a 'damned whore' and to knock her down. . . . Other things I saw pleased me better than this. I saw that the police were afraid; I saw on more than one occasion that the officials had to strike their free British men to make them obey orders. . . . The tops of the houses and hotels were crowded with well-dressed women, who clapped their hands and cheered with delight when some miserable and half-starved working-man was knocked down and trodden under foot.

At another point Annie Besant hurled herself bodily at the police cordons in an effort to break through. After it was all over, *The Times* rejoiced at the firm handling of the situation by Sir Charles Warren. 'Putting aside mere idlers and sight-seers . . . and putting aside also a small band of persons with a diseased craving for notoriety . . . the active portion of yesterday's mob was composed of all that is weakest, most worthless, and most vicious in the slums of a great city', ran next day's leader.

The following day, *The Times* reported great rejoicing all over London, especially in the West End. Next Sunday it was the police who demonstrated in Trafalgar Square, galloping about and chasing straggling crowds of hapless by-standers. One of these, a young man named Alfred Linnell, ridden down by a mounted policeman in Northumberland Avenue, died soon after in hospital from his injuries. For his funeral, staged by W. T. Stead and Annie Besant's Law and Liberty League on 18 December, Morris wrote ' A Death Song', printed and sold as a 1*d.* leaflet, with a woodcut by Walter Crane, for the benefit of Linnell's children.

In pouring rain, an enormous procession wound slowly from Soho to Bow Cemetery. For pall bearers the obscure Linnell had Cunninghame Graham, Annie Besant, Stead, Herbert Burrows, Frank Smith of the Salvation Army. and Morris. The streets were lined with sympathizers and the police were greeted with cries of 'That's your work !' The burial service was read by Stewart Headlam. 'There was to me', Morris wrote afterwards, 'something aweful (I can use no other word) in such a tremendous mass of people, unorganized, unhelped, and so harmless and good-tempered.'

At the graveside, Morris said (as reported in *The Commonweal* for 24 December):

> our friend who lies there has had a hard life, and met with a hard death; and if society had been differently constituted, his life might have been a delightful, a beautiful one, and a happy one to him. It is our business to try and make this earth a very beautiful and happy place. We are engaged in a most holy war, trying to prevent our rulers making this great town of London nothing more than a prison. I cannot help thinking that the immense pro-cession in which we have walked this day will have the effect of

teaching a great lesson . . . and we should begin to-morrow to organize for the purpose of seeing that such things shall not happen again.

The mildness of the speech is evidence that Morris was now dis-illusioned with the immediate prospects of revolutionary socialism. He was attacked in the press for his part in Linnell's funeral, but it nevertheless helped to make him the most beloved figure in the English Labour movement. For many weeks he remained active, speaking for the Law and Liberty League in defence of free speech. But John Burns and Cunninghame Graham were charged at the Old Bailey with taking part in a riot and unlawfully assaulting the police in the discharge of their duty. While they were sentenced to only six weeks' imprisonment, a stonemason named Harrison was given five years' penal servitude for assaulting a policeman.

In February next year, Morris went to Pentonville gaol early in the morning to greet Burns and Graham on their release, and he wrote to Jenny on the 19th:

I walked down the street to look at the miserable place and it made my blood boil to think that men should elaborate such a monument of folly, and thought how I should like to pull it down and turn it into a floor-cloth factory or something of that sort. . . . I should tell you that in spite of these shabby dogs there was a good gathering at the gates to meet the prisoners, and that some of them had been so thoughtful as to bring meat-pies with them which they thrust into their hands, and their dignity did not prevent them from 'wolfing' them, as Harry called it, at once: and they had a good time in a coffee shop just opposite the prison.

In the evening Morris helped May and Harry Sparling to serve teas at a social in the prisoners' honour. Two days later at the riding school in Seymour Place, Hyndman attacked the Radicals and the meeting broke up in disorder, with one of the Radicals shouting 'You infernal firebrand!' and rushing the platform. Thus ended the temporary union of the Radicals and the socialists.

Shaw says that the free speech contests with the police 'were perhaps the worst worries which Socialism brought on Morris' and that Mackail underrates the burden to such a character of the feeling, whenever a poor man went to prison, that 'he should have gone instead'. Morris loathed going to police courts and was very nervous of the officials, and Shaw thinks that the physical worry of this sort of thing to a man of Morris's temperament was much greater than that of open-air speaking. But then, as he points out, Morris brought to the professed socialists of the League and Federation 'a conception of life which they never assimilated and concerning which they could teach him nothing; whilst on the general public, already educated to some extent by Ruskin, it gained to an extent which Morris himself was the last to realize.'[12]

In March Morris wrote to Georgie:

> I am not in a good temper with myself: I cannot shake off the feeling that I might have done more in these recent matters than I have; though I really don't know what I could have done: but I feel beaten and humbled. Yet one ought not to be down in the mouth about matters; for I certainly never thought that things would have gone on so far as they have in the last three years; only, again, as opinion spreads, organization does not spread with it.

This month he read both *War and Peace* and *Anna Karenina*. He 'got through' *War and Peace* 'with much approbation but little enjoyment', he tells Georgie in the letter quoted above, 'and yet . . . with a good deal of satisfaction'. During this month's Scottish tour he wrote to Jenny: 'I have nearly read out "Anna Karenina": I think it better than "War and Peace" as a work of art, but I find it heavy reading some times. . . .' In fact, Morris seems to have had small interest in the greater novels of his time, with their analysis of adult human relationships. He turned for refreshment rather to the more adolescent adventure world of Dumas, whose novels he read over and over again, and to the knock-about humour of Surtees's Mr Jorrocks and Dickens's Joe Gargery, whom he was fond of impersonating, ending many of his letters to his daughters with Joe's favourite exclamation 'Wot larx!' He delighted in Mark Twain for much the same reason. Meanwhile in Scotland he went to Penkill, the Ayrshire castle of the Boyd family for whom William Bell Scott had carried out extensive restorations. 'The house at Penkill has been so much spoiled', he wrote to May, 'that one can take but little pleasure in the architecture thereof.'

Back in London, he found trouble brewing with the Bloomsbury branch of the League, among whose members were Eleanor Marx, Edward Aveling and A. K. Donald and most of those in favour of putting up candidates for parliamentary and municipal elections in conjunction with the SDF. The Bloomsbury branch had, in fact, begun to lead a largely independent life and had lately put down a resolution for the fourth annual conference for the federation of the various socialist bodies. Morris did not like the look of this at all and saw the League losing its identity in the SDF. The other most influential group within the League were the anarchists, who were all for direct, violent action. This did not meet with Morris's approval either, though he was on very good terms with Prince Kropotkin, the most urbane and gentle of anarchists, who published a monthly paper *Freedom*. As Morris had written earlier, trying to get these rival factions to agree was 'something like the worst kind of pig-driving'.

But the anarchist tendencies within the League continued to grow. After the trial and execution of the Chicago anarchists, their biographies appeared in *The Commonweal* and in November 1888 the League organized the visit to England of the widow of one of them, Lucy Parsons, who addressed commemorative meetings in London, Edinburgh, Ipswich and Norwich. She also spoke at Kelmscott House. 'Mrs Parsons' lecture was a great success here – the room was crammed', Morris wrote to Jenny on 17 November. 'May was in the chair: I was not present, as I had to go to a meeting of the Arts and Crafts. She is a curious woman: no signs of European blood in her, Indian with a touch of negro; but she speaks pure Yankee. I was much tickled by her indignation at the barbarous and backward means of communication in London.'

In the previous July Morris had written to Georgie:

I am a little dispirited over our movement in all directions. Perhaps we Leaguers have been somewhat too stiff in our refusal to compromise. I have always felt that it was rather a matter of temperament than of principle; that some transition period was of course inevitable, I mean a transition involving State Socialism and pretty stiff at that; and also, that whatever might be said about the reception of ideal Socialism or Communism, towards State Socialism things are certainly tending, and swiftly too. But then in all the wearisome shilly-shally of parliamentary politics I should be absolutely useless: and the immediate end to be gained, the pushing things just a trifle nearer to State Socialism, which when realised seems to me but a dull goal – all this quite sickens me. . . . Preaching the ideal is surely always necessary. Yet on the other hand I sometimes vex myself by thinking that perhaps I am not doing the most I can merely for the sake of a piece of 'preciousness'.

Four letters which Morris wrote to the Rev. George Bainton this year represent the most reasoned statement of his beliefs as a socialist.[13]

> Socialism is a theory of life, taking for its starting point the evolution of society; or, let us say, of man as a social being. Since man has certain material *necessities* as an animal, Society is founded on man's attempt to satisfy those necessities; and Socialism, or social consciousness, points out to him the way of doing so which will interfere least with the development of his specially human capacities, and the satisfaction of what, for lack of better words, I will call his spiritual and mental capacities. . . . Socialism aims, therefore, at realizing equality of condition as its economical goal, and the habitual love of humanity as its rule of ethics . . . In such a state of Society laws of repression would be minimised. . . .

August saw him marching through Richmond with the Leaguers, with band and banners, to Richmond Park, where he joined in the foot-race; he was 'rather tired' when he got home. He also spent some days at Kelmscott, enjoying the river. On the 24th he wrote to Jenny:

> Altogether a very pleasant river to travel on, the banks being still very beautiful with flowers; the long-purples & willow herb, and that strong-coloured yellow flower very close and buttony, are the great show but there is a very pretty dark blue flower: I think mug-wort, mixed with all that besides the purple blossom of the horse mint & mouse ear & here and there a bit of meadow-sweet belated. . . .

It was the treatment of the banks by the Thames Conservancy Board, which regularly cut down all the flowers and cleared the stream of its pleasant flowering reeds and rushes, which so enraged Morris. There was no evidence, of course, that under socialism, the Board would have had any more consideration for flowers.

But Morris had other enemies besides the Conservancy Board. As he complained to Georgie at Easter next year:

315

Some damned fool has been bullying our rooks so much that they have only got six nests, so that we haven't got the proper volume of sound from them.

One grief, the sort of thing that is always happening in the spring: there were some beautiful willows at Eaton Hastings which to my certain knowledge had not been polled during the whole 17 years that we have been here; and now the idiot Parson has polled them into wretched stumps. I should like to cut off the beggar's legs and have wooden ones made for him out of the willow timber, the value of which is about 7s. 6d.

From Kelmscott in August 1888 he wrote:

We have had all the birds here again. The herons have been stalking about the field in the gravest manner; and I have seen the kingfishers very busy. One ducked down into the water before me and came out again with a little fish. I saw an owl last night come sailing along, and suddenly turn head over heels and down in the grass; after a mouse I suppose: such a queer action I never saw.

One Sunday this month Emery Walker, who was staying at Kencott, cycled over to Kelmscott to find the following charac- teristic note fastened outside the front door.

In case you come over here while we are away, I tell you that we are going at eleven o'clock towards Inglesham, and shall be back at 5 p.m. or thereabouts: so if you come over in the afternoon *please* wait and take a drink of tea or wine or beer, and a bite of what may be handy. But if you come in the morning you would probably soon catch up with us by walking *up* the tow path (i.e. towards Lechlade), as we are going in a heavy boat against wind & stream. Note that the tow path breaks off just below St John's Lock and you will have to walk a few hundred yards by road to the lock.

I should be sorry to miss you if you come over so do as you are told. We can give you a bed. . . .

In August, too, we find him writing to Georgie:

I am prepared to see all organized Socialism run into the sand for a while. But we shall have done something even then, as we shall have forced intelligent people to consider the matter; and then there will come some favourable conjunction of circumstances in due time which will call for our active work again. If I am alive then I shall chip in again, and one advantage I shall have, that I shall know much better what to do and what to forbear than this first time. . . .

During the summer of 1889, Wilfrid Scawen Blunt records in his diary that he 'spent many pleasant days gudgeon fishing' at Kelmscott. He had, he says, known the Morrises for some years, Mrs Howard having asked him to Naworth specially to meet Jane in 1883, when he spent a week in her company. But of her husband he had hitherto seen little. Of his Kelmscott visit of 1889 he says:

> Morris was at that time in a mood of reaction from his socialistic fervour. He had quarrelled with Hyndman, and was disgusted at the personal jealousies of his fellow-workers in the cause and at their cowardice in action. He never got over the pusillanimity they had shown at the Trafalgar Square meeting two years before, when a few hundred policemen had dealt with thousands of them as though they had been schoolboys. Morris was too loyal and obstinate to abjure his creed, but the heart of his devotion to the cause of the proletariat had gone. In some ways our two positions were the same. We had both of us sacrificed much socially to our principles, and our principles had failed to justify themselves by results, and we were both driven back on earlier loves, art, poetry, romance.[14]

Blunt had perhaps suffered more than Morris for his convictions, having served a sentence of two months' hard labour in Galway gaol for speaking on behalf of the Home Rule Union against the eviction of Irish peasants by Anglo-Irish landlords. His intervention in Egyptian affairs had also got him into bad odour with the authorities.[15] He had now driven over to Kelmscott in style with a four-in-hand of Arabian mares, bred at Crabbet Park, Sussex. Of a subsequent visit in 1894 he records that he drove his Arabs across the Berkshire downs, travelling over grass through a quite uninhabited country, 'as desolate as parts of Mesopotamia'. In the evenings he and Morris read poetry together. Of Morris's reading of his own poems he says: 'He did it as if he were throwing a bone to a dog, at the end of each piece breaking off with, "There, that's it", as much as to say "you may take it or leave it as you please." '[16]

The fact is, Morris had a poor opinion of his early poems and it embarrassed him to be asked to read them.

Unlike most people, Blunt was not intimidated by Morris and he told him that 'he and Ruskin had done more harm than good by their attempt to make English people love beauty and decorate their houses. He defended himself good-humouredly, but I think has doubts, for we are engulfed to-day in a slough of ornament.' Blunt also records a visit to Merton Abbey in the summer of 1892, when he met Morris's brother

> working in the dye vats there, a dreamy man in workman's clothes, with his shirt sleeves turned up, and his arms blue with indigo to the elbows. I asked Morris about him and he tells me that having begun life with a good fortune – he had a country place in Herefordshire – he has gradually fallen in the world, and after trying one thing and another to get a living is now glad to be employed on weekly wages. He lives at Merton, and is quite happy, indeed he looked so, dipping wool all day in the vats, in a shed open on to the garden.[17]

This was 'Uncle Edgar'.

In March 1890 Morris wrote to Bruce Glasier that he was paying for the League and *The Commonweal* at the rate of £500 a year. Obviously he could not keep this up indefinitely. He had lately also paid out £1000 in a libel action. But by the spring of 1889 Morris had already abandoned all hope for the League, though he con-tinued to finance it. The anarchists, who had captured control of the executive, had removed him from the editorship of *The Common-weal* in favour of the extremist Frank Kitz. Moreover, old friends were beginning to fall away. Emery Walker, of whom Morris said that he regarded that day as lost on which he did not see him, was now too occupied with the Arts and Crafts Society to devote much time to politics. Charles Faulkner had been struck down with paralysis in 1888 and was slowly dying. 'I try not to think of it too much', Morris wrote miserably to Georgie the following year, 'lest I should give way altogether, and make an end of what small use there may be in my life.' Philip Webb, for a time treasurer of the League, was also preoccupied with his own profession. Even Scheu, the redoubtable Marxist, who at one time had reproached Morris for lack of backbone, now confessed to being disappointed in the English working-class, and was travelling in Jaeger. Belfort Bax had rejoined the SDF; Joynes was ill and in retirement and Edward Carpenter was becoming less and less political in his interests, being more concerned with achieving recognition for 'the third sex' in *Love's Coming of Age*. In the event, Morris was left with a small band of more or less uneducated firebrands. As he wrote to Glasier in March 1890:

> Socialism is spreading, I suppose on the only lines on which it could spread, and the League is moribund simply because we are outside those lines, as I for one must always be. But I shall be able to do just as much work in the movement when the League is gone as I do now. The main cause of the failure (which was obvious at least two years ago) is that you cannot keep a body together without giving it something to do in the present, and now, since people will willingly listen to Socialist doctrine, our rank and file have nothing to do.

Socialism was, in fact, spreading through such bodies as the Independent Labour Party and the newly created London County Council, which Morris had already stigmatized as 'the wearisome shilly-shally of parliamentary politics' and 'gas and water Socialism'. In fact, when John Burns was elected Liberal-Labour member of the LCC in 1889, Morris wrote to Glasier: 'You see John Burns has got some of his desire – rather him than me in the position – ugh!' – though he admitted that the LCC was 'an amazing improvement on the old red-tape bodies'.

The Socialist League had, Shaw admits, its share in the making of socialists, which was, as Morris held, the real business of the movement,

> but its attempt to extract from its proletarian members a Socialist Constitution was a grotesque failure. He bore with them for years, giving them every means of excogitating some plan that would hold water. Unfortunately they had no experience of the government of anything more complicated than a coster's barrow; and they were romantic anarchists to a man . . . strong on the negative side, but regarding the State as an enemy, very much as a child regards a policeman. Morris, like all original artists and thinkers, had a good deal of this feeling too.

A very amateurish plan was finally worked out, Shaw tells us, called Anti-State Communism.

319

Its author, after spending a good deal of Morris's money, suddenly became aware that the logic of their plan involved the repudiation of Morris's directorship (and money) which was keeping the whole affair together. So Morris, who had been holding the League up by the scruff of its neck, opened his hand, whereupon it dropped like a stone into the sea, leaving only a little wreckage to come to the surface occasionally, a demand for bail at the police court or a small loan.[18]

In contrast, the Fabian Society, with Shaw, the Webbs, Sydney Olivier and Graham Wallas, consisted of trained minds, those thoroughly familiar with the machinery of local government. It was Sidney and Beatrice Webb who, in fact, did the fundamental brain-work which made socialism in England possible at all.

But there still remained the romantic example of William Morris and his Sunday evenings at Kelmscott House. Here the little coach house, once the scene of passionate debates between the Fabians and the Anti-State Communists, now became a meeting place for the progressive intellectuals of the time – austerely and simply furnished, with its rush-bottomed chairs and wooden forms, its white-washed walls covered with rush matting and hung with engraved portraits of Sir Thomas More and other 'socialist' pioneers, and its speaker's platform at one end over which hung Crane's banner.

The Congress of Socialists held in Paris in 1888, to which Morris had gone as a delegate, had not, Mackail says, inspired him with very much confidence in either the future of the cause or the wisdom of its leaders. For the proceedings were marked by the usual bitter recriminations characteristic of those who are supposed to be working for the brotherhood of man. The dock strike of the following year appeared to him as a more hopeful sign of labour's ability to organize itself, but Morris did not delude himself that it was the beginning of the revolution. He got far more excited about the monuments in Westminster Abbey, as witness his letters to the *Daily News* of 30 January and 17 April 1889, and the threatened rebuilding of the west front of Peterborough Cathedral (*Pall Mall Gazette*, 10 September 1889).

By this time *The Commonweal* had practically ceased to sell at all and in May, Morris appeared on the stage for the second time in the one-act play, *The Duchess of Bayswater & Co.*, performed by the members of the League, in support of the fast-sinking funds of the journal, in a hall in the Tottenham Court Road. This time Shaw also took part. Meanwhile articles in the journal itself were becoming more and more violent, openly urging insurrection and the use of dynamite, and in July 1890 Morris wrote to its proprietor, D.J. Nicoll:

> I must say that I think you are going too far: at any rate further than I can follow you. You really must put the curb upon Samuel's blatant folly, or you will *force* me to withdraw all support. I never bargained for this sort of thing when I gave up the editorship. . . . Please understand that this is meant to be quite private, and do your best not to drive me off. For I do assure you that it would be the greatest grief to me if I had to dissociate myself from men who have been my friends so long and whom I believe to be at bottom thoroughly good fellows.

But, as Shaw remarks, 'The Socialist League contained many obscure tragic comedians, who were at first taken by Morris with perfect seriousness and whose subsequent development opened his mind as it had never been opened before.'[19]

May Morris gives an account of the last annual conference of the Socialist League this summer, which lasted from 10 a.m. to 10 p.m. in the Socialist Hall in the Farringdon Road.

> And there we were 'stewing in our own juice' that hot summer day in the bare long room above the clatter of the street. . . . The discussion of rules and amendments, the hair-splitting, the long reports, the harangues, all the proceedings were as wearisome as those of other societies that are composed of many and varied elements that won't mix. . . . The windows had to be open to let in the air, and the speakers must now and then raise their voices above the thundering of the great wagons over the granite setts in the street below. It is four o'clock; the air is heavy with tobacco smoke, with dust and London dullness; the person who has the floor is driving us almost to tears of boredom by a long discourse on ill-digested political economy, under cover of speaking to a resolution. On the platform the Chairman fidgets with his agenda-paper and the Treasurer with raised eyebrows draws flower-patterns all over the margins of his sheet of notes. Suddenly he flings himself back in his chair which creaks under him, and exclaims in a voice which rolls all down the long dull room:

'Mr Chairman, *can't* we get on with the business? I want my TEA!'

Everyone laughs, and good humour settles down on us for a while. Earlier in the proceedings the Treasurer has been inter-locuted on the subject of his Financial Report, which a captious questioner found insufficient or unsatisfactory in some way. 'Well, Mr Chairman,' he said drily, with his hand busy with the usual marginal decoration on the said Report, 'I can't see that it matters a damn; for I receive £10 in one hand, and with the other I pay out £50.'

After the conference, Morris and his branch returned to Hammer-smith on the District Railway and walked down to Upper Mall and the river.

We stand a moment in the bastion under the elms, looking out onto the stretch of black water all a-dance in the night breeze. The moon is up and the lights beyond the opposite bank strike long jagged spears across the dark. The city that never sleeps is murmuring, but Farringdon Road has vanished and the serenity of the summer night is like an echo of *News from Nowhere*. . . . 'The wind's in the West,' says my Father, taking a deep breath: 'I can almost smell the country. . . .'[20]

Bruce Glasier, who had come down from Glasgow for the con-ference, was also one of the party to return to Hammersmith. Morris had invited him to stay the night and, before going to bed, went to his room to read *Huckleberry Finn*. 'It will get the nasty taste of to-day's squabbling out of our minds', he said. He sat down by the candle on the dressing-table, opened the book and then suddenly asked Glasier what he thought of Burne-Jones's pictures at the New Gallery. Thinking of the conventionalized waves of *The Sea Nymph*, Glasier unluckily replied that it seemed to him as if the artist were trying to imitate some very early style rather than nature itself.

Hardly had I completed my sentence, than Morris was on his feet, storming words at me, that shook the room. His eyes flamed as with actual fire, his shaggy mane rose like a burning crest, his whiskers and moustache bristled out like pine-needles. 'Art for-sooth!', he cried, 'where the hell is it? where the hell are the people who know or care a damn about it? This infernal civiliza-tion has no capacity to understand either nature or art. . . . Look at your West End art – the damnable architecture, the damnable furniture, and the detestable dress of men and women. . . .' In this strain he continued for I don't know how long, flashing his wrath in my face, and moving round the room like a caged lion. Eventually there was a tap at the bedroom door, and it was opened slightly from the outside, and a voice expostulated: 'Really, the whole house is awakened. What is the matter? Do speak more quietly and let us go to sleep.'

This was Janey. At once Morris 'quietened down as suddenly as he had flared up . . . and making a turn round the room, he offered me his hand in the most friendly manner, remarking simply: "I *have* been going it a bit loudly – don't you think? I hope I have not upset you – I didn't mean to do that – and that you will have a sound sleep. Good-night and good luck."

'Next morning', Glasier continues, 'he came to wake me at seven o'clock, and was as cheery and charming as a man could be. Later, Jane remarked: "I knew when I heard him boasting last night of his good behaviour at the Conference that somebody would have to pay for it." Morris looked a bit shamefaced, but affected not to acknowledge his delinquency, and appealed to me that we were merely having "a little chat over art matters". His daughter Jenny said: "Oh you wicked, good father", and put her arms round his neck.'

Evidently Morris felt that some reparation was due to young Glasier for his outburst and, cancelling his other engagements, he devoted the rest of the day to entertaining him. 'He took me for a row on the river,' says Glasier,

> and on our return after lunch he sat with me in the garden – a long orchard glade with lawn, fruit trees and flowers behind the house – telling me of the change that had taken place in fruit and vegetable cultivation from the olden days, and giving me many curious instances of the feasting habits in the monasteries. After-wards, he sat smoking with me in the library, showing many of his rare book treasures, drawing my attention to the pages of illumination and typography, and reading to me one of the chapters in manuscript of his forthcoming first volume of prose romances, 'The House of the Wolfings'.

Morris was as sensible to the charm of young men as he was gruff and awkward with women. And when Glasier finally left, Morris stuffed his pockets with cigars, nuts and fruit, and wanted to give him a flask of whisky or brandy, 'in case of accidents'. He even walked to Hammersmith Broadway with him and saw him off at the Underground station, loading him with magazines from the bookstalls.[21] The whole incident, with its little domestic scenes, is typical of both Morris's irascibility and his generosity, of the suddenness of his rages and their equally sudden disappearance.

In November 1890, Morris and the Hammersmith branch with-drew from the League to form the Hammersmith Socialist Society. Here Morris gathered his friends round him in one last effort to make socialists. The little Sunday morning meetings at the foot of Hammersmith Bridge or at the corner of Weltje Road continued under another name, with Sunday afternoon trips to Victoria Park and Sunday evening lectures in the coach house. Walter Crane designed a new banner for the Society and it was worked by May Morris. 'Speaking and lecturing as much as sickened human nature can bear', Morris wrote to Glasier in December, 'are the only things as far as I can see.'

In August he had written a withering letter to *The Times*, in his capacity as secretary of the Society for the Protection of Ancient Buildings, about the proposed restorations in the parish church at Stratford-on-Avon, whose vicar had appealed for money to erect a copy of the original reredos in place of the existing one. Morris wrote:

I am glad the vicar talks about a 'copy' of the reredos, and not a 'restoration' of it: but may I ask why a copy of it should be 'erected in the old place'? Will not every fresh piece of modern work make 'the old place' (the church, I mean) look less old and more like a nineteenth-century mediaeval furniture-dealer's ware-house? There has been a great deal too much modernization of this fine church of Stratford-on-Avon already, and it is more than time that it should come to an end. Once for all I protest against the trick which clergymen and restoration committees have of using an illustrious name as a bait wherewith to catch sub-scriptions. Shakespeare's memory is best honoured by reading his works intelligently; and it is no honour to him to spend money in loading the handsome mediaeval church which contains his monument with trash which can claim none of the respect due to either an ancient or a modern work of art.

Morris in the 1880s, about the time
when he joined the Democratic
Federation. The portrait is by
W. B. Richmond (43).

A stone plaque carved by George
Jack, an artist employed by Morris
& Co., for the Memorial Hall at
Kelmscott, shows Morris in a
rural setting enjoying his
'Haven of rest' (44).

45

The family moved to Kelmscott
Manor, Oxfordshire, in 1871,
sharing the house with Rossetti. It
is a small Elizabethan manor-house
built in Cotswold stone and
enlarged in the seventeenth century
(46). *Above:* the staircase (45).
Below: the Tapestry Room (47),
the attic (48) and the Elizabethan
four-poster bed (49) with hangings
woven by May Morris and a sister
of W. B. Yeats.

46

47

48

49

50

An increasing demand for woven and printed textiles led Morris to move his factory
to Merton Abbey in Surrey (50). He himself was an enthusiastic weaver and gave
many lecture demonstrations. A sketch by Burne-Jones shows him in action (51).

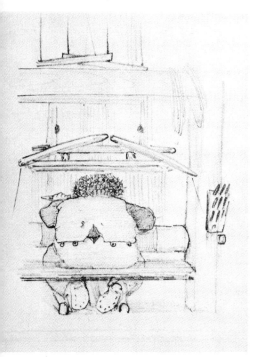

51   52

53   54

Two woven fabrics: 'Crown Imperial' (53) and 'Rose and Lily' (54). *Below:* two chintzes, 'Tulip' (52) and the fine 'African Marigold' of 1876 (55). Nearly all designs were produced in a variety of colours with Morris supervising the dyes.

55

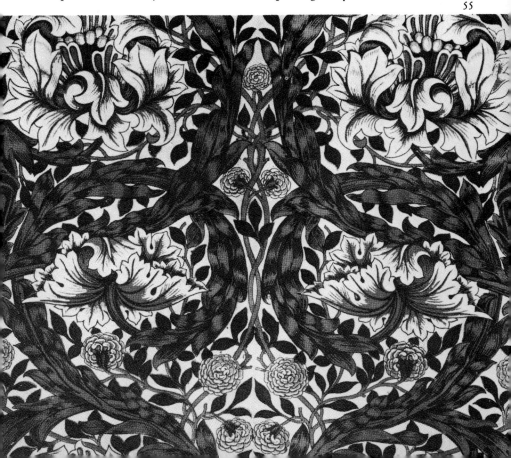

Kelmscott House, Hammersmith: a plain-fronted Georgian house overlooking the Thames, which Morris bought in 1878 (57). The drawing-room (56) contained the 'Bird' hanging, the 'Lily' Wilton carpet, the 'Chaucer' wardrobe and Philip Webb's settle. These are now in the Victoria and Albert Museum (see colour plate VII). (58) At the other end of the drawing-room a massive table by Webb was covered by an oriental carpet. (59) In the dining-room the wallpaper is 'Pimpernel', and the dresser contains an impressive display of china.

56

58

57

59

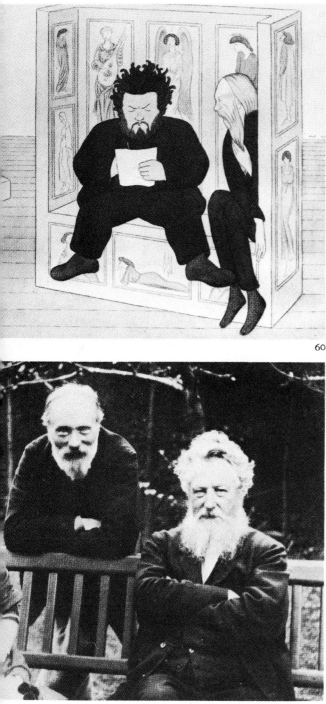

'Topsy and Ned settled on the settle in Red Lion Square.' A characteristic comment by Max Beerbohm (60). A photograph (61) shows them together in the garden of The Grange, Fulham, home of Burne-Jones and his family, where Morris was a frequent visitor.

60

Two interiors of The Grange: In the studio (62) several paintings can be seen against the walls, including a panel from the 'Briar Rose' series for Buscot Park (*left centre, behind the easel*). In the drawing-room (63), the wall is papered with Morris's 'Jasmine' pattern and the settee in the foreground is upholstered in his 'Honeysuckle' chintz. Over the fireplace hangs W.B.Richmond's portrait of Burne-Jones' daughter Margaret.

61

62, 63

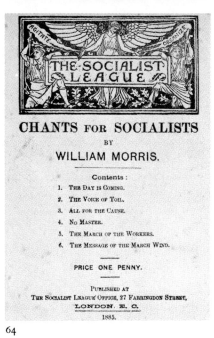

64

'Chants for Socialists' (64) were intended to be sung by choirs at Socialist meetings. The heading for this pamphlet was designed by Walter Crane (67) who also drew *Labour's May Day* (65) for the 1889 issue of *Justice*. Bernard Shaw (66) was an enthusiastic associate of Morris in the early days of the Socialist movement.

66, 67

LABOUR'S · MAY · DAY
DEDICATED · TO · THE · WORKERS · OF · THE · WORLD

65

68

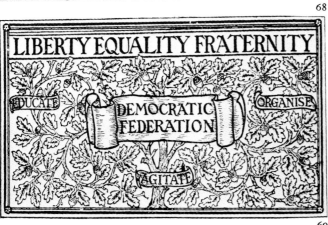

69

The Attitude of the Police, an ironic comment on Morris's apparently preferential treatment by the magistrate at the time of the Dod Street free speech campaign. His fellow demonstrators were imprisoned and heavily fined. The 'Paradox' is a pun on 'The Earthly Paradise' (68). Morris designed the membership card (69) for the Democratic Federation.

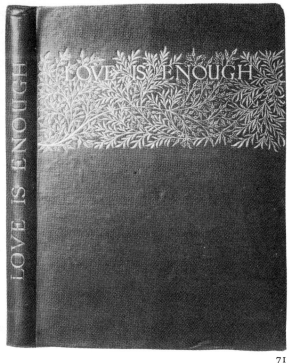

Morris became a keen collector of illuminated manuscripts and early printed books, some of which appear in a contemporary photograph (70) of his library at Kelmscott House, Hammersmith. (The walls are papered with 'Trellis', his first wallpaper design.) *Love is Enough*, an 'Interlude in the late Medieval manner', was published in 1872 with an elegant binding (71) which marks the beginning of Morris's interest in book production. This interest later blossomed into the famous Kelmscott Press. *The Story of the Glittering Plain* was printed in 1894 using Morris's own 'Troy' type. It is his only prose romance directly influenced by his Icelandic travels. The opening shown here (much reduced) contains borders by Morris and a woodcut by Walter Crane (72). Two printers are seen at work on the Kelmscott Chaucer in the photograph on the right (73).

71

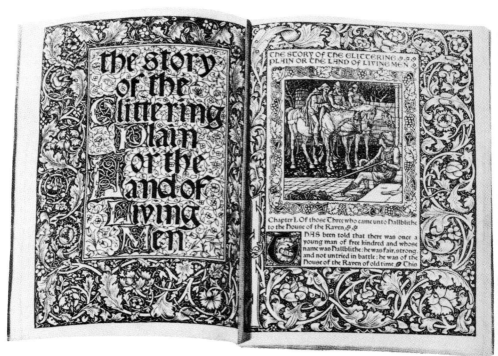

72, 73

Three generations of the Morris family. Morris's mother (74) and (75) the Morris and Burne-Jones families in the garden of The Grange. Morris (right) stands next to Burne-Jones. Seated in front of him are Jane and their elder daughter May. Mrs Burne-Jones (left) sits next to Jenny Morris who has Margaret Burne-Jones on her knee. Philip Burne-Jones (profile) stands behind his mother. Behind them is Burne-Jones' father. Mrs Burne-Jones was painted by F. J. Poynter in 1870 (78).

74, 75

77

The romantic drawing of Jenny Morris (76) is by Rossetti – seen in a photograph (77) taken by Lewis Carroll in 1863.

76

78, 79

80

An outing of members of the Kelmscott Press in September 1895. May Morris is sitting next to her father. Behind her is her husband Halliday Sparling. Emery Walker is standing behind Morris's right shoulder. Mrs Coronio (née Ionides) was a close friend of Morris. She too was drawn by Rossetti (79).

81

William Morris died at Kelmscott Manor in October 1896. He was carried to his grave in a decorated farm wagon (81) and buried in Kelmscott churchyard (82). By a strange coincidence the near-by church of Great Coxwell contains two Tudor brasses of 'Willm Morys', lord of the manor of Coxwell, and his wife 'Johane'.

82

PART THREE

UTOPIA

1890–1896

CHAPTER FOURTEEN

1890–1893

News from Nowhere: The Kelmscott Press

I T WAS DURING 1890, from 11 January to 4 October, after he had been deposed from the editorship by the votes of his own comrades, that Morris contributed his curiously naïve and innocent Utopia, *News from Nowhere*, to the pages of *The Commonweal*. It appeared first in book form in America (pirated from *The Commonweal*) and in the following year in England with grey paper covers at one shilling. Mackail writes of its 'refined rusticity'. If its male characters, with their jolly good-fellowship and arch humour, suggest youth club leaders, the young women, in their 'dainty raiment', recall the damsels of Walter Crane, that gentle Arts and Crafts socialist in his Liberty silk shirt and velvet knee-breeches.

News from Nowhere is peculiarly youthful in feeling for a man of fifty-seven, at times almost embarrassingly so with its 'light chaff', though Morris is throughout only too conscious of himself as an 'oldster' among all these happy young folk. This, however, does not prevent him from being very susceptible to the charm and grace of all the young women, who treat him with the kindness and sympathy evidently denied to him by his own wife. In fact, one is struck in all Morris's late prose romances by the prevalence of these compliant, white-armed maidens, who make up to him in imagina-tion for what, one suspects, he had been too shy to claim in his own life. *The Story of the Glittering Plain*, written immediately after *News from Nowhere* and the first book to be published at the Kelmscott Press in 1891, is a story of the search for the land of eternal youth, though, characteristically, Hallblithe, like Pharamond before him in *Love is Enough*, is only bent upon his quest for a lost maiden whose image he is shown in a painted book – 'standing in a fair garden of the spring with the lilies all about her feet, and behind her the walls of a house, grey, ancient, and lovely.'[1]

It would seem that Morris, whether because of unhappiness in marriage or because of some basic inhibition, was incapable of accepting the actual reality of any woman and so was driven con-tinually to idealistic compensations. In his letter to Charles Faulkner of 16 October 1886, giving his views on sex and marriage in general, he refers to 'the mere animal arrangement' and 'the grotesquery of the act', from which one might infer that in his own marriage the fault was not all on Janey's side, though he says that man has always 'adorned the act variously as he has done the other grotesque act of eating and drinking'.[2] His general view of modern marriage as 'legal prostitution' is very similar to that expressed by Shaw in *Mrs Warren's Profession* and other early plays, though in writing of the physical side of marriage, Morris goes on to refer to what he calls 'the decent animalism plus the human kindliness'.

Morris wrote *News from Nowhere* in a mood of reaction after reading Edward Bellamy's *Looking Backward*, an American socialist Utopia glorifying machinery and the great cities of the future. In contrast, we are given a picture of a largely pastoral community and a general revival of handicrafts, the disappearance of all the machinery of government, the abolition of laws and money, and the spread of mutual tolerance and universal good-humour. It would be an insult to Morris's intelligence to suppose that he really believed in the possibility of such a society, where the only work that appears to be going on is a little haymaking at Kelmscott. And yet one frequently finds *News from Nowhere* seriously discussed as though it were a blue-print for a communist future. It should be obvious enough that here Morris was merely abolishing everything he disliked in the nineteenth century and replacing it by everything he nostalgically longed for. In reality it is an Arts and Crafts Utopia with very little relation to anything that we know as communism, though in its account of 'How the Change Came' Morris makes use of Marxist analysis.

News from Nowhere provides an interesting parallel to Edward Carpenter's *Civilization: Its Cause and Cure*, for the general outlook of Morris and Carpenter was in many ways similar. Significantly, the shortest chapter is that 'Concerning Politics', where Old Hammond says: 'We are very well off as to politics – because we have none.' After a visit to Carpenter in December 1884, Morris had written:

It seems to me that the real way to enjoy life is to accept all its necessary ordinary details and turn them into pleasures by taking an interest in them: whereas modern civilization huddles them out of the way, and has them done in a venal and slovenly manner till they become real drudgery which people can't help trying to avoid. Whiles I think as in a vision, of a decent community as a refuge from our squabbles and corrupt society. . . .

It is this vision that he embodied in *News from Nowhere, or, An Epoch of Rest, being Some Chapters from a Utopian Romance.*

Basically, Morris viewed politics as a philosophical pursuit of happiness, and it is as visions of happiness and of a regenerated humanity that his later prose romances should be viewed. Certainly it is impossible to accept the kind of society lightly sketched in *News from Nowhere* as a picture of the final stage of communism in which the state, we are told, will wither away. 'We are for the withering away of the state', said Stalin at the Sixteenth Party Congress, adding with a certain grim humour, perhaps: 'To keep on developing state power in order to prepare for the withering away of state power – that is the Marxist formula.' So far, such has been the 'formula' followed by communist countries in our own time. We have yet to see any body of men, corrupted by almost unlimited power over their victims, voluntarily relinquishing that power and so, in effect, signing their own death warrants.

Morris's interest in printing dates from the first Arts and Crafts exhibition of 1888 and, more particularly, from Emery Walker's lecture on this subject delivered on 15 November of that year. By means of lantern slides, Walker made a detailed examination of incunabula, 'of manuscripts that had, or might have been, taken as models by the early printers, as well as later examples of what ought or ought not to have been done, and discussed all the factors that tell for beauty or the reverse in the printed book'.[3] It was after this lecture, Sparling adds, that Morris resolved upon designing and possessing a fount of his own. The project appeared to him simply 'as an endeavour . . . to re-attain a long-lost standard of craftsmanship of book printing'.

In December 1888, Morris brought out his prose romance, *The House of the Wolfings*, in a type originally chosen for the abortive folio edition of *The Earthly Paradise*, Whittingham's fount from an early Basel model. The same month he wrote of it to F. S. Ellis:

I am very glad that you like the new book. I quite agree with you about the type; they have managed to knock the guts out of it somehow. Also I am beginning to learn something about the art of type setting; and now I see what a lot of difference there is between the work of the conceited numskulls of today and that of the fifteenth and sixteenth century printers merely in the arrangement of the words, I mean the spacing out. . . .

From Morris's point of view, printing suffered from the disadvantage of having come into being on the eve of the Renaissance. The types that appealed to him most, therefore, were the Gothic founts of the early German printers, which were in effect an extension of manu-script. But a year was to elapse before he actually undertook the task of type designing, a year of inquiry and research into paper-making, binding and all the arts of the book. At the same time, he began collecting fifteenth-century books as models of type and ornament. The general run of books produced in the late nineteenth century appeared to him in their dreariness a counterpart of the dismal meanness of the late Victorian suburb, the deserts of Wands-worth, Balham and Putney. It was against such a drab poverty of design, with its thin, pinched type-faces, its characterless title-pages, its miserable papers and binding-cloths (usually of dirt colour) that Morris asserted his heavy black type, his thick paper, his exuberant decoration of title-pages, his bindings of plain light blue boards and canvas spines.

It is impossible to judge the Kelmscott Press books without actually handling them, turning their leaves and contrasting the highly decorated title-pages with the plain and simple lay-out of the pages which follow. It is only then that one can come to a full sense of their greatness and feel the extent of Morris's achievement. It may be argued that Morris only produced books for wealthy collectors and that his example only led to the proliferation of the small private press. But at least one direct outcome was J. M. Dent's Everyman's Library, started in 1905, whose original decorated title-pages and endpapers derive directly from Morris's example. Another logical outcome of his example were the admirably designed title-pages of the first editions of Bernard Shaw's plays. For it is a mistake to think of all the Kelmscott books as over-decorated. Most of them are relatively plain, with ornamental initials and occasional borders. Morris used woodcuts for his illustrations because the fifteenth- and sixteenth-century printers did so, but also as a protest against the spidery quality of contemporary illustrations printed on smooth paper by the new line-block process.

When designing the lay-out of his type, Morris treated the double page as a unit, regarding the verso and recto as two columns of type and making the inner margin of each page half the width of the outer; the bottom margin was deeper than the top, so that the hand which held the book should not cover the type. If the Kelmscott books have a fault, it is that the absence of a gutter makes them difficult to open fully without risking damage to the spine, particularly in those copies bound in vellum, so that they are liable to the charge of being decorative rather than functional. The same difficulty is not, of course, encountered in the case of canvas spines.

Of the two founts designed for the Kelmscott Press, the first to be cut, by Edward Prince of Islington, was a Roman type modelled upon that of Nicolas Jenson, the fifteenth-century Venetian printer. This came to be known as Golden type, since it was used for *The Golden Legend*, printed in 1892. 'By instinct rather than by conscious thinking it over', says Morris, 'I began by getting myself a fount of Roman type.' Had he done otherwise and produced only a Gothic type, his influence as a printer would have been far less. Morris's version of Jenson was, as Will Ransom remarks in his *Private Presses and their Books*, 'not only a magnificent gesture of dissent from the weak and awkward faces of the period: it was also a pattern for future development'.

Since Caxton's *Recuyell of the Histories of Troy* was the first book to be printed in England, Morris would have liked it to have been the first to be done at his own press, and for it he designed a Gothic type, modelled upon that used by the early German printers. This came to be known as Troy type; Chaucer type was a smaller variant and was used for the Kelmscott edition of *The Works of Geoffrey Chaucer*. In the event, as has already been noticed, *The Story of the Glittering Plain* was the first book to be completed at the Kelmscott Press in May 1891, followed by *Poems by the Way* in October. Issued by Reeves & Turner, they were both printed in Golden type, the latter in black and red. Another edition of *The Glittering Plain* was done in 1894 in a mixture of Troy and Chaucer type in black and red, lavishly decorated with borders and initial letters by Morris and twenty-three woodcuts by Crane.

Morris's method of type-designing was to study photographic

enlargements of the founts he most admired, then to modify them. Thus Golden type is Jenson's Roman fount slightly gothicized. The paper for the Kelmscott books was made from linen rag by Batchelor & Son of Little Chart, near Ashford, after an Italian pattern of the fifteenth century supplied by Morris. So closely were medieval models followed that the wire moulds were woven by hand so as to give a slight irregularity in the texture, as in the papers used by the earliest printers. Accompanied by Walker, Morris went to Little Chart to supervise its manufacture. He took off his coat and tried to make a sheet of paper himself, and at the second attempt succeeded in doing very creditably what it is supposed to take several months to master.

On 12 January 1891, a cottage was taken at 16 Upper Mall, a few doors from Kelmscott House, and the Kelmscott Press came into being, William Bowden, a retired master printer, who had printed *News from Nowhere* for Reeves & Turner, having already been engaged as compositor and pressman. A room upstairs was fitted with racks, cases, imposing stone and so on; in another stood the Albion hand-press, bought second-hand. 'Except for the change from wood to iron,' remarks Halliday Sparling in *The Kelmscott Press and William Morris*, 'and substitution of levers for the screw, this press was essentially similar to Caxton's; indeed, at the end of an hour or so, Caxton would have been comfortably at home with the Press as a whole.'

The first sheet of *The Glittering Plain* was printed off on 2 March and the last on 4 April; the twenty decorated initials were cut by George Campfield. The first edition was issued on 8 May, a small quarto with a single border engraved by Morris. Two hundred copies on paper and six on vellum were printed. Originally only twenty copies were to have been printed for distribution among Morris's friends, for at this time he still regarded his printing as a private and personal experiment. Rumours about the Press, however, led, much to Morris's annoyance, to an announcement in the *Athenaeum* that 'Mr William Morris is getting his press into working order'. This gave rise to many inquiries and requests for copies to be made available for sale. So, with many misgivings, Morris had an additional 180 copies printed for sale through Reeves & Turner. He feared, Sparling tells us, 'lest the pressman succumb to the monotony of his task, and, printing the same sheet so many times over, should fail to exercise the same scrupulous and minute care throughout.' His fears proved groundless and the 180 copies were sold out within a few days of publication, the paper copies at two guineas and the vellum at fifteen guineas – these prices covering little more than the production cost. The Kelmscott Press was never looked upon by Morris as a commercial enterprise.

Before the end of May 1891, the Press moved to larger premises next door, to Sussex Cottage, 14 Upper Mall, a part of a large old family mansion, Sussex House, occupied by the photo-engraving works of Walker & Boutall. William Bowden senior now retired and his son, W. H. Bowden, became overseer and several new compositors were engaged, among them Thomas Binning, late of *The Commonweal*. Today Sussex House is in a derelict condition; there is nothing to show that it ever housed the Kelmscott Press, and one fears that it is only too likely to fall into the hands of the developers.

Early in February Morris had delivered one of his broadsides to *The Times* about the proposed addition to Westminster Abbey of a memorial chapel, in the course of which he said:

We in the metropolis have treated our most beautiful building but ill for centuries. We have allowed its lovely interior to be cluttered up with a huge mass of the ugliest and vilest undertakers' masonry that can anywhere be seen. We have patched and cobbled its exterior with restorations, and restorations of restorations, till it has been half destroyed as a work of art; we keep the interior, again, in a state of sordid dirt, which is disgraceful both to the Government and the Chapter. But there is still some of it left, and what is left is of the utmost importance, and we profess to think it so. Would it not be well if we were to show some of our boasted 'practical common sense' by not throwing the remains of this treasure away, at the dictate of mere inconsiderate whim?

Towards the end of the month, however, Morris was laid low with a severe attack of gout, complicated by kidney disease, and he was told, says Mackail, 'that henceforth he must consider himself an invalid to the extent of husbanding his strength and living under a very careful regimen'.[4] Writing to Ellis, he says: 'My hand seems lead and my wrist string. . . . Yes, 'tis a fine thing to have some interesting work to do, and more than ever when one is in trouble – I found that out the other day.' Possibly Morris's collapse was connected with his disappointment at the failure of the League, but even more, one may guess, with the sudden worsening of Jenny's health. Anxiety about Jenny, May Morris wrote to Glasier in the middle of March, 'had terribly upset my father's nerves'. He even talked about dying, Sparling told Glasier.

At Folkestone, where he and Jenny had gone to recuperate, Morris continued to work, designing the ornamental border for the first page of *The Golden Legend* and several floriated initials, or 'bloomers'. Visiting the Press on his return to London, he wrote to Georgie on 20 May:

> Pleased as I am with my printing, when I saw my two men at work on the press yesterday with their sticky printer's ink, I couldn't help lamenting the simplicity of the scribe and his desk, and his black and blue and red ink. I almost felt ashamed of my press after all. I am writing a short narrative poem to top up my new book with.

This was 'Goldilocks and Goldilocks' for *Poems by the Way*, which included poems written between 1867 and 1874, and those he had illuminated for *A Book of Verse* in 1870, a group of political poems beginning with 'Chants for Socialists', English ballad-type poems and translations from the Icelandic and Danish. Among the best short pieces in the book are those he had written for Merton Abbey tapestries, and for Burne-Jones's 'Briar Rose' panels at Buscot, and the charming lines woven round the hangings of his bed at Kelmscott.

Morris spent most of the summer of 1891 at Folkestone, where, in June, he was designing his Troy type. But at the end of July he writes to Georgie, just before setting off to Northern France with Jenny, to tell her that he is ashamed to say that he is still not as well as he would like to be. He and Jenny visited Abbeville, Amiens, Beauvais, Reims, Soissons and Laon. 'I have given myself up to thinking of nothing but passing the day and keeping my eyes open', he wrote, and in letters to Webb and Walker he gives detailed descriptions of all the cathedrals and churches they visited. From Beauvais he wrote to Webb on 11 August:

> Here I am after 33 years, and not yet as melancholy as I suppose I ought to be. The Cathedral here not having run away, nor indeed having changed at all that I can see may partly account for that. I think I like it better than ever with the little extra know-ledge I have got hold of since then. The town also is very pleasant

and full of old houses, and comes as a blessing after Amiens town, which is dull, bourgeois, and, in a word, gritty, and is much improved for the worse since I saw it last by the addition of some beastly buildings of the 3rd Napoleonic style inconceivable almost outside Zola's books. As for the Church, it must be said that it is not ruined by its restorations. . . . However we spent an hour over the stalls to our great pleasure. Jenny almost refused to leave the Church when we were going away: she was delighted and is well and very happy.

He also wrote to Walker from Beauvais: 'Certainly the Cathedral here is one of the wonders of the world: seen by twilight its size gives one an impression almost of terror: one can scarcely believe it.' He was delighted by the town of Laon, but adds, in a letter to Webb, that unhappily it is poisoned by the very bad restoration of the cathedral. In Soissons Cathedral he saw 'some fine tapestries hung up in the aisles . . . in very good preservation, *c.* 1520 I think. They make splendid ornaments. I intend studying them and the stained glass and the sculpture to-morrow properly.' Most of his time, he adds, is spent 'staring and walking and eating'.

Morris was refreshed by his holiday in France and by the autumn was ready to take up his work again in earnest.

> Though he enjoyed several years more of fair health, his bodily powers became gradually less able to respond to the calls of his unflagging intellectual energy. The amount of work he had already done, in literature, in art, in politics, in handicraft, was enough to fill not one, but many lives. . . . But in these later years his whole personality ripened and softened. The outbursts of temper so familiar to his earlier friends ceased. The impatience born of an intense craving for sympathy and understanding died away.[5]

And Selwyn Image, his colleague on the executive committee of the Arts and Crafts Society and in the Art Workers' Guild, records, as the deepest impression made upon him at this time, Morris's extraordinary patience and conciliatory attitude.

In our estimate of the phenomenal amount of work which Morris got through in his life, it should always be remembered that work was for him a pleasurable exercise of his energies: it actually re-freshed him; and that his idea of recreation, apart from spells of fishing and enjoyment of the country and of architecture, was simply a change of occupation. Most of his writing – his lectures always excepted – was a form of half-wakeful dreaming and, together with his designing, was done, as Yeats observed, 'with an unheard of ease and simplicity'. A great part of his designing was, in fact, a glorified form of doodling, with which he wove his cocoon as a protection against the world. Intellectual effort, therefore, scarcely entered into it: it was almost as natural to him as breathing. But while this process could produce marvellous designs, in poetry and prose it often led to a wearisome diffuseness. Except in his shorter pieces, the one thing that Morris's poetry lacks is concentration.

In October 1891 Morris opened an exhibition of Pre-Raphaelite painting in the Birmingham municipal art gallery, commending their example to all artists for 'patience, diligence and courage'. For him it was their decorative and illustrative qualities which princip-ally distinguished the Pre-Raphaelites: he sees them as 'nothing more or less than a branch of the great Gothic Art which once pervaded all Europe'. The characteristics of that art were, he says, 'Love of Nature as the only instrument for telling a tale of some sort or another. . . . Love of nature is the first element in the Gothic Art; next is the epical quality, and joined to those two things is what people very often think perhaps is the only quality it has got, and that is its ornamental quality.' The Pre-Raphaelites, however, added

> the *romantic* quality, as I must call it for lack of a better word; and this quality is eminently characteristic of both Rossetti and Burne-Jones, but especially of the latter. . . . And I must say, that you will find throughout the whole of the history of the Arts, that when artists are thinking in the main of consciously telling a story their works are really much more beautiful, much more fitted for the ornamenting of public buildings than when they are only thinking of producing works of *mere* ornament.[6]

But, principally, he commended the Pre-Raphaelites for their naturalism and for their revolt against academic tradition.

Morris's main interests were now S P A B, his own prose romances, the Kelmscott Press, and, of course, Kelmscott itself. He was too busy with the Press to do much pattern designing and during the last six years of his life produced only ten wallpapers and two chintzes, among them the 'Daffodil' of 1891. They show, as Peter Floud observes, a return to

336

a somewhat more flowing, less rigid, structure, with particular emphasis on designs with an upward movement swaying from side to side. . . . A marked characteristic of this last batch of designs is the blending in the same pattern of conventional sym‑ bols and naturalistically drawn flowers, or the superimposition of decorative details on naturalistically drawn petals or leaves. Morris appears to be striving to combine a return to his earlier naturalism with the formalism derived from his study of historic textiles.[7]

The general management of the firm was now in the hands of the Smith brothers, who had been made partners in 1890, and of J.H. Dearle, manager of the Merton Abbey works. After 1885 most of the designs for wallpapers and chintzes were contributed by Dearle and May Morris, but so closely had these two artists assimilated Morris's style that many of their designs have since been attributed to him. In any case, there is, it must be admitted, a perceptible falling off of originality in Morris's later wallpapers – such, for instance, as the 'Hammersmith' of 1890, the 'Lechlade' of 1893 and the 'Spring Thicket' of 1894, though the 'Compton' of 1896, that marvellous design of great poppies, flaring, full‑blown tulips, honeysuckle, speedwell and pimpernels, which once more recaptures all the pro‑ fusion of nature, is among his greatest triumphs. Dearle, however, went from strength to strength and ranks as one of the finest pattern designers of the late nineteenth century. Indeed, both his designs and May's are still being reprinted, in addition to Morris's, from the original pear‑wood blocks by Messrs Sanderson.

To February 1892 belongs Morris's preface to the Kelmscott Press reprint of Ruskin's chapter 'On the Nature of Gothic and the Role of the Workman Therein' from *The Stones of Venice*. 'To some of us when we first read it, now many years ago,' wrote Morris, 'it seemed to point out a new road on which the world should travel. The lesson that Ruskin here teaches us is that art is the expression of man's pleasure in his labour.' In this chapter, Morris implies, Ruskin had laid, once for all, the basis for a true socialism. 'For without art Socialism would remain as sterile as the other forms of social organization: it would not meet the real and perpetual wants of mankind.'

This preface was followed in March by one of the very best of Morris's papers for S P A B, on the proposed 'complete restoration' of Westminster Abbey, with the addition of a memorial chapel. Morris had already protested against any sort of addition to the fabric of the Abbey. He now reviewed once more what the Abbey had suffered at the hands of restorers, from Wren and Wyatt down to Pearson's 'dead⁄alive office work' covered with 'what is called ecclesiastical sculpture – so utterly without life or interest that nobody who passes under the portal of the church on which it is plastered treats it as a work of art any more than he does the clergyman's surplice . . . a joyless, putty⁄like imitation that had better have been a plaster⁄cast. . . . Re⁄write the lost trilogies of Aeschylus, put a beginning and end to the Fight at Finsbury, finish the Squire's Tale for Chaucer, and if you *can succeed* in that, you may then "restore" Westminster Abbey.'

In August this year Morris invited the young Sydney Cockerell, who had been assiduously cultivating him, to spend a week at Kelmscott. 'Except Hever and Ightham I don't think I have ever seen any house so beautiful', Cockerell wrote. 'It looks as if it had risen from the ground with the old fruit trees about it – its grey stones like them, tinted yellow with lichen.' Morris sent his trap to pick him up at Lechlade station and met him at the door of the manor⁄house: 'burly and thick⁄set, but not tall', dressed as usual in a dark blue serge suit, 'a little untidy . . . a linen shirt dyed indigo in his own vats', and no tie.

Cockerell was so shy the first night that, rather than go through Morris's room to get to his own bedroom, he slept on the Tapestry Room sofa. But Morris soon put him at his ease. Together they visited Great Coxwell barn and some of the local churches, and fished. In the evenings, they played whist or 'twenty questions' in company with Jane and May. The visit was repeated in October and before it was over Cockerell found himself invited to catalogue Morris's library at Hammersmith at a salary of two guineas a week. 'I was never so happy in my work before', he records in his diary. The work was often quite arduous, Morris sending him off to the British Museum to verify details. 'It took me three whole weeks to count and tabulate for the first time the 1,809 woodcut illustrations in the *Nuremberg Chronicle* of 1493,' he notes, 'of which as many as 1,164 are repeats.' He also ran errands between Morris and Burne⁄Jones – 'the Bart', as they called him after he had accepted a baronetcy in 1890. 'Almost imperceptibly', Cockerell says, he found himself promoted to be Morris's private secretary, and in 1894 he was

338

officially appointed secretary to the Kelmscott Press.[8] 'He was', says May Morris, 'my father's right hand.' After Morris's death, Cockerell made himself indispensable to the family, becoming almost a son to Jane, and after her death the fierce guardian of her and her husband's memory.

The third book printed at the Kelmscott Press was Wilfrid Scawen Blunt's *Love Lyrics and Songs of Proteus*. 'I was much with him [Morris] in connection with it', Blunt notes. 'Politically he is in much the same position as I am. He has found his Socialism impossible and uncongenial, and has thrown it up wholly for art and poetry, his earlier loves.' Nevertheless, Morris was present at the May Day demonstration that year and on 3 May spoke alongside Aveling, Cunninghame Graham and Shaw, with Engels on the platform. He still spoke regularly at open-air meetings, carrying the banner of the Hammersmith Socialist Society to the foot of Hammersmith Bridge or to Latimer Road arches. Sometimes he carried the platform as well. In October 1892 the *Hammersmith Socialist Record* began publication. The same month he lectured to Charles Rowley's Ancoats Brotherhood, Manchester, on the principles of socialism.

It is true that we find him writing to Bruce Glasier refusing to lecture on art at Glasgow:

At present the absolute *duties* of my life are summed up in the necessity for taking care of my wife and daughter. . . . My *work* of all kinds is really simply an amusement taken when I can out of my duty time. . . . I must say no to the art lecture: it is with the greatest difficulty that I can get to you at all, and I must cut it as short as I possibly can. I understand that I am to lecture at Edinburgh on the Saturday evening: so I shall start from London that morning & go back to London as early as I can on the Monday morning. I am less troubled at not being able to give the art lecture as I am rather sick of putting matters before people which they cannot attend to under the Present State of things – let 'em turn Socialists!

What a set of ninnies the papers are about the Laureateship, treating it with such absurd solemnity! Bet you it is offered to Swinburne! Bet you he takes it. . . .

But Swinburne was considered unsuitable and Morris was sounded privately as to whether, if it were offered to him, he would accept. But he refused, remarking to his family that he could not see himself 'sitting down in crimson plush breeches and white silk stockings to write birthday odes in honour of all the blooming little Guelflings and Battenbergs that happen to come along'.[9]

Morris was at this time building up his magnificent collection of thirteenth-century manuscripts and early printed books. To cele-brate the completion of the printing of *The Golden Legend* in September 1892, he bought a vellum copy of Jenson's *Clementis Constitutiones*. He also possessed copies of the Nuremberg Bible, the Ulm *Renowned and Noble Ladies*, Aesop's *Fables* and a *Speculum Humanae Vitae* (both printed at Augsburg). One evening, when Sydney Cockerell, who had been working in the little room next to Morris's study, went up to the great drawing-room on the first floor at Kelmscott House to say good-night, he saw Morris and Janey playing draughts, with large ivory pieces, red and white. 'Mrs Morris was dressed in a glorious blue gown, and as she sat on the sofa, she looked like an animated Rossetti picture or a page from some old MS of a king and queen' – Sire Degrevaunt and his Bride, in fact, as pictured by Burne-Jones thirty years ago on the wall at Red House.

In October Caxton's *Historyes of Troye* was issued by the Press and published by Bernard Quaritch in two volumes, three hundred paper copies at 9 guineas each, with five on vellum at £80 a piece. Morris designed a large quantity of initials and ornaments for it. But by November, Jane was ailing again and Morris took her over to Bordighera and then hurried back anxiously to Jenny. Christmas 1892 was spent at Kelmscott. Writing to J. L. Joynes on 27 December, Morris said: 'Shaw is happy because (as he sleeps with his window wide open) his water-jug is frozen deeper than any one else's. This is the first time I have been here in mid-winter and I think I rather enjoy the frost as a change; though not so much as I should have done 40 years ago.' According to Sparling, Shaw spent his time at Kelmscott 'amusing himself by pasting into a scrapbook all the Press notices of his play [*Widowers' Houses*]. . . . Morris has just gone off to try for a pike, having vainly endeavoured to get either Shaw or myself to share his fishing enthusiasm. . . . He is extremely well and hearty.'[10]

Books now began to flow from the Kelmscott Press. The year 1893 began with a reprint of Caxton's *Reynard the Foxe* of 1482 in Troy type. It was followed in February by two books in Golden type, Shakespeare's poems and *News from Nowhere*. Then followed

Caxton's *Order of Chivalry*, together with Morris's verse translation of 'L'Ordene de Chevalerie', a thirteenth-century French poem which may have been the original of Caxton's prose treatise. For this volume the Chaucer type was used. Then came Cavendish's *Life of Wolsey* and, in April 1893, a reprint of Caxton's *Godefrey of Boloyne*, in Troy type, with an elaborately decorated title-page by Morris and chapter headings and glossary in Chaucer type. This was the first book both printed and sold at the Kelmscott Press. So far the medieval flavour of the Press was pretty consistent. It was reinforced by Morris's translation of a series of short thirteenth-century French romances, though he reprinted most of his own poems at the Press, as well as two volumes of Rossetti's, Swinburne's *Atalanta in Calydon*, and Tennyson's *Maud* among the moderns. The Press was not run as a business, but it brought in a profit which represented a fairly adequate salary for Morris. Cockerell's appoint-ment as secretary in 1894, however, relieved Morris of most of the administrative work. 'For the first time in his life', comments Mackail, 'his papers were kept in order.'

Morris began designing the ornament for the Chaucer in February 1893. 'Finished ornamental design for 1st page of Chaucer & big border, picture do and big Whan [the first word of the Prologue to *The Canterbury Tales*] going on with border', reads an entry in his diary for 16 February. The entry for the 25th reads: 'Finished the first lot of Beo [his *Beowulf* translation] about 100 lines. Wrote Wyatt.' Between February and April he paid Burne-Jones £200 for the Chaucer plates, making £300 up to date. By the summer he was regularly reading his *Beowulf* translation to Burne-Jones on Sunday mornings. A. J. Wyatt of Christ's College, Cambridge, supplied him with a prose translation which he proceeded to 'rhyme up' at his usual speed. Mackail admits the *Beowulf* to be one of Morris's 'few failures . . . in his desire to reproduce the early English manner he allowed himself a harshness of construction and a strangeness of vocabulary that in many passages go near to making his version unintelligible'.[11] After all, Anglo-Saxon was a closed book to him. Writing to Wyatt in February 1893, Morris said: 'if we read over the original I shall soon I think begin to appreciate the language'. But even the sagas were more accessible.

The difficulty of getting Burne-Jones's plates for the Chaucer satisfactorily rendered on wood caused much delay and disappoint-ment. 'We shall be twenty years at this rate in getting it out', Morris complained in May. Another disappointment of this year was the failure of his attempt to save the medieval statuary round the base of the spire of St Mary's, Oxford. Morris went up to Oxford in June to speak in their defence on behalf of SPAB, but his motion was heavily defeated in Convocation. 'You see the worst of it is', he wrote to Webb, 'the dons don't care one damn about them.'

Earlier in the year there had been a meeting at Kelmscott House between the Hammersmith Socialist Society, representatives of the SDF and the Fabians to try and achieve some sort of unity, and a manifesto was drafted to this end by Morris, Hyndman and Shaw. But as soon as it was drawn up, Hyndman, according to Shaw, immediately proposed the omission of the Fabian programme of municipal socialism. Shaw, in return, was equally determined not to endorse the policy of the SDF. 'There was nothing for it', says Shaw, 'but to omit both policies and to substitute platitudes that any church congress could have signed.'[12] Later Shaw confessed that he did not believe in the union and was determined that it should not be carried out.

Yet *The Manifesto of English Socialists* was issued on 1 May 1893, embodying such unequivocal Marxist principles as: 'Our aim, one and all, is to obtain for the whole community complete ownership and control of the means of transport, the means of manufacture, the mines and the land. Thus we look to put an end for ever to the wage system, to sweep away all distinctions of class, and eventually to establish national and international Communism.' Certainly no church congress would have signed that. Even Mackail says that the manifesto 'fairly represents the moderate and practical views which Morris held in the last years of his life'.[13] But Shaw and Olivier resigned from the joint committee and Morris's attitude is clear from his letter to Emery Walker of August: 'Whatever other people do, we the Hammersmith people must be careful to make as little quarrel with either party as we can help. More and more I at any rate want to see a due Socialist party established.'

By that time, however, the Independent Labour Party had emerged in the north of England, and Morris invited both Keir Hardie and Shaw Maxwell to speak on their aims at Hammersmith, which they did, though they were bitterly opposed by Hyndman in the pages of *Justice*. In 1893 also there appeared Morris and Bax's *Socialism: Its Growth and Outcome*, which gives the central place to Marx and Engels. Next year Morris spoke in Hyde Park on May

Day and may be seen in Walter Crane's drawing, a white-bearded, bespectacled figure, in a large black hat, leaning on a stick and addressing a crowd of workers from a cart decorated with spring flowers, the red flag and (oddly enough) the Socialist League banner floating over his head.[14]

Morris had already become reconciled to the SDF, writing an article for the June number of *Justice*, 'How I Became a Socialist'. Blatchford, in the *Clarion*, called upon him to take his rightful position as leader of the Independent Labour Party, an honour he declined. Earlier, in February, he had spoken for George Lansbury, the SDF candidate, at Walworth in a by-election, and at Manchester in March he admitted that Hyndman had been right all along.[15] 'We are now hand-in-glove', he said. Next year he spoke again for Lansbury, and in the general election of that year, he was invited by the South Salford branch of the SDF to become their parliamentary candidate! He headed the subscription list for Hyndman's fight at Burnley and gave the largest individual subscription to Lansbury's fund. On May Day 1895 he spoke once more from the SDF platform in Hyde Park.

None of this is mentioned by Mackail, but it may be found fully documented in E. P. Thompson's book. It is therefore quite untrue to think that Morris became any less of a socialist in his last years. It is simply that with his declining health he was unable to take such an active part in the movement as heretofore and that socialism can scarcely be detected in such works as *The Water of the Wondrous Isles* and *The Well at the World's End*. It is, however, true that Morris had become reconciled to the policy of permeation, of putting up socialist candidates for local elections and parliament, which he had earlier rejected.

Sydney Cockerell's diaries give us a good idea of Morris's outlook on the drama of his time. He did not altogether admire Ibsen's work, notes Cockerell, 'but he considered it powerful, and an interesting sign of the times. But disagreeable persons should not be introduced and heroines should always be pretty' – hardly a revolutionary view! Morris seldom went to the theatre, though he sometimes took his daughters, and when he did, he was liable to make audibly insulting remarks about the actors and actresses. 'Damned little pink TOAD!' he would growl at some leading lady.[16] One suspects that, apart from anything else, he found it irksome to have to sit still for so long without anything to do, and doubtless he found the theatre disagreeably hot. But he made an exception in the case of the first night of Bernard Shaw's *Widowers' Houses* at the Royalty Theatre in December 1892. Cockerell, who records this, adds: 'In the evening W.M. was at a party of Walter Crane's (in dress clothes)' – a curious sequel.

In general, however, Morris objected to realism in both the drama and the novel. He thought that the actors should wear masks and that scenes and costumes should be simple and symbolic, in which he anticipated Gordon Craig and W.B. Yeats. Shakespeare he thought altogether unfit for the modern stage. 'Shakespeare's genius', he said, 'has consecrated by its poetry and insight what was really a very bad form of drama' – a point of view taken up and amusingly exploited by Shaw in his dramatic criticisms for *The Saturday Review*, reprinted in *Our Theatres in the Nineties*.

Morris's attitude to the novel was similar. Cockerell told Mackail that when Thomas Hardy sent him *Tess of the D'Urbervilles*, in consequence of a lecture in which he had said that no one ever described real life in England, he thought it 'grim' and 'did not take to it'. George Borrow, however, was a firm favourite, whereas Henry James he dismissed as 'the clever historian of the deadliest corruption of society, the laureate of the flirts, snakes and empty fools of which that society is mostly composed. . . .' Yet, when he went on a railway journey, he seldom failed to buy the cheapest of yellow-back novels – in the same way as many addicts of crime fiction are now found among even the most intelligent people.[17]

In art criticism, Morris went no farther than to assert that

all worthy schools of art must be in the future, as they have been in the past, the outcome of the aspirations of the people towards the beauty and true pleasures of life. And further, now that democracy is building up a new order, which is slowly emerging from the confusion of the commercial period, these aspirations of the people towards beauty can only be born from a condition of practical equality of economical condition amongst the whole population. . . . The first step, therefore, towards the new birth of art must be a definite rise in the condition of the workers.[18]

This anticipates much of the Marxist criticism of the 1930s. But in spite of the tremendous rise in the condition of the workers that has taken place in our 'affluent society', the 'new brutalism' of our architecture expresses a greater dominance of commercialism and the machine than ever and a style more appropriate to the world of Edward Bellamy's *Looking Backward* than to the 'refined rusticity' of *News from Nowhere*. Unfortunately, it is Bellamy rather than Morris who has proved the better prophet. Nevertheless, our contemporary architecture is the inevitable outcome of a mass civilization and hence of socialism, while the menacing yet vacuous international style in painting would seem to reflect the gigantic forces of destruc-tion inherent in a scientific age which has now developed the means of abolishing life on this planet altogether. The sweet reasonableness, the universal tolerance and good-humour, the harmony of man and nature, art as 'an expression of the general pleasure of life' forecast by Morris now seems to be indeed news from nowhere.

CHAPTER FIFTEEN

1894–1896

Last Years

BY THE AUTUMN of 1894, Morris's strength was visibly failing. 'A certain physical feebleness had now become his normal condition,' Mackail tells us, 'he was seldom able to take long walks, or to spend whole days fishing; but he delighted in driving among the beautiful and familiar villages, and in shorter walks near home.' One day, during a walk to Buscot Wood, he talked for two hours on the principles of conducting business 'with all his old keen insight and fertility of illustration', but it was noticeable 'how he seemed to speak of the whole matter as, for himself, a past experi‐ ence'.[1] Insomnia grew upon him and he now got up regularly at three or four in the morning to continue one of his prose romances, which thus came nearer to being an expression of his unconscious mind than anything else he wrote. Sometimes, when it required more intellectual effort, Morris found writing exhausting, especially such things as his letters to the *Athenaeum* of August 1895 in defence of the Gothic tapestries in the South Kensington Museum.

In February 1894 Morris was surprised and touched by Swin‐ burne's dedication to him of his *Astrophel*, writing to him on the 16th:

as I knew your friendly feeling to me I ought not to be surprised at the expression of your kindness: but as a matter of fact it did take my breath away. A thousand thanks, my dear fellow, for both the art and the affection in it.

I am so glad you like my printing: I almost thought you would as I have known you for so long to have had an eye for an *old* book.

The printing of the Chaucer began on 8 August 1894. Morris had originally intended to have it published by Bernard Quaritch and then in July finally decided to publish it himself. 'The number of the Chaucer is to be 325 paper, and 13 (or 14?) vellum', he wrote to Cockerell on 30 July. 'The price £20, done up in boards like

The Golden Legend. Having gone over the number of lines with Ellis, I find it will not make more than 600 pages, which will go into one volume.' The number printed was subsequently raised to 425. 'They are printing the Chaucer very well', he wrote to Jenny on 22 August. 'Item it is all sold except 3 vellum copies & people are quarrelling over the privilege of buying it.'

Morris now was regularly buying manuscripts from Quaritch and Leighton and attending sales at Sotheby's and Christie's. He wrote to Ellis on 19 March 1895:

> I bought for £15 10s. (much too dear) a Guldin Bibel (Augs-burg, Hohenwang, *circa* 1470), a very interesting book which I much wanted. Also I bought for £25 (much too dear) a hand-some 13th century French MS., but with little ornament; because it looked so handsome I hadn't the heart to send it back. The Mentelin Bible Quaritch bought for himself: 'tis a *very* fine book, and I lust after it, but can't afford it. The prices were preposterous. There's a sale at Sotheby's this week, and I am just going up there, tho' I don't expect much in my way. I expect to meet Mr James there with the two leaves from the Fitzwilliam.

This was M. R. James, then director of the Fitzwilliam and a great authority on medieval manuscripts. Of another sale on 23 March Morris writes:

> Two books I bid for. A 13th century Aristotelian book with three very pretty initials, but imperfect top and tail; I put £15 on this with many misgivings as to my folly – hi! it fetched £50!! A really pretty little book, Gregory's Decretals, with four or five very tiny illuminations: I took a fancy to it and put £40 on it, expecting to get it for £25 – ho!! it fetched £96!!! Rejoice with me that I have got 82 MSS., as clearly I shall never get another. I have duly got my two leaves, and beauties they are.

In the previous July, Morris had bought, Mackail tells us, for upwards of £400 an English Book of Hours written about 1300 in East Anglia whose two missing leaves were traced to the Fitzwilliam Museum. Finally it was agreed that he should sell the book to the Fitzwilliam for £200 and have possession of it during his lifetime. During the course of the next two months, Morris added the twelfth-century Huntingfield Psalter and the fourteenth-century Tiptoft Missal to his collection. But his idea of bargaining for any book he wanted was to keep it tucked under his arm while he argued about the price, making it plain to the dealer that he intended to have it in any case.

In designing the Kelmscott Chaucer, Morris followed medieval precedent just as much as in *Jason* and *The Earthly Paradise*. Yet undoubtedly it is one of the great books of the world, a superb production, from the beautiful design on the white pigskin binding with its silver clasps, executed at Cobden-Sanderson's Doves Bindery by Douglas Cockerell, to each double-page spread, with its sturdy Gothic type, splendid Morris borders and the 87 Burne-Jones pictures cut on wood by Hooper. Morris has impressed his personality on this great folio so powerfully that its impact almost knocks one down. 'To me', writes Will Ransom in his *Private Presses and Their Books*, 'there are three kinds of Kelmscott books. In one group are the small quartos and 16mos, such as the first six and the Old French Romances; jolly, friendly, humanistic little volumes. Then the rest of the list, except one. And the Chaucer. . . . For monumental splendour and vivid beauty it has not been and can hardly be surpassed – that is, among modern books.'

The effect of brilliancy in the Kelmscott books is achieved by the thick and very black letters on the white page, reinforced by initials and foliage of white upon a dark background. Morris designed his title-pages with the all-over effect of one of his chintzes. Today, with our emphasis on plainness and functionalism, it is at first a little difficult to appreciate Morris's achievement at the Kelmscott Press, for it is the restraint and simplicity of Cobden-Sanderson's and Emery Walker's Doves Bible of 1903–5, rather than the bold flamboyance of Morris's books, which has had most influence on subsequent fine printing and has been taken as the example of perfection. The Doves type was designed by Walker and based on the Jenson letter to which Morris had given a Gothic twist. In-evitably our taste today is founded on the great eighteenth- and early nineteenth-century printers and typefounders, Caslon, Baskerville and Bulmer, rather than on the heaviness of black-letter type, with all its romantic connotations.

Morris's contribution to the future of printing was his awakening of public interest in the production of fine books, and his direct influence is seen at work in the productions of such small private presses as the Vale Press of Charles Ricketts, Lucien Pissarro's Eragny Press, and C. R. Ashbee's Essex House Press. Decadence is already evident in the Dent edition of the *Morte d'Arthur* with Aubrey Beardsley's illustrations and designs of 1893, where the limp knights are even more feminine than those of Burne-Jones, from whom they derive. Understandably, Morris disliked Beardsley's work and rejected his illustrations for the Kelmscott Press edition of *Sidonia the Sorceress* (1893), when submitted on Oscar Wilde's recommendation.[2]

Between 1891 and 1897 the Kelmscott Press produced fifty-three works in sixty-six volumes, a remarkable achievement for six years' work with only three hand-presses. A complete Shakespeare was planned and two pages of *Macbeth* were actually set up. Morris was also engaged on a selection of ballads, which he spoke of as the finest poems in the language, for a projected edition of a *Book of Romantic Ballads*. He asked Cockerell if he would continue the press with Walker, but Cockerell wisely declined. 'I said I was in favour of its ceasing,' Cockerell notes in the diary, under 30 August 1898, 'otherwise it would fizzle out by degrees, and the books already issued would suffer by inferior ones following them.' Unfortunately, Morris did not live to see the great folio edition of his *Sigurd* of February 1898 in Chaucer and Troy type, black and red.

Morris's mother died in the winter of 1894 in her ninetieth year and was buried at Much Hadham. Morris wrote to Georgie of the occasion: 'Tuesday I went to bury my mother: a pleasant winter day with gleams of sun. She was laid in earth in the churchyard close by the house, a very pretty place among the great wych-elms, which, if it were of no use to her, was softening to me. Altogether my old and callous heart was touched by the absence of what had been so kind to me and fond of me.'

At Whitsun he took a holiday in northern France; in July he appeared as a witness in court at the trial of Tom Cantwell, an old member of the Socialist League council and the compositor of *The Commonweal*. Cantwell was charged with 'soliciting the murder of members of the Royal Family' in a pamphlet *Why Vaillant Threw the Bomb*, defending the assassination of Carnot in Paris the previous month. When the Prince and Princess of Wales opened Tower Bridge in June, Cantwell and Charles Quinn held an open-air meeting near the bridge at which they sold the inflammatory pamphlet.

There was at this time an epidemic of anarchist bomb-throwing on the Continent, which Morris regarded, as he said in an interview in the *Justice* of 27 January, simply as a disease – 'a social disease caused by the evil conditions of society. . . . Of course, as a Socialist I regard the Anarchists – that is, those who believe in Anarchism pure and simple – as being diametrically opposed to us. . . . Anarchism, as a theory, negatives society, and puts man outside it.'[3] Feeling as he did about the anarchists who had taken over *The Commonweal* and were still desperately trying to keep it alive, it says much for his generosity that Morris should have allowed himself to be cited as a witness in this particular case, especially as in April 1892 Nicoll, the proprietor, had been sentenced to eighteen months' imprisonment for his article on the pathetic Walsall anarchists headed 'Are These Men Fit to Live ?' – meaning the police and the judge who had passed savage sentences of ten years' penal servitude on those involved in the manufacture of a bomb, which they believed was destined for Russia. Yet on this occasion Morris had come before the court and entered into surety for Mowbray, the publisher of *The Commonweal*, for £500, so that he might attend his wife's funeral.

At the beginning of 1895, Morris resumed work with Magnusson on the translation of the *Heimskringla*, which they had begun over twenty years before, for the Saga Library in course of production by Quaritch. Meanwhile, the third hand-press at Hammersmith, which printed the smaller books, was turning out the selected poems of Coleridge. Of this volume Morris wrote to F.S.Ellis, who was editing it, as well as a Keats and a three-volume Shelley:

> Coleridge was a muddle-headed metaphysician who by some strange freak of fortune turned out a few real poems amongst the dreary flood of inanity which was his wont. It is these real poems only that must be selected, or we burden the world with another useless book. 'Christabel' only just comes in because the detail is fine; but nothing a hair breadth's worse must be admitted. There is absolutely no difficulty in choosing because the difference between his poetry and his drivel is so striking.

The volume, *Poems chosen out of the Works of Samuel Taylor Coleridge*, finally included only thirteen poems. Morris explained to Ellis that there was no necessity to select from Keats, as he was 'a great poet who sometimes nodded' and evidently no selection was considered necessary in the case of Shelley.

One of the loveliest and most successful of the smaller books of the Kelmscott Press is the *Psalmi Penitentiales*, printed in black and red in Chaucer type, and published in 1894 at seven shillings and sixpence, with vellum copies at three guineas. The verses were taken from a manuscript Book of Hours written at Gloucester in the first half of the fifteenth century, but actually copied from a MS of about a century earlier.

By April 1895, Kelmscott Manor, 'of which his tenure had hitherto been precarious,' writes Mackail, 'had, by an arrangement made the month before, passed practically, though not formally, into his ownership'.[4] The manor had been leased from Charles Hobbs of the Manor Farm and, after his death, Morris lent his son, R. W. Hobbs, £6000 so that he could buy the whole Kelmscott estate of 275 acres on the understanding that Morris's lease of the manor should be renewed for another twenty years. In effect, Hobbs mort-gaged the Kelmscott estate to Morris, and May Morris at her death still owned a great part of the village as well as the manor-house.[5]

Next year, Morris decided to have the floors of several of the rooms renewed. He drew a plan of the ground floor from memory and sent it to Webb, who was in charge of the work, on 8 November 1895 with the following note: 'I should like those beastly machine-made tiles supplemented by flags, & have marked it so.' Against the plan of the Small Parlour he wrote: 'I want this room, which is now tiled with machine-made tiles, to be flagged. . . . Entrance is wood at present: it should be paved.' When work began, a stone floor was found under the boards in the Dining Room and Passage and, though the builder wrote to say that this seemed 'fearfully damp', Morris decided to re-use the existing old flags after they had been dried out. New wood floors were laid in other rooms, however, and on 17 April 1896, Webb wrote to the Acme Flooring Co. of London to say that he hoped that these would be laid by the end of the week as Morris's doctor was sending him to Kelmscott on the 22nd.[6]

There is a local tradition that the Morris family were regarded as decidedly odd and were not popular at Kelmscott. Morris's socialism was regarded as an unbecoming eccentricity in a man of means and it was looked upon as disgraceful that he should have allowed his wife to live there quite openly with Rossetti. Resentment at this can still be felt in the village. There was trouble (as there still is) about a right of way at the side of the manor-house which Morris had closed. This action was looked upon as not sorting too well with his socialistic principles, though it is understandable that Morris should have been jealous of his privacy in his 'harbour of refuge'. In London he was accessible to all and sundry. The country people, however, he found both servile and insolent – though he lectured to farm labourers at Buscot on the evils of the party system – and the farmers quite insensitive to the beauty of the ancient stone buildings they had inherited. Instead of reroofing their barns with expensive Cotswold stone tiles, they preferred to use cheaper materials such as zinc or corrugated iron. Even when the great wooden doors of their barns began to rot with age, they replaced them with these ugly modern materials. And once, on a visit to Burford, the rustic carles had openly jeered at the Guenevere-like appearance of Jane.

By the end of April 1895 Morris had finished the *Heimskringla*, as well as his own romance *The Water of the Wondrous Isles* and was working harder than ever for Anti-Scrape, unsuccessfully defending Peterborough Cathedral against Pearson's restorations and writing furiously to *The Times* in June on the subject of the proposed restoration of the tombs of the medieval kings at Westminster – 'to foist a patch of bright, new work, a futile academical study at best, amidst the loveliness of the most beautiful building in Europe'.

In July he went to Blythburgh to see

> a huge fifteenth-century church built of flint after that country manner: a very beautiful church, full of interest, with fine wood-work galore, a lovely painted roof, and some stained glass; the restora-tions not much noticeable from the inside: floor of various bricks, a few seats in the nave, all ancient, similar ones in the chancel, and the rest open space. . . . The place is close to Southwold on the little tidal river Bly at the end of the marshland valley, where they were busy with their second crop of hay. Little spits of sandy low upland covered with heather and bracken run down to the marsh, and make a strange landscape of it; a mournful place, but full of character. I was there twenty-five years ago; and found I remembered it perfectly.

This was when he was staying at Southwold with Jane and the children and writing 'October' for *The Earthly Paradise*. Rossetti, who had stayed there earlier the same year, describes it in one of his letters as a dull, dead-and-alive place. Fortunately Southwold is still one of the very few unspoiled little seaside towns of England, since there are almost no 'amusements' there.

The same month Morris wrote in unusually moderate terms to the Thames Conservancy Board about the proposed rebuilding of the lock-keeper's cottage at Eaton Weir near Kelmscott, explaining patiently that

> one of the characteristic and beautiful features in this neighbour-hood is the prevalence of old houses built of the stone of the district and roofed with *stone* – slates or slabs: and I have noticed that any intrusion of other materials materially injures the land-scape. This would be certainly the case if a building of red brick covered with ordinary slate took the place of the present cottage at Eaton Weir.

Considering the immoderate language he habitually used to many of the Thames Conservancy men he happened to meet on the river, it is amusing to find Morris hoping that he 'may be excused for troubling the Conservancy in this matter'. But in this instance the moderate tone of his letter achieved its object. He also, incredible as it may seem, prevailed upon the Conservancy to instruct their men who cut the weeds on the river to spare the flowers on the banks.

But, as he knew, he was fighting a losing battle. Few people cared about the things that made life worth while to him and to people like him, so that we find him writing to Georgie from Kelmscott in August:

> It was a most lovely afternoon when I came down here, and I was prepared to enjoy the journey from Oxford to Lechlade very much: and so I did; but woe's me! when we passed by the lovely little garth near Black Bourton, I saw all my worst fears realised; for there was the little barn we saw being mended, the wall cut down and finished with a zinced iron roof. It quite sickened me when I saw it. That's the way all things are going now. In twenty years everything will be gone in this countryside, which twenty years ago was so rich in beautiful building: and we can do nothing to help it or mend it. The world had better say, 'Let us be through with it and see what will come after it!' In the mean-time I can do nothing but a little bit of Anti-Scrape – *sweet to eye while seen*. Now that I am grown old and see that nothing is to be done, I half wish that I had not been born with a sense of romance and beauty in this accursed age. . . .

Perhaps it is just as well that Morris did not live on to see 'what will come after' in his beloved countryside. Nevertheless, his protests were not entirely vain, for it is to them that we owe such a body as the National Trust, which has succeeded in preserving at least small parts of our countryside from commercial exploitation, caravan sites and the scourge of development, though it cannot save our pleasant old towns, for where there is money to be made beauty is 'no stronger than a flower'.

Earlier in the year reports of excessive tree-felling in Epping Forest took Morris there in company with Webb, Walker, Ellis and Cockerell. One can see the party arriving – Morris, white-haired, tieless, in slouch hat, with his satchel over his shoulder, Walker and Ellis probably in velveteen jackets, Webb more formal with stiff collar and bow tie, a grave, bearded figure in tweeds. 'My diary records that it was a warm and cloudless day,' writes Cockerell, 'and that the young green of the beeches, mingled with the darker tone of the hornbeams, was very beautiful; also that we heard nightingales. We walked from Loughton via Monkwood, Theydon Bois, High Beech, and Bury Wood, to Chingford, and laughed and talked and enjoyed every moment.'[7] They do not seem to have been unduly dashed by what they saw, for the reports had been exaggerated.

Nevertheless, Morris wrote two long letters to the *Daily Chronicle* on the subject, which appeared on 23 April and 9 May 1895. After pointing out that the special character of Epping Forest was derived from its hornbeams, he went on:

But the hornbeam, though an interesting tree to an artist and reasonable person, is no favourite with the landscape gardener, and I very much fear that the intention of the authorities is to clear the forest of its native trees and to plant vile weeds like deodars and outlandish conifers instead.

We are told that a committee of 'experts' has been formed to sit in judgement on Epping Forest: but, Sir, I decline to be gagged by the word 'expert', and I call on the public generally to take the same position. The Committee of the Common Council has now had Epping Forest in hand for seventeen years, and has, I am told, in that time felled 100,000 trees. I think the public may now fairly ask for a rest on behalf of the woods.

For Morris woods and forests still had much of their ancient magic and in such prose romances as *The Wood Beyond the World* and *The Water of the Wondrous Isles* Yeats detected a deeply religious feeling for the Green Tree and the Waters of Abundance. Of the peculiar innocence of their love stories he says: 'The desire seems not other than the desire of the bird for its mate in the wood.' And again: 'It was his work to make us, who had been taught to sympathise with the unhappy till we had grown morbid, to sympathise with men and women who turned everything to happiness because they had in them something of the abundance of the beechen boughs or of the bursting wheat-ear.'[8]

Morris now grew very excited at the prospect of Burne-Jones doing twenty-five or thirty illustrations for the projected folio edition of *Sigurd*. Burne-Jones had promised to do this because he knew it would please Morris more than anything else. But he disliked the task and when the book finally appeared in 1898 he had only done two illustrations, one of the Hall of the Volsungs, with the mighty tree springing up from the middle of the floor and the wild hawks nesting in its branches, and the other of Atli's hall in flames and Gudrun with her torch, possibly because he had seen a similar scene in *Götterdämmerung*.

In May a week was spent with Walker, John Carruthers and Cockerell in northern France, at Cockerell's suggestion, so, he tells us, that he might have 'the felicity of seeing Beauvais with Morris'. Crossing from Newhaven to Dieppe, they stopped at Eu and Abbeville.

> On the first morning after we reached Beauvais, Morris rapped on my door soon after 7 o'clock and summoned me to 'come out and buy a manuscript'. . . . By an extraordinary stroke of luck we found a thirteenth-century Justinian going for a song at an old curiosity shop and carried it back in triumph to the Hôtel de France et d'Angleterre, where our two companions were just starting breakfast. It was Sunday and we went on to High Mass at the Cathedral. . . . After lunch we walked to S. Lazare and saw with excitement a thirteenth-century tithe-barn, which is, if still intact, even more superb than that of Great Coxwell with great arches of stone. Days were spent at Amiens and Senlis. The Mackails turned up at Beauvais on the last evening. . . . Most of the old streets that we explored together were destroyed by German conflagrations early in the last war.[9]

During the autumn and winter of 1895, Morris continued to attend book sales and to lecture, mostly at Hammersmith, but occasionally elsewhere too. In October he gave an address to inaugurate the newly founded Oxford Socialist Union and in November he spoke in the foggy drizzle outside Waterloo station at the funeral of Sergius Stepniak, the Russian writer who had been knocked down by a train on the level-crossing at Shepherd's Bush. He lectured twice in London in December, on English architecture and on Gothic illustrations to printed books – the latter lecture, given at the Bolt Court Technical School was, according to Mackail, the last he gave with his old vigour.

On 3 January 1896 he attended the New Year's meeting of the SDF at the Holborn Town Hall, 'and there made a short, but noble and touching speech on behalf of unity'. Two days afterwards, he gave the last of his Sunday-evening lectures at Kelmscott House, 'One Socialist Party'. Next day he noted in his diary: 'Could not sleep at night; got up & worked from 1 to 4 at Sundering Flood.' At the end of the month he attended a meeting at the Society of Arts of the National Society for Checking the Abuses of Public Advertising and seconded the resolution, 'That it is a national interest to protect rural scenery from unnecessary disfigurement and to maintain dignity and propriety in the aspect of our times.' This was the last time that Morris spoke in public. The day before he had been to his last Anti-Scrape meeting. Afterwards, on his way up Buckingham Street, noticing his obvious weakness, a friend ventured to remark that it was the worst time of the year. 'No, it ain't,' Morris replied, 'it's a very fine time of the year indeed: I'm getting old, that's what it is.' But he was still only sixty-two.

In the previous November he had gone down to Rottingdean to stay at the Burne-Joneses' house on his own, writing to Georgie on the 27th:

To-day has been quite mild, and I started out at ten and went to a mountain with some barns on the top, and a chalk pit near (where you took me one hot evening in September, you remem-ber), and I walked on thence a good way, and should have gone further, but prudence rather than weariness turned me back. They were ploughing a field in the bottom with no less than ten teams of great big horses: they were knocking off for their beaver just as I came on them, and seemed very jolly, and my heart went out to them, both men and horses.

I brought my University book [Rashdall's *Universities of Europe*

in the Middle Ages] down with me, but deserted it yesterday afternoon for Jane Austen's 'Pride and Prejudice', which I have just
finished. I am getting better here, but was better on Sunday for
the matter of that. The doctor called on Monday, and told me it
was good for me not to be victimised by bores, and that I had
better not be: this seems to me such good advice, that I pass it on
to you; but I am just struck with fear that you may begin the
practice of it on me. Anyhow I will be cautious enough of it not
to make this letter longer.

In December Morris designed the binding for the Chaucer, but he
was beginning to be worried lest he should not see it completed. At
the beginning of 1896, Burne-Jones wrote: 'Last Sunday, in the
very middle of breakfast, Morris began leaning his forehead on his
hand, as he does so often now. It is a thing I have never seen him
do before in all the years I have known him. . . . I am getting very
anxious about Morris and about the Chaucer. He has not done the
title-page yet, which will be such a rich page of ornament with all
the large lettering. I wish he would not leave it any longer.' But by
the end of February it was finished. Then on the 23rd Morris failed
to go to breakfast at the Grange. Soon after Burne-Jones wrote:
'Morris has been ill again – I am very frightened – better now, but
the ground beneath one is shifting, and I travel among quicksands.'[10]
Earlier that month there had been a Punch and Judy show in
the garden at the Grange for Denis Mackail's birthday and when
Morris came to see them next day, Burne-Jones said: 'I say, old boy,
I saw a play yesterday you would have liked – Punch.' The last
time he and Burne-Jones went anywhere together was to the Society
of Antiquaries to look at illuminated manuscripts. But Morris found
even this exhausting and Burne-Jones says that he could not look
at them for more than five minutes together. From Kelmscott Morris
wrote to the anxious Georgie on 27 April:

> I cannot say that I think I am better since I saw you a week ago,
> & I hope I am no worse. . . . However, I am getting on with my
> work, both drawing and writing, tho' but little of the latter, as
> Walker was with me Saturday & Sunday, to my great comfort.
> Ellis comes on Saturday, & will stay till I go back. . . . I have
> enjoyed the garden very much, & should never be bored by walk-
> ing about and about in it. And though you think I don't like
> music, I assure you that the rooks and blackbirds have been a

great consolation to me. We are still between flowers, for nothing stirs this beastly weather. The thing that was the pleasingest sur⁄prise was the raspberry⁄canes, which Giles has trellised up neatly, so that they look like a medieval garden. . . .

Moreover Hobbs has been re⁄thatching a lot of his sheds & barns which sorely needed it, & used to keep me in a fever of terror of galvanized iron: so that this time at least there is some improvement in the village.

In March Morris had bought from W.A.S.Benson a fine folio Testament of the twelfth century. But the Easter holidays had been a sore trial to him – 'four mouldy Sundays in a mouldy row,' he wrote, 'the press shut and Chaucer at a standstill'. On his last visit to Kelmscott in May he had written a brief article for the May Day number of *Justice*. But he was now subject to an exhausting cough, 'with bellyache and pains in the limbs'. He wrote to Webb on 4 May:

I am coming back on Tuesday, & shall see Broadbent as soon as I can. Now let that flea stick on the wall. Ellis here till Tuesday, when he goes back to Torquay: he amuses me considerably & is very friendly & considerate. Cockerell comes here to⁄morrow: he brings with him the said book [a twelfth⁄century English bestiary]. I had a letter from him yesterday in which he spoke of it in measured terms; but we take it that was to prevent dis⁄appointment, as he would hardly have bought it then & there if he had not thought it was worth the sacrifice of £900. There, the murder is out. But you see it will certainly fetch something when my sale comes off.

This fine English bestiary, which Cockerell had gone over to Stutt⁄gart with a blank cheque to buy for Morris, contained 106 miniatures, and is now in the Pierpont Morgan Collection in New York. A contemporary note in the book itself says that it had been given in the year 1187 to Worksop Priory by one Philip, Canon of Lincoln. Even the British Museum had nothing finer.

When Morris had consulted Sir William Broadbent earlier in the year, the diagnosis had been diabetes and other complications, but no immediate danger. However, he was steadily losing ground, though his condition fluctuated with slight improvements followed by relapses. He was now exhausted by a walk round his garden at Hammersmith. However, when he returned there on 6 May, he was greeted with the joyful news that the picture sheets of the Chaucer had been printed off and that the block of the title-page was ready for approval. Two days later the printing was completed.

Towards the end of May, Morris and Jane went to stay with Wilfrid Scawen Blunt at Newbuildings Place. 'The Morrises have been here at Newbuildings since Tuesday. He, poor man, very feeble and aged', Blunt notes in his diary under the 29th. 'I fear from the look of things that it is some form of consumption, and that he will not recover. But his spirits are fairly good, and he talks at times as brilliantly as ever. The new piece of tapestry he has made for me, Botticelli's Spring, is up and is very decorative and brilliant in the drawing-room, though the faces are hardly as good as they ought to be. It has been a great difficulty to execute it, he says, and has turned out better than he expected.'

Blunt records that he and Morris had 'many interesting talks on art, politics, and religion. As to the last he does not believe in any God the Creator of the World, or any Providence, or, I think, any future life. But he is not a pessimist, and thinks mankind the "crown of things", in spite of man's destructive action and his modern craze of ugliness.' Morris told Blunt that his father was a bill broker and that he himself was destined for the trade, adding: 'If I had gone on with it, I should have broken the bills into very small bits.' When he inherited his shares in Devon Great Consols, he sold them, he said: 'My relations thought me both wicked and mad.' This statement rather conflicts with the accounts of both Mackail and May Morris which represent Morris resigning from his directorship of Devon Great Consols in 1876 and afterwards sitting down on his top hat. It seems that he only sold the shares when their value began to go down.

On 31 May Blunt records: 'I took him yesterday to see Shipley Church, a fine old Norman tower, injured with restoration. He was very indignant, swearing at the parsons as we walked up the nave: "Beasts! Pigs! Damn their souls!"' Of his visit to Canterbury Cathedral as a boy and his first sight of an illuminated manuscript, he said, 'These first pleasures which I discovered for myself were stronger than anything else I have had in life', but neither his father, nor his mother, nor any of his relations had the least sense of beauty. 'He talked much about his Iceland journey, as he often does, and has a sick man's fancy to go there again. . . . "I am a man of the North", he said. "I am disappointed at the fine weather we are having here. I had hoped it would rain, so that I could sit indoors and watch it beating on the windows."'

On 30 June the first copies of the Chaucer came from the binder, one for Morris, the other for Burne-Jones. Morris's copy is now in the library at Exeter College, Oxford. The great folio was issued without introduction, notes or glossary – 'So that all is prepared for you to enjoy him thoroughly', Burne-Jones wrote to his daughter Margaret, now Mrs J. W. Mackail, when sending her his own copy as a birthday present in June.

The Chaucer, which had been projected five years earlier, was three years and four months in production, the actual printing occupying a year and nine months. In a revealing letter to Swinburne, quoted by E. P. Thompson, Burne-Jones wrote in August that he had 'abstained from decorating certain of the Canterbury Tales. . . . Morris has been urgent with me that I should by no means exclude these stories from our scheme of adornment – especially he had hopes of my treatment of the Miller's Tale, but he ever had more robust and daring parts than I could assume.'[11] This explains why the majority of the Chaucer illustrations are pitched in the romantic key of the Knight's Tale, as though they were illustrations to Malory.

'Every morning we drive down to the Harbour (it is too far for me to walk) and then I toddle about, and sit down, lean over the chains, and rather enjoy it, especially if there is any craft about', Morris wrote to Philip Webb on 14 June from Folkestone. 'The Harbour is the only decent place in the town, that and the view of the downs thence. It is very rough, not at all polite, all mixed up with the railway, which comes right up to the pierhead. We are going a bit of a drive after tea to Caesar's Camp, which is a fine point of the hills behind: all of which would be very beautiful still if it were not for the almost incredible squalor & hideousness of the miles of squattering new buildings.'

Morris had gone to Folkestone to try the effect of a change of air, with Sydney Cockerell, and other friends came to keep him company – the Burne-Joneses, Blunt, Ellis, Walker, Catterson-Smith. Expeditions included a trip to Boulogne and to Lympne Court, an early fifteenth-century farm-house: 'a most exceedingly lovely house knocked about as a farm-house but quite unrestored', he wrote to Webb. 'It is within a few feet of the W of the church once a noble

EE. & Norman ruined by fakement various. The whole ch. yard
lies all along the brow of the steep hill. It is a strange and very
beautiful place. We didn't get inside, being afraid of Sundayfied
farmers; the dog made friends.'

On his return to London, Sir William Broadbent suggested a
sea-trip to Norway. 'Dined with the Morrises', Blunt noted in his
diary under 12 July, 'to wish him good-bye, as he sails for Norway
next week. The garden at Kelmscott House is lovely with hollyhocks.' Before going, Morris sent a copy of the Chaucer to Swinburne, inscribed by himself and Burne-Jones. 'So I am going with
what amount of hope I can muster, which varies, to say sooth, from
a good deal to very little', he wrote.

He set off with John Carruthers on 22 July. The journey was not
a success. Morris missed his books and his illuminated manuscripts.
He felt weary and restless. He was terrified by the coils of rope
lying on deck, as they 'appeared to his disordered mind like a great
serpent preparing to crush the life out of him', and, according to
Mrs A. M. W. Stirling, they haunted him till Mary de Morgan, who
nursed him in his last illness, succeeded in ridding him of the
obsession. 'You have rid me of the coils', he said to her one day.[12]
It was as though all that side of his nature which Morris had denied
and suppressed throughout his life, now, as death approached, rose
up to strangle him.

In Norway he was unable to make any excursions and was
depressed by the melancholy of the firths. He stayed at Vadsö, near
North Cape, for a week, then returned to England. Afterwards
Carruthers wrote to May Morris that her father was cheerful during
most of the voyage, joked with other passengers, and on deck
always asked to have his chair put near the youngest and prettiest
of the women.[13]

Morris reached Tilbury on 18 August and from Hammersmith
wrote at once to Webb:

My dear Fellow,
I am back. Please come and see me. I saw Throndhjem – big
church, terribly restored, but well worth seeing; in fact, as
beautiful as can be. It quite touched my hard heart.
Yours affectionately,
W. M.
P.S. Somewhat better, but hated the voyage; so glad to be home.

His one wish, Mackail tells us, was to go to Kelmscott. But a day or two afterwards he became too ill to make the journey and wrote to Jenny:

Dearest own child,

I am so distressed that I cannot get down to Kelmscott on Saturday; but I am not well, & the doctors will not let me; please my own dear forgive me, for I long to see you with all my heart. I hope to get down early next week, darling. I send you my very best love & am

Your loving father

W.M.

To Thomas Wardle of Leek, who had written inviting him up to Derbyshire, he dictated a letter saying that he was now too weak to walk over his own threshold. But he concluded: 'The Manifold is the same river, is it not, which you carried me across on your back, which situation tickled us so much that, owing to inextinguishable laughter, you nearly dropped me in. What pleasant old times those were.' On 8 September Morris dictated the last few lines of *The Sundering Flood* to Cockerell. 'Come soon,' he wrote to Georgie, in the last letter he was able to write with his own hand, 'I want a sight of your dear face.' Ellis was with him daily, and together they worked on a selection from the Border Ballads, Morris doing a recension from the different texts. Another project which had to be abandoned was the *Morte d'Arthur*, with at least a hundred illustrations by Burne-Jones. This, had it been achieved, might very well have proved to have been the most magical production of the Kelmscott Press, eclipsing even the Chaucer. But congestion of the left lung had set in, and with it general organic degeneration. Morris was now known to be a dying man.

'It is an astonishing spectacle', Cobden-Sanderson observed in his journal on 12 September. 'He sits speechless waiting for the end to come. . . . Darkness soon will envelop all the familiar scene, the sweet river, England green and grey, Kelmscott, Kelmscott House, the trees . . . the Press, the passage, the Bindery, the light coming in through the windows . . . the old books on the shelves. . . .' 'But', he said to Mary de Morgan, 'I cannot believe that I shall be annihilated.' And Mackail says: 'As the powers of self-control slackened, the emotional tenderness which had always been so large an element in his nature became more habitually visible.' Arnold

362

Dolmetsch came with a pair of virginals and played sixteenth-century music. Morris was greatly moved by a pavan and galliard of Byrd and broke into a cry of joy at its opening phrase, but after the two pieces had been repeated could not bear to hear any more. It has often been said that Morris had no feeling for music, but May was an accomplished performer on the lute and frequently played and sang early music to him.

Webb and the Burne-Joneses were now with Morris daily and, Mackail says, Emery Walker 'nursed him with the patience and tenderness of a woman'. R. H. Benson brought him thirteenth-century manuscripts to look at from the Dorchester House library. Under 29 September Cockerell notes in his diary:

W. M. said he felt much better. It was a bright morning, and we took him out in the bathchair. We went into Ravenscourt Park and round by the library, the longest run we have had – and W. M. was in good spirits and declared that he was not a bit tired, and that he felt able to do some walking. At 4.45 I went to the post and on returning found W. M. upstairs with blood streaming from his mouth. F. S. Ellis was with him: we helped him downstairs and put him to bed. Dr Hogg came soon after.

Four days later, at 11.15 on 3 October, at the age of sixty-two, William Morris peacefully died. Almost his last words were: 'I want to get mumbo-jumbo out of the world.' Jane, Georgie, May, Detmar Blow and Mary de Morgan were in the room. Mary de Morgan and Walker went to Kelmscott to break the news to Jenny; Fairfax Murray and Richmond made two drawings of Morris on his death-bed, one of which Murray gave to Cockerell, who was startled to see how little the dead face resembled the living Morris. 'The face was singularly beautiful,' he notes in his diary, 'but the repose of it made it more unlike what I had known.'[14]

When Burne-Jones came, he asked Cockerell to lead him by the hand into the death-chamber and to leave him there alone. Earlier, when Cockerell had been left alone there, he had burst into an uncontrollable paroxysm of tears and had to be led back into the study by Catterson Smith, where, he says, 'for some time I went on sobbing. When it abated I set to work on all there was to be done.'

To Sydney Cockerell, Morris was always the greatest man he had ever known. Wilfrid Blunt also recorded in his diary under 4 October:

He is the most wonderful man I have ever known, unique in this, that he had no thought for anything or person, including himself, but only for the work he had in hand. He was not selfish in the sense of seeking his own advantage or pleasure or comfort, but he was too absorbed in his own thoughts to be either openly affec-tionate or actively kind. . . . He was generous and open-handed in his dealings, and I fancy did many kindnesses in a money way for people in distress, but he fashed himself for no man and no woman. . . . It will be a great grief for Jenny, a great break-up for Janey, and a great loss for the world at large, for he was really our greatest man.

Next day, Blunt came up to London and called on Burne-Jones, who told him 'that his interest in life had come to an end with Morris, as all their ideas and plans of work had been together all their lives. . . . Then I went on to Hammersmith. The coffin, a very plain box, lay in the little room downstairs, with a beautiful old embroidered cloth over it and a small wreath of leaves and sad-coloured flowers. It was the room which was his bedroom, and where he died, with his best and favourite books around him.'[15]

Morris was buried in Kelmscott churchyard on 6 October. It was a suitable day for the burial of an autumnal poet – a day of storms, with south-westerly winds at gale force, as Mackail records in his fine description. The waters were out over the low-lying river meadows and 'all the little streams that are fed from the Cotswolds ran full and deep brown. The noise of waters was everywhere. Clumps of Michaelmas daisies were in flower in the drenched cottage gardens, and the thinning willows had turned, not to the brilliance of their common October colouring, but to a dull tarnished brown. The rooks were silent in the elms about the Manor House.'[16]

The coffin was met at Lechlade Station. 'No red-faced men in shabby black to stagger with the coffin to the hearse,' wrote Cunning-hame Graham, 'but in their place four countrymen in moleskin bore the body to an open hay cart festooned with vines, with alder and with bullrushes and driven by a man who looked coeval with the Anglo-Saxon Chronicle.' A wreath of bay was laid on the coffin of unpolished oak with its wrought-iron handles. 'The group of mourners followed it along the dripping lanes, between russet hedgerows and silver-grey slabbed stone fences, to the churchyard

gate, and up the short lime-avenue to the tiny church.'[17] 'E. B-J.
standing by grass with Mrs Morris, seemingly 6 feet high & broad in
proportion,' Mackail notes. 'She like the photograph of her as a very
young woman with the same sway to the folds of her cloak from the
neck to the ground.'[18]

Inside, the church was decorated for the harvest festival, the oil-
lamps wreathed with ears of corn and barley, with pumpkins and
carrots round the font, and sheaves of corn. The service was read by
the Rev. Adams, Vicar of Little Faringdon, an old Marlborough
schoolfellow of Morris. Among the mourners were the workmen
from Merton Abbey, the Kelmscott villagers and members of the
Art Workers' Guild, all of them in their daily working clothes. 'It
was', says Lethaby, 'the only funeral I have ever seen that did not
make me ashamed to have to be buried.'[19]

The gravestone was designed by Philip Webb, low on the ground,
with a coped top like a house roof. In this it followed the local
Cotswold tradition. The fine, bold lettering and the simple design
of a spray of grass was Webb's last offering to his friend. He had
built his first as well as his last house. After that Webb virtually
gave up his practice. 'My coat feels thinner', he said. 'One would
think I had lost a buttress.' He lived on in retirement at Caxton's, a
cottage at Worth on Wilfrid Scawen Blunt's estate in Sussex, until
1915. 'You cannot lose a man like that by his death,' said Burne-
Jones, 'but only by your own.' Two years later Burne-Jones himself
was dead.

We are left with a picture of Morris as one of his friends remembers
him, walking through the streets of London – 'The figure . . . in
the cloak and satchel, the soft hat pulled down over his eyes and
the stick firmly grasped and held point forward as he walked straight
on, seeming to see nothing of what was round him – yet in fact seeing
it and taking it all in with incomparable swiftness – through the
glare and bustle of the Strand, was like one other person and one
only, Christian passing through Vanity Fair.'[20]

After her husband's death, Jane Morris went to stay in Egypt for
six months with Wilfrid Scawen Blunt and his wife. Her health
improved; she became more serene, even talkative. Young Will
Rothenstein, watching her as she signed a copy of the Kelmscott
Chaucer at May's house on Hammersmith Terrace, writes: 'She
looked like a splendid Sibyl from the Sistine Chapel. I had heard
and read of her moving, a noble figure, among the great people

about her husband – noble but silent. I found her serene indeed, but interested in a thousand things: an admirable talker, wholly without self-consciousness, always gracious, and in her person beautifully dignified. In Mrs Morris's presence I seemed to be living in a dream.'[21] In a late photograph, however, taken in the Tapestry Room at Kelmscott, she looks as unhappy and haunted as ever.

Jane Morris's letters to Cockerell, which he bequeathed to the Victoria and Albert Museum, reveal her as practical and hard-headed, but on the anniversary of Morris's death in 1898 she wrote: 'I perceive that I am really rich, but feel inexpressibly poor today.'[22] Of her friendship with Rossetti, the cause of so much unhappiness to all concerned, Moncure Conway, the American Nonconformist minister who came to live at Hammersmith, wrote in his *Auto-biography* of 1904: 'I have not in my long life known anything more quasi-miraculous than this re-appearance in modern London of Dante and Beatrice. . . . The superb lady, great-hearted, and sincere, recognised the fine spirit to which she was related, and responded to his visions and ideals. . . . She was honoured by all who knew her and Dante Rossetti as one who thought for herself and was great enough to live in accordance with her own heart.'[23]

The Hammersmith house was sold and Jane retired to Kelmscott with Jenny, dividing her time between Oxfordshire, rooms in London, and Lyme Regis, where she stayed with Morris's widowed sister Emma, who lived in a house on the cliffs, surrounded 'by her brother's yellow Marigold wallpapers and his blue carpets and chintzes'.[24]

Conclusion

THERE CAN REALLY be no conclusion to a book on William Morris, since so many of the things he fought for are still our problems today. One can say of his achievement, in the words of his own John Ball: 'men fight and lose the battle, and the thing they fought for comes about in spite of their defeat, and when it comes turns out to be not what they meant.' Undoubtedly the world, as it has developed since Morris's time, is in many respects not what he meant. How could it be? We are now oppressed with a complexity and superabundance he never envisaged. Two possible futures are open to us – total annihilation, in which we can scarcely believe, and, on the other hand, the possibility of a fuller, richer life for all men. Many things that Morris loathed have grown to monstrous proportions since his time, so that the simplicity, harmony and fellowship which he longed for, and the healing influence of nature in our lives, seem farther off than ever.

But we are still tantalized by his vision of a world as it might be. For it is only the noblest spirits in any age who conceive Utopias. Curiously enough, it was Oscar Wilde who wrote in *The Soul of Man Under Socialism*: 'A map of the world that does not include Utopia is not worth even glancing at, for it leaves out the one country at which Humanity is always landing. And when Humanity lands there, it looks out, and, seeing a better country, it sets sail. Progress is the realization of Utopias.' Morris would surely have agreed with that, for it is the essence of his vision. Bernard Shaw, who worked with him in the political field, wrote in 1935: 'With such wisdom as my years have left me I note that as he has drawn further and further away from the hurly-burly of our personal contacts into the impersonal perspective of history he towers greater and greater above the horizon beneath which his best-advertized contemporaries have disappeared.'

And yet, in many ways, Morris was a contradictory, volcanic and baffled character. Emotionally he was attached to the past, to an unchanging order: intellectually he was convinced of the necessity of a new order, and in social revolution he saw the only hope for the future. He appears now as a Janus figure facing both ways. His work is that of a traditionalist: as a thinker he was in the vanguard of the most progressive movements of his time.

367

Nevertheless, he had rather more than his share of the inconsistencies that afflict those who try to impose their dogmas upon art and life. In fact, Morris's social theories of art had little relation to his actual practice. We may ask how a man 'careless of metaphysics and religion . . . but with a deep love of the earth and the life on it', as he once described himself, could have spent so much time decorating churches, for which he himself had no use. But his church decoration – that is, that carried out by his own hands – belongs to the earlier part of his career. As a man of business, he was fulfilling the demands of the mid-nineteenth-century Anglo-Catholic revival, as well as practising the type of medieval decorative art he admired. In this he was only one of a number of artists of the High Victorian Gothic Revival. It may be questioned, too, how Morris, as a militant socialist, could have accepted commissions to decorate Balmoral, St James's Palace and the houses of wealthy capitalists and Liberal politicians. But here again, as a business man, he could scarcely have refused such orders, since he was, after all, living in a capitalist and monarchical society, and these were his patrons.

More serious, however, are the inconsistencies at the root of his work as an artist-craftsman. In lecture after lecture, Morris defined beauty in art as the direct outcome of the workman's pleasure in his work. There could be no art without this pleasure, he said, for art should be 'a joy to the maker and to the user'. Yet we find that more than half of his designs for wallpapers and textiles were not produced at Merton Abbey at all, or even under his direct supervision, but by outside firms. As Peter Floud has pertinently remarked, how did Morris know whether the anonymous workmen who laboriously printed his designs by hand-block were happy in their work or not? – however 'ideal' working conditions at Merton may have been. Here Morris was surrendering to the very evil he most passionately condemned, and which, he said, was responsible for the decadence of all design since the days of medieval craftsmen – the division of labour. In any case, the printing of wallpapers and textiles by hand from wood-blocks is far more laborious than printing them by machinery. Certainly the results are better in the matter of colour, which is why Sandersons now print all Morris's designs from the original pear-wood blocks. But as far as actual drudgery is concerned, the machine has the advantage over hand-work every time, so that, according to Morris himself, the inevitable boredom and weariness of printing endlessly repeating patterns by hand should manifest itself by a certain lifelessness in the final product. Oddly enough, it does not. It is the abounding life and freshness and the sense of natural growth that delights us in the best of Morris's patterns. All the same, as Floud in his talk, 'The Inconsistencies of William Morris', concludes: 'This is a strange paradox: that the man whose work, above that of all other designers, was best adapted to that undeviating and infinite multiplication which is the special virtue of the machine should at the same time have been the most eloquent protagonist of hand-crafts as opposed to machine-production.'

Fortunately, these inconsistencies do not diminish Morris's stature as the greatest pattern designer we have ever had. He made no claim to originality: he claimed only to be taking up and developing the tradition of English design from the point at which it had languished at the close of the Middle Ages. One has only to compare his recurring acanthus motive with similar decoration on the great early sixteenth-century memorial brass of Sir Thomas Bullen at Hever to see that. 'That talk of inspiration is sheer non-sense,' he once said impatiently, and perhaps defensively, of his own poetry, 'I may tell you that flat. There is no such thing. It's a mere matter of craftsmanship.' But craftsmanship on the level at which Morris practised it in his finest designs, though not so much in his poetry, did amount to inspiration. Though he rejected his age and rebelled against the society that bred him, he still felt bound to justify himself in its own terms. 'Just because I string a few rhymes together, they call me dreamy and unpractical', he protested. 'I can't help writing verses, I must do it, but I'm as much a man of business as any of them.'

NOTES AND SOURCES

Quotations from the writings of William Morris are principally from the *Collected Works*, 24 vols., edited by May Morris, 1910–15, and from the two Supplementary volumes, *William Morris: Artist, Writer, Socialist*, 1936, referred to as Sup. I and II. Letters to his wife and daughters are quoted from the Family Correspondence, British Museum Add. MSS 45,338–45,341 and others from *The Letters of William Morris*, edited by Philip Henderson, 1950. Otherwise references to both published and unpublished material are given in the notes to each chapter. This includes the 40 vols. of the May Morris Bequest to the British Museum, Add. MSS 45,298–45,337, the recently released letters of Dante Gabriel Rossetti to Mrs Morris, also catalogued under the William Morris Papers, vol. xxv, Add. MSS 52,333A and B, Add. MSS 52,332A and B, Philip Webb's letters to the Morris family, Add. MSS 45,342, in which a number of William Morris's letters are included, the Shaw Papers vol. xxxiv, Add. MSS 50,541, which include several of Morris's letters, the Cockerell Papers, Add. MSS 52,734. Other MSS collections drawn upon are those in the Victoria and Albert Museum, the William Morris Gallery, Walthamstow, and at Castle Howard.

CHAPTER I: *1834–1852*

1 J.W. Mackail, *The Life of William Morris*, London 1901 ed., I, 2.
2 Ibid., 1, 5.
3 Letter to Andreas Scheu, 5 September 1883, in which is included 'a rather long-winded sketch of my uneventful life'.
4 Typed extracts from a letter from Effie Morris. 'Friends and Relations of William Morris', William Morris Gallery, Walthamstow, MSS 106–9.
5 W.S. Blunt, 'A Few Words About William Morris'. British Museum, Add. MSS 45,350.f.33.
6 Mackail, op. cit., I, 137.
7 Ibid., I, 16.
8 Letter to Andreas Scheu, 5 September 1883.
9 Mackail, op. cit., I, 17.
10 Ibidem.
11 W.S. Blunt, *My Diaries, 1888–1914*, 1932 ed., 231–2.
12 Mackail, op. cit., I, 17.
13 Ibid., I, 25.

CHAPTER II: *1853–1856*

1 Georgiana Burne-Jones (G.B-J), *Memorials*, London 1904, I, 75.
2 Canon Dixon's reminiscences of Morris and his friends. William Morris Gallery, Walthamstow, MS J189.
3 William Gaunt, *Oxford*, London 1965, 147.
4 Mackail, op. cit., I, 35.
5 Ibid., I, 35.
6 Ibid., I, 35–6.
7 Montague Weekley, *William Morris*, London 1934, 22.
8 Mackail, op. cit., I, 37.
9 Marx had also written in *The Communist Manifesto* of 1848: 'Owing to the extensive use of machinery and to the division of labour, the work of the proletarians has lost all individual character and consequently all charm, for the workman. He becomes an appendage of the machine.'
10 Dixon's reminiscences (see note 2 above).
11 G.B-J, op. cit., I, 104.
12 Mackail, op. cit., I, 51–2.
13 May Morris, *William Morris, Artist, Writer, Socialist*, Oxford 1936, I, 376. Subsequently referred to as: May Morris, Sup. I and II.
14 British Museum, Add. MSS 45,298.

15 Mackail, op. cit., I, 64-5.
16 G.B-J, op. cit., I, 111.
17 Ibid., I, 115.
18 Mackail, op. cit., I, 78.
19 G.B-J, op. cit., I, 116.
20 *The Oxford and Cambridge Magazine*, 1856, 559.
21 Barbara Morris, *Victorian Embroidery*, London 1962, Chap. 6, *passim*.

CHAPTER III: *1856–1859*

1 Mackail, op. cit., I, 113.
2 Rosalie Glynn Grylls, *Portrait of Rossetti*, London 1965, 120.
3 An early example is the illuminated page of Gothic script from Grimm's tale 'The Iron Man'. British Museum, Add. MSS 45,347. f. 63.
4 G.B-J, op. cit., I, 147.
5 W.M.Rossetti, *Ruskin, Rossetti and Pre-Raphaelitism*, London 1899, 194.
6 Ford Madox Hueffer, *Ford Madox Brown*, London 1896, 154. In 'The Paintings of William Morris', *Journal of the William Morris Society*, II, No. I, Spring 1966, 4-8, Janet Camp Troxell points out that Mackail confused this painting with the later portrait of Jane Burden, *Queen Guenevere*, which came to be known as *La Belle Iseult*.
7 G.B-J, op. cit., I, 159.
8 Ibid., I, 161.
9 Mackail, op. cit., I, 121.
10 W.R.Lethaby, *Philip Webb*, London 1935, 21.
11 Mackail, op. cit., I, 129.
12 Ibid., I, 126.
13 Ibid., I, 111.
14 Ibid., I, 126-7.
15 G.B-J, op. cit., I, 161-2.
16 Notes of a conversation with Bliss, 30 June 1897. Two notebooks and manuscript notes compiled by Professor J.W.Mackail for his *Life of William Morris*. William Morris Gal-

lery, Walthamstow, MSS J163-6. Mackail wrote to Sydney Cockerell in September 1898: 'What I feel is that it does great injustice to Morris himself to slur over the fact that he married "beneath him" and did so with perfect simplicity and as a thing which he had no reason whatever to feel ashamed of in any way. I have been obliged to some degree to slur it over, and the loss will be the book's and Mrs Morris's own, if she knew it.' British Museum, Add. MSS 52,734.
17 Lethaby, op. cit., 34.
18 Janet Camp Troxell, 'The Paintings of William Morris' (see note 6 above). An account of these 'negotiations' is given in John Ingram's *Life of Oliver Madox Brown*, London 1883.
19 Cockerell's introduction to the World's Classics reprint of Mackail, 1950, VII.
20 Oswald Doughty, *A Victorian Romantic: Dante Gabriel Rossetti*, London 1949, 369. 'The Cup of Cold Water' was written as the background to a projected painting, since for the Pre-Raphaelites every picture told a story, though its significance is by no means always clear. Rossetti was in the habit of giving his own pictures resounding Italian titles, which impressed an uncultivated public.
21 George Saintsbury, *History of English Prosody*, London 1906-10, III, 322.
22 Walter Pater, *Appreciations*, London 1889.
23 Jack Lindsay, *William Morris, Writer*, William Morris Society, London 1961, 7-8. Lindsay finds Morris's Guenevere 'the most rounded and convincing image of the Queen in all literature'.
24 British Museum, Add. MSS 45,321.
25 Lethaby, op. cit., 23.

CHAPTER IV: *1859–1865*
1 John Brandon-Jones, 'Philip Webb', *Victorian Architecture*, London 1963, 250-1.
2 G.B-J, op. cit., I, 212.
3 Mackail, op. cit., I, 144.
4 G.B-J, op. cit., I, 208.
5 May Morris, Sup. I, 395-6.
6 G.B-J, op. cit., I, 210-11.
7 Grylls, op. cit., 77.
8 G.B-J, op. cit., I, 213.
9 Theodore Watts-Dunton, *Athenaeum*, 10 October 1896.
10 Mackail, op. cit., I, 145.
11 *An Exhibition of Victorian and Edwardian Decorative Arts*, catalogue, Victoria and Albert Museum, 1952.
12 N. Pevsner, *Pioneers of Modern Design*, London 1960, 49.
13 Lethaby, op. cit., 39-40.
14 Mackail's notes of a conversation with Arthur Hughes, 9 April 1897. William Morris Gallery, Walthamstow, MSS J163-6.
15 Mackail, op. cit., I, 152.
16 Peter Floud, 'The Wallpaper Designs of William Morris', *Penrose Annual*, LIV, 1960.
17 Mackail, op. cit., I, 152-3.
18 *The International Exhibition of 1862*, catalogue, Victoria and Albert Museum, 1962.
19 Lethaby, op. cit., 39.
20 Elizabeth Aslin, *Nineteenth Century English Furniture*, London 1962, 56.
21 A.C.Sewter, 'William Morris's Designs for Stained Glass', *Architectural Review*, March 1960: 'Morris & Co. Windows', *Architectural Review*, December 1964.
22 May Morris, Sup. I, 17.
23 Ibid., I, 25.
24 A.C.Sewter, 'William Morris's Designs for Stained Glass' (see note 21 above).
25 'Drawings (88) of figures and details of painted decoration from the rood-screens, roofs etc. of Norfolk churches ... made for Messrs. Morris, Marshall & Co., 1865-6.' Victoria and Albert Museum, 94.J.31.
26 British Museum, Add. MSS 45,350.
27 G.B-J, op. cit., I, 226.
28 Ibid., I, 284.
29 Ibid., I, 297.

CHAPTER V: *1865–1871*
1 Mackail, op. cit., I, 174.
2 G.B-J, op. cit., I, 298-9.
3 Letters from Warington Taylor to Philip Webb, 1866-9, Victoria and Albert Museum, Reserve Case JJ35. Also contains letters to Rossetti and Morris, as well as others from Rossetti and Burne-Jones to Webb, annotated by Sir Sydney Cockerell. Extracts were quoted by Lethaby, op. cit., Chap. 4, *passim*.
4 Charles Mitchell, 'William Morris at St James's Palace', *Architectural Review*, January 1947.
5 Aymer Vallance, *The Art of William Morris*, London 1898, 60.
6 May Morris, Sup. I, 401.
7 Ibid., I, 402.
8 E.P.Thompson, *William Morris, Romantic to Revolutionary*, London 1955, 150-1.
9 Mackail, op. cit., I, 210.
10 E.P.Thompson, op. cit., 159.
11 British Museum, Add. MSS 45,298.
12 The last six lines of this poem appear in the *Collected Works*, XXIV, 358, as the last verse of 'May Grown A-Cold'.
13 Letter in author's collection. First quoted in *Times Literary Supplement*, 7 September 1951.
14 British Museum, Add. MSS 45,298. These lines appear in a revised form with the refrain 'Half-forgotten, unforgiven and alone!' as 'Song' in *Collected Works*, XXIV, 360-1.

15 British Museum, Add. MSS 45,298. *Collected Works*, xxiv, 262–3.

16 Doughty, op. cit., 453–5.

17 Percy Lubbock (ed.), *The Letters of Henry James*, London 1920, I, 17–18.

18 Mackail, op. cit., 11, 349.

19 Hueffer, op. cit., 237–8.

20 Grylls, op. cit., 118.

21 Sidney Colvin, *Memorials and Notes of Persons and Places*, London 1922, 61–2.

22 H. Allingham and D. Radford (eds.), *William Allingham: A Diary*, London 1907, 181–2.

23 Oswald Doughty and Robert Wahl (eds.), *Letters of Dante Gabriel Rossetti*, Oxford 1965, 11, 685.

24 Letter in author's collection.

25 Lubbock, *The Letters of Henry James*, I, 17–18. By 'tapestry' James means embroidery. Morris did not begin his experiments in tapestry weaving until ten years later.

26 British Museum, Add. MSS 52,333 A.

27 British Museum, Add. MSS 45,342. Morris's letters are bound up with Webb's letters to the Morris family. May Morris printed a few extracts in *Collected Works*, v.

28 British Museum, Add. MSS 52,333 A.

29 *Collected Works*, vii, xvii.

30 British Museum, Add. MSS 52,333 A.

31 Ibidem.

32 Ibidem.

33 W. J. Stillman, *The Autobiography of a Journalist*, London 1901, Chap. 24, *passim*.

34 Ibid., 90–1.

35 City Museum and Art Gallery, Birmingham, MS 983.27.

36 British Museum, Add. MSS 45,347.

CHAPTER VI: *1871–1875*

1 *Collected Works*, viii, xxvi.

2 Iceland journals 1871, 1873. British Museum Add. MSS 45,319, A, B. 'Journal of Travel in Iceland', *Collected Works*, viii.

3 *The Icelandic Jaunt*, William Morris Society, 1962, 20.

4 Mackail, op. cit., I, 262.

5 Ibid., I, 280.

6 Ibid., I, 281.

7 *Athenaeum*, 10 October 1896.

8 British Museum, Add. MSS 45,328.

9 Doughty, op. cit., Chap. 11, *passim*. In a long review of this book in *Encounter*, November 1961, Geoffrey Grigson commented: 'I suspect that Buchanan's attack was in reality supported on a fairly exact knowledge of Rossetti's fleshly and a little crawly relationships.' Grigson goes on to attack Rossetti as a 'faker' and a 'beauty hypocrite'. Rossetti haunted Cremorne Gardens in search of models and on one occasion is reported to have bought an Indian bull because its eyes 'reminded him of Janey Morris'. At one time his private zoo at Cheyne Walk grew to alarming proportions.

10 Grylls, op. cit., 152. The original is in Mrs Troxell's collection, New Haven, Connecticut.

11 Ibid., 155.

12 Ibidem, 155.

13 Philip Webb's letters to the Morris family. British Museum, Add. MSS 45,342–4.

14 *Collected Works*, viii, xxv.

15 Webb's letters to the Morris family (see note 13 above).

16 This letter, originally in the collection of Mrs Rossetti Angeli, was quoted in part in Grylls's *Portrait of Rossetti*, 160. I am indebted to Mrs Troxell for the complete text.

17 E. V. Lucas, *The Colvins and Their Friends*, London 1928, 35.

18 Helen Rossetti Angeli, *Dante Gabriel Rossetti: His Friends and Enemies*, London 1949, 115.

19 Luke Ionides, *Memories*, Paris 1925, privately printed.

CHAPTER VII

1 Peter Floud, 'William Morris as an Artist: A New View', *The Listener*, 7 October 1954.

2 Lethaby, op. cit., 94.

3 Asa Briggs (ed.), *William Morris: Selected Writings and Designs*, with a supplement by Graeme Shankland, London 1962, 'William Morris Designer', *passim*.

4 Robert Schmutzler, *Art Nouveau*, London 1964, 100.

5 Peter Floud, 'Dating Morris Patterns', *Architectural Review*, July 1959.

6 Peter Floud, 'English Chintz: The Influence of William Morris', *CIBA Review* No. 1, 1961, 21–3. The article was edited for press by Barbara Morris.

7 Typescript of sixty-one letters from William Morris to Sir Thomas Wardle, 1870–96. Victoria and Albert Museum, Box II. 86. zz.

8 G.B-J, op. cit., 11, 58–9.

9 Bernard Shaw, 'More About Morris', *Observer*, 6 November 1949. Shaw says that Morris's rages were epileptic and left him humbled and shaken as after a fit. He also says that he had a rich man's petulance when thwarted.

10 D.M. Hoare, *The Works of Morris and Yeats in relation to Early Saga Literature*, London 1937, 76.

11 John Robert Wahl, 'No Idle Singer: *The Lovers of Gudrun* and *Sigurd the Volsung*', inaugural lecture delivered before the University of the Orange Free State, Cape Town, in 1964.

12 Bernard Shaw, 'Morris As I Knew Him', May Morris, Sup. 11, xxxvii.

13 *Collected Works*, XII, xxiii.

CHAPTER VIII: *1876–1879*

1 Letter to Sydney Cockerell, 24 August 1898. May Morris, Sup. 11, 602–6.

2 Undated letter at Castle Howard. From the burlesque tone, and knowing Burne-Jones's shyness, it is doubtful whether he actually did speak in public, even though he went to meetings.

3 Philip Henderson (ed.), *The Letters of William Morris*, London 1950, Appendix II, 388–9.

4 Castle Howard collection.

5 British Museum, Add. MSS 52,333 B.

6 Castle Howard collection.

7 Ibidem.

8 Grylls, op. cit., 178.

9 British Museum, Add. MSS 52,332 A.

10 G.B-J, op. cit., 11, 106–7.

11 Castle Howard collection, where there are many letters from Webb and Burne-Jones about their work at Palace Green. Mackail quoted from Morris's letters.

12 *Collected Works*, XIII, xviii–xix.

13 Mackail, op. cit., 1, 372–3.

14 *Collected Works*, XIII, xxi.

15 Victoria and Albert Museum, MS 86. L. 79.

CHAPTER IX

1 Sir Kenneth Clark, *The Gothic Revival*, London 1928, 228.

2 Letter of 10 February 1881 to Mrs William Morris. British Museum, Add. MSS 52,332 B.

3 Rupert Hart-Davis (ed.), *The Letters of Oscar Wilde*, London 1962, 174–5.

4 J. Brandon-Jones, 'Philip Webb', *Victorian Architecture*, London 1963, 255.

5 Ibid., 258.

6 Ibidem, 258.

7 Ibid., 262.

8 Emile Mâle, *The Gothic Image: Religious Art in France of the Thirteenth Century*, London 1961 (French edition: Paris 1902).

9 Jean Gimpel, *The Cathedral Builders*, London 1961, 104–5.

10 Morris's somewhat confused views on architecture were the subject of Dr Pevsner's lecture to the RIBA reprinted in their *Journal*, March 1957.

11 Conclusion to 'The Revival of Architecture', *The Fortnightly Review*, May 1888.

CHAPTER X: *1879–1883*

1 Mackail, op. cit., 11, 7.

2 Lubbock, *The Letters of Henry James*, I, 80.

3 British Museum, Add. MSS 52,332 A.

4 These are mostly in Mrs Troxell's collection. Some passages were quoted in Grylls's *Portrait of Rossetti*.

5 British Museum, MSS Ashley A 1964, ff. 37–8.

6 Mrs Troxell's collection. This is the unpublished part of the letter printed in Bell Scott's *Autobiographical Notes* edited by W. Minto, London 1892, 11, 319.

7 James Mavor, *My Windows on the Street of the World*, London 1923, I, 201.

8 This letter, with others to Scott, is at Penkill (Miss Courtney-Boyd). Ellis asked that his letters to Scott be burned. Quoted by Grylls, op. cit., 240.

9 British Museum, Add. MSS 45,353, f. 30.

10 'Description of an expedition by boat from Kelmscott House, Upper Mall, Hammersmith, to Kelmscott Manor, Oxfordshire, with critical notes', British Museum, Add. MSS 45,407. The notes are by Morris. May Morris wrote later of this trip: 'Remembering

how we disliked the crowds of Henley or the "cockney waters" of Pangbourne (we always required the full stretch of the river to ourselves for pure enjoyment) it is pleasant to turn over the leaves of a diary of our first journey in the Ark from Hammersmith to Kelmscott written by one of the party, and to find in certain notes in my father's hand traces of the quiet affection he bore for our small river.' *Collected Works*, XXIII, xxii.

11 Manuscripts at Newnham College, Cambridge. I am indebted to Lady Mander for drawing my attention to this.

12 Madeleine Smith, the central figure of a sensational Edinburgh trial, had been charged with the murder of her lover by arsenic. The verdict was returned 'not proven'. She married George Wardle, Morris's general manager, in 1861 and later died in New York under another name.

13 Annual report, William Morris Society, 1959.

14 E. M. W. Stirling (ed.), *The Richmond Papers*, London 1926, 317–18.

15 Ibid., 315–16.

16 Sir Arthur Richmond, *Twenty-Six Years, 1879–1905*, London 1961, 9.

17 Ibid. This story about Morris and Wilde is also to be found in *The Richmond Papers*, 317.

18 Hart-Davis, *The Letters of Oscar Wilde*, 290–1 and note.

19 *Collected Works*, XXII, xxvii. But usually he preferred the more knockabout humour of Surtees's Mr Jorrocks. In any case, Morris was not sufficiently detached from socialism to feel ironical about it, as he might have been had he lived longer.

20 Hesketh Pearson's letter to *The Times Literary Supplement*, 12 August 1962, and subsequent correspondence. There is a letter of Morris's to Wilde

of 5 January 1893, now in the Miriam
Lutcher Stark Library, University of
Texas, asking permission to reprint
Lady Wilde's translation of *Sidonia
the Sorceress* at the Kelmscott Press.
The tone is courteous and formal.
21 British Museum, Add. MSS 45,407
B.
22 Alfred Slinger, 'The Firm of Messrs
Liberty & Co. Ltd., Merton Abbey',
A History of Merton and Morden, edited
by Evelyn M. Jowett, Merton and
Morden Festival of Britain Local
Committee, 1961, 130.
23 Mackail, op. cit., II, 38.
24 Floud, 'English Chintz: The Influence of William Morris' (see Chap.
VII, note 6, above).
25 British Museum, Add. MSS 45,350.
26 Mackail, op. cit., II, 58–9.
27 May Morris, Sup. I, 53.

CHAPTER XI: *1883–1884*
1 Letter to Sydney Cockerell, 24
August 1898. May Morris, Sup. II,
602.
2 'How I Became a Socialist', *Justice*,
No. 544, 1894. *Collected Works*,
XXII, 271–81.
3 May Morris, Sup. II, 603–6.
4 Bernard Shaw, *Sixteen Self Sketches*,
London 1949, 67. It was while staying with Salt in Surrey that Shaw
began to write his *Plays Pleasant and
Plays Unpleasant*.
5 R. F. Rattray, *Bernard Shaw: A
Chronicle*, London 1951, 52.
6 Shaw, *Sixteen Self Sketches*, 59.
7 H. M. Hyndman, *Record of an Ad-
venturous Life*, London 1911, 350–1.
8 Letter to Laura Lafargue of 13
September 1886: 'Morris is a settled
sentimental Socialist; he would be
easily managed if one saw him
regularly a couple of times a week,
but who has the time to do it and if

you drop him for a month, he is sure
to lose himself again. And is he
worth all the trouble even if one had
the time?' *Frederick Engels to Paul and
Laura Lafargue*, Moscow 1959, I, 370.
9 *The Manchester Examiner*, 14 March
1882.
10 *New Statesman*, March 1934.
11 G. B-J, op. cit., II, 97.
12 Quoted by May Morris in her introduction to *Collected Works*, XIX,
xix–xx.
13 May Morris, Sup. II, 164.
14 E. P. Thompson, op. cit., 160 note.
15 Floud, 'Dating Morris Patterns' (see
Chap. VII, note 5, above).
16 Mackail, op. cit., II, 126. Letter to
Georgiana Burne-Jones?
17 E. P. Thompson, op. cit., 395.
18 May Morris, Sup. II, 226.
19 Bruce Glasier, *William Morris and the
Early Days of the Socialist Movement*,
London 1921, 31–2.
20 Dr John Glasse, Minister of the old
Greyfriars Kirk, Edinburgh, was
very sympathetic to socialism. Morris
often stayed with him on his visits to
Edinburgh. R. Page Arnot, *Unpublished Letters of William Morris to
Glasse*, Labour Monthly pamphlet,
Series No. 6, 1951.

CHAPTER XII: *1885–1887*
1 The manifesto of the Socialist League
is given by Thompson, op. cit., 849–
57, with selections from the annota-
tions by Morris and Bax to the second
edition.
2 E. P. Thompson, op. cit., 341.
3 May Morris, Sup. II, 188–9.
4 W. B. Yeats, 'Four Years: 1887–
1891', *Autobiographies*, London 1926,
182.
5 *The Commonweal*, June 1885.
6 *Ibid.*, October 1885.
7 *Daily News*, 20 November 1885.

8 Tom Mainwaring, *Freedom*, January 1887. Quoted by Thompson, op. cit., 472.

9 *The Commonweal*, 24 July 1886.

10 William Morris's lecture engagements, diary for 1887. British Museum, Add. MSS 45,408.

11 Glasier, op. cit., 80–2.

12 Castle Howard collection.

13 Letter in author's collection.

14 Bernard Shaw, 'Morris as I Knew Him', May Morris, Sup. 11, xxvi–xxxi.

15 British Museum, Add. MSS 45,412.

16 Sir Basil Blackwell, 'More About Miss Lobb', *The Bookseller*, 27 October 1962. Mr Robert Lusty, Mr Hobbs's grandson, writing in *The Bookseller* for 20 October, is less complimentary: 'Certainly what strange freak of nature brought together this brutish, foul-mouthed creature with the gracious delicacy and refinement of May Morris into a partnership of 40 years must remain a psychiatric problem.' According to the same source, on May's death Miss Lobb retired to bed with a bottle of brandy and threatened all comers with a loaded pistol.

17 Nevertheless, Blunt records that Morris disapproved of the marriage. 'He had a strong affectionate heart and had centred his home affection on his two children.' *My Diaries*, 1, 23.

18 Shaw, *Sixteen Self Sketches*, *passim*. May Morris's letters to Shaw (British Museum, Add. MSS 50,541) are enough to show that she was piqued and fascinated by him.

19 Wilfrid Blunt, *Cockerell*, London 1964, 65–6.

20 *The Bookseller*, 27 October 1962.

CHAPTER XIII: *1887–1890*

1 H. H. Sparling, *The Kelmscott Press* and *William Morris, Master Craftsman*, London 1924, 103–4.

2 Yeats, op. cit., 184.

3 Ibid., 178.

4 Ibid., 175–6.

5 Ibid., 180.

6 W. B. Yeats, 'The Happiest of the Poets', *Ideas of Good and Evil*, London and Stratford-upon-Avon 1903, 51.

7 Shaw, 'Morris As I Knew Him', May Morris, Sup. 11, i.

8 'Maid for Morris', interview by Andrew Lawson, *Isis*, 11 November 1965.

9 Sparling, op. cit., 37.

10 'The Tables Turned or Nupkins Awakened', May Morris, Sup. 11, 528–67.

11 Ernest Rhys, *Everyman Remembers*, London 1931, 205.

12 Bernard Shaw, *Pen Portraits and Reviews*, London 1949, 205. A review of Mackail's *Life of William Morris*, reprinted from the *Daily Chronicle*, 2 April 1899.

13 Henderson, *The Letters of William Morris*, 282–91.

14 W. S. Blunt, *My Diaries*, 23.

15 Blunt was arrested under the Crimes Act, in October 1887, in Ireland just after he had been playing tennis at Clouds House with Balfour, the Irish Chief Secretary in Lord Salisbury's government. He had a small estate at Sheykh Obeyd just outside Cairo, supported Egyptian nationalism and was much beloved in Egypt, where he lived for a large part of each year. Yet all his relatives and intimate friends were, as he confessed, in the Tory camp. See the Earl of Lytton, *Wilfrid Scawen Blunt, a Memoir by His Grandson*, London 1961.

16 W. S. Blunt, op. cit., 57.

17 Ibid., 67.

18 Shaw, 'Morris As I Knew Him', May Morris, Sup. 11, xvi.

19 Shaw, *Pen Portraits and Reviews*, 207.
20 May Morris, Sup. II, 321–4.
21 Glasier, op. cit., 51–6.

CHAPTER XIV: *1890–1893*

1 Indeed the late prose romances recall Sir Walter Raleigh's description of their author: 'a hale old party, with a skipper's beard and a loud voice, but I cannot get rid of the impression that there was a strain of the school-girl in his soul. A little, just a little, silly, I think. Everyone who writes about him is just a little silly too.' Letter to Percy Simpson, 4 September 1913, *Letters of Sir Walter Raleigh*, edited by Lady Raleigh, London 1926, II, 396. *The Water of the Wondrous Isles* begins: 'Whilom, as tells the tale, was a walled cheaping town hight Utterhay . . .'.
2 This letter is printed in full in Thompson, op. cit., 818–20, from the original in the Bodleian Library.
3 Sparling, op. cit., 8.
4 Mackail, op. cit., II, 255.
5 Ibid., II, 266.
6 Address on the collection of paintings of the English Pre-Raphaelite School in the City of Birmingham Museum and Art Gallery on Friday 24 October 1891. May Morris, Sup. I, 296–310.
7 Floud, 'Dating Morris Patterns' (see Chap. 7, note 5, above).
8 Blunt, *Cockerell*, 59.
9 Sparling, op. cit., 7.
10 Sparling to Ernest Radford, 24 December 1892, quoted by Thompson, op. cit., 717–18.
11 Mackail, op. cit., II, 284–5.
12 Shaw, 'Morris As I Knew Him', May Morris, Sup. II, xxxvi.
13 Mackail, op. cit., II, 289.
14 Walter Crane, *William Morris to Whistler*, London 1911, 15.

15 Hyndman, op. cit., 362.
16 *Collected Works*, XXII, xxviii. Occasioned by 'a French woman of dreadful archness' during a musical comedy to which Morris had been prevailed upon to take his daughters.
17 Mackail's notebooks. William Morris Gallery, Walthamstow, MSS J163–6. Cockerell's 'Boswell notes' were made use of by May Morris in her introductions to the *Collected Works* and in Sup. I, 84–93.
18 'The Deeper Meaning of the Struggle', letter to *Daily Chronicle*, 10 November 1893.

CHAPTER XV: *1894–1896*

1 Mackail, op. cit., II, 307.
2 'Beardsley – hm – I can only say that the illustrations to the M.D.A. which I saw were quite below contempt', Morris wrote to Shaw on 16 October 1894. 'Obviously *nothing* in them, except an obvious desire to be done with the job, but he *may* have got better since – tho' I don't think so.' British Museum, Add. MSS 5,054. Beardsley himself said that he found the illustrations to the *Morte d'Arthur* tedious to do. Morris's attitude to Ricketts and Shannon was similar. Writing to thank them for a copy of *The Dial* in 1893, he says: 'I confess that I looked at the art portion of it with somewhat mixed feelings, as the talent and the aberration of the talent seemed to me in about equal proportions.' *Letters and Journals of Charles Ricketts, R.A.*, collected and compiled by T. Sturge Moore, edited by Cecil Lewis, London 1939, 20.
3 E. P. Thompson, op. cit., 685–7.
4 Mackail, op. cit., II, 312.
5 I am grateful to A. R. Dufty of the Society of Antiquaries, the present owners of Kelmscott Manor, for this information.

6 Bodleian Library, MS. Top. Oxon, d. 347.

7 Cockerell's introduction to the World's Classics reprint of Mackail, 1950, xiii.

8 Yeats, 'The Happiest of the Poets' (see Chap. XIII, note 6, above).

9 Cockerell, op. cit., xiii–xiv.

10 G. B-J, op. cit., II, 277.

11 Brotherton collection, Leeds. Letter of 3 August 1896.

12 A. M. W. Stirling, *The Merry Wives of Battersea*, London 1956, 146. Mrs Stirling evidently had this from her sister, Mary de Morgan.

13 Memorials of William Morris, British Museum, Add. MSS 45,350.

14 Blunt, *Cockerell*, 63. There is a photograph of one of these drawings in the central library, Hammersmith.

15 W. S. Blunt, *My Diaries*, 240–1.

16 Mackail, op. cit., II, 348.

17 R. B. Cunninghame Graham, 'With the North-West Wind', *Saturday Review*, 10 October 1896.

18 Mackail's notebooks. William Morris Gallery, Walthamstow, MSS J163–6. Among the other mourners were: F. S. Ellis, Walter Crane, W. B. Richmond, Cockerell, Arthur Hughes, T. Armstrong, Webb and Emery Walker. Another account of the funeral has recently come to light in a letter from Arthur Hughes of 25 November 1896, to Alice Boyd of Penkill, quoted by William E. Fredeman, 'William Morris's Funeral', *The Journal of the William Morris Society*, vol. II, No. 1, Spring 1966, 32–5. 'Mrs. Morris very broken down, May bearing up well, but poor Jennie weeping piteously', notes Hughes.

19 Lethaby, *Philip Webb*, 195.

20 Mackail, op. cit., II, 345.

21 Sir W. Rothenstein, *Men and Memories*, London 1931, I, 288.

22 Letters from Mrs William Morris and others to Sir Sydney Cockerell. Victoria and Albert Museum Reserve Case JJ.34.

23 Quoted by Grylls, op. cit., 240.

24 Effie Morris, 'Notes on Members of the Morris Family'. William Morris Gallery, Walthamstow.

Acknowledgements

It is a pleasure to record my indebtedness to those who have helped me in collecting material for this book by their kindness, advice and hospitality. I would mention in particular: Lady Rosalie Mander; George Howard; Lord Baldwin of Bewdley; Professor Oswald Doughty; Dr Paul Thompson, who generously allowed me to read *The Work of William Morris* in proof; A.C.Sewter; Paul Bloomfield; Professor Norman Kelvin; Mrs Barbara Morris; Richard Ormond; Ronald Briggs, Hon. Secretary of the William Morris Society; J. Brandon Jones; John Gere; A.I.Stewart Liberty; A.Slinger of Messrs. Liberty's Merton Abbey Print Works; Dr and Mrs D.C.Wren, late of Kelmscott Manor; Mr and Mrs Edward Hollamby of Red House; Lionel Lambourne; Mrs Clare Sitter of the Miriam Lutcher Stark Library, University of Texas; A.R.Dufty, Vice President of the Society of Antiquaries of London; Mrs Elizabeth Wood; Nomi Durrel; Peter Calvocoressi; Colin Franklin; and Ken Goodwin.

For permission to reproduce copyright material I am indebted to: Mrs Helen Rossetti Angeli; George Howard; Mrs Janet Camp Troxell; Rupert Hart-Davis; Denis Mackail; Sir Basil Blackwell; Andrew Lawson; The Principal, Newnham College; the Society of Antiquaries of London; the British Museum; the Victoria and Albert Museum; and the William Morris Gallery, Walthamstow.

The publishers and I would also like to express our thanks to the owners and photographers who have kindly supplied, or permitted us to reproduce, the illustrations: City Museum and Art Gallery, Birmingham, 2; Bradford Corporation Libraries, Art Gallery and Museums Committee, 30; British Council, 27; Trustees of the British Museum, London, 17; *Country Life*, 18, 22; the Vicar of All Saints, Jesus Lane, Cambridge, 34; Syndics of the Fitzwilliam Museum, Cambridge, 9; Dennis Frone, 19, 34, 44, 45, 47, 49, II, III; Gernsheim Collection, University of Texas, 77; Central Library, Hammersmith, London, 56, 57, 58, 59, 61, 70, 73; William Heinemann Ltd., 60 (from *Rossetti and his Circle* by Max Beerbohm); National Monuments Record, London, 3, 4, 8, 21, 26, 32, 48, 62, 63, 82; National Portrait Gallery, London, 43, 80; H.F.Rossetti, 17; St Bride Printing Library, London, 2, 13, 14, 15, 23, 74, 76; A.C. Sewter, 35; Edwin Smith, 5, 41; Society of Antiquaries of London, 13, 76; Trustees of the Tate Gallery, London, 11, 12, 60; Victoria and Albert Museum, London, 28, 38, 39, 40, 42, 52, 53, 54, 55, 75, 79, IV, V, VI, VII; John Webb, Brompton Studio, IV, V, VI, VII; Whitworth Art Gallery, University of Manchester, VIII; John Evelyn Society, Wimbledon, 50; William Morris Gallery, Walthamstow, 1, 16, 36, 51, 68, 71, 81. We should finally like to thank the Vicars of Christ Church, Albany Street, London and Christ Church, Southgate, and the Rector of Clewer, for kindly permitting us to reproduce stained glass in their churches (35, II, III, 32).

Index

Numbers in *Italic* refer to illustrations

ABBEVILLE, 25, 355
Academy, 11, 113–14
Adams, W. Bridges, 274
Aeneid, 160–1
'Aims of Art', 18
Allingham, William, 86
Amiens, 26, 34, 56, 256, 335
anarchism, 349–50
Anti-State Communism, 319–20
armour, designed by M., 44–5
Arnold, Matthew, 241
'Art and Democracy', 254 ff
'Art and Labour', 268
'Art and Socialism', 262
'Art, Wealth and Riches', 247–50
Artists' Corps of Volunteers, 66
Arthur's Tomb, see *King Arthur's Tomb*
Arts and Crafts Essays, 203
Arts and Crafts Exhibition Society, 157
Astarte Syriaca (Rossetti), 151
'At Last' (Rossetti), 103
Attitude of the Police, 68
Austin, Alfred, 105
Aveling, Edward, 246, 264, 266–7, 271, 279–80, 281, 313

BALDWIN, Louisa, 130, 143
Balfour, A. J., 296
Ballads and Sonnets (Rossetti), 218
Balmoral Castle, 152
Barton Turf Church, 76
Batchelor & Son, 332
Bax, Belfort, 260, 271, 274, 278, 295
Bell, Margaret, 156
Bell, Sir Lowthian, 153
Bell Street, London, 289
Bellamy, Edward, 328
Benson, W. A. S., 251
Bentley, J. F., 207
Beowulf, 341
Besant, Mrs Annie, 246, 264, 308, 311
Birmingham, St Philip's, glass, 197
Blackwood's Magazine, 28–9
Blencowe, Agnes, 36
'Blessed Damozel' (Rossetti), 24, 33

Bliss, W. H., 9, 138
Bloody Sunday, 308 ff
Blue Closet (painting by Rossetti and poem by M.), 51–2, 54, *12*
Blue Dress (Rossetti), *13*
Blunt, Wilfrid Scawen, 317–18, 339, 359
Blythburgh Church, 199, 352
Bock, Dr, 251
Bodley, G. F., 70, 71, 211
Book of Verse, 115–16, 334, *IV*
bookbinding, 115, *71*
Borrow, George, 344
Bowden, William, 332
Boyd, Miss Alice, 102
Bradfield College, 9
Bradlaugh, Charles, 267
brass-rubbing, 26
Briar Rose (Burne-Jones), 202, 334, *41*, *62*
Bright, James F., 258
Bright, John, 264
Brighton, St Michael's, 71; glass, 72, 73, *36*
'Brotherhood', 14, 22–3
Brown, Ford Madox, 24, 37, 66, 69, 72 ff, 149
Brown, Lucy, 145
Browning, Robert, 34, 35
Bryce, James, 197
Buchanan, Robert, 130
Burden, Elizabeth, 61, 69, 110, 134
Burden, Jane, see Morris, Jane
'Burden of Nineveh' (Rossetti), 33
Burford Church, 194
Burges, William, 70, 71
Burne-Jones, Edward, with M. at Oxford, 6 ff, 22 ff; shares lodgings with M., 37 ff; decorates Red House, 59; glass, 72 ff; *A Book of Verse*, 115; tapestry, 236–7; painting, 322 ff; illustration, 355 ff; and socialism, 258–9; *24, 51, 60, 61, 75, VIII*
Burne-Jones, Georgiana, 6, 23–4, 60, 77–8, 98, 115–16, 135, 142–3, 165, 177–8, 186, 362

Burns, John, 264, 312, 319
Burrows, Herbert, 311
Buscot Park, 202, 334, *41*
Butterfield, William, 11, 22, 36

CAINE, Hall, 218
Cambridge, 24
　All Saints, 71; glass, 73, 74, *34*
　Jesus College, 80, 202
　Peterhouse, 74
　Queens' College, 75
Cambridge Camden Society, 194
Campfield, George, 69, 273
Canterbury Cathedral, 6, 359
Canterbury, St Augustine's, 35
Cantwell, Tom, 349
Carlyle, Thomas, 15, 29, 197
Carpenter, Edward, 247, 260, 271-2,
　319, 328-9
carpets, 153, 190-1, 233, *56*, VII
　'Bullerswood', 191
　'Clouds', 191, 207, *42*
　'Naworth', 230
　'Orchard', 222
Carruthers, John, 287ff, 361
Champion, H.H., 244, 260
'Chants for Socialists', 238, 264, *64*
Chaucer, Geoffrey, 61, 88-90
Chaucer, Kelmscott Press edition, 341,
　346-7, 348, 357, 359, 360, *73*
Cheddleston Church, glass, 75
Chicago Anarchists, 314
chintzes, 153, 155
　'African Marigold', *55*
　'Bird and Anemone', 234, 260
　'Borage', 234
　'Brother Rabbit', 234
　'Corncockle', 234
　'Cray', 234, 263
　'Daffodil', 336
　'Evenlode', 234, VI
　'Eyebright', 234
　'Honeysuckle', 155, *63*
　'Kennet', 234
　'Rose', 234
　'Strawberry Thief', 234, 251, 260
　'Tulip', 154, *52*
　'Tulip and Willow', 155, 157
　'Wandle', 234, 263
　'Wey', 234, 263
　'Windrush', 234
Christian Socialists, 283

Clarke, W.J., 270, 271, 274
Clarkson, Thomas, 154, 157
Clay Hill, Walthamstow, 3
Clayton & Bell, 68
'clearances', 267
Clouds, 207
Cockerell, Douglas, 348
Cockerell, Sir Sydney, 302, 338, 363
Cole, Sir Henry, 64, 65, 82
Coleridge, Kelmscott Press edition, 350
Collins, Charles, 25, 26
Combe, Thomas, 23
Commonweal, 272, 273ff, 320-1
'Concerning Geffray Teste Noir', 53
Congress of Socialists (Paris 1888), 320
Cooper, J., 264, 271, 274
Cornforth, Fanny, 136
Coronio, Mrs Aglaia, 112, 134-5, 142,
　146, 160, 162, 183, *79*
Craig, E.T., 274
Crane, Walter, 273, 302, *65*, *67*, *72*
Crayford, 231
Crimean War, 21
'Cupid and Psyche' (Burne-Jones), 87-8,
　186, *37*
'Cup of Cold Water' (Rossetti), 50-1

Daily News, 173, 285
Dalziel, Messrs., 32
Dannreuther, Dr Edward, 169
Day Dream (Rossetti), 217
Dearle, J.H., 68, 236, 337
'Death Song', 311
'Decorative Arts: Their Relation to
　Modern Life', *see* 'Lesser Arts'
'Dedication of the Temple', 21
Dedworth Church, glass, 72
Defence of Guenevere, 6, 19, 29, 51ff
Democratic Federation, 176, 241, 244ff,
　260ff, *69*
De Morgan, William, 69, 189, 220
Devon Great Consols, 4, 63, 359
Dickens, Charles, 313
Disraeli, Benjamin, 173-5, 177
Dixon, R.W., 11, 13, 29, 56, 147
Dod Street, London, 281-3, *68*
Donald, A.K., 313
Doves Bindery, 348
'Dream', 34
Dream of John Ball, 11, 273, 301
Dresser, Christopher, 64-5, 70-1
Duchess of Bayswater & Co., 320-1

Dumas, A., 313
Dunn, Henry Treffry, 182
Dürer, Albrecht, 16
dyeing, 157 ff, 164–5, 235, V

Earthly Paradise, 78, 86–92
Eastern Question Association, 175, 179
East London Radical Club, 283
Ellis, F. S., 105, 112, 186, 219, 358
Ely Cathedral, 233
embroidery, 46, 60–1, 69–71, 153, 224,
    233, *39, 40,* VI
Ems, 99 ff
Engels, F., 250, 261, 265–6, 272, 277–8
engineering, 208
Epping Forest, 6, 354
Evans, W. H., 119 ff
Everyman's Library, 330
Exhibitions
    Art Treasures (Manchester 1857), 42
    International (South Kensington 1862),
        70, *28*
    International Health (1884), 205
    Royal Academy Summer, reviewed by
        M., 264

FABIAN SOCIETY, 247, 320, 342
fabrics, *see also* chintzes, embroidery,
    tapestry
    'Bird', 188, 260, *56*
    'Dove and Peacock', 260
    'Dove and Rose', 192
    'Flower Garden', 192
    'Forest', 237
    'Peacock', 231
    'Rose and Lily', *54*
    'Willow', 192
'Fair Traders', 286
Faulkner, Charles J., 6, 13, 44, 66, 76,
    119 ff, 140 ff, 161, 274, 318, *25*
Faulkner, Kate, 68, *40*
Federation of Radical Clubs, 308
Fildes, Luke, 202
'Fleshly School of Poetry' (Buchanan),
    130–1
Foster, Birkett, 74
Fouqué, Friederich, 16
France, M.'s visits to, 18, 25 ff, 55 ff,
    334 ff, 355
Freiheit, 241
Frith, W. P., 202
Froissart, 52, 303

Fulford, William, 13, 25–6, 33
furniture, 39–40, 67, 70, 71, 233
    'Chaucer' wardrobe, VII, *56*
    Red House Settle, 71, 224, VII
    Red Lion Settle, 39–40, 60, 62, *22*
    'St George' cabinet, 70, *28, 40*
    Sussex elbow-chair, 71, VII

GANDISH'S, 38
Garda, Lake, 183
Garden Cities, 144
George, Henry, 241, 246, 254
Gerard's *Herbal*, 157
Gladstone, William, 215
Glasier, John Bruce, 267–8, 322–3
glass
    painted, 233
    stained, 67, 72 ff, II, III, *30, 32, 35, 36*
Glasse, Dr John, 270
Gobelins, factory, 192
Godefrey of Boloyne, see *History of Gode-
    frey of Boloyne*
Godwin, E. W., 206
Goethe, J. W. von, 103
Golden Legend, 331, 334
'Golden Wings', 54
Goodman, Major, 207
Gosse, Edmund, 95
'Gossip about an Old House', 119
'Gothic Architecture', 208
Gothic Revival, 210
Graham, Cunninghame, 308, 310–12
Graham, William, 131
Great Coxwell, 225–6, *5*
Greek architecture, 209
Green Dining Room, *see* Victoria and
    Albert Museum
Gregynog Press, 86
Grosvenor, Hon. Richard, 220
Gunner, Floss, 303–4
'Gunnlaug the Wormtongue', *see* Sagas
Guy, Rev. F. B., 9, 68

HAKE, Dr George, 131, 147
Hall Place, 231
Hammersmith Socialist Record, 339
Hammersmith Socialist Society, 324, 342
Hampstead Liberal Club, 262
Harden Grange, 42, 74, *30*
Hardie, Keir, 342
Hardy, Thomas, 344
hautelisse loom, 192

'Haystack in the Floods', 53
Headlam, Stewart, 247, 308
Heal, Ambrose, 204
Heckmondwike Manufacturing Co., 153
Heeley, Wilfred, 23
'Hill Of Venus', 112
'Hints on House Decoration', *see* 'Making the Best of It'
History of Godefrey of Boloyne (Caxton), 299, 341
'History of Pattern-Designing', 155, 190, 238
Histories of Troy, see *Recuyell of the Histories of Troy*
Hogg, Gordon, 295
Holiday, Mrs Henry, 154, 156, V
Holst, Gustav, 264
Hooper, W.H., 348
'Hope Dieth: Love Liveth', 143
Hopes and Fears for Art, 199
Horace, *Odes* copied by M., 160
Horrington House, 137
Houghton, Richard Monckton Miles, Baron, 197
House of Life (Rossetti), 118, 131, 218
'House of the Wolfings', 329
Howard, George and Rosalind, 147–8, 149, 184–5, 216, 240
Howell, C.A., 98
'How I became a Socialist', 343
'How Sir Palomydes loved La Belle Iseult', 44
Hudson, W., 274
Hueffer, Ford Madox and family, 112, 133
Hughes, Arthur, 32, 37, 43, 51, 66, 73
Hughes, Thomas, 287
Humanitarian League, 247
Hunt, Violet, 223–4
Hunt, William Holman, 17, 22, 197
Hyndman, H.M., 241, chapter XII *passim*

IBSEN, H., 343
Iceland, 119ff, 140ff
'Iceland First Seen', 120
illumination, 115, 160–1
Image, Selwyn, 335
Impressionism, 203
Ina, Kathleen, 264
Independent Labour Party, 319, 342
Inglesham Church, 199

International Workingmen's Club, 281
Ionides, Aleco, 112
Ionides, Luke, 98, 151
Irish Coercion Bill, 215
Iseult on the Ship see *Tristram and Iseult on the Ship*
Italy, 138ff, 183ff

JACK, George, 44
James, Henry, 98–9, 216, 344
James, M.R., 347
'Janey Morris and the Wombat' (Rossetti), 17
Japanese style, 206
Jason, 87–8
Jefferies, Richard, 278–9
Jeffreys of Islington, 68, 153
Jenson, Nicolas, 331, 332
'Jingoism', 177
Johnson, Florence, 156
Jones, Edward, *see* Burne-Jones, Edward
Jones, Owen, 64–5, 152
Joynes, J.L., 246, 260
Justice, 261, 270, 272

KEATS, John, 350
Keene, Charles, 197
Kelmscott Church, 364–5, *82*
Kelmscott House, Hammersmith, 180–2, 187–90, 303–4, *56–9, 70*
Kelmscott Manor, 117ff, 300, 351, *15, 45–9*
Kelmscott Press, 327ff, *72, 73, 80*; see also individual works
'King Arthur's Tomb' (poem by M. and painting by Rossetti), 51–4, *11*
King's Walden Church, glass, 75
Kitz, Frank, 288, 318
Kropotkin, Prince, 302

La Belle Iseult, see *Queen Guenevere*
Labour's May Day (Crane), 65
La Pia (Rossetti), 95–6
Lachmere, Sir Edmund, 196
Ladies' Ecclesiastical Embroidery Society, 36
'Lady of Shalott' (Tennyson), 14
Lady Place, Hurley, 221
Lancelot's Vision of the Sancgrael (Rossetti), 44
Lane, Joseph, 266, 271
Lansbury, George, 343

Law and Liberty League, 308, 312
le Strange, H.S., 233
Leclaire, 245
Leeds, St Saviour's, glass, 73-4
Leicester Secular Society, 262
'Lesser Arts', 6, 199, 238
'Lesser Arts of Life', 155, 192
Liberal Party, 174
Liberty, Arthur Lazenby, 238
Life of William Morris (Mackail), binding, 129
Life of Wolsey (Cavendish), 341
'Lindenborg Pool', 34
Linnell, Alfred, 311
Lithend, 120, 122
Liverpool Cathedral, glass, 74
Llandaff Cathedral, triptych (Rossetti), 38, *2*
Lobb, Mary, 299
London
    Christ Church, Albany Street, glass, 35
    Hammersmith Church, 259
    Hampstead Church, 194
    St Alban's, Holborn, glass, 75
    St Giles, Camberwell, glass, 74-5
    St James's Palace, 80, 153, 215, *33*
    St James-the-Less, Thorndike Street, 36, *4*
    St Paul's Cathedral, 210
    St Peter's, Vere Street, 197
    St Thomas's, Fulham, 86
    South Kensington Museum, *see* Victoria and Albert Museum
    Westminster Abbey, 233, 333, 338
    Westminster Cathedral, 207-8
London County Council, 319
London Trades Council, 264
London Trades Guild of Learning, 246
'Love and Death', IV
'Love Fulfilled', 142
Love is Enough, 128-9, *71*
'Lovers of Gudrun', 109
'Love's Gleaning Tide', 136
Lubbock, Sir John, 197
luxury, M.'s views on, 153
Lyons, Lewis, 281-2

MCALPIN, Stead, 157
Macdonald, James, 260
Maclise, Daniel, 25
Magnusson, Eirikr, 107, 109, 119 ff, 350

Maguire, Tom, 274
Maids of Elfenmere (Rossetti), 32, 33
Mainwaring, Sam, 289
'Making the Best of It', 154, 190-1, 202-3
Malory, Sir Thomas, see *Morte d'Arthur*
Manet, Edouard, 202
Manifesto of English Socialists, 342
Mann, Tom, 264
Marks, Newman, 198
Marlborough College, 7-9
marriage, M.'s views on, 328
Marshall, P.P., 60, 69
Marx-Aveling, Eleanor, 246, 261-2, 271, 274, 281
Marx, Karl, 241, 244, 263
Mavor, James, 269, 274
Maxwell, Shaw, 342
'Maying of Guenevere', 54
Men and Women (Browning), reviewed by M., 34, 35
Merton Abbey, 153, 231 ff, 250 ff, *50*
Metropolitan Radical Association, 308
Middleton, John Henry, 141, 251
Millais, Sir John, 16, 23, 25, 26
Moore, Albert, 69
Morgan, William de, *see* De Morgan, William
Morris & Co., 63 ff, 76-8, 149-50, 176-7, 286, *31*
Morris, Edgar (M.'s brother), 5, 318
    Emma (Oldham, M.'s sister), 4, 19, 366
    Emma (née Shelton, M.'s mother), 3, 30-2, 41, 74
    Jane, at Oxford, 42, 48, 49-51; marriage, 56-7; at Red House, 60, 62-3; birth of Jenny, 65; illness, 81, 98, 143, 185, 216-17; trip to Italy, 182-5; impressions of, 98-9, 114, 216, 223, 224, 304, 306, 340, 352, 365-6; 323; *13-17*, *75*, I. See also Rossetti, Dante Gabriel
    Jenny, 65-6, 165-6, 223-4, 334, *75*, *76*
    May, 68, 298-300, 307, *49*, *75*
'Morte d'Arthur', glass (Burne-Jones), 74
Morte d'Arthur (Malory), 29
Most, Johann, 241
Mrs William Morris (Rossetti), 95
'Ms at Ems' (Rossetti), 103
Mundella, A.J., 175, 178
Munro, Alexander, 43

Index

Murray, Charles Fairfax, 83, 115
'Music', glass (Rossetti), 74

NAIRNE, W. J., 268-9
National Liberal League, 214
National Secular Society, 267
National Society for Checking the
    Abuses of Public Advertising, 356
Naworth Castle, 147, 185, 216
'Near but Far Away', 92
News from Nowhere, 118, 187-8, 219-22,
    273, 327 ff, frontispiece
'Nibelungen', translated by M., 106
Nicholson, Mrs Mary ('Red Lion Mary'),
    40-1, 224
Nicoll, D. J., 321, 350
Norway, 361
'Nuptial Sleep' (Rossetti), 103
Nuremburg Chronicle, 338

O'BRIEN, William, 308
Odyssey, translated by M., 291, 304-6
'Of Dyeing as an Art', 157
Olivier, Sydney, 247, 320
Oneglia, 185
'Orchard Pit' (Rossetti), 104
Ordene de Chevalerie (Caxton), 341
Ormond Yard, 190, 191-2
Owen, Robert, 259
Oxford, 285-6, 254 ff
    Christ Church, 72; glass, 233
    Exeter College, 10, 11-12, 14, 238,
        244
    Keble College, 36
    Magdalen College, 22, 211
    Merton College, 11, 3
    New College cloisters, 11
    SS. Philip and James, 22
    Union, 6, 43 ff, 144, 7
    University Museum, 45-6, 8
Oxford and Cambridge Magazine, 23, 24,
    26, 29, 32
Oxford Movement, 11

PALACE GREEN (1), 186
Pandora, M. paints Jane as, 95
'Parable of the Vineyard', glass (Rossetti),
    70
Paris, 26
Parsons, Lucy, 314
'Parted Love' (Rossetti), 131
Pater, Walter, 53-4, 228

Patmore, Coventry, 197
Pattison, Mark, 197
Paxton, Sir Joseph, 211
Penkill, 102-3, 313
Peterborough Cathedral, 320, 352
'Pilgrim in the Garden', see 'Romaunt of
    the Rose'
Pilgrims of Hope, 291-2
Pliny, 157
Poems by the Way, 120, 334
Pollen, Hungerford, 11, 43
Poynter, F. J., 70, 82, 78
Pre-Raphaelites, 16 ff, 202, 243, 336
Price, Cormell, 6, 13-14, 19, 24, 29, 30,
    78, 220
Prince, Edward, 331
Prinsep, Valentine, 43, 47-8
printing, see Kelmscott Press
Proserpine (Rossetti), 189
'Prospects of Architecture', 204
Psalmi Penitentiales, 351
Pugin, A. W. N., 7, 152

QUEEN SQUARE, chapter V passim,
    26
Quinn, Charles, 349

Recuyell of the Histories of Troy (Caxton),
    299, 331, 340
Red House, 56, chapter IV passim, 18, 19,
    21, 22
Red Lion Square, chapter III passim, 60
Reeves & Turner, 331, 332
'Revival of Architecture', 208, 211
Reynard the Foxe (Caxton), 340
Richmond, Sir Arthur, 227-8
Richmond, Sir W. B., 226-7, 43, 63
'Riding Together', 20
Robson, E. R., 211
Roman art, M.'s views on, 208
'Romaunt of the Rose', 156, 202, 39
Rossetti, Dante Gabriel, M.'s early
    admiration for, 24, 32, 33; helps M.,
    37 ff; and Red House, 60-1; with
    Morris & Co., 63, 66-7, 71-4, 149-
    50; and Jane Morris, 50-1, 93 ff,
    109 ff, 117-18, 131 ff, 140, 150-1,
    217-19, 351, 366; poems, 111 ff;
    illness, 131 ff, 145, 147, 186; death,
    218; 2, 9, 11, 12, 13, 14, 17, 77, VII
Rossetti, William Michael, 76-7, 145
Rouen, 18, 56

Rounton Grange, 153, 156
Rubaiyat of Omar Khayyam, 115–16
Ruskin, John, 12ff, 42–3, 241, 254ff, 337, *6*
Russell Club, 254

SAGAS
Egils, 106
Eyrbyggja (Story of the Dwellers at Eyr), 115
Grettis, 109, 124
'Gunnlaug the Wormtongue', 107
Heimskringla, 109, 138, 350
Laxdaela, 108, 109, 125
'St Olaf', 109
Volsunga (Sigurd the Volsung), 106, 107, 162, 167–9
Saga Library, 350
'St George and the Dragon', glass (Marshall), 69
Salisbury Cathedral, 197, 209
Salt, Henry, 246–7
Sanderson, Cobden, 263
Scalands, 109
Scarborough, St Martin's, 71; glass, 72, 74
Scheu, Andreas, 251, 260, 265ff, 318
Scott, Sir George Gilbert, 12, 194ff
Scott, Sir Walter, 6
Scott, William Bell, 133, 313
Scottish Land Restoration League, 267
Seddon, J. P., 70, 259
Selsley, All Saints, 71; glass, 72, 73
'Shadows of Amiens', 34
Shakespeare, 17–18, 344
Shaw, G. B., 170, 247, 264, 298, 340, *66*
Shaw, Richard Norman, 207, 211
Shipley Church, 359
'Short Poems and Sonnets', 92
Siddal, Lizzie, 45, 50, 60, 66
Sienna, 140
'Sir Peter Harpdon's End', 53, 224
'Sir Tristram after his illness...', 42
Skalaholt Press, 260
Smeaton Manor, 207
Smith, Frank, 311
Social Democratic Federation, 261ff, 286ff
socialism, 148–9, 241ff, 253ff, 315ff
Socialism: Its Growth and Outcome (M. and Bax), 244, 342
Socialist League, 271–2, 321ff

Society for the Protection of Ancient Buildings, 195ff, 214, 324, 342
Soldan's Daughter in the Palace of Glass, 42
Solomon, Simeon, 69
South Kensington Museum, *see* Victoria and Albert Museum
Southgate, Christ Church, glass, 72, II, III
Sparling, H. H., 273, 298–9
Spartali, Marie (Mrs W. J. Stillman), 114, 133, 223
'Staff and Scrip' (Rossetti), 33
Stanhope, Spencer, 43
Stanley, Dean, 233
Stead, W. T., 242, 308
Stephen, Leslie, 197
Stepniak, Sergius, 356
Stillman, W. J., 114
Story of the Dwellers at Eyr, see Sagas, *Eyrbyggja*
Story of the Glittering Plain, 143, 327, 332, *72*
'Story of the Unknown Church', 32, 34–5
Stratford-on-Avon Church, 324
'Stream's Secret' (Rossetti), 101–2, 104, 113
Street, George Edmund, 22, 29, 32, 38, 208, 210, *4*
Summary of the Principles of Socialism, 252
Summerly's Art Manufactures, 64
Sunday Lecture Society, 268
Sundering Flood, 362
'Supreme Surrender' (Rossetti), 103
Surtees, R. S., 313
Sussex House, 333
Swinburne, A. C., 47, 105–6, 113, 239, 261, 339, 346

Tables Turned, or Nupkins Awakened, 306
tapestry, 192–3, 233, 236ff
'Botticelli's Spring', 359
'Cabbage and Vine', 154, 190
'Flora', 236
'Goose Girl', 236
'Holy Grail', 236
'Orchard', 237
'Pomona', 236, 237, VIII
'Star of Bethlehem', 238
'Vine and Acanthus', 260
'Woodpecker', 237, 260, *38*

Taylor, Warington, 80 ff
Temple Bar, 105
Tennyson, Alfred, Lord, 17, 33, 258, 306
Tewkesbury Abbey, 195-6
'Textile Fabrics', 205
Thames Conservancy Board, 227, 315, 353
Third Reform Act, 264
Thorpe, Benjamin, 15
'Thunder in the Garden', 142
tiles, 133
Tite Street, London, Whistler's house, 210; Wilde's house, 206
Tolstoy, Leo, 313
Toynbee, Arnold, 254
Tristram and Iseult on the Ship, 42, 48, 10
Turkey, M. opposed to war with, 173 ff
Twain, Mark, 313
typefaces, 329-32
Tyrwhitt, St John, 44

Unjust War, 175
'Useful Work *versus* Useless Toil', 262

VENICE, 183, 214
Verona, 183
'Verses for Pictures', 237
Victoria and Albert Museum, foundation, 64-5; M.'s love for collections, 65, 158, 189, 190, 263, 294, 346; Green Dining Room, 61, 81-3, 40

WAGNER, Richard, 168-70
Wales, 161-2
Walker, Emery, 302, 316, 318, 363
Wallas, Graham, 247, 320
wallpapers, 152 ff; substitute for tapestry, 205; classical motifs in Morris & Co.'s, 208
    'Acanthus', 161
    'Bird', 86
    'Chrysanthemum', 176
    'Compton', 337
    'Daisy', 60, 68, 27
    'Fruit' ('Pomegranate'), 68, VII
    'Hammersmith', 337
    'Indian', 86
    'Jasmine', 115, 128, 159, 63
    'Lechlade', 337
    'Pimpernel', 59

'Powdered', 154
'St James', 215
'Spring Thicket', 337
'Trellis', 67, 70
'Vine', 154
'Willow', 154
'Willow Boughs', 154
'Wreath', 29
Wardle, George, 76, 115, 149
Wardle, Mrs George (Madeleine Smith), 69, 224
Wardle, Sir Thomas, 153, 155, 216
Warner, Metford, 68
Warr, Professor G. C. W., 246
Warren, Sir Charles, 307
Water House, Walthamstow, 8
Water Lily (Rossetti), 118
Water of the Wondrous Isles, 343, 352
Watson, Edward, 274
Watts, G. F., 109-10
Watts-Dunton, Theodore, 129
weaving, 190 ff, 51
Webb, Philip, 35, 44, 56, chapter IV *passim*, 81-4, 86, 150, 188, 207, 210, 318, 351, 354, 365, 20, 33, 40, VII
Webb, Sydney, 247, 320
Wedgwood Institute, Burslem, M. speaks to, 242
Well at the World's End, 343
Whistler, J. McN., 203, 206, 210
'Why Dost Thou Struggle?', 93-4
Wilde, Oscar, 206, 228-30, 304-5, 367
Wilding, Alexa, 133, 136
Williams, Jack, 264 ff, 289
'Willow and the Red Cliff', 19-20
'Willow-wood' (Rossetti), 101-2
'Winter Weather', 33
Woodford Hall, 3-4
Woodward, Benjamin, 43, 7, 8
Workmen's Neutrality Demonstration, 177
Wren, Sir Christopher, 198
Wright, Aldis, 197
Wyatt, Matthew Digby, 64-5
Wyndham, Hon. Percy, 191, 207

YEATS, W. B., 277, 302-3
Yonge, Charlotte, 16

ZAMBACO, Mrs Marie, 97-8
Zola, Emile, 335